THE NATURE OF THE ITALIAN PARTY SYSTEM

THE NATURE OF THE ITALIAN PARTY SYSTEM

A REGIONAL CASE STUDY

GEOFFREY PRIDHAM

ST MARTIN'S PRESS NEW YORK

©Geoffrey Pridham 1981

All rights reserved. For information, write:
St. Martin's Press, Inc., 175 Fifth Avenue, New York, NY 10010
Printed in Great Britain
First published in the United States of America in 1981

Library of Congress Cataloging in Publication Data

Pridham, Geoffrey, 1942–
   The nature of the Italian party system.

   Bibliography: p.272
   Includes index.
   1. Political parties – Italy. 2. Political
parties – Italy – Tuscany. I. Title.
JN5655 1981.P74   324.245   80-22750
ISBN 0-312-56194-6

CONTENTS

List of Abbreviations
Preface

1. The Nature of the Italian Party System — 1
   (a) Italian Political Parties: the Historical Perspective — 2
   (b) Classifying the Italian Party System — 11
   (c) The Political Parties and the Regional Structures — 19
   (d) The Changing Socio-economic Environment of the 1970s — 24
   References — 26

2. The Region of Tuscany: the Case-study Presented — 29
   (a) Why a Regional Case-study? — 29
   (b) Political Traditions — 31
   (c) Socio-economic Structure — 38
   Notes — 42
   References — 43

3. The Tuscan Communists: the Party of Integration on the Left — 45
   (a) Evolution as Party and Movement — 45
   (b) The PCI's Mass Base: its Integrative Capacity and Way of Life — 50
   (c) The PCI's Structural Character: Patterns of Change and Continuity — 77
   (d) The 'Party of Government and Struggle': the Internal Dimension — 100
   Notes — 112
   References — 112

4. The Tuscan Christian Democrats: the Party of Catholic-Conservative mobilisation — 120
   (a) Party, Movement or Electoral Association? — 120
   (b) The DC's Mass Character: between Socio-political Movement and Clientilist Formation — 126
   (c) The DC as a Structured Party: the Formality and Reality — 144

	(d) The Question of Party Identity and the Problems	
	of *Rapprochement* with the PCI	167
	Notes	179
	References	179
5.	Inter-party Relationships and the Politics of Convergence:	
	the Tuscan Experience	184
	(a) The Evolution of Party Strategies: Converging in	
	the Same Direction?	187
	(b) Inter-party Relationships: the Case of Local	
	Government	199
	(c) Inter-party Relationships and the New Regional	
	State Structure	225
	Notes	242
	References	243

Conclusion: Change and Continuity in the Italian Party System	249
Note on Sources	259
List of Tuscan Communes Visited for Research and Interviews	260
List of Interviews	265
Published Sources and Bibliography	272
Index	279

ABBREVIATIONS

CL	Comunione e Liberazione (Catholic association)
CGIL	Confederazione Generale Italiana dei Lavoratori (PCI-allied trade union organisation)
CISL	Confederazione Italiana Sindacati Lavoratori (Catholic trade union organisation)
DC	Democrazia Cristiana (Christian Democratic Party)
FGCI	Italian Communist Youth Federation
GIP	Gruppi di Impegno Politico (Groups of Political Involvement) — DC organisation in the factories
MILLE	Movement for a Free Italy in a Free Europe
MSI	Movimento Sociale Italiano (Italian Neo-Fascist Party)
PCd'I	Partito Comunista d'Italia (name of Communist Party before Mussolini)
PCI	Partito Comunista Italiano (Italian Communist Party)
PdUP	Partito di Unità Proletaria (Left-wing Communists)
PLI	Partito Liberale Italiano (Italian Liberal Party)
PPI	Partito Popolare Italiano (pre-Mussolini Catholic Party)
PR	Partito Radicale (Italian Radical Party)
PRI	Partito Repubblicano Italiano (Italian Republican Party)
PSDI	Partito Socialista Democratico Italiano (Italian Social Democratic Party)
PSI	Partito Socialista Italiano (Italian Socialist Party)
PSIUP	Partito Socialista Italiano di Unità Proletaria (Italian Socialist Party of Proletarian Unity)
PSU	Partito Socialista Unificato (name of the temporary merger between the PSI and PSDI in the later 1960s)
UDI	Union of Italian Women (collateral organisation of the PCI)
UIL	Unione Italiana del Lavoro (trade union association of the Centre-Left, including Socialists, Social Democrats and Republicans)

COMMUNES IN TUSCANY

SEE OVER FOR REFERENCE GUIDE

REFERENCE GUIDE TO TUSCAN COMMUNES BY PROVINCE

Province of Massa-Carrara

Aulla 11
Bagnone 5
Carrara 15
Casola in Lunigiana 14
Comano 8
Filattiera 4
Fivizzano 12
Fosdinovo 13
Licciana Nardi 9
Massa 16
Montignoso 17
Mulazzo 3
Podenzana 10
Pontremoli 2
Tresana 7
Villafranca in Lunigiana 6
Zeri 1

Province of Lucca

Altopascio 52
Bagni di Lucca 40
Barga 38
Borgo a Mozzano 41
Camaiore 44
Camporgiano 27
Capannori 49
Careggine 32
Castelnuovo di Garfagnana 31
Castiglione di Garfagnana 28
Coreglia Antelminelli 39
Fabbriche di Vallico 42
Forte dei Marmi 18
Fosciandora 30
Gallicano 37
Giuncugnano 22
Lucca 47
Massarosa 46
Minucciano 21
Molazzana 33
Montecarlo 51
Pescaglia 43
Piazza al Serchio 24
Pietrasanta 35
Pieve Fosciana 29
Porcari 50
San Romano in Garfagnana 25
Seravezza 19
Sillano 23
Stazzema 34
Vagli Sotto 20
Vergemoli 36
Viareggio 45
Villa Basilica 48
Villa Collemandina 26

Province of Pistoia

Abetone 74
Agliana 65
Buggiano 57
Chiesina Uzzanese 53
Cutigliano 73
Lamporecchio 63
Larciano 62
Marliana 70
Massa e Cozzile 58
Monsummano Terme 61
Montale 66
Montecatini Terme 59
Pescia 55
Pieve a Nievole 60
Pistoia 68
Piteglio 71
Ponte Buggianese 54
Quarrata 64
Sambuca Pistoiese 67
San Marcello Pistoiese 72
Serravalle Pistoiese 69
Uzzano 56

Province of Florence

Bagno a Ripoli 101
Barberino di Mugello 77
Barberino Val d'Elsa 103
Borgo S. Lorenzo 82
Calenzano 86
Campi Bisenzio 109
Cantagallo 75
Capraia e Limite 120
Carmignano 121
Castelfiorentino 117
Cerreto Guidi 124
Certaldo 114
Dicomano 91
Empoli 118
Fiesole 100
Figline Valdarno 96
Firenze (Florence) 107
Firenzuola 78
Fucecchio 125
Gambassi 115
Greve 102
Impruneta 106
Incisa in Val d'Arno 97
Lastra a Signa 111
Londa 92
Marradi 80
Montaione 116
Montelupo Fiorentino 119
Montemurlo 88
Montespertoli 113
Palazzuolo sul Senio 79

(Province of Florence, cont'd)

Pelago 94
Poggio a Caiano 122
Pontassieve 99
Prato 89
Reggello 95
Rignano sull'Arno 98
Rufina 93
San Casciano in Val di Pesa 105
San Godenzo 90
San Piero a Sieve 84
Scandicci 112
Scarperia 83
Sesto Fiorentino 108
Signa 110
Tavarnelle Val di Pesa 104
Vaglia 85
Vaiano 87
Vernio 76
Vicchio 81
Vinci 123

Province of Livorno (Leghorn)

Bibbona 169
Campiglia Marittima 174
Campo nell'Elba 181
Capoliveri 179
Capraia Isola 184
Castagneto Carducci 170
Cecina 168
Collesalvetti 165
Livorno (Leghorn) 166
Marciana 183
Marciana Marina 182
Piombino 175
Porto Azzurro 178
Portoferraio 180
Rio Marina 176
Rio nell'Elba 177
Rosignano Marittimo 167
San Vicenzo 173
Sassetta 171
Suvereto 172

Province of Pisa

Bientina 129
Buti 130
Calci 132
Calcinaia 137
Capannoli 150
Casale Marittimo 164
Casciana Terme 160
Cascina 136
Castelfranco di Sotto 127
Castellina Marittima 159
Castelnuovo in Val di Cecina 145
Chianni 158
Crespina 153
Fauglia 154
Guardistallo 163
Lajatico 148
Lari 152
Lorenzana 155
Montecatini in Val di Cecina 147
Montescudaio 162
Monteverdi Marittimo 146
Montopoli in Val d'Arno 139
Orciano Pisano 156
Palaia 141
Peccioli 142
Pisa 135
Pomarance 144
Ponsacco 151
Pontedera 138
Riparbella 161
San Giuliano Terme 133
San Miniato 140
Santa Croce sull'Arno 126
Santa Luce 157
Santa Maria a Monte 128
Terricciola 149
Vecchiano 134
Vicopisano 131
Volterra 143

Province of Grosseto

Arcidosso 199
Campagnatico 195
Capalbio 211
Castel del Piano 197
Castell'Azzara 203
Castiglione della Pescaia 193
Cinigiano 196
Civitella Paganico 190
Follonica 185
Gavorrano 191
Grosseto 194
Isola del Giglio 212
Magliano in Toscana 208
Manciano 206
Massa Marittima 186
Monte Argentario 210
Monterotondo Marittimo 187
Montieri 188
Orbetello 209
Pitigliano 205
Roccalbegna 201
Roccastrada 189
Santafiora 200
Scansano 207
Scarlino 192
Seggiano 198
Semproniano 202
Sorano 204

Province of Siena

Abbadia San Salvatore 215
Asciano 232

(Province of Siena, cont'd)

Buonconvento 226
Casole d'Elsa 247
Castellina in Chianti 242
Castelnuovo Berardenga 239
Castiglione d'Orcia 223
Cetona 217
Chianciano Terme 220
Chiusdino 236
Chiusi 219
Colle Val d'Elsa 246
Gaiole in Chianti 240
Montalcino 225
Montepulciano 221
Monteriggioni 243
Monteroni d'Arbia 233
Monticiano 235
Murlo 234
Piancastagnaio 213
Pienza 222
Poggibonsi 244
Radda in Chianti 241
Radicofani 216
Radicondoli 248
Rapolano Terme 231
San Casciano dei Bagni 214
San Gimignano 245
San Giovanni d'Asso 227
San Quirico d'Orcia 224
Sarteano 218
Siena 238
Sinalunga 230
Sovicille 237
Torrita di Siena 229
Trequanda 228

Province of Arezzo

Anghiari 257
Arezzo 255
Badia Tedalda 286
Bibbiena 279
Bucine 259
Capolona 270
Caprese Michelangelo 283
Castel Focognano 271
Castelfranco di Sopra 268
Castel San Niccolo 274
Castiglion Fibocchi 266
Castiglion Fiorentino 250
Cavriglia 262
Chitignano 281
Chiusi della Verna 280
Civitella in Val di Chiana 258
Cortona 249
Foiano della Chiana 251
Laterina 265
Loro Ciuffenna 267
Lucignano 252
Marciano della Chiana 253
Montemignaio 275
Monterchi 256
Monte San Savino 254
Montevarchi 261
Ortignano Raggiolo 273
Pergine Valdarno 260
Pian di Sco 269
Pieve Santo Stefano 284
Poppi 278
Pratovecchio 276
San Giovanni Valdarno 263
Sansepolcro 285
Sestino 287
Stia 277
Subbiano 282
Talla 272
Terranuova Bracciolini 264

To Pippa

PREFACE

This book originated in a long-standing academic and personal interest in Italian affairs, while the idea for this subject crystallised during a visit to Tuscany in the summer of 1975, which formed the preparatory stage for the research work which followed. This was conducted essentially during two visits to Italy in the summer and autumn of 1977 on sabbatical leave and in the summer of 1978, accompanied by correspondence and telephone contact with useful sources both in between and since these visits for the purpose of updating.

The period 1975-1980, during which this book was researched and written, itself featured many important changes in the Italian party system. These provide the central theme of the present study, and are introduced in an historical and comparative setting in the first chapter and elaborated on in later sections of the book. The value of a regional case-study approach is discussed in Chapter 2, while the main part of the book consists of three chapters dealing separately with the development of the PCI and DC as political forces; and then their political strategies, together with those of the smaller parties, are examined comparatively in the final chapter. A strong argument of the whole study is that political parties should not be analysed too exclusively as autonomous entities as so much academic work on them has tended to do, but consideration should also be given to the political environment and to their political roles and strategies. The nature of Italy's multi-party system dictates that major account should be taken of inter-party relationships and the effect on them of the internal relationships and general evolution of individual parties, and vice versa. The focus of this study has been on these aspects of party-political behaviour rather than on a detailed discussion of policy implementation or electoral support. In short, it investigates the application of the 'historic compromise' strategy of the PCI, the central theme of political strategy debate during the period in question, from the perspective of a particular chosen region.

The stimulus for this work has derived therefore not merely from a need to update on party development in Italy, but also from the necessity of questioning many previously held assumptions about that country's party system in the light of political and socio-economic change during the decade of the 1970s. Indeed, while there was in general a shortage of academic analyses of Italian party development (apart from a few accomplished examples) at the outset of this study, the subsequent years in which it was researched have evidenced a growth of interesting and perceptive literature on the subject in both Italian and English. Undoubtedly, the changes in the Italian party system already noted have been a major reason for this new interest. Selected titles on Italian parties in general are mentioned in the Bibliography along with publications relating to the case of Tuscany. The author has benefited above all from the availability of both published and documentary as well as personal sources on this region — on which see the Note on Sources, List of Communes Visited and List of Interviews as well as Bibliography at the end of this book. He would like especially to draw attention to the plentiful and systematic publications of the statistical department (SEDD) of the Tuscan region, which has distinguished itself in this respect among the new Italian regions. These have provided rich and accurate data on both electoral behaviour and local administrations throughout Tuscany, and have been supplemented by a new journal on the former published since 1977 (see Bibliography, p. 273). A map of Tuscany is provided to help the reader, who is informed that the province of towns mentioned in the text is usually given in brackets. He or she may also refer to the introductions to the Appendices for the specific use made of the various forms of research material.

In collecting this variety of source material, the author was assisted generously by research and travel grants from the Nuffield Foundation (Social Sciences Small Grants Scheme) for his sabbatical stay in Italy in 1977 and by the British Academy (West European Grants) for the subsequent visit in 1978. Thanks are given for their interest and patience to all interviewees mentioned in the list on pp. 265-71, but many personal acknowledgements deserve to be mentioned. This book must refer to the friendship and memory of Sergio Marchetti, whose hospitality to Pippa and myself at Lo Spugnaccio in 1975 did so much originally to encourage the first tentative steps in embarking on this research project; and also to those whom we met through him, Flavio and Anna Mocenni of S. Piero in Barca, Giorgio and Elli Bianchi of Radda in Chianti and Mario Ciappi of Siena. I should also like to thank in particular Mario Gabelli of the Tuscan region's SEDD, Paolo Giovannini of Florence University and Mario Caciagli of Catania University, as well as Giuseppe Matulli of the Tuscan DC and Vannino Chiti of the Tuscan PCI. Finally, our stay in Tuscany would have been much less enjoyable without the company and hospitality of all our friends (especially the Cesarini family and Margerita Falciani) in Montalcino (Siena), of the Cardi family at Peccioli (Pisa), Domenico and Gabriella Corradini at Pisa for several lively lunchtime conversations and Celia and John Turvey for allowing us to live in their serenely located house near Lucca as well as many other friends and acquaintances in Florence and the Tuscan countryside. We are also glad that my sister, Pop, joined us for Christmas and was responsible for our gastronomic delights.

The final production of this work can hardly pass without special mention of Anne Merriman, whose excellent typing skills have once again transformed a much-rethought manuscript for the author — and that, despite repeated promises of an earlier delivery of the manuscript. Mary Woods of the Department of Politics also helped with the final stage of typing.

By far the greatest individual debt and thanks go to Pippa, to whom this book is also dedicated. The reasons are innumerable and include her editing and interpretative criticism of the whole of the original manuscript (a task which she has patiently performed on numerous other occasions), her understanding for a husband too often closeted in his own world but also for her company on both visits to Italy and sharing in laughs and adventures around Tuscany.

Geoffrey Pridham
Bristol

1 THE NATURE OF THE ITALIAN PARTY SYSTEM

The thesis of this book is that the Italian party system has undergone a process of unprecedented change during the decade of the 1970s which requires not merely an updated survey of its development but rather a re-interpretation of the nature of that system. It is of course a truism to say that party systems do or should change in that they are required as viable frameworks for political development — that is, expecially in democratic systems political parties are central to the process of socio-political integration and interest aggregation. However, in the Italian case many assumptions made about its party system based on the experience of its operation in the postwar decades preceding the 1970s have to be reviewed and modified. This qualitative transformation in the nature of the Italian party system has derived both from the evolution of the different parties, individually and in relation to each other, and from the changing socio-political and economic environment in Italy.

While therefore 'political change' is somewhat relative as a term of reference, when applied to an evolutionary situation, there are many indices which support the conclusion that change in Italian party development during the 1970s has been of fundamental importance. The most obvious evidence has come from the uncustomary mobility in voting behaviour compared with the previously extremely stable patterns. The continuously dominant role of the DC since the late 1940s has been significantly weakened, even though it has remained the senior party in national government; while at the same time the PCI as the other main party has increasingly assumed positions of political authority at different levels of the state structure, more than ever since the War. Furthermore, this latter development in particular has involved a new departure in inter-party relationships with the replacement of the former polarised divide between the DC and PCI with a more competitive situation. While it may be said of the PCI's strategy of the 'historic compromise' that as a proposition it is indeed 'historic' because of the new governing role claimed and partially acquired by that party, as a form of 'compromise' in practice it is not so essentially new. Thus, the Italian party system has in the 1970s featured the same political parties as earlier, but their positions and courses have altered as a major component of the new situation.

2 The Nature of the Italian Party System

Italy has not been exceptional in Western Europe, where many other national party systems have faced erious problems of change partly arising from similar causes (notably common economic pressures from world inflation), but the quality of her party system has been particularly essential to the functioning of Italy's relatively young parliamentary democracy. It is important, however, to establish to what extent this process of political change in the 1970s may be a long-term development and not just a passing phase. This process will therefore be placed in the broader context of the historical evolution of Italian political · parties especially since Fascism, reference will be made to different theoretical interpretations of the Italian party system while establishing the latter's interest for the comparative study of political parties, the question of regional government will be examined as a test case of the attitudes and positions of the various parties towards institutional reform and, finally, the impact on party development of social and economic changes in the 1970s, and what problems these present for a re-interpretation of the party system in Italy, will be discussed.

(a) Italian Political Parties: the Historical Perspective

Far from presenting a detailed account of the historical development of Italian parties from pre-Fascist times, it is considered necessary here in view of the approach of this study to focus on various key questions relating to this entire period for the purpose of outlining the main *leitmotivs* and aspects of party development in Italy. The most suitable framework of reference is that offered by Eckstein and Apter, who identify three essential relationships when examining the general role of political parties: their relationship to the state, to the national community and between themselves.[1] It will be seen that in all three cases the crucial historical watershed in Italy was the Fascist period, as this not only interrupted previous patterns of party development but also provided through the subsequent consensus of anti-Fascism a basic point of ideological reference for the postwar period as well as reinforced features of mass politics in Italy inadequately developed in a democratic context before the rise of Mussolini.

Looking at the first of these criteria, it clearly emerges that the principal difference between the pre-Fascist and post-Fascist periods in the relationship between the parties and the state lies in the degree of centrality of the former's role with respect to the latter. While Italian political parties acting as the predominant channel of political communication, policy-making, leadership recruitment and access to public office have been in existence since the Second World War, they did not essentially perform that function before the advent of the Fascist state. This difference becomes evident when turning to the role of parties in the earlier period.

The salient characteristic of the half-century or more from the unification of Italy to Fascism was the dominance of an exclusive political class enjoying control of the centralised state machine without reference to a mass political base and without challenge from an effective opposition. This political class, called the 'historic Right' (or later the Liberals), which ruled Italy from the time of Cavour, was drawn from the landed and commercial bourgeoisie, notably from Piedmont, but in strictly party-political terms was little more than an incohesive collection of political groupings held together by the habit in government of arriving at *ad hoc* or pragmatic policy arrangements to the mutual satisfaction of the different interests represented by this class — a system generally known as *trasformismo*. The Liberals' control of the state and monopoly of parliamentary representation was made possible by a highly restricted franchise and facilitated by the weakness or virtual absence of opposition. As Salomone has written, this period was marked by the fact that there was 'no organised opposition to factions, cliques and camarillas, which skirmished in Parliament until the rise of the Socialists at the end of the century'.[2] Moreover, even with the appearance of this first organised political force in modern Italian history, the two traditional political sub-cultures of Socialism and Catholicism (represented by various Catholic associations which amounted to a loose movement at this stage) were located on the periphery of the political system until the end of the First World War. In particular, the Catholics as a political movement were restrained by the Vatican prohibition on their political participation as a consequence of the Papal non-recognition of the newly unified Italian state. The consequence was a Liberal regime but one with a pronounced lack of socio-political integration and a potentially vulnerable state of legitimacy. The enlargement of the franchise under Giolitti in 1913 and the early political success of the Catholic Popular Party (PPI), founded in 1919 after the lifting of the Papal ban, came too late to strengthen the party-political basis of the parliamentary state and check the destabilising impact of the First World War on Italian politics. The Fascist period followed with the proscription of other parties under the one-party state.

Party development after two decades of Fascist rule was

qualitatively very different from that prevalent during the Liberal period. First, the Fascist state had introduced the concept and practice of the party acting as a pervasive capillary organism present throughout different levels of society and enjoying an intensive relationship with the state apparatus. This precedent, fostered in a one-party framework, influenced postwar party development in the new democratic context most conspicuously in the elaborate organisational presence of the DC and PCI in Italian society since the Second World War. Furthermore, during the Fascist period the hostility between the Roman Catholic Church and the Italian state had been solved through the Concordat of 1929, which was incorporated in the postwar Constitution of 1948. Secondly, as this Constitution underlined in its Article 49 ('All citizens have the right to associate freely in political parties in order to contribute through democratic procedure to the determination of national policy'), the primacy of competitive political parties as channels of political communication was already established before the inauguration of the postwar political system and they came to dominate its functioning. This dominance developed to such an extent that it became known as *partitocrazia* ('rule by parties'); that is, a system in which the political parties are not only the controlling power in the decision-making processes of the state, but also permeate the activities of public life in general.[3]

The question of the centrality of the parties' role may be taken one stage further by asking whether they have also had a unifying or legitimising effect on the Italian political system by way of counterbalancing the renowned inefficiency of the Italian state administration, such structural and social cleavages as those reflected in the north/south divide, centrifugal factors like regionalism and the provincialism of Italian life and, above all, the lack of popular attachment to the nation-state to which Almond and Verba paid attention.[4] This question has been often raised and contested. On the one hand, Galli and Prandi have argued positively that the PCI in particular has acted 'as a primary force in the process of "nationalisation of politics", that is, of the progressive spreading throughout the country of national political agencies and issues',[5] and that the DC has performed similarly through its network of Catholic associations. Although this organisational penetration of Italian public life by the main parties is undeniable, other writers (notably Sartori) have maintained that the confusion engendered by Italian party life has acted as a factor promoting alienation from the system;[6] while it has also been argued that the weak internal cohesion of the ruling parties, especially the DC, has detracted from the performance of successive Italian governments.[7] One important approach, often overlooked in general studies of Italian politics, is to examine the sub-national levels of party activity for this allows a more profound, as well as specific, survey of the organisational presence of the respective parties and its political importance, the extent to which they penetrate or absorb Italian provincial life and whether their individual strategies are more than just political arrangements devised in Rome. In short, these levels of activity reveal more than national politics, whether the political parties are centripetal or centrifugal agents in the operation of the political system. Sidney Tarrow has already indicated the value of this approach in his discussion of centre-periphery relations in Italian politics.[8]

Finally, one major reservation must be noted about the competitive basis of the relationship of parties to the state. The DC has been the senior governing party of Italy continuously since 1945, not merely because of its electoral strength — which has remained around 40 per cent, except for its one absolute majority in 1948 — as the fact that its power position has been sustained ideologically by an anti-Communist consensus involving an alliance with smaller parties and that it has consolidated its tenure of office through 'populating' the politico-economic establishment, notably the bureaucracy, the public corporations and the judiciary. It is in this sense that the dictum 'with 40% of the votes, the DC controls 80% of the power' has its application. Consequently, while electorally the DC and PCI have been the two dominant forces in Italy it is the former which has dominated within the political structure, so that it is permissible to speak of a 'DC regime' or even 'DC state'. The extent to which this dominance has differed from the Liberal and Fascist regimes will be shown by the next section, and the way in which it has come under challenge is a theme of this book.

The second form of relationship, that of the political parties to the national community, once again underlines the importance of the Fascist period as the principal historical turning-point in party development. Mussolini's regime discredited not only Fascism as a political force but also traditional political classes like the Liberals which had collaborated with it, thus creating an immense vacuum on the Centre to Right of the political spectrum only too readily occupied by the newly founded *Democrazia Cristiana* (DC), which succeeded in mobilising both Catholic and conservative elements. In 1946 the DC won 35 per cent of the vote compared with the 20 per cent of its Catholic predecessor, the PPI, prior to Fascism. The experience of the Resistance gave the Left in particular an important opportunity for organisational mobilisation at a mass level unprecedented in Italian politics, an event which distinctly favoured the Communists with their strong ideological commitment and external support from the USSR. As a result, the basis for the superior strength of the DC and PCI in the emerging postwar party system was created. Hence, the two political forces based on the Catholic and Marxist sub-cultures which had been relegated to the margin of the pre-Fascist political system became dominant in the new postwar one.

It is worth glancing briefly at the pre-Fascist period to record other features which reinforce the picture of contrast. First, it is at the very least dubious to talk about an Italian party system before Mussolini — if only because of the absence of what may be referred to as 'movements' and 'parties' at the societal level. The ruling Liberals were neither one nor the other but essentially an elite group at best loose-associational in its construction, whose 'social presence' derived from little more than the influence of local notables. The moderate groups on the Left, such as the Republicans and Radicals, could also not claim any form of mass-party linkage with the public. It was only with the founding of the Italian Socialist Party in 1892 that there occurred the beginning of an organised political movement, though it never achieved before the First World War the same degree of structural intensity as its German counterpart, the SPD, which became the model for Michels' classic study of oligarchy in political parties.[9] Secondly, the established political groups of the Liberal period accordingly failed to promote the legitimacy of the political system. This was necessarily a reflection of the highly restricted franchise in Italy, which in the later nineteenth century had risen from only 1.92 per cent at the time of unification to 9.57 per cent in the year of the formation of the Socialist Party and to 25 per cent with the extension of male suffrage in 1913. Turnout in these elections never moved out of the range of 50 per cent to 60 per cent, in contrast to the regular 92 per cent and over in elections since the Second World War, at the conclusion of which the granting of the vote to women brought the first genuine introduction of universal suffrage. Before Fascism, therefore, political participation in the most elementary sense was highly circumscribed. More seriously, social changes and pressures, deriving long-term from the impact of industrialisation from the late nineteenth century and short-term from the economic and psychological consequences in Italy of the First World War, were hardly absorbed into the pre-Fascist 'party system'. The only pointer to the post-Fascist future was the success of the Catholic PPI and the Socialists in winning over half of the votes and parliamentary seats following the introduction of proportional representation in 1919. The Socialists acted as an integrative force in harnessing support from industrial workers, but they were not admitted to any decision-making role in the political system.

Looking again at post-1945 Italy, the decisive question when estimating the relationship of the party system to the community must be how far the role of individual parties in the state is based on the strength of their social roots and their integrative capacity. This is a particularly telling question in view of the accelerated process of social change in postwar Italy, witnessed by the impact of growing industrialisation and the high degree of internal population mobility, not to mention further socio-political pressures emanating later from the protest movements of the late 1960s and persistent inflation and unemployment in the 1970s.

This problem may be approached in a variety of ways, ranging from analysing patterns of electoral behaviour to evaluating the resilience of the parties in response to social change and their bridging of socio-economic divisions. Italy has since Fascism demonstrated a remarkably high degree of electoral stability, where with a few exceptions the margin of fluctuation of support for individual parties between national elections has been at the most three per cent to four per cent. This may of course disguise cross-voting between parties and a wider margin at the sub-national levels, but the Galli and Prandi study — based on the Cattaneo Institute's analysis of 7,144 of the country's 8,000 communes for the elections of 1946-1963 — confirmed this electoral stability at the local level, although it was more marked in the northern and central regions, especially where there were strong Catholic and 'Red' traditions to reinforce voting affiliation, than in the south.[10] This stability has usually been attributed *inter alia* to such factors as the strong political traditions of the two leading parties and their extensive network of party auxiliary organisations. However, in the 1970s these patterns have been altered by greater voter mobility as shown transiently by the rise of the neo-Fascist vote in the early years of the decade but, more significantly, by the major advance of the PCI electorate in the mid-1970s. At the same time, while the DC's vote has remained pertinaciously around its usual level, there were signs by the end of the decade of qualitative changes in voting behaviour and a loosening of party support which have increased mobility.[11]

Party identification can be further ascertained by considering membership recruitment. By West European standards, Italy has evidenced a strong level of registration in parties. Adams and Barile wrote in 1966 that 'both for its procedure and for the quality of commitment it entails, membership in an Italian political party is not dissimilar to membership in an American church . . . party flags are carried in funeral processions of ordinary party members'.[12] This tendency is generally explained by the *tessera* (membership card) mentality — of party adherence as a ticket to employment — conditioned by the Fascist experience, a habit utilised by the postwar parties. This feature must not be overrated since party membership is obviously a largely passive affair, though there are significant variations between the parties of the Left and Right as to the motive of ideological commitment. Nevertheless, the durability of party ties has been noted in the face of continuous or new social tensions up to the earlier 1970s,[13] and there has since been a remarkable stability even with evidence of some relapse in PCI recruitment in the later 1970s.

It must finally be asked how the parties have managed as agents of social integration in ameliorating or containing cleavages in the Italian community. Kirchheimer's sometimes overrated thesis of 'catch-all parties' presented in the mid-1960s[14] has a particular application in the Italian case, for once the DC's electorate stabilised from 1953 this party's maintenance of inter-class support and ability to aggregate different interest claims has been gradually matched by the PCI's success in mobilising wider support. The PCI's vital role in integrating the lower social strata and the Left electorate generally is undeniable and may be illustrated by the enlargement of its basin of support after the War in the south as well as north[15] and among middle-class voters, not to mention its absorption of much of the extra-parliamentary Left of the late 1960s. Although many potential factors of cleavage have continued to exist, such as Church-state relations and foreign policy differences, these have more recently been underplayed by the parties in their desire for accommodation. This has been achieved, however, at the cost of stagnation in the political system. The social links of the individual parties do not therefore provide the complete picture of how the state and community relate through their medium, for just as crucial an aspect is how they conduct themselves as competitive or co-operative 'gatekeepers' or channels of political activity. To what extent can they together promote or produce social and political cohesion in the wide sense of stability of the political system? This leads us to the third of the principal relationships — that between the political parties themselves.

As with the other two historical approaches to Italian party development, the Fascist period was the real watershed. Inter-party relationships hardly developed before Mussolini, if one excludes the practice of *trasformismo* as being between parliamentary figures or unformulated political groupings rather than party leaders with organised support. During the brief period of turmoil following the First World War the new parliamentary weight acquired by the Socialists and the PPI with proportional representation did not modify traditional patterns of political arrangement, even though government was impossible without their consent. The determination of these parties to assert their positions, coupled with the reluctance of Giolitti and other established leaders to accept the changed party-political balance, created an unstable situation already made ripe for exploitation by the Fascists through sociopolitical tensions caused by the War and the traditional ideological antagonism between Socialists and Catholics.

Postwar Italy has been different since organised political parties have become an established and central part of the policy-making process and of government/opposition relations. Indeed, Italy has been noted among West European democracies for the pronounced influence exerted by party organisations over parliamentary groups. This has been particularly true of the PCI as a machine party whereby the position of national deputy is regarded as functional rather than prestigious. Even though a parliamentary deputy enjoys a higher standing in the ranks of the DC, this party's laborious process of forming an internal policy consensus has accorded the party secretary and executive bureau a special place in decision-making. It is because of this area of bureaucratic party politics that any historical comparison with the Giolittian system of *trasformismo* strictly falls down, however much some parallels may be drawn with the method of obtaining a wider consensus at the cost of distinct or innovative policy lines taken by the parties concerned.[16]

Two main questions concerning inter-party relationships need to be briefly reviewed. First, these have at the governmental level usually taken a heterogeneous form. The DC has admittedly been the dominant partner in all coalitions since 1945, but it has invariably been forced to rely on the support of other parties and, even after De Gasperi's electoral triumph of 1948, the government was widened to include Republicans, Liberals and Social Democrats. Efficiency in policy-making has too often been sacrificed to the dictates of seeking a broad consensus. This was strikingly the fate of the Centre-Left governments of the 1960s which, after some initial successes, decelerated to a policy stalemate. A notable feature of Italian parties in government has been their internal factionalism, which has been the source of checking or counterchecking influences in policy-making. The power of the factions has become such an entrenched part of the Italian political scene — hence the term *correntocrazia* — that they have been also a significant factor in inter-party relationships both in establishing policy preferences and in the selection of Cabinet personnel, including prime ministers.[17]

The second question relates to whether inter-party co-operation has promoted loyalty to the political system or otherwise. Historically, the practice of political accommodation has continued to derive some inspiration at moments of national crisis from the common wartime starting-point for the parties in the Resistance, whose anti-Fascist motif has remained an implicit focus for regime loyalty even though the individual parties have expressed a varied degree of ideological commitment to an anti-Fascist purpose (it is felt most keenly on the political Left). This motif was, however, strongly overlaid by anti-Communism among the parties of government from the time of the Cold War. At the level of individual policy matters, the treatment by the parties especially in more recent times of factors of potential polarisation has been conditioned by their fear of treading on a tinderbox of potentially controversial issues and igniting emotional fallout. This preference for convergence has derived from a concern about the negative effects of socio-economic crisis in the 1970s on the system's legitimacy and has been notably illustrated by the PCI's 'historic compromise'. On the other hand, elite-level accommodation has also heightened a feeling of confusion and apathy among the Italian public and hence increased the risk of alienation from the established political parties. Inter-party relationships have ultimately to be accountable to both party members and electorates.

In conclusion, it becomes clear that, while the Fascist period was the crucial historical dividing point in Italian party development, all three relationships of political parties — with the state, with the national community and between themselves — have undergone a significant transformation during the course of the 1970s. Many assumptions long held about the nature of the postwar Italian party system — such as the dominance of DC rule, the factor of electoral stability and the state of polarisation — have had to be questioned, not least because socio-economic change has been greater than in any previous decade since the republican system of government was established in the later 1940s. Since the consequent political change has been not so much abrupt as evolutionary, the fundamental question arises of how this change has related to continuity — which is the central theme of this book.

(b) Classifying the Italian Party System

The foregoing historically-based discussion helps us now to assess the Italian party system along more comparative lines, bearing in mind such questions as: to what extent is the Italian case elucidated by the comparative study of political parties in being unique or representative, or both; and, therefore, to which classification of party system does it approximate? Various theoretical interpretations of the postwar Italian party system seem all the more to have a relative value in the light of the aforementioned factors of political change evident during the course of the 1970s.

The hypothesis of this study is that no individual model of interpretation is applicable without significant modification, just as no party system is literally a 'classic' example of any particular form. Apart from the overriding purpose of the comparative approach to formulate through the method of categorisation a workable and reasonably accurate conceptual basis for measuring the nature and activity of political parties, it also provides a useful framework of analysis for illuminating the national case-study — which is the chosen focus here.

Moreover, flexibility in the use of models is obviously dictated by the need to take account of evolution in party systems. It is here that the Italian case has caused problems of interpretation. Aside from comments on the 'Byzantine' nature of the country's politics,[18] which refer especially to complex internal party procedures as in the ruling DC as well as the extensive practice of *sottogoverno*, we are thinking of wider structures where the impact of political re-alignment has produced an admixture of types of party system. In a study of new trends in West European party systems, Gordon Smith for instance concluded in 1978 that Italy was an ambivalent example since elements of all four of his types of party system were present there: dominance, fragmentation, balance and diffusion.[19]

The Italian party system is difficult to categorise for a number of specific reasons, which do not exclusively relate to the circumstances of the 1970s. First, if the DC is an example of a dominant party, for which it must be a serious candidate in view of its protracted period of national rule, then this is not convincingly established as a straightforward case by the conventional standard of continuous and overriding electoral superiority if one omits its absolute majority gained in 1948 and lost in 1953. Hence, alliance partners have been essential to its maintenance of dominance.

Secondly, the PCI's particular strategic evolution whereby it has combined adaptation (as to the national political environment) with radical propositions (e.g. the re-structuring of the socio-political system) has through its consequent ambiguity led to differing and sometimes conflicting explanations of its role; all of which goes to show that stereotyped definitions cannot be used in this particular case. This reflects in turn on the problem of measuring the exact form of polarisation endemic in the Italian polity and hence the precise nature of its party system, for, as seen in the 1970s, substantial political 'distance' between parties is not always in practice incompatible with varying degrees of inter-party relationships.

Thirdly, the role of ideology in Italian politics is difficult to evaluate. Political positions may often be couched in ideological language, but, as Barnes has shown in his 'in-depth' study of one party's provincial federation, ideology is not an undifferentiated concept and that generally ideological sensitivity is more a preserve of middle-class leaders than it is of rank-and-file members.[20] Converse's preference for the term 'belief system' when applied to the lower levels of political participation[21] has a special relevance in the Italian case with the relatively limited degree of political education in that country. Tarrow has provided a refreshing antidote to some of the misleading assumptions about the role of ideology in Italian politics with his emphasis on examining partisanship and political dialogue locally. He suggests that 'in a system governed by a paralysed bureaucracy and by a national elite whose ideological cleavages are intense, integration may take place more readily at the foundation than at the top, in the hollows between ideological polemics and in the interstices of the bureaucracy that a resourceful local elite can manage to find'.[22]

Fourthly, conventional definitions of the multi-party character of the Italian system are confounded especially by the clear electoral and structural predominance within it of the DC and PCI together, but also by the persistent presence and not negligible influence of the small parties, whether through the forcefulness of individual political figures or their representation of political traditions or minority interests, out of proportion to their limited individual numerical strength.

Fifthly, the picture in Italy of serious social disharmony on the one hand and relative stability of established party-political structures on the other remains a seeming paradox until one looks at the sub-national level of politics, for this indicates the extent to which the parties have provided a uniform and durable framework for political development and change.

All this adds up to a situation demanding discriminating interpretation, though not to the picture of unqualified confusion portrayed by Sartori. The Italian version is not necessarily more complex than some other West European party systems. There is at least a consistency in the presence of the various party-political forces, more so than in France where there has usually been a fluidity in the way political traditions have been expressed through parties as organised entities. In its structural and political forms it is certainly not comparable to the German Weimar Republic, a model sometimes adopted by less sophisticated observers in view of Italy's problems of government competence and socio-political dysfunction. When applied specifically to the 1970s, all the five factors mentioned above do have a poignant relevance suggesting a party system in the process of transformation. This still leaves us with the problem of actually defining the Italian party system. For this reason it is useful to record the main theories which have been presented and to ask how much they need re-interpretation or modification in the light of trends in this party system since the late 1960s.

There have been two classic lines of interpretation about the nature of the Italian party system: as a case of 'polarised pluralism', and as an example of an 'imperfect two-party system'. The first of these expounded by Sartori has maintained that a system of 'polarised pluralism' is one characterised by the existence of many parties located along an ideological arc which stretches from extreme Right to extreme Left.[23] This produces an 'encirclement' of the political system in Italy by pro-system, half-way and anti-system parties, which combined with other cleavages promotes heterogeneity and hence centrifugal tendencies. The key factor for him is 'not only the number of the poles, but the distance between them'.[24] Sartori is most open to criticism for his placing the PCI alongside the neo-Fascist MSI as an 'extreme' party, a judgement very questionable in taking account of the 1970s when the PCI's changing role has tended to encourage centripetal rather than centrifugal tendencies.[25] At a theoretical level, Sartori's usefulness is to have emphasised the different kinds of multi-party system — 'for there is a world of difference between the bipolar pattern of moderate pluralism and the multipolar features of extreme pluralism'[26] — but even so, in the Italian case, the increased or sustained aggregation by both major political forces in the 1970s and the PCI's greater legitimacy have required a re-definition of the multi-party character of its party system.

The other principal line of interpretation has been followed by Galli, who has argued the existence of an 'imperfect two-party system' (*bipartitismo imperfetto*) because of the electoral predominance of the two main parties as representatives of the Catholic and Marxist subcultures, while at the institutional level there has been neither a homogeneous majority nor an opposition which can form an alternative government.[27] Variations on this theme have been discussed by others, such as Allum's comparative reference to the Namierite model drawn from eighteenth-century England of a permanent 'Court' party and a permanent 'out' party, each allied with minor parties.[28] Allum has also gone further in arguing the case for an 'imperfect one-party regime' (*monopartitismo imperfetto*) in view of the special ideological and political factors buttressing the power-bloc of the DC.[29]

The electoral predominance of the DC and PCI goes without saying, though it is instructive to note the consistency of it by recording its statistical strength. Table 1.1 details the combined vote of the two parties in national elections throughout the postwar period:

Table 1.1: Combined Vote of DC and PCI, 1946-1979

	%		%
1946	54.1	1968	66.0
1948*	79.5	1972	66.0
1953	62.7	1976	73.1
1958	65.1	1979	68.7
1963	63.6		

* Combined vote of the Communists and Socialists, who formed a Popular Front alliance in this election.

This combined strength of the two main parties falls, however, significantly short of that generally attained by their equivalents in Britain and West Germany as major examples of two/three-party systems. Hence, it is useful to indicate the total vote of the three main parties in Italy considering the triangular relationship which has existed throughout between the DC, PSI and PCI and as these are the only parties acting as fully organised channels of political participation at the grass-roots (see Table 1.2). This has left a total of more than 20 (though less in 1976) obtained by the smaller parties.

The lack of real alternation in government is obvious from the DC's longevity as senior party in government and the PCI's continued position as senior party in opposition from 1947 to 1976. This absence of change has had some basis in the electoral distance maintained by the DC as the stronger party from the PCI until the mid-1970s (see Table 1.3). Of course, the trend reducing this electoral distance was reversed some-

The Nature of the Italian Party System

Table 1.2: Combined Vote of the DC, PCI and PSI, 1946-1979

	%		%
1946	74.8	1968*	80.5
1948	79.5	1972	75.6
1953	75.5	1976	82.7
1958	79.3	1979	78.5
1963	77.4		

* Includes the combined Socialist vote as the PSI and PSDI campaigned together as the PSU

what in 1979 and future developments here remain to be seen. All the same, the Galli thesis, while applicable up to the mid-1970s, has none the less to be revised both in the light of this electoral mobility and the stronger political role acquired by the PCI; equally, the case for arguing an 'imperfect one-party regime' is much weakened. But the question of the DC's dominance must be examined in a wider frame of reference before assessing the state of transformation in the Italian party system.

The model applied here is that formerly used by Heidenheimer to evaluate the one-party imbalance favouring the West German CDU/CSU during the 1950s,[30] because when applied to the Italian situation it effectively shows the degree of change that has occurred in the space of the 1970s. Heidenheimer offers five main criteria for assessing a case of party dominance: the institutional; the socio-economic and ideological; leadership; foreign relations; and constitutional and political rules of the game.

First, the relationship between party and state has been unquestionably a predominant one in the case of the DC, not only because of its permanency as leading party in government but also as it has been in a privileged position to impose its own interests and values on the postwar republican system. The DC's privileged role has in particular been

Table 1.3: Difference between Votes of DC and PCI, 1946-1979

	%		%
1946	16.3	1968	12.2
1948*	17.5	1972	11.6
1953	17.5	1976	4.3
1958	19.7	1979	7.9
1963	13.0		

* This is the difference between the DC and the combined vote of the Communists and Socialists.

supported by its traditionally close relationship with the Roman Catholic Church and its roots in the extensive patronage system of the centralised state as well as its economic agencies. The term 'iceberg' is aptly descriptive of the visible and invisible sides of the DC's position in relation to the Italian state.[31] During the 1970s, this situation had to be significantly modified at the political-institutional level even though the DC has remained the senior national governing party. The gradual though substantial insertion of the PCI in greater positions of authority in the state structure, ranging from a co-decisional though not formal role in national government during the latter half of the 1970s to a much enlarged position in both local and regional administration (whereas previously it had been essentially confined to local government in the 'Red' belt), involved a qualitative even if not radical change in the party/state relationship. This change was facilitated by structural reform in the state machine with the introduction of regional governments throughout Italy in the early 1970s, and promoted by the PCI's new electoral success and its formation of alliances, especially with the PSI. At the same time, the position of the Church in society came under serious challenge, which in turn affected the role of the DC.

Secondly, the socio-economic and ideological factor provided a clear-cut case of party dominance when looking at the earlier period of DC rule. This criterion relates to the ability of the governing party to harness and integrate different interests and generally identify with the socio-economic development of the country. In this sense, the 'DC state' was also an economic system, a definition encouraged by the divergent economic 'philosophies' of the DC and PCI. Ideologically, this system was constructed on the basis of anti-Communist consensus, which had as its purpose the exclusion of the PCI from power once the party was expelled from the government in 1947. However, the 'economic miracle' of the 1950s and earlier 1960s finally collapsed by the late 1960s, so that economic performance in the 1970s has generally been marked by a turnabout with rampant inflation, persistently high unemployment and a marked vulnerability to the energy crisis. This has inevitably weakened both the standing of the DC and its resources for economic patronage. The PCI's new prominence in Italian politics undoubtedly has benefited from the difficulties of the DC, and it has argued the case strongly for the 'historic compromise' on grounds of this economic instability. It is significant that some economic elites have become less averse to the PCI's playing some part in economic policy formulation.

Thirdly, the leadership factor as a projection of authority has much less application than in West Germany, where charisma has been directed through the 'Chancellor effect'. De Gasperi was himself able to strengthen the appeal of his party, partly because of his integrative role, not matched by any of his successors in the DC; for the proliferation of *correnti*, each with leading figures vying for power, has prevented any such repetition. All the same, leadership credibility — whether individual or of a group — may assist a governing party's appeal, but this has been less likely than ever before in the 1970s because of the moral and political discredit attached to so many DC leaders in this decade. This only contributed to that party's general loss of credibility.

Fourthly, the identification of a governing party with national security interests is very relevant as a factor explaining the predominance of the DC in postwar Italy because of the profound impact of East-West antagonism on Italian domestic politics. The anti-Communist consensus behind the government was supported by the Atlantic Alliance, of which Italy was a founding member with the establishment of NATO, and reinforced by the USA's moral and financial support of the DC and its allied parties. Just as postwar Italy's external relations have always demonstrated a strong interlinkage with her internal affairs, so the process of the 'historic compromise' has inevitably had its international repercussions, as indeed it has its counterpart in the PCI's 'European road to socialism'. Significantly, the PCI's move away from a pure opposition force has been accompanied by its espousal of the cause of European integration by the late 1960s as well as acceptance of Italy's continuing membership of NATO in the mid-1970s. Traditional suspicions of the PCI's long-term purpose, should it fully enter government, have nevertheless remained at home among the DC and Centre-Right parties and abroad in Washington and some West European capitals where the DC is still regarded as the guarantor of Italy's national interests.

Fifthly, the use of constitutional and political rules of the game to support DC dominance was aptly illustrated by the Scelba Law of 1953 (popularly called the 'swindle law') introduced to manipulate the electoral system in the DC's favour at a time when its chances of retaining its absolute majority were declining. Similarly, the long delay in introducing regional government, provided for in the 1948 Constitution, was motivated on the DC's part by its desire to restrict the scope of the PCI's role in administrative politics. In the 1970s the PCI's increasing participation in government at different levels of the political system has weakened the possibility for politically discriminatory measures against it and increased its own scope for the distribution of patronage as well as its share in policy-making.

From this five-point model, it becomes evident how much the dominance of the DC has declined in the 1970s compared with its position in the two preceding decades. Admittedly, in applying these five criteria the result combines likely long-term or permanent features with possibly short-term trends, but the former are sufficiently important to suggest that the changed situation is a qualitative one. Thus, on the one hand, PCI electoral advances might recede (as indeed happened in 1978-1980, though not so far as the pre 1975-1976 level): East-West relations might worsen (as from the end of the 1970s) with possible effects on the PCI's standing; and the DC's credibility might improve though probably remain fragile. On the other hand, the regional structures are permanent, allowing an outlet for a PCI governing role here, its electoral support and alliance partners permitting; the precedent of the PCI's co-determining role in national government has been established and PCI strategy has despite difficulties continued to evolve offering 'constructive opposition' if not involved in government; while structural problems in the Italian economy show every sign of being long-term.

With this changed situation in mind, the deficiencies or outdatedness of the Sartori and Galli interpretations are clear. The former underestimated the consequences of the PCI's strategy and its emergence from polarised opposition, while the latter's thesis predated the substitution of convergence for alternation between the parties and in any case has to be modified to take account of growing signs in the 1970s of erosion in the sub-structures. Moreover, both interpretations conceived in the 1960s are that much less pertinent in view of other trends in the 1970s, such as a new flexibility in alliance formations following the DC's exhaustion of coalitions other than some agreement with the PCI as well as unprecedented electoral fluidity indicated both by the rise and partial fall of support for the PCI and re-emergence of smaller even regionalist parties.

Trends in the 1970s do not of course predict trends in the 1980s and beyond, so partly for that reason it is difficult to construct a model of the Italian party system guaranteed to carry conviction for the future. It is the intention in any case of this study to focus attention on the sub-national level of Italian politics in order to assess more accurately the precise importance of the aforementioned changes. However, as previously noted, some re-definition of the multi-party nature of the Italian system is necessary. Contrary to widespread belief, this never has been a classic or literal example of a multi-party system, even though it possesses some of the qualities of one — e.g. the proportional representation election system and the normal rule of coalition politics. A more suitable definition is a modified multi-party system with dominant elements, which allows for the combined electoral strength of the DC and PCI and, unlike the Sartori and Galli theses, takes account of the PCI's emergence from exclusive opposition. It is not merely the number of parties in a system (one factor of continuity in the Italian case) that determines its description, but also their relative strength (changed in the 1970s), their ideology (less pronounced as a factor dividing the main parties), the nature of their popular support (significant changes or fluctuations in the 1970s) and the structure of their organisations (more of a constant, though under some challenge during this decade).[32] Altogether, the outcome is a more competitive rather than a polarised party system in Italy.

(c) The Political Parties and the Regional Structures

One area of special relevance to the decline in DC dominance in the state and the emergence of a more competitive party system has been the institutional change commencing with the establishment of regional government throughout Italy in the early 1970s and the party-political battle before this was effected. The issue at stake was not so much the initiation of the idea of the regions as the much belated implementation of the provisions for its introduction which were contained in the Italian Constitution of 1948, Title V, Articles 114-33.

While special statutes enacted these provisions for the five frontier and island regions of Trentino-Alto Adige, Friuli-Venezia Giulia, Val d'Aosta, Sicily and Sardinia, partly in response to postwar ethnic and possible separatist pressures, for the remaining 15 'ordinary' regions in the rest of Italy the Constitution remained inoperative for over two decades. Because of the close relationship of some of the parties, particularly the DC, with the centralised state, the issue of implementing regional government must be considered a question of vested interests. It is therefore worth examining this issue both to show the extent to which the different political parties handled and controlled it, and as introductory background to the regional case-study approach of this book.

Historically, the idea of the regional structures was broadly conceived after the Second World War as an answer to Italy's geographical and cultural diversity and strong feelings of local patriotism.[33] The concept and tradition of local autonomy deriving from the role of the medieval city-states had been given new impetus by republican thinkers like Mazzini in the nineteenth century, but the creation of a unified centralised state under Piedmontese leadership by 1870 foreclosed the federal possibility except when fluctuating moods of regionalism occurred because of its espousal by opposition groups notably from the islands.[34] The regions therefore remained a 'statistical fiction' until the end of the Second World War, for they had been invented as an administrative convenience for data-collecting purposes at the time of unification and had consisted merely of clusters of provinces.[35] The reaction to the Fascist state undoubtedly produced a more thorough support for regionalism than had ever existed previously since the Risorgimento. Anti-Fascist figures like the historian Salvemini and Luigi Sturzo, ex-leader of the Catholic Popular Party, whose programme had advocated 'the construction of the regions', lent respectability to the idea. On a more popular level, the discredit associated with central government, the traumatic experience of the Resistance and Italy's collapse in the War combined, with the emergence of local political groups through the Committees of National Liberation, to foster a tendency for local autonomy which passed over into the immediate postwar period.[36]

The general picture of the postwar parties' attitudes towards regional government is well-known with the reversal of pro- and anti-positions between the DC and PCI once the former became entrenched in and the latter excluded from power. Unlike the West German Federal Republic, where a similar case of party dominance was mitigated by the role allowed the national opposition party in the government of the *Länder*, the postwar Italian political system consequently offered no equivalent outlet for a co-determining influence in policy-making by the opposition. In view of the later discussion in this book of their activity in regional politics, it is relevant to trace the respective positions of the various parties on regional reform from the late 1940s through to the 1970s to show how these related to their wider national strategies.

The major proponent of regionalism immediately after the War was the DC in accordance with the demand for decentralisation voiced by it its predecessor, the pre-Fascist PPI, and with its concept of autonomous social groupings.[37] Following its election triumph of 1948, the DC exercised a turnabout and became reluctant to implement the constitutional provisions for regional government, although it never went so far as to declare outright opposition to the idea but rather argued the need to wait for the 'right time' before establishing the new structures. In reality, this reluctance stemmed from a firm dislike of the prospect of Communist-led governments at least in the traditional 'Red' belt of north-central Italy. It was also coloured by the fear that the existence of regional governments, especially in the south, would free that part of the country from its dependence on the national bureaucracy and with it the multifarious forms of DC patronage.[38]

During the 1950s and 1960s, DC leaders indulged in stale rhetoric on the issue though were increasingly forced to take a defensive position in response to mounting pressure from the Left to introduce the regional structures not only from the PCI but also the PSI now in coalition with the DC at Rome. For some time, the DC was assisted in its stand by other sources of resistance to change, notably from the national bureaucracy, which it permeated, the general indifference of public opinion, a tendency to criticise the performance of the five existing special regions as well as a broad unwillingness to envisage any dismantling of established administrative procedures.[39] The anti-Communist motive within the DC still persisted even after the formal introduction of the 'ordinary' regions in 1970, and continued to affect its outlook. For instance, a series of conferences was held by the DC in the light of the discussion about regional powers prior to the forthcoming elections to the regional assemblies in 1975, at which speakers repeatedly expressed their concern about the growth of Left-wing influence in the regional structures. At a session of the party national conference at Rome in May 1975, which concluded this series, one speaker accused the Left of having 'used the communes and the provinces as a seat for collision with the state'.[40] Another intervention from Paolo Semama, provincial secretary of the Livorno DC, concluded with the remarks:

> Is it really so possible that in many Italian regions, especially the so-called Red regions, the day nursery has become a party instrument considered and propagandised above all for the purpose of obtaining electoral consensus and for systematising the enrolment of members and guaranteeing supplies to the co-operatives which bring money to the PCI and PSI? And that the same is happening in the infant schools or junior schools, which are already an ideological channel and an incubator of Soviet man?
> We have not wanted the regions for this reason, for with them it would be a matter of replacing the impartiality of the state by the party-political choice of the local majority in the public institutions, and this is a delicate matter.
> We believe in units of local autonomy, but we do not want them to be transformed into a pretext for giving an uncontrolled power

over everything to one side. Therefore, it is necessary to be vigilant.[41]

Despite the Christian Democratic partiality for 'apolitical' arguments, it was clear from the strident tone of such statements that DC leaders viewed the new regions as a potential power instrument for the PCI and certainly as a new area for party competition.

The same political assumption about the importance of the regions was contained in the PCI's motivation on this issue and explains its movement in the opposite direction to that of the DC. Originally, the PCI with the PSI were opposed in principle to any diminution of national parliamentary sovereignty and thought regionalism might impede the execution of necessary social and economic reforms,[42] but they departed from their Jacobin tradition once it became clear from 1948 that the Left was being left 'out in the cold' in Italian politics. Both parties became ardent supporters of regionalism, so that when the PSI formed Centre-Left coalitions with the DC in the 1960s it stipulated as a precondition the establishment of the 'ordinary' regions as one major item of government policy. The PCI, now left alone in opposition but desirous of claiming a greater determining role, meanwhile continued to make this a propaganda issue. At the time of the first regional elections in 1970, the PCI leader, Pietro Ingrao, bluntly asserted that he viewed the new regions as an 'instrument for the conquest of power by the working classes'.[43]

Since then this view has been elaborated by various PCI statements on the subject. At a party national conference on 'Decentralisation and Participation' at Bologna in November 1976, Renato Zangheri, PCI mayor of that city, argued that the extension of local autonomy was essential for the renewal of democratic institutions and would accordingly provide 'closer contact with the basis of society'.[44] Marcello Stefanini, a member of the PCI Central Committee, told the same conference that this 'renewal of the state' was not only 'a purely institutional question, but strengthens the type of economic and social development that we want to impress on the country'.[45] A more specific political purpose was offered at a further conference on regional problems the following year by Pancrazio De Pasquale, PCI president of the Sicilian regional assembly, when he said that through the various institutional levels of local and regional autonomy:

> We have begun to exist . . . not only as a force of opposition and protest, but as a constructive force of government, as a stable point of reference for every form of political and social aggregation . . .

We are beginning to perceive — not only among the leadership, but also at the mass level — the institutions as the natural location for our political and social involvement, as something that belongs to us no less than to the other democratic forces . . . I mean that this present starting-position of our long and victorious struggle against discrimination . . . represents for us Communists an irreversible conquest, a choice of battleground, a policy that we mean to advance by successive stages through an increasingly full assumption of responsibility.[46]

The regional structures were therefore viewed as a central forum for the pursuit of PCI involvement in policy-making and the strategy of the 'historic compromise'. As one PCI leader noted at the time of the transfer in 1977 of powers to the regions under Law 382 of 1975, this represented in the institutional field 'an important step forward towards the liquidation of a system of power that has been created and utilised by the Democrazia Cristiana'.[47]

With this conflict over the regions between the DC and PCI, the positions of the smaller parties have largely gone unnoticed. These have been more consistent and more in line with the parties' respective traditional inclinations. Only the Republicans initially rivalled the DC in their advocacy of regionalism after the War, but they have remained a strong apostle of autonomy and decentralisation since then. On the other side of the political argument, the Liberals accompanied by the neo-Fascists and Monarchists firmly opposed the institution of the 'ordinary' regions on grounds of maintaining the centralised state and opposing the Left. The positions of these parties were generally marginal to the process which led to the formation of new regional entities in the early 1970s.

This belated institutional reform owed something to changing social and economic circumstances — with rapid industrialisation and large-scale internal migration strengthening the need for greater co-ordination with local planning bodies — in addition to factors of political pressure such as the PSI within the Centre-Left.[48] The powers of the ordinary regions were not clearly defined or granted when the first elections took place in 1970, nor were their administrative structures yet developed. According to the provisions of the 1948 Constitution, the regions have a significant degree of authority to legislate in a number of areas ranging from the police and health services to town planning and tourism, although all these are subject to strong supervisory powers by the central government and ultimately dependent on the state for financial support.[49] In 1977, an important transfer of direct powers from the state to the regions and communes finally occurred in the fields of economic development and the social services.

The institution of the ordinary regions was the most acknowledged feature of the new 'participation' in institutional arrangements that has occurred in Italian politics in the 1970s, owing something to the protest movements of the late 1960s but essentially harnessed by the political parties, especially the PCI. Other channels of wider policy consultation have been initiated with the 'mountain communities' (*comunità montane* — involving co-ordination between groups of neighbouring communes), the city district councils (*quartieri*) under the Law of April 1976, the factory and zonal councils and the school district councils. There has, however, been marked variation in the application of these new institutional structures between north and south in Italy; while some disillusionment in the light of the high ideals and 'spontaneity' of the 'participatory movement' has been accompanied by the inevitable control of these new institutions by the political parties.[50]

From the point of view of party development, the establishment of regions throughout Italy has had the undoubted effect of introducing a new arena for competition between the various parties. At the same time, it has complicated the pattern of inter-party relationships by offering new possibilities for differentiation in political alliances. This and the question of the modifying influence of the developing regional structures on the parties themselves will be discussed later in this study.

(d) The Changing Socio-economic Environment of the 1970s

If there has nevertheless been a strong consistency in the political and institutional structures of Italy, the same cannot be said of the country's social and economic development particularly since the late 1960s. The events of 1968–1969, with the widespread student protests of 1968 followed by unprecedented trade union militancy in the 'hot autumn' of 1969, have commonly been seen as a watershed in the country's development, because combined with longer-term factors of social pressure and economic performance they marked the beginning of both new forms of socio-political mobilisation and the first serious reversal of Italy's economic patterns since the War. These changes in turn reflected or reinforced inadequate social conditions, leading to a pronounced rise in demands for reform of all kinds and to the questioning of traditional values (as evident in the success of the Divorce Referendum in 1974).

Pronounced social dislocation, notably present in the vast extent of internal population movement increasingly under way since the early 1960s, was having a more visible impact on the worsening conditions of urban life. Finally, the year 1969 saw the beginning of the growth of political violence and terrorism as a major new problem which became a constant trend through the 1970s and derived impetus from the combination of social unrest, chronic unemployment and political frustration with the failure of ruling elites to offer any coherent solution to the changing socio-economic environment.

This is not the place to include detailed discussion of the various aspects of what is commonly called 'the Italian crisis'.[51] It is all the same important to establish the main features and general salience of this changing environment as a context to the case-study of party development in the 1970s which follows. First, and most crucially, the turnabout in Italian economic performance provided the key determinant in the different interlocking factors in this new situation. Briefly, the postwar 'economic miracle' had evaporated as the factors which had created it — such as export-oriented expansion, the continuing availability of cheap labour and government-promoted industrialisation — no longer existed. International causes were paramount in Italy's high inflation and unemployment of the 1970s, but that country was particularly vulnerable to the world recession with severe domestic repercussions. Secondly, while some factors contributing to social tension had existed before this decade they had largely been held in check by the compensations of Italy's economic expansion after the War. Italian society therefore became considerably more unstable in the 1970s compared with the two earlier decades, to which should be added a growing public awareness of and dissatisfaction over backwardness in modernising social structures and values. Thirdly, the last problem related to the issue of the 'reform of the state' much voiced during the 1970s, especially by the political Left, for all these various basic sources of discontent and unrest have increasingly emphasised the inadequacy of the traditional state institutions. This criticism has been justified in that the political and administrative system of the country has been proverbially sluggish in responding to the need for change or adaptation.

Hence, the onus for answering this need has ultimately fallen on the role of the political parties, both individually and in common, which only confirms their centrality in the functioning of the postwar political system in Italy. This leads of course to the question of how much the 'Italian crisis' might be political in terms of party behaviour as well as socio-economic and institutional. Apart from the negative impact of socio-economic changes on the standing of the DC as governing party already noted, it is fundamental to question and examine the degree of political change that has been necessary and possible in this review of the Italian party system. As one Italian political scientist wrote in the mid-1970s: 'The prospects for the evolution of the Italian political system, opened up by the crisis of the DC as party, as government and as regime, have imposed not only the problem of the internal transformation of a system of polarised pluralism, but also the problem of an alternative system and therefore of the elaboration of models, scenarios and strategies of transition.'[52] It is no longer possible to say, as could be said at the end of the 1960s, that the Italian party system was 'static' even though the economic and social framework in which it was operating was already 'changing'.[53] It appeared, furthermore, by the end of the 1970s that not only the role of the DC in particular but also that of the established parties in general was being called into question as effective channels of political communication and as agents for policy-making (as evidenced by the 1978 referendum on public financing of the parties). In short, the very capacity of the political parties to respond to, direct and absorb pressures deriving from the changing socio-economic environment was under greater scrutiny than ever before. The outcome depended on whether the more competitive party system was in any better position to meet this challenge than its polarised version of former decades.

References

1. H. Eckstein and D. Apter, *Comparative Politics: a reader* (1963), p. 329.
2. W.A. Salomone, *Italy in the Giolittian Era: Italian Democracy in the Making, 1900-1914* (1960), p. 14.
3. See G. Galli and A. Prandi, *Patterns of Political Participation in Italy* (1970), Chapter 5.
4. G. Almond and S. Verba, *The Civic Culture: Political Attitudes and Democracy in five Nations* (1963), esp. pp. 402-3.
5. Galli and Prandi, *Patterns of Political Participation*, p. 21.
6. See G. Sartori, 'European Political Parties: the case of polarised pluralism' in J. LaPalombara and M. Weiner (eds.), *Political Parties and Political Development* (1966), pp. 151-2.
7. On this see Antonio Lombardo, 'Sistema di correnti e deperimento dei partiti in Italia' in *Rivista Italiana di Scienza Politica*, April 1976, pp. 139-61.
8. See Sidney Tarrow, 'The Italian Party System between crisis and transition' in *American Journal of Political Science*, May 1977.
9. R. Michels, *Political Parties* (1962), first published in German in 1911.

10. See Galli and Prandi, *Patterns of Political Participation*, pp. 47-55.
11. A. Parisi and G. Gasquino, 'Changes in Italian electoral behaviour: the relationships between parties and voters' in *West European Politics*, October 1979.
12. J.C. Adams and P. Barile, *The Government of Republican Italy* (1966), pp. 160-1.
13. See, for instance, G. Sani, 'L'immagine dei partiti nell'elettorato' in M. Caciagli and A. Spreafico, *Un sistema politico alla prova* (1975), esp. pp. 110-14., which looks at this problem in the light of the 1972 election.
14. Otto Kirchheimer, 'The Transformation of the West European Party Systems' in LaPalombara and Weiner, *Political Parties*, pp. 177-200.
15. See Sidney Tarrow, *Peasant Communism in Southern Italy* (1967).
16. For a discussion of the practice of *trasformismo* in reference to the PCI's policy of the 'historic compromise', see Hansjakob Stehle, 'The Italian Experiment and the Communists' in *World Today*, January 1977, pp. 7-16.
17. See Lombardo, 'Sistema di correnti e deperimento', pp. 143-7.
18. According to Sartori, 'the net result is a Byzantine and undecipherable party system whose end product is overcomplication and confusion — at least, this is how the polity must look to the ordinary voter'. In LaPalombara and Weiner, *Political Parties*, pp. 151-2.
19. Gordon Smith, *Development in West European Party Systems*, paper presented to the Political Studies Association conference, 1978, pp. 8-9. See published version in *West European Politics*, January 1979.
20. The study is on the PSI on the Tuscan province of Arezzo; See Samuel Barnes, *Party Democracy: Politics in an Italian Socialist Federation* (1967), esp. Chapter 10.
21. Philip Converse, 'The Nature of Belief Systems of Mass Publics' in D. Apter (ed.), *Ideology and Discontent* (1965), pp. 206-61.
22. Sidney Tarrow, *Partisanship and Political Exchange in French and Italian Local Politics: a contribution to the typology of party systems* (1974), p. 49.
23. See Sartori, in LaPalombara and Weiner, *Political Parties*, Chapter 5.
24. Ibid., p. 138.
25. Sartori has partially revised his view of the PCI, as having become 'semi-integrated' within the Italian political system, in F. Cavazza and S. Graubard (eds.), *Il caso italiano* (1974).
26. Sartori in LaPalombara and Weiner, *Political Parties*, p. 137.
27. See G. Galli, *Il bipartitismo imperfetto* (1966).
28. P.A. Allum, *Italy – Republic without Government?* (1973), pp. 63-6.
29. P.A. Allum, 'Italy' in Stanley Henig (ed.), *Political Parties in the European Community* (1979), p. 135.
30. See Arnold Heidenheimer, 'Der starke Regierungschef und das Parteien-System' in *Politische Vierteljahresschrift*, 1960–1961, pp. 242-3.
31. The phrase is G. Tamburrano's in *L'Iceberg Democristiano* (1974).
32. Criteria used by J. Blondel and V. Herman, *Workbook for Comparative Government* (1972).
33. Peter Nichols, *Italia, Italia* (1973), p. 243.
34. P.A. Allum and G. Amyot, 'Regionalism in Italy: old wine in new bottles?' in *Parliamentary Affairs*, Winter 1970–1971, p. 55.
35. Martin Clark, 'Italy: Regionalism and Bureaucratic Reform' in James Cornford (ed.), *The Failure of the State* (1975), p. 45.
36. R.C. Fried, *The Italian Prefects* (1963), p. 227.
37. Ibid, p. 228.
38. Tarrow, *Peasant Communism*, pp. 315-16.
39. Fried, *The Italian Prefects*, pp. 239-40, 244-5.
40. See the selection from the speeches at these conferences in *Regioni, enti*

locali per lo sviluppo nella libertà (1975), p. 175.
41. Ibid, pp. 202-3.
42. Fried, *The Italian Prefects*, p. 228.
43. *Le Monde Weekly*, 10 June 1970.
44. See Zangheri's speech in A. Cossutta, M. Stefanini and R. Zangheri, *Decentramento e Partecipazione: l'iniziativa dei comunisti per l'attuazione della legge sui consigli di circoscrizione* (1977), pp. 3-16.
45. Ibid, p. 19.
46. *Bollettino della sezione regioni ed autonomie locali del Comitato Centrale del PCI*, No. 4, 1977, p. 50.
47. Ibid, No. 8, 1977, p. 12.
48. Clark, 'Italy: Regionalism and Bureaucratic Reform'. pp. 51-2.
49. On the powers of the ordinary regions, see Allum, *Italy – Republic without Government?* pp. 228-32; and Clark, 'Italy: Regionalism and Bureaucratic Reform', pp. 54-60.
50. For an analysis of these problems in relation to the schools councils, see Pippa Pridham, 'The Problems of educational reform in Italy: the case of the *decreti delegati*' in *Comparative Education*, October 1978.
51. On this, see L. Graziano and S. Tarrow (eds.), *La Crisi Italiana* (1979); also, M. Salvati, 'Muddling through: economics and politics in Italy, 1969-1979' in *West European Politics*, October 1979, pp. 31-48, for a survey of economic development during this decade.
52. G. Pasquino, 'Crisi della DC e evoluzione del sistema politico' in *Rivista Italiana di Scienza Politica*, No. 3, 1975, p. 472.
53. P.A. Allum, 'Italy' in S. Henig and J. Pinder (eds.), *European Political Parties* (1969), p. 252.

2 THE REGION OF TUSCANY: THE CASE-STUDY PRESENTED

(a) Why a Regional Case-study?

There is no watertight argument in favour of any particular case-study, although it should be adequately representative of the wider theme to which it is devoted and of the particular problems to which it is addressed. While each case-study must have its unique features, the degree of its relevance is determined by the special focus of the subject it is examining. In other words, it offers advantages over a more general approach as a 'laboratory' for analysing the theme and its accompanying questions, and compensates in depth for what it lacks in scope and breadth.

The method chosen for this investigation has been influenced by a number of considerations. In a centralised state like Italy's (though one now modified by devolution), it is important to examine both vertical political relationships between sub-national and national levels and also horizontal political relationships sub-nationally. The first shows how much the parties have strengthened the state structure by acting centripetally or otherwise by acting centrifugally; while the second focus directs attention to the parties' integrative role at the lower reaches of the political system and allows more specific treatment of their organisational importance and strategy behaviour. Both angles facilitate, the latter especially, an analysis of the party system as a uniform, durable and responsive framework for political development, an essential question in Italian politics because of the inadequacies of the state administrative system. A regional rather than local study provides sufficient geographical range to include different levels of party activity and structure (regional, provincial as well as local) and encompasses more variety of social conditions and party-political strength.

There may be additional reasons for taking a case-study approach for a particular country. With Italy, a regional case-study is on different grounds appropriate and justifiable. First, it allows much greater scope for an 'in-depth' treatment than would a simply national overview of the subject — particularly necessary in view of the complex or supposedly 'Byzantine' character of Italian politics. Secondly, the importance of regional and local political traditions in Italy has meant that both the electoral strengths and the ideological and social dimensions of the parties have been significantly affected by this factor. Thirdly, the regional approach is favoured because of the presence of the new regional administrative structures in the 1970s which, as already discussed in the preceding chapter, provide a useful area for looking at the ability of the parties to adapt or reorientate themselves to institutional change.

There are several arguments in favour of selecting Tuscany, although it is true that no individual region can be regarded as a fully representative example of political-cultural patterns in Italy. In view of the prominence of 'political change' in the theme of the book, it was decided it was vital to discuss the performance of the Communist Party in relation to its role in government, as this is important to an understanding of the 'historic compromise'. Therefore, the choice settled on a 'Red' region, although one with a sufficient variety of social and political conditions to allow for a reasonably representative approach. Tuscany is preferable to the other traditionally 'Red' region of Emilia-Romagna, which is far more compact in both its socio-economic structure and its political tradition (it was, for instance, a more substantial stronghold of the Left before Fascism than was Tuscany), while Umbria as the third region in the 'Red' belt is very much smaller in population than Tuscany and less representative of national conditions. The classic case of Bologna, regarded widely as a show-case of PCI local government since the War, is not, however, very typical of Italian politics especially in the new situation of the 1970s. It is more instructive to examine the PCI's role in administration where it has both long held office and come to power more recently, therefore having to face immediately all the mounting problems of Italian city government — with incessant indebtedness and lack of financial resources, the pressures of urban development and housing shortage and problems of law and order and social mobility — without the advantage of having been in a position to control early development after the War. Tuscany provides a useful amalgam of new PCI-led administrations (most importantly Florence) alongside other more established municipalities of the Left (notably Livorno as well as Siena) in addition to a regional government led by a coalition of the Left since 1970, a notable instance where the PSI's coalition with the PCI (not so then in Emilia-Romagna) occasioned serious dispute with the DC over the Centre-Left arrangement at the national level. Moreover, unlike its regional neighbour Tuscany does include an important area of 'White' dominance in the province of Lucca (not to mention DC strength in other less concentrated parts of the region), thus offering some diversity of party-political balance and hence of inter-party relationships.

There are other intrinsic reasons which make the case of Tuscany an interesting and important one. Although Tuscany possesses more of a cultural and regional identity than many of the other newly constituted regional structures in Italy, deriving from its earlier status as a Grand Duchy and its prominence as the birthplace of the national language (spoken in its pure form extremely widely throughout the region), there is also a remarkable incidence of local traditions with a continuing political impact. In the notable cases of Florence, Pisa and Siena this may be traced back to their role in the Middle Ages as independent and rival city-states, while more generally a mosaic of political tendencies is identifiable when looking at both the nine different provinces of Tuscany and the mixture of heterogeneous cultural and geographical zones within them. All this amounts to a different and necessary forum for examining party development from that obtained by a national study, for such localised factors are influential in Italian politics.

From a comparative perspective, Tuscany demonstrates as a fairly representative case some characteristics of an intermediary area between north and south, even though distinguished by its individual features. With its strategically central geographical position in the Italian peninsula, Tuscany has faced many similar problems as other parts of the country, such as its experience of major social change (a considerable internal movement of population since the War, bringing with it the predictable problems of growing urban life), and its mixed industrial-agricultural economy occasioning some comparisons with the depressed rural zones in the south and with the pressures of rapid industrial development as in the north, although clearly in the latter case Tuscany has not matched the economic dynamism of Lombardy and Piedmont. In the words of Lelio Lagorio, first president of the Tuscan region, 'Tuscany is a divided region . . . it knows all the problems of metropolitan areas and all the problems of depressed areas — our task is to reunify them.'[1]

(b) Political Traditions

Tuscany is, as noted, a predominantly 'Red' region but one with interesting variation within it, making possible as examination of different political developments at the local and provincial levels. This sub-regional variation merits closer attention in view of the influential variable of local as well as regional political traditions which have helped to mould the relative strengths of the various parties and to some extent their ideological and social character. It is in particular relevant to this study to note briefly the factors which have historically favoured a predominance of the political Left and given the Communist Party its early strength after the Second World War.

In the generation since the War the 'Red' tradition in Tuscany has been almost monopolised by the PCI, which already emerged as the strongest party in the 1946 elections to the Constituent Assembly while gaining an absolute majority of votes in a large number of communes. During the decades which followed the PCI has gradually assumed a position of increasing dominance *vis-à-vis* the PSI at the same time as the combined vote of the Left has remained consistent at around 60 per cent, with a small margin of fluctuation between individual elections. The 'Red' tradition, however, has itself a longer history dating back to the 1870s, when the Italian section of the Socialist International movement enjoyed one of its largest concentrations of membership implanted in Tuscany along with Romagna, Naples, Sicily and the Marches.[2] The relatively powerful organisational presence of the Left from this time onwards rested on a number of general features of Tuscan political development.

The outstanding quality of this 'Red' tradition has been its appeal in rural areas drawing on a long record of agrarian socialism, which has its firm roots in two interconnected socio-economic phenomena: the system of sharecropping or *mezzadria* (predominant in Tuscan agriculture until the aftermath of the Second World War) and anti-clericalism. The former as an economic system is discussed below,[a] except that it should be emphasised in this political context that the subordinate relationship it had established since the Middle Ages between landowning class and tenant farmers became an element in the class struggle promoted by the Socialists from the early twentieth century, which saw the appearance of rural agitation involving the *mezzadri*. Religious attachment was traditionally low among the sharecroppers, especially in those provinces like Florence, Siena and Pisa where the system was strongest, as a natural consequence of the anti-clericalism which derived much of its force in Tuscany from the association between the local clergy and the landowning class in the nineteenth century following the impoverishment of the Church with the confiscation of its lands during the Risorgimento. From the end of that century, Socialism became virtually synonymous with anti-clericalism, thus lending the latter more political impact, so that in areas of Socialist strength in particular party adhesion was an act simultaneous with a break with the Church.³ Anti-clericalism therefore took root in Tuscany for a number of social and political reasons, although it never reached the vibrant form it assumed in Emilia-Romagna for, as Burgalassi the expert on Tuscan religious life has indicated, it has been expressed through a generic indifference towards the clergy sometimes accompanied by a sympathy for the local priest.⁴ In other words, while religious life itself has been less affected by anti-clericalism, it has nevertheless deprived the Church of a significant influence in political affairs, and so removed a powerful socio-political obstacle in rural community life to the advance of the Left. While anti-clericalism has provided an important background against which the 'Red' tradition has been established in Tuscany, the latter was reinforced by the beginnings of a popular Marxist culture in the form of assistance and mutual credit societies and, more notably, the Socialist recreation centres in the Case del Popolo, often regarded by the clergy as a threat to the 'unity of parish life'.⁵

Certain historical patterns had promoted a marked Leftward tendency in Tuscan politics, but it took the forceful experience of Fascism and its culmination in the Resistance to make the 'Red' tradition an integral part of political life in the region in a manner which, combined with general postwar developments, produced a situation of political dominance by the PCI. Tuscany was the scene of some of the worst excesses of Fascist violence just prior to Mussolini's rise; for the sharp increase there in the Socialist vote in 1920 resulting in the Socialists' assuming authority in a large number of local administrations (in fact 149 out of 290 in Tuscany) provoked a reaction from the Right in circumstances already highly charged with bitter tension over possession of the land following the rural strikes of 1920.⁶ At the same time, the split in the Left with the founding of the Italian Communist Party (PCd'I) at Livorno in early 1921 was already having negative repercussions on Socialist organisation in Tuscany. The new party took rapid advantage of the PSI's organisational and other weaknesses — notably its inability in spite of its recent electoral successes to overcome the strong impact of Tuscan localism on its very uneven distribution of membership — to establish several important bridgeheads, especially in the province of Florence, and attract large numbers of particularly younger members from the PSI.⁷ What emerged during the following two decades of Fascist rule was that the PCI was the only non-regime political organisation in Tuscany to maintain some effective structural network based on its system of cells and practice of extensive penetration above all at places of work.⁸ This established practice of organisational tenacity welded during the time of political suppression imposed under Fascism placed the postwar PCI in a position of considerable advantage with regard to becoming an aggregative force in Tuscan politics. The extent to which the newly founded PCI was able to harness opposition to conservatism on anti-Fascist grounds was reflected in the fact that Tuscany was one of the regions with the highest anti-monarchy vote in the 1946 Referendum. This showed a clear correlation between Communist voting strength and support for a republic (76.1 per cent in the province of Siena; 71.4 per cent in the province of Florence).

The effect of the Fascist experience in Tuscany on politics at the grass roots predominantly worked in favour of the PCI (with the important exception of the province of Lucca, discussed below) and was solidified by the catalytic influence of the Resistance in promoting not only the 'reality' of the PCI's political presence but also the 'myth' surrounding its image. It contributed an heroic dimension to the political role of the Left in particular (hence the tendency of many PCI activists in Tuscany to refer to the Resistance as the 'second Risorgimento'). One of the regions most affected by physical war destruction, which brought the harsh effects of hostilities to the doorstep of ordinary families, Tuscany also witnessed a strong incidence of Resistance activity. The Tuscan Committee of National Liberation (CTLN), which originated in Florence and acquired social prestige through the adherence of many luminaries of Florentine intellectual life, was, however, more relevant politically in acting as the spearhead of the maze of partisan actions which occurred in the different localities of the region. The role of the 'Red' Garibaldi brigades especially was a crucial factor in profoundly affecting the political colouring of various zones after the War, including areas like the isolated Pisan hills where the PCI had not previously established a foothold, through their local control for several months after hostilities ceased and their success in 'interpreting' the new political situation for the resident and often traumatised population.

Indeed, the period of the German occupation was not easily forgotten in the rural areas of Tuscany, more so perhaps than in the cities, for it established in the individual memory an identification with concrete events in the community at a moment of historical political importance. Although peasants were traditionally less involved in active politics than urban circles, their passive contribution to the Resistance effort with their hospitality to both partisans and escaping prisoners-of-war[9] had some socialising effect in the light of their later strong commitment in most parts of Tuscany to Communism. Predictably, the village angle on the Resistance was kept alive by political parties long after the War with the production of local histories commemorating individual episodes and persons as well as Nazi atrocities. Twenty or thirty years after the event, local or district symposia have continued to record these experiences in faithful detail, which has tended to reinforce the sense of traditional solidarity on the Left of Tuscan politics.[10] The impact of the Resistance has been particularly noticeable in Tuscan parochial life because it became rooted in local folklore.[b]

The preceding discussion of the historical roots of the 'Red' tradition, which applies to much of Tuscany, has ignored so far the presence of an important though localised 'White' tradition which, represented through the second strongest political party (the DC), has nevertheless made its own substantial contribution to the political development of the region. No complete picture of political traditions in the region can be given without reference to the display of 'White' islands throughout Tuscany at the communal and sub-communal (i.e. individual village) level. Their location and concentration is of course in inverse proportion to the degree of 'Red-ness' of the different provinces of the region, with Siena and Livorno overwhelming in their Left orientation, while the provinces of Florence, Arezzo and Massa Carrara have evidenced distinct areas of traditional DC allegiance such as in the mountainous communes of the Apennines, not to mention the city of Florence itself. A different but relevant feature of the Catholic tradition has been its active contribution to political thinking.[11] The end of the Second World War saw a revival in Catholic intellectual thought with the growth of several reviews based in Florence (such as *Testimonianze* founded by Don Balducci) and it was encouraged further by the evangelistic form of progressive Catholicism espoused by Giorgio La Pira (mayor of Florence, 1951-1957 and 1961-1964).

For the purpose of this general outline of Tuscany's political traditions, attention should focus on the province of Lucca as providing a contrast to the rest of Tuscany because of its separate and cohesive 'White' tradition analogous to such a region as the Veneto. For here the PCI has faced persistent problems for cultural as well as economic-structural reasons in 'penetrating' society and establishing its legitimacy as a political force in the sense that, as in north-eastern Italy, the social environment, especially its religiousness, has traditionally buttressed the hegemony of the DC.[12] This applies most of all to the Lucchesia, the eastern half of the province, rather than to the western coastal area of the Versilia, where the impact of social change since the War has tended to promote the interests of the Left. As with the 'Red' tradition elsewhere in Tuscany, historical explanations provide the basic key in understanding why Lucca — sometimes referred to as 'the white handkerchief in the large red cloth of Tuscany' — has a divergent political orientation.

Lucca was the only state in Tuscany not to succumb to Florentine dominance in the Middle Ages, and remained as an independent republic until the Napoleonic occupation before its final annexation to the Grand Duchy of Tuscany in 1847. Even today, the sense of identity as separate from the rest of Tuscany is evident in the area's reputation of isolated tranquillity and its state of being relatively untouched by mass tourism and the major communication lines.[13] In socio-economic terms, the distinctive character of the Lucchesia has appeared in the prevalence of peasant smallholders (*coltivatori diretti*) as opposed to the *mezzadria* elsewhere in Tuscany,^cthe positive relationship between Church and society uncomplicated by the rural class struggle and the accordingly higher level of religious practice.[14] As with the 'Red' tradition, this 'White' tradition was visible politically following the rise of mass democratic parties before Fascism in that the Lucchesia was the only area where the Catholic PPI was not a minority party in Tuscany.[15] Similarly, too, the Resistance played an essential part in crystallising the Catholic tradition to the benefit of the postwar Christian Democrats for it was led by local cadres of Catholic activists, mainly former protagonists of the PPI, and assisted by the rural clergy, which suffered its own record of local martyrs.[16]

Sub-regional variations in party strength which relate to the factor of political traditions as generally described are illustrated by Table 2.1 on electoral support for the main parties in the nine provinces of Tuscany.

Finally, the overall relative strength of the three main parties in Tuscany is indicated by the results of national elections since the Second World War (Table 2.2).

This section has concentrated on the aspect of political traditions as of fundamental importance in understanding the dominant 'Red' and minority 'White' tendencies in Tuscany as a starting-point for examining the role of political parties there since the Second World War. It has not touched on the theme of postwar change, which will now be introduced in a brief discussion of Tuscan society and economic development.

Table 2.1: Votes for PCI, DC and PSI in Provinces of Tuscany, National Election 1979 (%)

	PCI	PSI	DC
Arezzo	46.2	9.7	33.0
Florence	48.3	9.2	29.0
Grosseto	43.0	12.7	25.8
Livorno	52.5	8.9	23.2
Lucca	27.9	10.1	45.1
Massa Carrara	34.7	13.3	32.4
Pisa	47.0	10.4	28.5
Pistoia	48.7	7.8	29.8
Siena	56.5	8.8	24.2
Tuscany	45.8	9.8	30.1
Italy	30.4	9.8	38.3

Source: Regione Toscana/Giunta Regionale, dipartimento statistica, elaborazione dati, documentazione, *Elezioni Senato e Camera del 3-4 giugno 1979* (1979), p. 62. The above figures are for the election to the Chamber of Deputies.

Table 2.2: Votes for PCI, DC and PSI in National Elections in Tuscany, 1946-1979 (%)

	PCI	PSI	DC
1946	33.6	21.9	28.2
	(18.9)	(20.7)	(35.2)
1948	..... 48.1		39.0
	(31.0)		(48.5)
1953	35.0	15.4	34.3
	(22.6)	(12.8)	(40.1)
1958	34.4	16.8	35.3
	(22.7)	(14.2)	(42.4)
1963	38.5	14.7	30.5
	(25.3)	(13.8)	(38.3)
1968	41.0	13.7*	31.0
	(26.9)	(14.5)	(39.1)
1972	42.2	9.0	31.0
	(27.2)	(9.6)	(38.8)
1976	47.5	9.8	31.4
	(34.4)	(9.6)	(38.7)
1979	45.8	9.8	30.1
	(30.4)	(9.8)	(38.3)

* PSI and PSDI combined as PSU.
Note: Their overall national votes are given in brackets.
Sources: V. Capecchi et al., *Il comportamento elettorale in Italia* (Bologna, 1968), pp. 334-5, 338; publications of Regione Toscana/Giunta Regionale, SEDD, on national election results in Tuscany.

(c) Socio-economic Structure

This study's focus is on the party-political dimension of change, so that it is necessary to present the economic and social setting in which the parties operated in this region and the changing reality to which they had to adjust. Far from being a static society, Tuscany has experienced since the early 1950s the most rapid socio-economic change in its whole history — a process sometimes called the 'Tuscan miracle', though this was essentially part of the postwar Italian economic miracle. Until the Second World War, Tuscany's economic system remained largely unchanged, having been untouched by early industrial development in Italy following unification, though there had been some signs from the early twentieth century of moving away from a purely agricultural-mineral region.[17] By contrast, Tuscany has demonstrated during the recent postwar period an exceptionally high rate of industrial growth which has continued into the 1970s.[d] In order to put this recent decade into a wider perspective it is obviously important to look at developments in the preceding years.

Tuscany's economy, as indicated, underwent no major change in the present century until after the Second World War. The most radical form of postwar change has been the disintegration of the *mezzadria* system and the consequent rural exodus. During the two decades of Fascist rule the identification in the rural areas between the Fascist elite and the landed nobility noticeably in the appointment of members of the aristocracy to head local administrations had engendered a demand for socio-economic change.[18] However, the conditions which gave way to change in Tuscany in agriculture and industry must be attributed to postwar factors prevalent in Italy as a whole: the rapid expansion of the foreign as well as domestic market, especially for consumer goods; the growth of mass tourism; industrial promotion from state investment; as well as the initiative shown by traditional working-class and artisan sectors in the entrepreneurial sphere. The outcome has been what is customarily referred to as the 'two Tuscanies', the one backward and represented by the medieval museum-like towns in the hills with their retention of traditional peasant culture, and the other modern and located in the plains where cities have expanded outside their walls and villages have become metamorphosed.[19] The latter is most striking in the Florence basin, when travelling the autostrada from Florence westwards towards the sea, especially when the night is brightened by the 'luminous publicity' of new industrial establishments.

The Region of Tuscany: the Case-study Presented

The starting-point for examining this change must be the postwar revolution in Tuscan agriculture. The vast majority of Tuscan peasants had been involved in the sharecropping method or *mezzadria* – with the notable exception of the province of Lucca, already mentioned – a system also found outside Tuscany in the other 'Red' regions of Emilia-Romagna and Umbria. It was a system which had conditioned the social structure of rural Tuscany for centuries, having operated since the late Middle Ages as a method based on the unit of a family-sized tenancy whereby the *mezzadro* farmed the section of land belonging to the landowner and shared the crops on a 50–50 arrangement (the name came from the word *mezzo*, or 'half'). It worked on an annual renewal of contract and ensured a full year's work and food supply, but the system was paternalistic and had feudal undertones which, as the twentieth century progressed, became more and more anomalous. Discontent became channelled through politics because of the experience of the Fascist period, so that protest against the system was easily monopolised after the War by the Left. Although the Catholic organisations had before Fascism advocated reforming the *mezzadria*, the postwar Christian Democrats were unable to match the clear challenge to the system from the Communists and Socialists because of their own inter-class social composition and, in particular, their ties with conservative groups in Tuscan society. DC-sponsored agrarian reforms in Tuscany in the 1950s failed really to break the superiority of the Left, especially the PCI, in mobilising this agrarian sector, for in this major case of economic and social transformation the Communists were able to count on the fact that the deep roots of political tradition favouring them could withstand its subsequent impact.

The result of the eclipse of the *mezzadria* system has been a massive exodus from the land, beginning in the early 1950s but accelerating swiftly from the early 1960s. This reflected a growing lack of confidence in the agricultural sector as well as expressing an outburst of accumulated discontent.[20] This process gained further momentum from the attractions of modern urban life, especially for young members of peasant families; the dissemination of new social values, facilitated as this was by the arrival of television; and the growth and improvement of communications which hardly penetrated central Tuscany until the mid-twentieth century. The consumer society therefore affected Tuscany profoundly after the Second World War, bringing radically different social aspirations for the introduction to a new style of life made the old one less acceptable, above all to the younger generations.

The flight from the land reduced the number of those employed in agriculture in the region from 305,000 in 1963 to 133,000 in 1973 (or by 56.4 per cent)[21] compared with the national figures of a decline from 6.6 to 3.6 million (or by 45.4 per cent) for the period 1960-1970.[22] So far as the changes relating to the sharecropping system have been concerned, these have been in three directions — to *coltivatori diretti*, to a salaried status in employment by large farming enterprises and to industry and partly the tertiary sector in the urban areas — though the last course has been the predominant one. Table 2.3 shows the degree of structural change in agriculture in the postwar period.

Table 2.3: Stratification of Tuscan and Italian Agriculture, 1901-1971
(Figures as a % of total employed population)

	1901	1921	1951	1961	1971
Tuscany					
Direct cultivators	10.3	10.4	13.2	9.6	5.8
Sharecroppers	32.2	29.6	20.4	10.6	2.7
Agricultural labourers	15.0	13.2	5.2	3.5	3.3
Italy					
Direct cultivators	21.0	22.4	21.6	15.2	Figures
Sharecroppers	12.5	8.6	6.4	2.9	not
Agricultural labourers	26.4	24.5	13.6	10.5	given

Source: Giacomo Becattini (ed.), *Lo Sviluppo Economico della Toscana* (1975), p. 82.

The Tuscan path of postwar economic development has taken various forms, but clearly the predominant feature has been the concentration on light and to some lesser extent medium-sized industry. The region includes some element of most industrial sectors, except notably car construction, though in a differing degree from the national average with an under-representation of some of the more dynamic sectors, like electronics and chemicals, and an emphasis on the more traditional ones.[23] Tuscany has drawn on her rich natural resources to develop the extractive industries (notably iron ore on the island of Elba and marble in Massa-Carrara) as well as expand a whole range of small and medium concerns, some of them based on skills with a traditional background in Tuscany: such as leather goods and shoes (which have benefited considerably from the growth of an export market), the textile industry especially around Prato and furniture and the building trade with its several localised centres.[24] This rapid growth of industry has made it the preponderant sector in the Tuscan economy (45 per cent — 1971 figure) though only just ahead of the equally expanding tertiary sector (42.6 per cent), while agriculture has declined to 11.5 per cent.[25]

It is worth noting briefly the main zonal concentrations to give some indication of sub-regional variation.[26] As a supreme example of impetuous postwar growth, the Florence basin including the cities of Florence, Prato and Pistoia and the intermediate areas has seen intense specialisation and a multiplication of small firms, though with the mechanical industry as the strongest single element (e.g. Nuova Pignone at Florence). The zone between Florence and the sea along the lower Arno valley has been characterised by a series of different centres rather than a homogeneous concentration, notably Empoli (glass), Santa Croce (leather goods) and of course Pontedera as one of the more dynamic industrial localities with the Piaggio establishment (the production of the Vespa and other motorised vehicles like the Ape delivery van). Other cases of local industrial growth would include Poggibonsi and Valdelsa, in the northern part of Siena province, for furniture and glass manufacturing — an important area because it features industrialisation based on a working-class tradition — as well as the Italsider ironworks complex at Piombino on the coast. Metallurgy, mechanics and petroleum are present around Livorno and small industry is found around Pisa as two important communications centres (respectively a major port and strategic railway junction); while, finally, the Versilia along the north-western coast has also seen much recent industrialisation as well as the growth of the tourist trade. Because of this localisation of industrial development in Tuscany and the fact that it has not manifested itself in the form of large modern urban centres (apart from a few smaller exceptions like Pontedera), the traditional critera for separating 'town' and 'country' do not easily apply.

No discussion of light industry in Tuscany can conclude without mention of the active artisan trade as the prime example of where a very traditional sector has expanded in response to postwar growth. Indeed, Tuscany is often viewed as the artisan region *par excellence* in Italy for it now counts some 110,000 such enterprises.[27] With its origins tracing back to the medieval corporations, the artisan business is far from dying, having experienced some renewal in the nineteenth century, but the real boom came after the Second World War as a consequence of both foreign demand and the tourist trade. Special note should be made of such traditional types of work as alabaster production at Volterra (Pisa) which originally flourished under the Etruscans and Romans. The crucial factor in boosting the contribution of this sector to the postwar economy has been the rise of mass tourism in Tuscany, for, originally confined to Florence, the spa of Montecatini Terme and parts of the Versilia, it has since the early 1950s spread extensively throughout the region with the impact of new communications to include many other localities, large and small.[28] Now Florence's role as the main Italian centre for the export of artisan goods as well as their promotion directly through the tourist trade is widely recognised. Furthermore, mass tourism has been instrumental in the expansion of the tertiary sector of the Tuscan economy, involving the retail business and other forms of commerce, the tourist agencies and banks and the public services.

In conclusion, it must be added that the rapid economic change occurring in Tuscany since the Second World War has entailed considerable social dislocation through demographic movements and the growth in various parts of population density. This has led to predictable problems of urban life, a matter of increasing concern in the 1970s with the high level of unemployment. The rural haemorrhage has inevitably had a demoralising effect on the depopulated communes in the country with the constriction of their economic situation, a tendency only modified by the high incidence in Tuscany of commuting workers (*pendolari*) who live in 'rural dormitories' and work in the cities, a way of life often requiring long hours of travel to and from work.

All these new social conditions return us to the role of the political parties, since a crucial aspect of the examination of their development is how in the context of such change they have acted as forces of integration or sought to exploit new tensions arising in society. The postwar economic growth of Tuscany has been largely unplanned, so that the parties of the Left in particular have been inclined to respond by emphasising the need for structural reforms, a demand that has had some bearing on their policies following the inauguration of the regional government.

Notes

a. See Chapter 2(c), p. 39.
b. The author's investigations in selected representative communes in Tuscany

generally confirmed the importance of local Resistance activity as a major factor in reinforcing or modifying (and its absence otherwise) the political orientation of different localities or villages. In some cases, the Resistance factor was introduced in interviews not so much as one strengthening local solidarity as relating to traditional rivalry between neighbouring villages in the same commune — for example in Peccioli (Pisa), where the mayor (PSI) emphasised how the 'mentality of opposition to the *capoluogo* [i.e. Peccioli]' on the part of the village of Fabbrica, five miles away, had found its political expression in that the *fabbrichesi* were pronouncedly Christian Democratic in contrast to the *pecciolesi* who voted predominantly for the parties of the Left. During the Occupation, Peccioli had been a scene of some bitter partisan fighting including bombing by the Germans, while Fabbrica had been little involved in the Resistance and had escaped war damage (Interview with Luigi Arzilli at Peccioli, October 1977).

c. It is worthwhile noting the exception here of a couple of communes (Montecarlo and Altopascio) in the south-eastern corner of the province where their difference as 'Red' islands in this 'White' area of the Lucchesia has corresponded with the former local dominance of the *mezzadria* system in them.

d. For the period 1951-1961 Tuscany was in second place among the regions for regional industrial growth, after Emilia-Romagna; by 1961 was in fourth place for the number of industrial enterprises (after Lombardy, Piedmont and Emilia-Romagna); and in fifth place for the number of industrial employees (*Tradition et Changement en Toscane*, cahiers de la fondation nationale des sciences politiques, No. 176 (1970), pp. 134-5). With a population of nearly 3½ million (1971), Tuscany is the ninth largest region in the country.

References

1. Lelio Lagorio, *Presidente in Toscana* (1977), pp. 20-1.
2. C. Seton-Watson, *Italy from Liberalism to Fascism, 1870-1925* (1967), pp. 67-8.
3. See the study of the Socialist stronghold of Sesto Fiorentino (Florence) in Ernesto Ragionieri, *Storia di un comune socialista — Sesto Fiorentino* (1976), pp. 180-2.
4. Silvano Burgalassi, *Il Comportamento Religioso degli Italiani* (1967), pp. 118-19.
5. Ragionieri, *Storia di un comune socialista*, pp. 183-4.
6. *Tradition et Changement en Toscane*, cahiers de la fondation nationale des sciences politiques, No. 176 (1970), pp. 337ff.
7. See the useful tables by region and province of the relative strengths of PSI and PCd'I membership in Renzo Martinelli, *Il Partito Comunista d'Italia, 1921-1926: politica e organizzazzione* (1977), pp. 122-5, 134-6, 194-6.
8. See Carlo Francovich, 'Profilo dell'antifascismo militante toscano' in *La Toscana nel regime fascista, 1922-1939* (1971), proceedings of the 1969 conference on this theme in Florence, Vol. I, pp. 98-9. For a local study on this subject, see Sergio Gensini, 'L'Antifascismo in Valdelsa dal 1922 al 1939' in Ibid., Vol. II, pp. 723-51.
9. See especially the diary of Iris Origo, *War in Val d'Orcia* (1947), *passim*, for a descriptive account of the assistance given by the rural population to the Resistance activity in southern Tuscany.
10. See, for instance, the proceedings of the 1966 conference at Castelfiorentino (Florence), published as *Antifascismo e Resistenza in Valdelsa* (1971); Estevan Giuggi, *Peccioli nella Resistenza: la storia del comitato di liberazione*

(1976) on a town in the province of Pisa; and Vittorio Meoni, *Memoria su Montemaggio* (1975) on one particular Nazi atrocity in the north of Siena province written by the only survivor. In several cases, new incoming Left-wing local administrations formed in the wake of the PCI and PSI successes in the 1975 elections initiated the publication of such local histories of the Resistance.

11. See *Tradition et Changement en Toscane*, Chapter VIII, Section 2c.
12. For a case-study of the PCI in the Veneto, see Alan Stern, 'Political Legitimacy in Local Politics: the Communist Party in Northeastern Italy' in D. Blackmer and S. Tarrow, *Communism in Italy and France* (1975), pp. 221-58.
13. See the article on the city of Lucca in *L'Espresso*, 9 October 1977, pp. 28-32.
14. See Burgalassi, *Il Comportamento Religioso*, pp. 115-16.
15. See Mario Rossi, 'La Chiesa e le organizzazzioni religiose' in *La Toscana nel regime fascista*, Vol. I, esp. pp. 346-52.
16. The Catholic Resistance in Tuscany was commemorated by a 30th anniversary conference in Lucca in April 1975, the proceedings of which were published as *Il Clero Toscano nella Resistenza* (1975).
17. Giacomo Becattini (ed.), *Lo Sviluppo Economico della Toscana* (IRPET, 1975), pp. 39-41.
18. See Ernesto Ragionieri, 'Il Partito Fascista' in *La Toscana nel regime fascista*, Vol. I, pp. 70-1.
19. *Tradition et Changement en Toscane*, p. 220.
20. See Becattini, *Lo Sviluppo Economico della Toscana*, Chapter 4, on the crisis of the *mezzadria*.
21. Survey on Tuscany in *Financial Times*, 15 November 1974.
22. John Earle, *Italy in the 1970s* (1975), p. 104.
23. *Tradition et Changement en Toscane*, pp. 150ff.
24. For a discussion of the growth of light industry in Tuscany, see Becattini, *Lo Sviluppo Economico della Toscana*, Chapter 6.
25. Quoted in Luciano Cavalli (ed.), *Classe Dirigente e Sviluppo Regionale* (1973), p. 15.
26. For details on this, see *Tradition et Changement en Toscane*, Chapter VI, Section 3.
27. Survey on Tuscany in *La Stampa*, 24 August 1977.
28. For the relationship between tourism and small enterprise, see Becattini, *Lo Sviluppo Economico della Toscana*, pp. 125-40.

3 THE TUSCAN COMMUNISTS: THE PARTY OF INTEGRATION ON THE LEFT

(a) Evolution as Party and Movement

There is an obvious element of tautology in considering a political party's relationship with the party system, of which it may form an essential component, especially when the theme is the degree and quality of change occurring in this system. Nevertheless, the necessary starting-point for examining this question must be the nature and adaptability of the individual parties themselves, in particular their capacity for responding to, absorbing, directing and channelling socio-political pressures for change. Indeed, a stricter measure of their performance would include their ability to foresee necessary changes in society and their skill in initiating and promoting them.

In Italy's own form of multi-party system, the evolution of the various parties and especially the principal ones has to be judged in relation also to their strategies and how they inter-relate. There is consequently a two-way impact between a party's external relationships — notably, with other parties as well as with the state and national community — and its own internal relationships: the form and effectiveness of its own structure, the social composition of its membership and the importance of its own ideology, political traditions and modes of political behaviour. In short, party leaders are not free to pursue their strategic objectives out of the context of their internal party relationships. The extent to which the latter condition the former may of course vary, but this itself reflects on the nature of the party in question. It is therefore preferable to look first at the individual parties' own evolution and integrative capacity as their function here provides the necessary precondition for assessing the importance and success of their strategies, both in affecting the parties themselves and how their internal relationships influence the implementation of these strategies. It goes without saying that this order of discussion facilitates a thorough analysis of whether changes in the party system are more permanent than transitory.

Attention will focus first of all on the case of the PCI, not merely because, as in the region of Tuscany, it has been the strongest party and acted as an important integrative force, but primarily since it has emerged in the decade of the 1970s as the most consistent proponent of change in Italian society as well as in the method of government within a democratic framework. Moreover, the PCI's application of the 'historic compromise' increasingly to concrete political situations not only underlined its own success and greater prominence in the state institutions, but at the same time imposed problems of internal tension and adaptation with its move away from a position of long-term and exclusive opposition. It is hence crucial to look at its own qualities as a 'party' and 'movement' in estimating its importance as a force for political and social change.

There are different ways of analysing a political party during any given period of time — historically, organisationally and ideologically — but any approach must define how the party in question features within the comparative framework of political parties. Taking various basic criteria for establishing the classification of parties — ideological/non-ideological or ideological/programmatic/'pragmatic' or class/voter-oriented or mass-structured/loose-associational — the PCI approximates to an ideological, mass-structured and class party, though any such model should as always be employed with flexibility since qualifications are requisite in particular cases. For example, the PCI's class character has been evident from its placing the working class at the centre of its policies, but the uniqueness of the PCI as a party requires some modification of conventional categories to take account of its strategy of social and political alliances extending beyond its traditional social base.

The issue has also been raised in the context of the PCI's development in the 1970s whether or not it has lost something of its mass-party character and acquired some features of a 'catch-all' party,[1] a valid question to pose taking into account the PCI's rise in electoral support, its growing administrative role in the state structure and the consequences of its strategy for its internal life as a political force.

One possible hypothesis is to view the PCI as remaining structurally a mass-party while revealing electorally some signs of becoming a 'catch-all' party.[2] The possibility arises here of some conflict inherent in this analysis even when allowing for a certain flexibility in the application of our comparative criteria. To put it more succinctly, are there any basic contradictions in the PCI's presentation of itself as 'a party of government and struggle', since in the 1970s this has not been merely a label for its strategy and has gradually expressed more of a concrete reality?

For our purposes, it is necessary to clarify what is a 'catch-all' party as distinct from a mass-structured one. It is not sufficient to state that the former should be inter-class without examining the kind of relationship it forms with its social base. The following schema defines the qualities of a 'catch-all' party which distinguish it from a mass-structured one: a 'catch-all' party is preoccupied with the need to create as wide an electoral base as possible even at the cost of social coherence in its support, and where stated policy preferences are subordinated to this need; its social base is marked by its inclination to *collect* rather than *integrate* the groups it attracts; its ultimate purpose is the retention or acquisition of government office *per se* as distinct from the role of party ideology or policy strategy as the point of reference; and hence it follows that its organisational character is different in that party activities are less continuous (i.e. outside election periods) and its relationship with its membership is less structured.[3]

There are two aspects in applying such a schema to an individual party. First, there is the subjective aspect — namely, how a party conceives itself, which is an influential determinant in its political behaviour. Secondly, the objective aspect whereby academic analysis places the party in question in a particular classificatory division according to a systematic set of relevant attributes. It is obvious that, while these two aspects may well correlate, they will not necessarily harmonise.

With regard to the first aspect the PCI has, especially in the 1970s, shown a sensitivity about maintaining its traditional mass character. Respondents in interviews were noticeably and uniformly insistent on this when faced with the classificatory alternative of being or becoming a 'catch-all' party, thus underlining the continuing imprint of the party's self-image and the 'organic' view it holds of its social roots. One PCI leader with experience at both provincial and regional levels illustrated this outlook:

> We believe that the moment of the vote is an important verification, a moment of struggle. Therefore, we are seeking as much as possible to secure our base, but without modifying the fundamental characteristics of our party. That is, we do not want to be an electoralistic party, a party of opinion. We are an organised party, that organises the popular masses. We wish to enjoy a presence among all sectors of society, even if we call ourselves basically the central focus for the working-classes who produce consensus for changing the situation in the country.[4]

Electoral and political developments during the 1970s did, however, begin to call into question some features of the party's mass character. Berlinguer referred critically to this change in an important statement made to the PCI Central Committee following the party's loss of votes in the June 1979 national election, alluding to the fact that the membership was not entirely unaffected by electoralistic tendencies:

> In assessing the election results, we must guard against all tendencies to minimise the scope and significance of the fall in support we suffered. But it would also be misleading to concentrate attention exclusively on this loss, and see winning back these votes as the only task facing the party today. There are comrades who reason as if this were the only aspect of the election outcome and the only problem it raises. They argue more or less as follows: since we lost 4% and this loss occurred in the popular strata and among youth and took the form of a left-wing criticism of our policy (and in particular, they add, of the policy of broad democratic unity), then all we have to do is change this policy, adopting a more closed one geared to the Left alternative, and everything will work itself out and our voters will come back to us.
>
> This reasoning, which some express very simply and others develop in highly sophisticated terms, is mistaken for many reasons.
>
> First of all, to place election results at the top of the list of our political concerns, making them the criteria for our choice of line and even strategy, means reasoning like Social Democrats. In this way, one overlooks all the other elements of the political and social struggle and battle of ideas that mark the life and successes of a Communist party like ours, a party that wants to transform society and overcome capitalism with the democratic method, but knows that there is more to this method than electoral battles alone.
>
> Furthermore, this reasoning is mistaken because it fails to consider the whole picture coming out of the results and the various and complex phenomena revealed by the vote. Finally, it is obvious that the party cannot decide its line solely in view of the goal — which we do, however, set ourselves — of winning back the votes it lost, but must bear in mind all the elements of the situation and not only the domestic situation, but also the European and international scene.[5]

Analytically speaking, it is somewhat misleading to talk too strictly of electorally-oriented parties as against other categories in the sense that all viable political parties are electorally-minded to some degree — it is,

The Tuscan Communists

in fact, the priority accorded the electoral function which differentiates them. As to the quality of the PCI's mass character, more specific examination will touch on regional variation here and hence introduce the question of how far the Tuscan PCI is representative or not of the party in other regions or Italy as a whole. Typical of the 'Red' areas in the country, the Tuscan PCI is more evidently a mass-structured party than, say, simply a mass movement with some structural framework, of which it has shown more signs of being in the south.[6] However, the Tuscan case offers the advantage of observing more easily the impact on a traditional mass-structured party of the implementation of its strategy of the 'historic compromise' and of its growing role in the state institutions. At the same time, the predominant role enjoyed by the PCI in postwar Tuscan politics must have conditioned its reception and interpretation of the general party line in the 1970s as well as influenced its outlook on the problem of party legitimacy. Some background comments on the PCI's evolution as a mass party in the region of Tuscany are necessary before turning to look at its social-integrative capacity there in the 1970s.

The Tuscan PCI established itself as a mass party rapidly after the Second World War. This was most notably so in the province of Florence, where its membership rose from 35,000 in March 1945 to 78,412 the following October, stabilising around 92,267 by December 1947 and constituting at this time a solid working-class base of about 50 per cent.[7] The membership total reached 13.1 per cent of the population in 1951 (14.6 per cent in 1954), with sharecroppers (*mezzadri*) providing the second largest sector of the membership (21.7 per cent in 1947; 21.5 per cent in 1953).[8] This development was in line with the argument that a large socialist party needs the presence of a sizeable and receptive proletariat as its initial basis.[9] But the PCI's organisational intensity was not uniform throughout Tuscany at this early stage, being among other things conditioned by the socio-economic factor of the predominance or not of the sharecropping system (at its strongest in the provinces of Florence, Pisa and Siena). The very strong correlation between PCI organisational dominance in rural areas and the prevalence of the sharecropping method is borne out by an examination of both factors at the level of commune.[10]

While strong concentrations of *mezzadri* allowed the PCI in rural areas to base its appeal on class conflict, the incidence of party mass membership also depended locally on a variety of other factors. The organisational impact of Resistance activity counted, especially where peasant-partisan links were strong, but also enabled the PCI to project its credibility as a political force among other social groups. This could on the other hand be reduced by the persistence of sectarian class attitudes among party militants during the years after the War, or alternatively enhanced by the role of a prominent ex-partisan as a 'father-figure' style mayor.[11] In order to complete this background, one should in fact trace back local party development to the immediate pre-Fascist period following the split in the Socialist Party in 1921 to note the extent to which ex-PSI activists established local strongholds of Communist organisation before the rise of Mussolini.[12]

By and large, the PCI in Tuscany emerged after the Fascist period as a mass-structured party, albeit with varying degrees of intensity at the local level. This variation illustrated the important interplay of organisational with socio-economic and political factors, which went some way towards supporting the thesis of Apter that political parties are dependent factors of their environments.[13] This line of reasoning has led to the misleading, if not mistaken, popular view that the Tuscan PCI is more 'conservative' than in most other parts of the country,[14] a term in any case provocative in Italian because it means association with the reactionary political Right and which is therefore anathema to Communist politicians. The PCI's traditional role in local administration and of consensus-formation in the region, as well as its appeal there to such middle-class groups as small and medium entrepreneurs, have undoubtedly influenced its own nature as a party, but all the same this popular view is based on a one-dimensional explanation of the PCI's relationship with society. Apter's thesis has a certain attraction, but environmental variables should not be treated too 'passively' or statically when discussing party development. It is equally important to ask whether and how the political party in question *acts* as a force for social change.

(b) The PCI's Mass Base: Its Integrative Capacity and Way of Life

There are two fundamental ways of viewing a party's base in socio-political terms: quantitatively as to the size of its support among different social groups and the balance between them within its membership; and qualitatively as to the nature or intensity of the party's link with these various groups and in particular the degree of coherence between them. These two points of focus form the background to the following discussion, which considers in turn general problems of membership composition and development, the PCI's relationships with

The Tuscan Communists

specific social groups and then the importance of party activities for its socio-political role. An examination of these aspects together allows conclusions about the PCI's success in maintaining its mass character during a period of challenge from social and also political changes.

Reflecting its mass character in the region since the Second World War, the Tuscan PCI has traditionally featured numerically as having the second largest total of membership after the other 'Red' region of Emilia-Romagna (Emilia-Romagna 447,516, Tuscany 256,880, followed by Lombardy with 217,087 — figures for 1976).[15] It follows that with its wide quantitative span of membership — out of Tuscany's population of around 3½ million (1971 census) one-fourteenth are registered in the party — the PCI has been particularly susceptible to any major demographic developments. In short, our examination must begin with how far these have left their imprint on the party's social composition, and the manner in which the party has reacted to these problems of adaptation.

The degree of social change is immediately apparent if one compares the composition of party membership across units of a decade or two. To take the province with the highest rate of economic growth in the postwar period, that of Florence, Table 3.1 bears out the extent of change in the relative strength of the different social groups.

Table 3.1: Social Composition of PCI Membership in the Florence Federation, 1947-1970

	1947 %	1970 %
Workers	54.1	44.0
Clerical workers	3.6	3.2
Professions	0.2	0.8
Small businessmen	1.7	3.6
Artisans	5.2	6.3
Agricultural labourers	2.3	1.8
Sharecroppers	21.7	9.0
Housewives	6.9	15.4
Pensioners	0.4	14.7
Students	0.2	0.6

Source: Neri Gori, 'L'Organizzazione del PCI a Firenze [1945-1971]' in *Rassegna Italiana di Sociologia*, 1974, p. 393.

The outstanding features of change are the relative decline of working-class membership with the cautious increase among the middle-classes, the sharp drop in sharecroppers and a concentration of older members (reflecting a stability of membership among ex-workers in particular). Substantial social change had occurred largely by the 1970s, arising from urbanisation with the growth of small and medium industry and the tertiary sector following the rural exodus. However, the significant trend in the 1970s has been the extension of PCI membership among the middle classes. This becomes evident if one compares figures across the whole postwar period, taking the province of Siena, which as the 'Reddest' of all in Tuscany (roughly one-sixth of the population being PCI members) has seen vast social change with considerable depopulation of the country areas and the virtual eclipse of the sharecropping system as well as the development of industry in certain areas.

Table 3.2: Social Composition of PCI Membership in the Siena Federation, 1948-1976

	1948 %	1976 %
Workers	20.0	33.27
Agricultural labourers	4.0	5.91
Sharecroppers	57.0	2.91
Direct cultivators	1.0	8.40
Middle classes	4.0	10.49
Students/housewives/pensioners	13.0	38.97

Note: Middle classes (*ceti medi*) = artisans, small businessmen, small entrepreneurs, clerical workers and the liberal professions all together, the figures for 1948 not being sub-divided. In the last category pensioners provided, in 1976, 21.71 per cent of the total membership.
Source: PCI Siena, *Dati Statistici*, 14th provincial congress, March 1977, pp. 14-15.

It was inevitable that the PCI membership composition should have been conditioned by such massive social change in the region, though whether one agrees with the proud assertion of one Tuscan party leader that the PCI has a 'great plastic capacity' in adapting to this depends on an estimation of the difficulties it faced in the process. It is worth dwelling on these in order to place in a broader perspective the PCI's evolution as a mass party during the 1970s, when further social and political challenges arose. The main importance of these earlier social changes as part of postwar Italy's industrialisation and demographic movement, which resulted in a severe reduction in the PCI's aggregative ability during the decade up to the late 1960s, was that the weakening — and in the case of the *mezzadri* the virtual decimation — of its two essential bases of class support in Tuscany created a crisis of identity for it as a mass party. In short, the degree and speed of social change which took place had political consequences because it uprooted the fundamental link between the Tuscan PCI's appeal to both the urban and rural proletariat which was clearly the factor and concept of class struggle. Having become in the rural areas 'the party of the sharecroppers', the PCI for a certain time found itself outdistanced by the dramatic rate of depopulation from the late 1950s and was unable to recoup its membership in the growing urban areas to balance its losses in the countryside,[16] a problem magnified by the impact of political developments, notably the Hungarian invasion of 1956 which, as elsewhere in Italy, occasioned a decline in party membership.

Similar problems have confonted the PCI in the 1970s, but for a different reason. This was the party's 'crisis of growth' originating in the student and working-class mobilisation of 1968-1969, and evidenced in the PCI's slow penetration of new sectors of urban society as well as the impact of its rapid rise in electoral support in the mid-1970s. The primary challenge to the PCI came from the fact that developing urban society presented a far more complex social environment in which to operate politically, for not only did traditional class-conflict appeals have less effect but also the growth of consumer values posed special problems of social coherence. By the early 1970s, it was still clear that PCI membership had not only not kept pace with urban growth, but had even stagnated. In Florence, for example, the population had risen during the decade 1958-1968 by 8.8 per cent while party membership had remained at a constant level and even declined in the later 1960s (from 18,494 in 1966 to 16,034 in 1970).[17] This feature, which hit the other parties too but the PCI most seriously because of its strong mass-party character, was attributed to social disintegration with the growing isolation of the individual in the large city and a visible disinterest of citizens to exert social and political influence, both of which had a profound effect on associational ties and hence on the PCI's capacity for political mobilisation.[18]

Special problems of membership instability were caused by the fact that a high proportion of workers who sought employment in large cities, notably so in Florence, did so while commuting from their 'dormitory' homes outside, thus inhibiting the maintenance of organisational links with the party. At the same time, the PCI was forced to re-consider its approach to the new middle-class groups it was beginning to attract. The difficulties of adjusting to this dual development were emphasised by party leaders, already concerned about the PCI's limitations in absorbing rapid social change through their experiences of the 1960s:

> Some things have to be taken into account: namely that student numbers are increasing, as are also those of white-collar workers, technicians and those working who have diplomas and degrees, while in the city the workers are declining. In addition, the existence of party sections at the place of work (*sezioni aziendali*) means that activity there is growing, while that of many Communist working-class militants is declining in the territorial sections (*sezioni di strada*). But let's ask ourselves, comrades, who are in large part these students who are working in the party sections. They are the sons of workers, labourers and artisans, they themselves are an expression of the popular strata of the city and the province. They are our sons who in 1968 troubled us, because they seemed to want to choose different paths from the main road followed by militants of the Italian Communist Party.[19]

This acknowledgement by the PCI federation (i.e. provincial) secretary for Florence of the need to avoid class tensions within the party by establishing a sense of social identity between traditional working-class militants and the post-1968 influx of young middle-class intelligentsia will be discussed below,[a] except that it is worth noting here that this involved more than a generational gap but also a class divide.

The need to adjust to urbanisation entailed adopting more sophisticated and flexible skills in projecting the PCI as a party as well as re-thinking its general approach to different social groups. This among other things included taking note of particular local conditions. At Sesto Fiorentino, on the outskirts of Florence and part of that circular belt around the Tuscan capital which has seen the greatest economic expansion, the problems posed for the party varied between localities. Common to them all was the imigration of southerners coming from a social environment not so conducive to PCI support, as Tarrow has shown. However, the PCI at Sesto was able to maintain a remarkably constant level of electoral support (at around 54 per cent during 1963–1972) during the decade when the population there more than doubled, partly through the influence of socialisation within a notably strong 'Red' sub-cultural setting but also as a result of the conscious effort by local PCI leaders to establish party organisational links in a differentiated manner. As one of them noted:

> The party in decentralising and operating on the basis of the city district (*quartiere*) allowed the party section to change its relationship with the population. It was directed in a way that political action could be applied differently. For example, districts like Campanello and Quinto Basso mean following a policy aimed at the middle classes, much more accentuated than in other districts. It is not as if things remain static.[20]

In neighbouring Scandicci, on the other hand, the growth of urbanisation had been more precipitate (population rise 1960-1973: 18,085 to 51,565) so that with weaker sub-cultural links the difficulties for party *aggiornamento* had been more pronounced, for the rise in PCI electoral support (from 12,461 in 1968 to 20,229 in 1976) was not accompanied by an equivalent strengthening of its membership base (ratio of 1 to 10 in 1976).

These instances, while being among the more disproportionate cases, nevertheless pointed to one major theme relevant to this discussion of the PCI as a mass party in the 1970s — the weakening ratio of party members to voters. A mass-structured party needs, in order to stabilise its social roots, as strong an organisational (i.e. membership-based, not just electoral) link with its supporters as possible, for the smaller the ratio of voters to members the more it is such a mass party. Applying this classic criterion to the PCI, there have been periods of fluctuation since the War, as during 1958-1963 when generally the ratio rose from 3 to 4.8, reflecting not only the marginal rise in votes but particularly the decline in party membership during this time. During the 1970s, the ratio of voters to members has risen again exclusively as a result of the unprecedented increase in the PCI's electorate, for it has in fact been accompanied by a growth of membership. Here the 'Red' regions of Italy have featured a greater stability than elsewhere in Italy (the national ratio rose from 5.6 to 6.6 in 1970-1975), especially than in the south (e.g. Sicily rose from 7.5 to 9.0), Tuscany itself rising only from 4.3 to 4.7.[21] It is often more instructive to note the differences that appear at the sub-regional or even local levels, for within the Communist stronghold of Tuscany there have been marked differences between the provinces (the ratio varying from 2.6 in Siena in 1975 to 7.8 in Lucca), but especially so between communes. Taking these two contrasting examples, the province of Siena showed on the basis of the data for the member/voter ratio for all the communes in the years 1963, 1972 and 1976 a cautious rise in most cases, though also a stability or even decline in several;[22] whereas the PCI federation of Lucca (for the Lucchesia) witnessed no dramatic overall rise in the ratio (because of a sharp rise in membership during 1970-1975), but a much wider margin of difference between the ratios of the various communes (from 3.2 in Careggine to 24.8 in Castiglione Garfagnana in 1976).[23]

This evidence points to a growing instability of the PCI's social links, for where the provincial level of membership rose most during the 1970s (i.e. Lucca 26.55 per cent in 1970-1975, Massa Carrara 20.59 per cent, contrasting with Siena 2.49 per cent)[24] this was on the basis of a weak numerical strength at the beginning. For a party, which pays such serious even symbolic attention to its membership recruitment, this general development occasioned a deep concern leading to an increased drive to improve the member/voter ratio in the annual recruitment campaigns.[25]

One factor which clearly emerges in assessing this instability is the importance of local political and cultural traditions, as featured in the presence of PCI-allied collateral associations, as well as variation in the extent of PCI dominance in different areas of the region. This is illustrated by looking at the ratio of population to PCI membership by party federation (Table 3.3). Whereas the greatest change in the first half of the 1970s occurred in the two provinces of Lucca and Massa Carrara, the PCI membership's share of the population still being proportionately weak, in the 'Reddest' provinces of Siena and Livorno there remained over this period a far greater stability in the PCI's organisational presence in society. In spite of all these difficulties and variations, it must nevertheless be emphasised that they arose from the electoral success of the PCI during 1970-1976 and not from any organisational decline, although trends since 1977 have indicated some reversal of this process.

In order to illustrate more specifically these problems of membership and in general the PCI's social-aggregative capacity, it is necessary to focus on certain specific social groups, noting the extent to which they have been integrated into the party in the 1970s and whether they have affected its social composition. In so illustrating the nature of the PCI's inter-class roots, attention should be given to both how these different groups inter-relate within the PCI and to the intensity of their own links with it.

First, since industrial workers have continued to form by far the largest individual section of the membership (accounting for some

Table 3.3: PCI Membership by Federation re: Ratio to Provincial Population, 1971-1975

	Membership		Ratio population/membership	
	1971	1975	1971	1975
Arezzo	21,345	22,561	11.0	10.4
Florence	65,754	69,585	11.6	10.9
Prato	10,625	11,411		
Grosseto	14,128	15,315	11.8	10.8
Livorno	28,555	31,595	9.0	8.2
Lucca	3,364	4,285	37.8	30.5
Viareggio	4,274	5,177		
Massa Carrera	6,626	7,837	22.7	19.2
Pisa	21,650	23,003	13.4	12.7
Pistoia	15,410	16,682	12.7	11.7
Siena	41,280	42,078	5.0	4.9
Tuscany	233,011	249,529	11.5	10.7
Italy	1,510,502	1,715,195	25.5	22.5

Source: PCI Ufficio Elettorale e di Statistica, *Raccolta di dati sull'organizzazione, 1971-1975*, November 1976, pp. 16, 18, 32-3.

37 per cent of it in Tuscany), the question is whether their numerical presence has been matched by their weight and role in party life. The point is relevant in view of the expansion of the PCI's electoral appeal and the pronounced growth of young middle-class intellectuals at the local and intermediary leadership levels.[b] As mentioned above, some working-class resentment was apparent in the early 1970s over this change, and was likely to increase as this trend developed.[c] It should not be forgotten that this change occurred at the same time as a rekindling of working-class militancy and sense of *operaismo* from the 'Hot Autumn' of 1969, though the impact of this on the PCI must be measured against the way in which this new militancy was channelled more through the trade unions, specifically the Communist-allied CGIL, with their growing autonomy from the political parties. Moreover, the particular structure of industrial growth in Tuscany itself, besides creating an enlarged working-class, also presented the PCI with certain difficulties in maintaining or establishing membership links with this sector. The main difficulty arose from the development of small and medium industry, hence the dispersion of new groups of

industrial workers among a multiplicity of firms rather than in urban industrial concentrations, where party organisation would have been easier. But the problems here were not purely geographical, for other factors entered the picture, as the Tuscan PCI review *Politicà e Società* noted:

> On the social level the extension of light industry changes the composition of the working-class; it enlarges female occupation and creates a younger generation of the working-class (there is much recourse to apprenticeship). The party encounters major difficulties of organisation with these new strata, whether because they are dispersed in a constellation of small firms or whether it is because they change their subjective outlook in matters of consciousness, culture and conditions of life.[26]

The basic difference emerging here is that the PCI has experienced much greater difficulty in areas where postwar industrial development has been new rather than based on an older tradition of industrial activity, as is notably the case with the port of Livorno, the Piaggio mechanical engineering factory at Pontedera and the historical centre of alabaster workers at Volterra. In the first instance, the problems are illustrated by Santa Croce sull'Arno (Pisa), where industrial development (notably leather and tanning) has mushroomed with the creation of some 3,000 firms employing 19,000 workers, with long working hours and a general practice of overtime. According to an analysis by two local party leaders, this created problems of party mobilisation in the factories, in spite of a strong tradition of local PCI organisation since the anti-Fascist strikes there in 1944, leading to a reduction in political militancy, a trend not unattached to the fact that some active involvement has been diverted to trade-union activity.[27]

In other areas, the problem has been not so much location as mobility. The secretary of the PCI's Lucca federation described the situation in the Garfagnana:

> In this zone there is very much commuting (*pendolarità*). There are many workers who travel by train and coach, work at Lucca, at Massa Carrara, at ENEL, in the quarries. When they return home there is no relationship between residence and political activity ... we have entire groups of leading activists in certain *sezioni* who leave on Mondays and return on Saturdays, who go to Pisa, to Florence. Let's take an example — Gallicano. Gallicano has a *sezione*

of comrades consisting half of workers who work away and half of students who study at Pisa. The party practically does not exist between one local congress and another.[28]

The difficulties of PCI organisational penetration in the Lucchesia also underlined the extent to which sub-cultural factors are reproduced in the process of industrialisation. In so far as new workers are ex-peasants originating in a strong Catholic environment, where ties with the Church and the DC have traditionally been strong, the PCI has been unable to make significant inroads in this sector, the notable case being the large industrial commune of Capannori. In the view of one party leader from that area, this had retarded the PCI's social aggregation in the Lucchesia as there was the 'danger of isolation' of those workers favourable to the PCI because there was little 'concrete possibility of a social and hence political alliance' between them and other strata, especially the peasants.[29] The sub-cultural explanation, however, worked in the opposite direction to the PCI's advantage in the many areas of 'Red' hegemony elsewhere in Tuscany, where ex-sharecroppers became workers. At Poggibonsi (Siena), for example, the postwar development of the metal industry has been based on a new labour force of exclusively sharecropping origin. In such a case as Poggibonsi, the more cohesive concentration of industrial workers has also facilitated the development of party membership. In short, this survey of the working-class base of the Tuscan PCI emphasises the considerable local diversification of party links with a general tendency in the light of industrialisation to move towards a more differentiated relationship than that encountered in major industrial centres. The ties between the PCI here and its working-class members have changed therefore not so much quantitatively as qualitatively, but nevertheless traditional working-class solidarity has helped in most areas to absorb the effects on the party of socio-economic change.

Secondly, the PCI's links with the urban middle classes (*ceti medi*) illustrate other important facets of the PCI's socio-political role, in particular the possibilities and limitations of its inter-class appeal. The PCI's relationship with this key sector started with the disadvantage that with one exception the party in Tuscany did not enjoy any traditional ties. The exception was the artisan class in certain areas, notably Florence (where they had played an important role as a channel of communication for the anti-Fascist Resistance) and at Volterra (Pisa), where the sub-cultural argument of 'Red' hegemony operated. There were other local instances of PCI organisational links with artisans, but these two were the most notable cases. In general, the PCI's strength among this particular group was shown by the vote of 58.7 per cent in Tuscany for the party-allied National Confederation of Artisans (CNA) in the elections to the artisan provincial committees in 1970.[30]

By and large, the *ceti medi* have not provided a substantial element of the party membership. For the whole of Tuscany, artisans consisted of 5.3 per cent of the membership, small businessmen 3.66 per cent and clerical workers 2.09 per cent (1974),[31] though in all cases there was very considerable local variation, thus tending to support the hypothesis of Hellman that local history and traditions in buttressing PCI hegemony are a crucial variable in winning middle-class support.[32] In the city of Livorno, with its long Left-wing tradition, PCI membership was particularly strong among the tertiary sector (24 per cent of new recruits in 1976), in particular among public employees.[33] Individual social conditions played a part such as at Cecina (Livorno), an example of a dramatic expansion of the tertiary sector and a population explosion, where the PCI has retained a strong presence among public employees and artisans because they largely come from working-class origins.[34] By contrast both groups form a minute part of the membership on the island of Elba, which lacks any such 'Red' tradition.[35] A similar examination of party membership composition for the province of Pisa by commune underlined the same theme about local variation,[36] though 'Red' dominance cannot be considered too exclusive a factor as the social composition of members also depends strongly on the incidence of local occupational structure as well as on the influence of family political attitudes (as the author's interviewees have recorded).

There are various reasons for the limited success of the PCI among the urban *ceti medi*. First and foremost, it is a question of overcoming traditional social and hence political attitudes. Outside the important artisan sector in Tuscany and the cities where Left-wing political tendencies are deeply-rooted (i.e. pre-Fascism), the PCI has had the problem of penetrating anew these various groups while retaining in their eyes traditional (working-) class associations — although this class reluctance is not so pronounced among those *ceti medi* from humble (worker or peasant) backgrounds. This reflects on the difficulties for the PCI in projecting its social-alliance strategy towards the 'productive middle classes', which has remained at least in part an expression of good intentions rather than of past achievement. In spite of the party line, old class antagonisms have persisted among working-class members and these have contributed to a certain ambivalence in the PCI's position. At a conference organised by the PCI on the subject of its alliance with the *ceti medi* at Empoli in July 1971, the official speech by the PCI communal *assessore* for economic affairs was followed by an intervention from one party member, who accused the PCI of looking after the interests of the 'little bosses' (*padroncini*) against those of the working-class. One local party leader then responded by justifying the party position as follows:

> I well understand that in saying these things I will perhaps appear just like someone who is concerned much with the interests of capitalists for comrade B., who spoke before, but I believe that all those who are militants in the Communist Party know that the Communist Party has long looked to the general interests of Italian society and does not assume a narrow class-conscious attitude; certainly, the PCI is the party of the working-class, but it is the party of the working-class which takes on responsibility for all the problems of Italian society.[37]

The PCI leadership has, however, striven to overcome the problems of contact with the urban middle classes, for, as one provincial party secretary commented: 'This is a problem area we are studying in a way different from that of the working-class.' The approach was different from that taken towards working-class members in that the PCI has attempted to capitalise on its increasing electoral appeal, the impact of economic crisis on the standing of the DC and the credibility acquired by the PCI from the 'historic compromise' to promote its organisational links among the *ceti medi*. Even in a PCI stronghold like Sesto Fiorentino the party has not found it less necessary to concentrate its energies in this direction. In a conscious reference to Togliatti's alliance strategy, the local party formed in the mid-1970s a special commission on the *ceti medi* with the aim of creating stronger links with 'artisan and tradesman members' and of 'articulating better our political proposals and improving penetration by the party of all levels and categories of the *ceto medio*'.[38] At the same time, the Sesto PCI continued to cultivate that sector of the middle classes where it had its strongest membership, the artisans, through municipal financing of their projects and exhibitions of work by both small businessmen and artisans.[39]

One group of the *ceti medi* worth special mention is that of small entrepreneurs (*piccoli imprenditori*), a much remarked-on feature of party membership in the 'Red' regions and Tuscany in particular because it poses the question of bridging an obviously strong class divide. Numerically, they have provided in fact a very small proportion of the PCI membership (0.39 per cent in the province of Florence, 0.94 per cent in the province of Siena), nor do they play a conspicuous or active role in the party. According to a study of party activism in the province of Florence, members from the entrepreneurial class tended to establish relations with the PCI that 'probably by-pass the level of *sezioni* so as not to provoke any reactions among grass-roots activists'.[40] A party review of PCI development in the Valdelsa (north-west corner of Siena province) admitted that the real problem in this respect was the surfacing of sectarian class attitudes among working-class members:

> In this area, the limits of the party's policy of alliances are reflected. The progress towards an open position *vis-à-vis* small and medium entrepreneurs encounters in fact serious obstacles in the way in which the working-class interprets its own role and defends its interests ...[41]

The possibility of polemical attitudes concerning the economic role of the *compagni imprenditori* has therefore discouraged their close participation in the party, reflected in their low level of financial contributions, but clearly another reason must be the impact of dynamic change in their economic status and activity as an example of postwar industrialisation.

The question of the nature of their party links must be investigated further at the local level, for it is a matter of taking those individual communes with a concentration of Communist entrepreneurs, whose contacts tend to focus on the PCI-led administrations rather than the party machine. One such example is Colle Valdelsa (Siena), where *imprenditori* account for roughly 5 per cent of the party membership (about 150 out of some 3,200). It is interesting to note why they have remained Communists. The factor of PCI hegemony with its control of public agencies and facilities for financing projects undoubtedly has helped to explain this phenomenon of Communist entrepreneurs, but other less obvious features have also been operative. At the human level, their family political traditions as ex-workers or ex-peasants have persisted in spite of the change in personal economic roles, although this has more to do with sentiment and general beliefs than strict adherence to an ideology for the local entrepreneurs are not really Marxist in outlook. 'They are enlightened petty bourgeois, whose social viewpoint is halfway between socialism and social conscience (*sta nel mezzo di socialismo e socialità*), I would say more social conscience than socialism,' according to one local party leader. The PCI mayor of Colle Valdelsa emphasised that in a relatively small town inter-class relationships were different from those in a large city, for 'at Colle everybody knows everybody else, 90% use "tu" to each other, we all went to school together and there is continuous contact between people'.[42] All the same, the growth of a local entrepreneurial class from the mid-1950s had been accompanied by some evidence of conflict between *imprenditori* and workers, and such a divergence of economic interests has tended to weaken the former's party ties. According to a local PCI leader:

> ... gradually these interests increase, conflict expands until there comes a point at which he [the *imprenditore*] leaves. Not in a vulgar manner, of resigning bluntly, but of maybe not renewing party membership, because it is a position that at times is discomforting for all; also as the Communist party itself finds itself between workers on the one side and some entrepreneur on the other, and sometimes has been forced to act as mediator . . . which is always difficult.

It is evident from this discussion of the PCI's links with the middle classes that there is a distinct difference of intensity in these links when a comparison is applied to the various component groups in this category. In other words, the hegemony argument as the basis for explaining the PCI's middle-class roots in a strong 'Red' region is relevant, but must be employed in a differentiating way: for example, political-cultural ties combined with local tradition to account for the fact that artisans have featured as the strongest element among the PCI's middle-class membership. In view of the attachment to locality in Tuscan society, PCI hegemony has more visible socialising effects in the smaller or medium-sized provincial towns, where the population is more cohesive, than in the larger towns which have been the focal point for the disorganised growth of an urban middle-class from the 1950s, and in Tuscany especially from the 1960s. In the latter instance, the PCI has had more problems in stabilising or expanding its support, even though it has worked hard at establishing its base among the urban *ceti medi*. It is significant that, while the Tuscan PCI has suffered from the virtual decimation of its natural rural constituency among the sharecroppers, it has managed to retain its traditional link with this class after the sharecroppers' transference to urban employment in a large number of cases, especially when they have become workers; but also this particular influence has extended within the tertiary sector. The fact that Communist Party associations have withstood economic change has ultimately much to do with the permeation of Communist 'values' at the familial level, not merely as a consequence of close family ties in Italian life but also of the marked propensity with PCI members for other members of their families to join the party (according to the 1977 Doxa survey of the PCI membership nearly 60 per cent had other PCI members in the family).[43] Another point of differentiation is that the PCI has encountered more problems of harmonising its links with both working-class and middle-class sectors in the larger cities, where class barriers are more pronounced and have indeed been acerbated by population growth. This is particularly true of cases like Florence and Pisa, but notably less so of Livorno, where traditionally Left-wing political-cultural ties have ...ed as an absorptive agent.

Noting such local and intra-class variation helps to place in a concrete perspective the PCI's strategy of social alliances, a strategy which is basic to the PCI's aggregative capacity as a mass party. Togliatti's concept of the 'new party' (*partito nuovo*) was constructed on the axis of the PCI's presence among all sectors of the population, those 'millions and millions of citizens who at any moment are ready to do something to improve their situation', for the PCI aimed at 'stabilising contact with them, giving the shape of organised movement to their aspirations'.[44] In effect, it was directed at virtually all Italians except for certain 'monopolistic' minority sectors (e.g. large landowners in the case of Tuscany). In practice, the projection of this social alliance was not so simple in the light of urbanisation from the early 1960s, especially where it was a question of forming organisational links with those middle-class sectors which lacked any obvious 'cultural' affinity with the party. These problems become clearer if we continue this examination of individual social groups by looking at those two further sectors, which as a consequence of social and political change since the late 1960s the PCI has found increasingly receptive as an audience — youth and women.

The PCI's relationship with youth provides a touchstone for measuring its ability both to respond to new, and in this case rather sudden, social upheaval and to harmonise this sizeable new element of membership with other social groups within the party. In short, has the PCI been successful in integrating youth since the movement of 1968, or has it merely 'collected' in a 'catch-all' fashion their adherence? This is a pertinent question in view of the problems of membership stability among this group which became more evident by the later 1970s. Although the unprecedented influx of younger party members left its mark quantitatively on the PCI, it is the qualitative consequences of this development which provide most interest, not only in reference to the nature of youth's links with the PCI but also their significance for the PCI's internal balance of class forces. More specifically, a distinction needs to be made in the case of the PCI between the growth of a young working-class and the rise of political militancy among that more vocal element of the higher-educated sections of the younger generation, the students. The former presented fewer problems of integration in the party, although several PCI leaders interviewed commented on the influence of consumer values in reducing political commitment in this group; while the latter, with their preponderantly middle-class background and different style of articulating political demands, forced the PCI to contend with internal tensions arising from traditional suspicions among working-class militants which were not only generational but also class-based. In other words, the rise of the student youth movement granted the party a unique opportunity for 'renewal' while occasioning within it abnormal problems of integration, all the more so as students had not been originally conceived of as part of the PCI's traditional social alliance strategy.

In terms of absolute numerical strength the influx of new young recruits after 1968 made less impact on the PCI in Tuscany, with its postwar record of mass membership and where a sizeable element had after thirty years in the party progressed to middle age and beyond, than in the regions of the south. This is clear if one compares Tuscany with a few southern regions and Italy as a whole a few years later (Table 3.4).

Table 3.4: Age Structure of PCI Membership, 1974 (%)

	Up to 25	25–40	41–60	60 and above
Tuscany	7.67	25.37	51.32	15.64
Campania	18.02	37.24	32.12	12.62
Calabria	15.74	34.57	39.07	10.62
Italy	11.28	30.70	40.11	17.91

Source: PCI Ufficio Elettorale e di Statistica, *Raccolta di dati sull'organizzazione, 1971-1975*, November 1976, pp. 124-6.

However, many of the same general problems of integrating these new members applied to Tuscany as becomes clear when focusing more specifically on certain areas or cities where the youth movement concentrated and presented the PCI with some challenge. In the province of Siena, for example, such a situation did not exist because of the predominance of members in the older age groups (87.65 per cent between 41 and 60 (1974), reflecting both the vast migration of young people to cities elsewhere in search of employment as well as the exceptionally strong record of a mass membership in that province. By contrast, the three party federations with the highest proportion of young membership (under 25) were Prato (as an economic growth area), Lucca (which saw a recoupment of party membership during the 1970s) and Pisa (with the presence of a large student population). In the Florence federation, this was less noticeable proportionately because of the high absolute number of party members.

While some integration of young, especially middle-class, activists has occurred at the intermediary leadership level,[d] so far as the social base of the party in general went various points should be noted. The PCI has undoubtedly benefited substantially from a growth in youth attachment since the *contestazione* of 1968, during which crisis the party responded with a sensitive awareness of the significance of the event combined with a certain perplexity about how to handle this wave of mobilisation. Based on research in the earlier 1970s, Hellman noted a marked hostility among local party leaders, especially those over 40, towards student activists, all the more when the latter criticised the 'revisionist' line of the PCI.[45] Since then the emergence of a young generation of leaders has reduced the generational gap problem, while the PCI during the time of its electoral surge in the mid-1970s reinforced its appeal to young people as a 'modern' force for change. However, the party's organisational as opposed to electoral links with youth have been less easy. This could be attributed in part to problems of youthful volatility, a reason particularly applicable in the 1970s with the high incidence of youth unemployment and other factors of youth disorientation (Florence, for instance, has the fourth highest rate of drug-taking among Italian cities). In the case of the university cities of Pisa and Siena, there were the special problems of student mobility with a high proportion of southerners and other non-locals among the student body. In the former case the body of about 25,000 students accounted for a quarter of the population. The Pisan PCI took various initiatives to try and solve the pressing question of student accommodation and other general problems arising from a large

The Tuscan Communists

floating student population in the city.[46] The communal conference of the Pontedera PCI, June 1977, underlined the difficulties of maintaining a party link with youth in general, and not just in reference to students:

> ... it is necessary to think of the problem of the young generation, which demands a constant initiative by the party, of a continuous battle at the level of ideas and politics, but in actual relations with youth this sometimes leads to harsh confrontation. We should be able to measure up to the problems of the future, since the most worrying cause of disorientation among youth is that today they think and act almost exclusively with the immediate situation in mind.[47]

However, this problem for the party was distinctly less pronounced among employed youth for, as one young party activist from Florence pointed out, 'when a youth enters productive work, his relationship with the PCI becomes more positive', especially as employment entails not only a psychological change but also establishes a trade union association.

The same interviewee also mentioned an attitude of 'diffidence' apparent among PCI clubs (*circoli*) with the habit of young people in the city of visiting the party recreation centres (*Case del Popolo*) but not being seen around party *sezioni* proper, indicating a loose rather than structured relationship with the PCI. Similarly, at the time of 1968 there had been a tendency at Florence by students and young teachers involved in the then controversy over Italian schools to see their point of contact at the *Case* and not the PCI *sezioni*.[48] These pointers to an 'associational' rather than 'communal' link with the party, to use Tönnie's distinction, help to explain the crisis undergone by the party's youth organisation, the Italian Communist Youth Federation (FGCI), during the 1970s. In the years immediately following 1968 there appears to have been a weakening of FGCI membership,[49] no doubt due to the initial inability of the party organisation to adjust to the challenge of the new student movement. During the years 1971-1975, the total of FGCI membership rose gradually in Tuscany as elsewhere (in Tuscany from 10,596 to 16,179), once the party's relationship with youth settled down, but since 1976 the instability of FGCI membership has again surfaced with a decline from 17,169 to 15,537 recorded for 1976-1977 and this trend continuing through 1978-1980. Party leaders have been only too aware of these difficulties, as any reading of the speeches of party secretaries at federation congresses in the spring of 1977 will show. According to the Lucca party secretary, the PCI had failed to appreciate fully the 'great discontinuity' in the youth movement and assist it with its 'considerable difficulty in developing organised structures for the movement, in identifying objectives with which to grow and continue'.[50] The secretary of the Florentine FGCI commented more fully in a review article on the subject:

> The FGCI has been (and continues to be) poised between two ways of existing: on the one hand, the organisation of cadres, thoroughly political, in certain respects quite closed and sectarian; on the other hand, the organisation is completely permeated by the logic of a movement, not always capable of performing a politically educative role, with an unambiguous and one-dimensional vision of the youth situation.[51]

These problems related to long-standing incongruities in the PCI's relations with youth, notably the acknowledged inhibiting effect of its bureaucratic structures on youth participation, especially as the post-1968 movement called into question traditional methods of political organisation.[52] The difficult situation from 1976 derived in fact primarily from the impact of national political events on this potentially unstable relationship — the Bologna student riots of March 1977, but also the adverse impression created among critical youth of the PCI's growing involvement in supporting a DC government at Rome. A year after the 1976 Election, the organisational conference of the Tuscan FGCI pinpointed 'new contradictions' in the PCI's relations with youth since the party's abstention in favour of the Andreotti government.[53] A contemporary round-table discussion of party leaders explained this by the fact that the PCI's approach of 'gradualism' in national affairs was not readily accepted by youth.[54] Such fluctuation in youth's political links with the PCI underlined the profound difficulties which it experienced in the 1970s in establishing a stable relationship with this group, whether in reference to the student population as a whole or unemployed working-class youth. The PCI has undoubtedly been the main political beneficiary quantitatively of youth mobilisation since 1968, but the latter has rather retained features of an amorphous 'movement' than submitted itself to the articulated discipline of party organisation. Only at the level of the leadership cadres has full integration of the 1968 youth generation occurred, which will be discussed in the next section.

The role of women members in the PCI illustrates similar problems encountered by the party in its attempt to harness and provide a structured relationship for new forms of political mobilisation during the 1970s. Once again, the PCI has benefited, though only partially, from the repercussions of the growth of the women's movement on Italian politics. The party's approach has been manifested in a cautious espousal in principle of the values of that movement combined with difficulties in practice of relating its organisational structures to it. A few years after the youth mobilisation of 1968, the women's movement crystallised politically with the Divorce Referendum of 1974, an occasion which, in the words of one PCI provincial secretary, allowed the party 'above all to reactivate its relationship with the female masses'.

In Tuscany, the PCI has traditionally been characterised by a strong quantitative presence among women as a reflection of the region's 'Red' sub-cultural ties which have buttressed party solidarity. Tuscany, together with Emilia-Romagna, are consequently the two regions in Italy where the proportion of female membership is substantially high in relation to the female population. However, problems concerning the qualitative link of female members with the PCI have been noted in Tuscany as elsewhere, notably a low degree of participation and minimal representation at the leadership cadre level.

The explanation for this must be sought primarily in the influence of various social factors, specifically in the persistence of conservative social attitudes about women's role in society, notably within working-class families, as the author's own impressionistic observations during personal interviews suggested. It is significant that, whereas women account for one-quarter of the PCI membership in Tuscany (1975 – roughly equal to the national average), over 60 per cent of them in the province of Pisa, for instance, are housewives, to which may be added another 20 per cent for female pensioners.[55] Moreover, an examination of the proportion of female members per commune in the same province reveals a striking contrast between the smaller rural localities (very low membership) and the larger, industrialised areas,[56] thus again underlining the impact of conservative rural values and a greater political apathy among the female population in the former case. As further evidence of this trend, it should be noted that among the small proportion of women functionaries in the party there is a distinct preponderance of those who are both middle-class and young. In the province of Florence, for example, in the earlier 1970s one-fifth of the female functionaries were students and nearly one-quarter were employed in white-collar positions,[57] again relating the degree of female activism to the incidence of female 'liberation' from traditional roles. It goes without saying, of course, that the impact of the women's movement was essentially middle-class, for, as the PCI federation secretary for Pistoia observed in his party congress speech of 1975, 'the inflow of young and politically versed female comrades in the *sezioni* and in the federation comes almost entirely from educated sources'.[58]

These tendencies have led the party to attempt to 'redefine' its relationship with women members. Only too conscious of the need to adapt party-political activity to individual social attitudes as here, PCI leaders have typically sought a solution through the elaboration of organisational structures. There has been a growth of women's committees at the *sezione* level during the 1970s to seek ways of promoting female activity, but the tendency has remained of female functionaries being concerned exclusively with the 'question of women' rather than with the general policies of the party. It might also be added that the PCI has not successfully bridged the gap between its politically articulate minority of female activists and the vast majority of its female members who remain as housewives. Even among the former there have been some signs of disillusionment with the PCI's inclination to compromise with the DC in Rome over such issues as shelving the question of abortion.[59]

This survey of the PCI's relationship with different social categories demonstrates the party's awareness, though in some cases belated, of the significance and problems of new forms of socio-political mobilisation in the 1970s. This has derived from its tradition, especially strong in Tuscany, of being a mass-structured party, but at the same time the PCI has often responded over-bureaucratically to such forms of social change. Moreover, while its membership has in the 1970s been strengthened quantitatively there have been tendencies for some weakening of its qualitative structural links with some elements in its membership. This development has undoubtedly taxed the party's integrative capacity.

Finally, it is relevant to look at the importance of party activites as a further measure of the PCI's socio-political role. Any estimation of the bearing of these on the PCI's mass-party character must start, especially in the case of a 'Red' region, with the question of 'institutionalised sub-culture'[60] — that is, the presence of collateral organisations allied to the PCI and representing various sectional interests which *in toto* give the party's social roots a 'cultural' dimension. In so far as these collateral organisations lend substance to the PCI's mass-party dimension they are relevant to the discussion of this chapter, although their general function in relation to the party is already well-known and hardly needs elaboration here.[61] Suffice it to say that in a region like Tuscany, where their articulation is intensive, they provide an element of stability for the PCI's social roots in the face of political change and electoral fluctuation as well as clearly reflecting the political dominance of the PCI itself.

The most notable case is the preponderant strength of the PCI-allied trade union, the CGIL, which in Tuscany has been numerically more than three times as large as the Catholic DC-allied trade union, the CISL: CGIL 396,656; CISL 120,535 (1974). Considering that the CISL has, relatively speaking, its strong points in the provinces of Lucca (especially in the Catholic Lucchesia, where it is dominant) and Massa Carrara and to some extent Florence and Arezzo, the positive correlation between CGIL strength and the degree of Marxist-oriented sub-culture is obvious. This is most notably the case in the province of Siena, with its pervasive 'Red' tradition, for here the CGIL outnumbers the CISL and Centre- or lay-Left UIL as follows: CGIL 47,250; CISL 7,000 and UIL 1,500 (1976). The massive presence of the CGIL is shown by a zone such as that around Montalcino/S. Quirico/Asciano, where there are 6,000 members to 30,000 inhabitants.[62] The CGIL is noted for its detailed articulation of sub-organisations for numerous sectors; e.g. the FIOM and FILTEA for metal and textile workers respectively, the Federmezzadri and Federbraccianti in agriculture, special organisations for railway and port workers and the variety of similar organisations for those employed in the public services — the SNS for schools, the FLELS for local government and the FIP for post and telephones. Altogether, Tuscany provides over ten per cent of the CGIL's total membership, although as with the other collateral organisations their level of articulation and numerical strength is considerably greater in Emilia-Romagna, where the tradition of 'Red' sub-culture is that much more developed and long-standing. This is particularly true of the National League of Co-operatives (Tuscany 951 units; Emilia-Romagna 1,911 (1976)) as well as the Union of Italian Women (UDI) and the National Alliance of Peasants. In short, the dominance of the Communist-allied collateral organisations and particularly the CGIL in the region solidifies the PCI's relationship with the working population. In spite of the development of trade-union autonomy since the late 1960s, the strong historical links binding the CGIL and the PCI in Tuscany have meant that their relationship has remained a close one.[63]

There is also well-established in Tuscany a tradition of popular, as distinct from interest-oriented, sub-culture which can trace its roots back to the later nineteenth century with the growth then of workers' clubs and mutual-help associations. Its most unique expression in Tuscany, as well as Emilia-Romagna, is the institution of the *Case del Popolo* as both a recreation centre and a point of congregation in the PCI for political discussions. There are some 1,200 of these in Tuscany,[64] with a concentration of them in the 'Red' provinces of Pisa (333), Florence and Pistoia and to some extent Siena, although their presence in the last instance is less extensive as they are essentially a working-class rather than peasant feature. At the other end of the scale, the PCI federation of Lucca (for the Lucchesia) has practically none, once again underlining the sub-cultural contrast between that area and the rest of Tuscany. The *Case del Popolo* became a recognised feature of Communist Party life very soon after the Second World War, taking over the role of the Socialist clubs which had existed prior to Fascism. Invariably they consist of such amenities as a bar, juke-box and billiards table and are often in the same building as the local PCI headquarters, though the more active party centres sometimes boast a separate building, such as a reconverted cinema, with neon lighting and a meeting-hall inside. The importance of the *Case* for party activities is essentially 'associational' rather than 'communal', such as a focal point for companionship among youth not necessarily Communist though usually Left-inclined, with the very active ones providing a touch of the 'communal' with regular debates on local political or economic issues.

Another special feature of party associational life in Tuscany is the existence in the main urban centres of party bookshops, either called officially *Librerie Rinascita* after the PCI weekly review (as at Florence, Sesto Fiorentino and Empoli) or represented by bookshops of the League of Co-operatives (as at Pistoia). Their aim is both to provide a local public service and to contribute a cultural dimension to political debate.[65] The *Rinascita* bookshop at Sesto, for instance, started originally as a party library for local workers in the mid-1950s, but it has now expanded into the main bookshop in this town of over 40,000 volumes displaying not just Marxist literature but also Catholic publications and a special display of school-books at the beginning of each school-year.[66] Clearly, however, the party bookshops are not a widespread feature of PCI life even in Tuscany for their viability depends on the dictates of local economic circumstances, which in earlier postwar years forced the closure of some of them.[67]

A further allied characteristic of the PCI especially in Tuscany, which may be grouped under the heading of institutionalised sub-culture, is the phenomenon of local party newspapers. Since this is in addition to the circulation of the party daily newspaper, *L'Unità*, and the weekly journal, *Rinascita*, efforts in this direction are dependent entirely on local enthusiasm and finance and in the majority of cases local PCI newspapers have exhibited a fluctuating record. Although *L'Unità* does feature four pages of Tuscan and Florentine news, local newspapers are generally regarded by activists as an important form of 'participation' by the membership, even if one must take this as meaning in a passive form. In effect, these newspapers — which range from the glossily produced *Nuovo Corriere Senese* to more primitive cyclostyled news-sheets — are more likely to have lasted where there are sufficient activists willing to devote time to such a venture and a guaranteed readership outside strict party circles; i.e. where PCI dominance is traditional.

This points to one clear reason for the peculiarity of this feature to the Tuscan PCI, for it has usually been combined with that historical parochialism, even municipal patriotism, in traditional Tuscan life called *campanilismo* (referring to the *campanile* commonly seen atop provincial Tuscan towns). As one local party leader in Montalcino (Siena), a medieval hilltop fortress town, put it:

> The *montalcinesi* feel attached to the town, so that we are more successful in publishing news of our locality which interests the population of Montalcino, not the news of [neighbouring] Buonconvento or S. Quirico.[68]

Indeed, the local PCI fortnightly cyclostyled *L'Informatore Politico* devotes the large proportion of its coverage to local issues such as extracts from sessions of the town council, the situation in the local schools and hospitals, the need to protect local fauna, the annual honey festival, the achievements of the Montalcino football team or recording tales of bravery by local Resistance fighters when anniversaries arise — with occasional attention given to national problems like terrorism, the suppression of the Chilean people and the flight of the SS General Kappler (as a reading of the issues for 1975-1978 shows). *L'Informatore Politico*, which has been published fortnightly since 1956, is almost an archetypal example of the more durable local papers, being distributed to all households in the town and available in all bars whatever the political leanings of the bartender. Another instance of such localism is the existence of party newspapers in three nearby PCI strongholds in Siena province — Poggibonsi, Colle Valdelsa and San Gimignano — although with varying degrees of success. The one at Colle has been virtually defunct, that at San Gimignano (*Il Campanone*) has kept going as an irregular monthly since 1957, and still retains subscriptions from some 40 *sangimignanesi* who have emigrated abroad, while *La Città* at Poggibonsi is a more recent endeavour, though by no means the first one there. In other cases, local newspapers have been born out of initial enthusiasm, but have folded up either through the lack of local journalistic talent or the preoccupation of party activists with their own work or other party activities, even in PCI strongholds.

Such fluctuation in local PCI papers is regarded higher up the party hierarchy with scepticism, not least on financial grounds, although in various cases *campanilismo* has been overcome to the extent of neighbouring *sezioni* co-operating to initiate zonal newspapers. Examples are also to be found in working-class areas, such as *Il Piaggista*, the monthly of the special PCI *sezione* for the Piaggio factory at Pontedera which has been published since this *sezione* was founded in 1974. However, the most successful local Communist Party newspaper in Tuscany has been the weekly *Nuovo Corriere Senese* (since 1967), which, although not an official party organ, is directed by provincial-level Communists, and with its established readership not only in the city of Siena but throughout the province may be said to reflect in a 'secular' way the traditional 'Red' sub-culture in that area. While its main rival is the Florence-based liberal-conservative *La Nazione*, with its special daily section on Sienese provincial news, the *Nuovo Corriere Senese* is readily available at local newsagents and features wide coverage of sports events, theatrical news with special daily editions devoted entirely to the annual *Palio* (medieval horse-race) at Siena during the summer.

As this description of the local PCI press shows, there is an evident preponderance of the 'communal' in the municipal sense over the 'associational' in the party sense.[69] Since the PCI as a mass party aims to act as a force for merging national and local political efforts and goals, one is led to ask whether the varied forms of popular activity categorised grandly under 'institutionalised sub-culture' are not more a means of passive communication with the party membership as a whole (e.g. the provision of information) rather than an active channel for promoting political activity.

The obvious occasion for maintaining or reinforcing the party's relationship with the passive membership is the annual event of the *Unità* festival held both locally and provincially as well as nationally: in the summer of 1974 890 such festivals were held in different Tuscan localities, with an increase in numbers during the course of the 1970s. Officially in support of the party daily newspaper, for which purpose they were introduced after the Second World War as a means of campaigning for subscriptions, the *Unità* festivals have increasingly acquired from the 1960s the gastronomic as well as the political touch. Since the 1950s, when the festivals were a more sombre occasion and largely attended by working-class members, there has been a growing inclination for them to assume a more middle-class character with a striking preponderance of young members.[70] This is particularly noticeable with the local versions, which invariably combine a speech from the provincial party secretary or one of his colleagues and a series of debates on issues of national or local concern with a wide variety of amusements like side-shows, tombolas, hunt the treasure, pop-groups and, of course, bars and a restaurant, so that one West German visitor felt compelled to comment that they had more in common with the mood of the (Munich) *Oktoberfest* than that of the October Revolution.[71] This lighter form of party socialisation could also be geared to local interests or 'culture', as was clear from the directions at the end of the festival programme at Montalcino (Siena) in August 1977:

For the whole duration of the festival:
— at supper you can find at the restaurant typical local and traditional dishes
— the bar will be open
— dancing before and after each political meeting
— various games and attractions — book-stand
— exhibition of local agricultural products, and of artisan work from the Socialist countries — huntsman's stand
— photographic exhibition 'Looking back on Montalcino life'
Citizens, read and support the press of the PCI![72]

Higher party officials have sought to emphasise in recent years that the *Unità* festivals are not merely another form of local saints' festivals,[73] but even at the provincial level these *feste* contain a very strong element of culture both popular and more classical — e.g. the Florentine provincial *Unità* festivals of 1978 held in the Cascine Park from 26 August to 10 September had five sections in its programme: political meetings and debates, cinema, general events (e.g. dances, jazz, pantomime, cabaret), artistic shows and sporting events. The importance of the *Unità* festivals is clearly in the category of party 'associational' life so far as it relates to the PCI's socio-political role. Party activists interviewed frequently emphasised the *Unità* festival as a 'form of identification' with the PCI among the mass membership. The 1977 Doxa survey of attitudes among party members noted the high rate of the membership's participation in the *feste* and also in the organisational arrangements.[74] They invariably also tend to attract Left-wing sympathisers in general as well as PCI members proper, though rarely are convinced Christian Democrats seen present.[75] Party leaders undoubtedly see this mild form of political socialisation as complementing the more serious and direct forms of party-political activity.

In conclusion, while it is true that every large political party is characterised by both 'communal' and 'associational' elements to varying degrees, the special feature of the PCI is that it has sought, if not to convert the 'associational' into the 'communal', then at least to maintain the former's links through continual forms of socio-political activity. This is of course one principal feature of mass-structured parties, and it is evident from our examination of the PCI during the 1970s that it has in a different and changing socio-political environment continued to satisfy the main conditions of being such a party. In doing so, it has been much easier for the PCI in Tuscany because here the traditions of the party's mass character are deeply rooted. This regional study confirms in general the assumption about the party's institutionalised sub-culture, except that a closer examination of this does yield some insights into the complexities of these sub-cultural influences while also questioning their effects in promoting an active party life. Furthermore, there was evidence during the 1970s of 'secular' trends replacing the traditional 'Marxist' nature of this sub-culture. The interest therefore lies not so much in whether the PCI has lost its mass character as such as that there has been in the course of the 1970s some modification in the quality of some of its mass features. More specifically, the PCI has broadened its social base, and hence its interclass links, and has endeavoured to do so in a way consistent with its usual organisational methods of social integration. At the same time, the coherence between the various social groups contained in its membership has suffered as a result of both the unprecedented form of social change in a developing urban society during this decade and of the less predictable nature of the social groups where it has expanded most. In short, the PCI has become more of a mass party quantitatively, but qualitatively speaking its structural links with its mass base have weakened relatively. This is because the PCI has tended more often to respond, indeed attentively, though more bureaucratically than spontaneously, to changes in the socio-political environment rather than to act as a channel for promoting them.

(c) The PCI's Structural Character: Patterns of Change and Continuity

While it may be sufficient in a general comparative setting to describe the PCI as a mass-structured party, it is necessary with reference to our theme of such a party in a period of unprecedented change to focus on the specific form of internal structural relationships within such a category in a way which avoids the academic 'sin' of regarding party structures in too static a manner. Two considerations are uppermost in viewing this aspect of party development: first, the interaction of organisational and political factors (of which the debilitating effects on the PCI's structures of its 'exclusion' from a leading role in the political system after the election defeat of 1948 and of the Hungarian crisis of 1956 are two noted earlier examples); and, secondly, that there is a distinct difference between the formality and reality of party structural relationships for, as Duverger has noted:

> The organisation of parties depends essentially on unwritten practice and habit. It is almost entirely a matter of custom. Constitutions and rules never give more than a partial idea of what happens, if indeed they describe reality at all, for they are rarely strictly applied. Moreover, party life is deliberately shrouded in mystery . . . It is only the old guard of the party that knows much about the ins and outs of its organisation . . . These people, however, rarely possess a scientific mind which allows them to retain the necessary objectivity, and they do not talk willingly.[76]

Duverger's point about statutory as against informal procedures is important, although the divergence between them does depend in the particular case on the degree of acceptance or imprint of its own bureaucratic norms and features on the party's internal life. With the PCI, we have a political party which has demonstrated a certain habit of structural self-criticism and a strong, almost 'social scientific', consciousness of the need to adapt party structures to new social and

institutional exigencies, as PCI documentation and interviews with
functionaries at different levels have underlined. Does this therefore
suggest that the PCI has been able to contain in any way the conservative dynamics operative in Michels's theory of party bureaucracies,[77]
or is this attitude of bureaucratic flexibility merely a profession of
intent? This question is especially relevant to the PCI's organisational
development in the 1970s regarding various problems: the impact of
social change and new forms of political participation on the party
structure; the latter's adaptation to institutional changes in the state
structure, notably regionalisation, as well as to the PCI's increasing role
in government at different levels; whether changes in the composition
of leadership cadres have produced any modification of structural
relationships; and the effects of all these developments on the PCI's
traditional modes of internal party behaviour based on the principle of
democratic centralism.

For analytical purposes, the question of the PCI's social-integrative
role has already been discussed separately from the organisational
consequences of the party's response to and particularly absorption of
factors of social change. Since in conventional PCI terms the 'party' is
seen as having a directing role over the 'movement' — according to
Gianni Cervetti, 'the party is the indispensable factor in the direction
of the movement of the masses, of theoretical consciousness, of the
organisation'[78] — it is important to note in what respects the PCI sees
structural adaptation as necessary. In the view of Cervetti, head of
party organisation at this time:

> What is required is to keep in mind . . . how much the phenomena
> of urbanisation and the changing relationship between town and
> country have pushed the method of organising communities towards
> two poles: on the one hand the city, and on the other the zone,
> the district.[79]

Taking the case of Tuscany, it is useful here to indicate briefly the
general features of structural adaptation arising from the earlier discussion of social change. Rapid urbanisation and the consequent
disequilibrium between town and country have in Tuscany, as elsewhere in Italy, forced the PCI to consider new or different forms of
structural articulation. An early instance of the PCI's structural
adaptation to a changing socio-economic environment was the
formation in the late 1950s of two new party federations within the
provinces of Lucca and Florence, the first for the Versilia in 1958 and

the other based on Prato in 1959. In both cases the party was taking account of a rapidly expanding area which economically was distinct from that of the rest of the province.

This organisational innovation, which departed from following strictly the territorial confines of the state structure (i.e. the provinces), was logical in that each federation has by and large catered for a definite socio-economic setting — the Florence one for a growing urban and tertiary centre, and the Siena one by contrast for a declining agricultural area. This logic was all the more compelling in a region like Tuscany with its pronounced local traditions, which had left their imprint on the early historical development of the workers' movement there. The party structure was therefore coloured by traditional factors as well as determined by the postwar state structure, but did this not also make for bureaucratic resistance to structural adaptation?

Although party leaders interviewed usually emphasised the PCI's ability to adapt its organisational structure to new social conditions 'on an analytical basis',[80] particular local conditions invariably intervened and made matters more complex. This has notably been the case where indiscriminate urban expansion and the growth of worker mobility had led to the party structure's being rapidly overtaken by events. This development entailed either a new flexibility in party organisation, such as the development since the late 1950s of *sezioni aziendali* (party sections based on the location of industrial firms), or alternatively the creation of further *sezioni* out of old ones simply to handle a mushrooming population. In the latter event the process of adaptation has not been easy, especially when it has been a question of dismembering the one *sezione* which had related to a commune as a whole and therefore raising the problem of co-ordinating the activities of the various new units for the purposes of local politics. These difficulties have continued into recent times, examples being the industrial commune of Santa Croce sull'Arno and other developing localities like Sesto Fiorentino.[81]

There have accordingly been two related but somewhat contrary pressures impinging on the party structure, the one promoting adaptation and the other inhibiting its application, the latter deriving partly from the prevalence at lower levels of the party organisation of Tuscan parochialism. In 1977, a regional PCI three-year plan for organisational development commented on the need to 'overcome elements of fragmentation and *municipalismo*, still existing in our work';[82] and it is significant that even in an area like Sesto Fiorentino, close to Florence, local leaders have drawn attention to the need of adopting 'a method of directing and operating that gets away from sectionalism and municipalistic visions, which very often multiply in the small localities at the expense of rationality'.[83] The difficulties of translating structural plans into practice have therefore arisen more commonly from the impact of these various socio-economic factors than from bureaucratic conservatism as such, although clearly party bureaucracies, like bureaucracies in general, are slow in their actual process of adaptation. In this context it is interesting to note a certain disparity between the initiating role of provincial party functionaries and the comparatively less flexible outlook of party activists at the infrastructural level outside the main urban centres.

However, what generally distinguishes party bureaucracies from, say, state bureaucracies is their more direct vulnerability to political pressures, whether these be electoral or socio-political or a changing political role for the party in question — a point particularly applicable to a party as highly articulated as the Tuscan PCI. But what has characterised the 1970s and marked off this period from preceding ones has been the development of institutional change in the state bureaucratic structure (i.e. decentralisation). This has necessitated an accompanying decentralisation of the party structure, but the motive here has been more than institutional in that decentralisation of the state has been linked to the increasing role in government and hence political legitimacy of the PCI during the 1970s. Decentralisation has taken various forms, most evidently with the establishment of the regions but also with the creation of zones or districts (*comprensori*) to facilitate inter-communal co-ordination in economic programming. Tuscany has been in the forefront of developing the latter, including too the creation of *consigli di quartieri* or neighbourhood councils with Florence being the first city in Italy to hold direct elections to these councils (autumn 1976).[84] The relevance of the *quartieri* to the party structure has been that they have begun to modify the traditional role of the PCI *sezioni* with less emphasis on propagandistic activities and more on the need to formulate policy in relation to the deliberations of the neighbourhood councils.[85] Equally, the PCI has formed zonal committees in the course of the 1970s in response to and to some extent in anticipation of this change in the state structure.

As the major party in Italy most committed in the 1970s to institutional decentralisation or 'reform of the state',[e] it is consequently instructive to record not only the PCI's influence in promoting this change but furthermore its own process of structural adaptation to accord with this development. Even though the political motivation behind the party's support for institutional change has been clear, its own adjustment has in many respects been slow for a certain gap has been visible between political will and concrete application in the regionalisation of the PCI's structure. Before proceeding to look at party regionalisation, an instance which provides recent insight into the PCI as a form of mass-structured party, a number of general points need to be established.

First, a full discussion of the problems of party bureaucratisation is not valid without taking into account the specific organisational values that permeate internal relationships within the given party. Within the PCI, which has such a strong sense of vocation as a mass party, one must suppose a high level of attachment to bureaucratic norms as a means both to reinforce party solidarity and to promote political action. The general prevalence of bureaucratic norms as such is suggested by the high incidence of bureaucratic language and terminology employed by party functionaries.[86] However, this is accompanied by an attitude geared to viewing the party structure not so much as an end in itself but as the channel for regulating party activity which requires regular attention to the need for adjustment to changing political conditions. In so far as this emphasis on bureaucratic flexibility is conditioned by any 'conservative' dynamics as identified by Michels this derives primarily from traditional modes of party behaviour, notably the value placed on party 'unity' as expressed in the 'organic' view of the different levels of the PCI's structure. In short, structural change in the PCI avoids disrupting this traditional feature of party life.

Secondly, despite the formal uniformity of party structures the reception of bureaucratic norms within the party as whole has been modified by geographical variation in the degree of organisational vivacity and intensity. The impact of local socio-economic factors, as already discussed, are some pointer to this, but it is worthwhile noting here that even in a 'Red' region like Tuscany this variation can be marked. Table 3.5 shows both the general incidence and specific density of party *sezioni* on the basis of federation.

What may be observed here is the extent to which organisational intensity has either followed new population growth, as in the supreme case of Florence, or maintained a relatively high level of articulation because of a strong local party tradition despite depopulation, as in Siena. Viareggio (the Versilia) is a case where party organisation has less history, but like the area in general is developing. On the other hand, the Lucca federation has continued to illustrate the difficulties of organisation penetration in an area where sub-cultural factors and

Table 3.5: Total of PCI *Sezioni* per Federation and Size of Membership, 1976

PCI Federations	Total no. of *sezioni*	Those with up to 100 members	With 101-200 members	With 201-500 members	With over 500 members	Sezioni being restructured
Arezzo	184	91	46	30	1	16
Florence	227	39	66	84	38	-
Grosseto	112	70	21	15	5	1
Livorno	96	27	14	32	23	-
Lucca	53	40	9	4	-	-
Massa Carrara	103	79	19	5	-	-
Pisa	144	63	43	31	4	3
Pistoia	103	38	38	23	3	1
Prato	81	25	32	16	-	8
Siena	162	50	46	37	29	-
Viareggio	33	17	7	8	1	-
Tuscany	1,298	539	341	285	104	29

Source: PCI Comitato Regionale, *Dati statistici elettorali e dell'organizzazione del partito in Toscana*, 1977, p. 4.

and geographical isolation inhibit this — which has occasioned concern among party leaders there about the Lucca PCI's deficiencies as a mass party and the consequent effect of this situation on its structural relationships.[87]

Turning now directly to the regionalisation of the party structure in response to the state's decentralisation, it becomes apparent that these conditioning factors of outlook and environment have impinged on this process. Party regionalisation accordingly offers a valuable case-study of the points of divergence between structural formality and its application in practice in a given setting like Tuscany. Moreover, the question arises whether this structural adjustment on the part of the PCI has had any centripetal or, alternatively, centrifugal consequences for the party's relationship with the state, hence underlining the umbilical link between party-organisational and party-political factors.

It is already evident that the regionalisation of the PCI's structure throughout Italy in the 1970s has occurred for two strongly related reasons: decentralisation of the state inaugurated in 1970, and the enlarged role of the PCI in government at the regional and also local levels. Whereas the one required an equivalent adaptation of the party structure, for the purpose of policy co-ordination, the other reinforced this change because of the aim of PCI leaders to strengthen the party's role in the policy-making process at the sub-national level. It is also worth adding that party regionalisation has developed in the context of a general organisational revival of the PCI after the stagnation of the 1960s, eliciting a new awareness of the socio-political importance of structural articulation. Party functionaries have, for instance, habitually coupled the question of regionalisation and other forms of structural change with the need to promote 'participation' and maintain adequate party links with different social strata.

In formal terms, regionalisation has involved a reactivation of pre-existing structures. Party regional committees were originally instituted by the PCI in 1948, later abolished in 1956 (save in the five special regions of Italy, where they had assumed some political authority in accordance with postwar decentralisation there) and reconstituted formally in 1966 as simple organs of organisational co-operation. After the establishment of regional governments throughout Italy, including Tuscany, in 1970 discussion occurred inside the PCI about granting the regional committees a political (i.e. directing) role, and after an interval this structural change was approved at the national congress in March 1975. The speech of Armando Cossutta, responsible in the national party for local and regional affairs, emphasised at this congress the political importance of this change in the party statutes:

> With this modification of the statutes, it is considered urgent and indispensible to assure for one of the executive organs foreseen in our present organisational structure a capacity for action and higher political direction. We are referring to the regional committees ... At the moment they are organs of co-ordination ... but the whole party should be able to elaborate and realise its policies taking account of the new dimension, the regional one, in which it should articulate its activity. The regions are a reality ... The party intends to adapt its organisational structure. The regional committees, transformed into real and proper institutions, can and must direct the organisations of the party in their regions, and at the same time must be effective agencies of decentralisation in elaborating and achieving national policy.[88]

During 1976-1977, there followed the series of first regional congresses (the Tuscan one, 31 March-3 April 1977), which implemented these changes with the election of the regional committees (as distinct from their previous nomination by the party federations) and the institution of regional commissions of control to monitor party policy at the regional level and of various regional policy committees.

This regionalisation of the party structure has nevertheless proceeded with a priority being accorded to avoiding any diminution of party unity: hence, the stress laid by party leaders on 'synthesis' in this process of structural change. An early and clear statement of this priority was made by Enrico Berlinguer at the PCI national congress in March 1972:

> The institution of the regional structure is the greatest reform of the Italian state achieved since the setting up of the Republic itself. It creates a new area and new possibilities for initiative by the popular and democratic forces for a policy of unity . . . From this comes the demand for giving our regional committees a new function, which requires the decentralisation of some functions that have been performed up to now by the national Directorate of the party. There could be risks here in weakening the political and operative unity of the party, but such risks must be overcome . . . In other words, while we must grant without hesitation fuller functions to the regional committees, we must at the same time affirm all the more rigorously our character as a national unitarian force . . . The capacity for synthesis, for political unification by the national Directorate of the party must be strengthened at the same time as we grant larger functions to the regional committees.[89]

Berlinguer's exposition of the party line has been the conceptual basis for the elaboration of structural change since. Indeed, the revised party statutes of 1975 continue to assert, as before, that the regional committee 'constitutes the principal channel whereby the national executive organs are bound to the local organisations and direct them, there still being the firm necessity for direct links between the national centre and the federations'.[90] This leads to consideration of two problems: how have the newly reinforced regional structures integrated into the established party structure; and to what degree have they acquired real political authority?

The main change in the 1975 statutes had specified that the regional committee should 'co-ordinate and direct the activity of the party group in the regional council'.[91] While this followed the established practice of the PCI at the national level, whereby the party organisation had controlling functions over the parliamentary group at the equivalent level in the state structure, the regional example in Tuscany has shown that this 'classical' model has not been easy to introduce. The PCI regional committee was involved in deliberations on the first programme of Tuscan regional development in the early 1970s,[92] but the election of a PCI regional group of councillors in 1970 before the formalisation of the new powers of the party regional committees several years later left an imbalance in their relationship with the former retaining a certain autonomy. Although programatic consultation developed between the PCI group in the regional council and the party's regional executive organs, this was not substantiated by much correlation of personnel. The PCI regional secretary (until 1978), Alessio Pasquini, was a regional councillor, but only five out of the 28 members of the Tuscan PCI regional directive committee and eight of the 83 members of its regional committee were also regional councillors.[93] It must of course be borne in mind that, as of the late 1970s, the decentralisation of the state structure was still in an incipient stage, despite the transfer of new powers to the regions in 1977, and that their restricted administrative and political role inevitably reflected on the limited scope for policy-making on the party of the PCI's regional structure.

A further feature of party regionalisation must of course be the functioning of the PCI regional organs themselves, and the development of a regional level of party leadership. The regional organs have not met on such a regular basis as, say, the equivalent organs at the federation (i.e. provincial) level, though more frequently than before 1975; the regional committee meets usually five or six times a year 'when problems arise', compared with 13 or 14 times in the case of, for instance, the Lucca federal committee; the regional directive committee meets about 20 times a year compared with 40 times on the part of the federal equivalent.[94] This difference has in turn echoed the greater internal bureaucratic and political weight still enjoyed by the longer-established federations within the PCI structure. The PCI regional organs have lacked a fully developed bureaucratic structure, with a role essentially that of co-ordination, although admittedly one with more prestige and formal authority than it had prior to the statutory change. As of late 1977, the regional secretariat consisted of eight full-time functionaries with responsibility for such areas as press and information, local government, education, party organisation, agriculture and problems of employment and the middle-classes together with the regional secretary and the office of the Tuscan PCI's review, *Politica e Società*. Regional policy-making within the PCI's structure is conducted by way of 'homogenisation' through liaison with the party federations and co-ordination through the five policy commissions of the regional committee (these are in most cases chaired by party federation secretaries). In the field of policy-making, therefore, the approach could be described as 'synthesis'. On administrative matters, however, the limited number of staff has tended in practice to force the regional secretariat to rely heavily on the federations. This is notably the case with the Florentine federation, in whose building the regional secretariat is housed on the fourth floor, giving it the advantage of everyday contact and consultation. In the words of one local PCI secretary in Tuscany, the regional committees of the party

> have not yet succeeded in performing completely that role which they have been assigned. On the contrary, it seems that the federations are still the point of reference and of essential political direction . . . whether from the organisational point of view or from that which is properly political: the zones, the communal committees and the *sezioni* see in the federation an element which is irreplaceable.[95]

The existence in Tuscany of several large federations like those of Florence, Siena and Livorno, each with their own traditional weight within the party structure, has reduced the potential interventionist role for the regional executive organs. It is the very *fact* therefore of the established position of the federations that would suggest a Michels-type 'conservatism' in the party organisation, although the slowness of regionalisation of the PCI's structure has been the object of some self-criticism in the Tuscan party on various occasions.[96] Indeed, the importance of creating an effective regional structure is widely accepted *conceptually* among party leaders and functionaries from the provincial level upwards.[97] The problem relates to traditional modes of internal party behaviour. As one local party secretary, who described himself as believing in party regionalisation, put it: 'Theoretically, everyone agrees, but there is not always the consequent political action responding to this necessity at different levels. It is not a question of internal interests, but of certain habits and conditioning.'

On the other hand, the integration of regional functionaries within the party career pattern has been easier to implement because of the practice of bureaucratic rotation, which has tended to increase during the course of the 1970s. As one party federation secretary appointed to a regional party responsibility commented:

> One can pass from the provincial level to the national level, or one can pass from the provincial level to the regional level, one can go from the regional level to the national level or return from the national level to the regional or provincial level. There is an

interlacing process rather than a line of continuity.[98]

In this sense, the prevalence of bureaucratic norms among the overall body of party functionaries has mitigated any strong possibility of personal vested interests being attached to specific posts in the party structure, and consequently facilitated the inclusion of regional functionaries and leaders along with other levels in this internal system of transference. This method of integrating regional functionaries in the party structure has worked in two vertical directions. Regional party leaders together with PCI heads of regional assemblies or governments are members of the party's Central Committee, a notable case being Alessio Pasquini who, besides being Tuscan regional secretary, has also been president of one of the Central Committee's five policy commissions. The integration of regional functionaries with federation party personnel is even more marked, and here a noted change has occurred in Tuscany. Whereas until the mid-1970s regional functionaries were almost all Florentines, the regional secretariat has since then been serviced by personnel with provincial party experience.[99] As of late 1977, four of the eight members of the Tuscan regional secretariat were former federation secretaries, Pasquini himself having held that post in the province of Arezzo. This has been a matter of deliberate party policy for, as Pasquini himself has emphasised, 'it is important to utilise secretaries of federations in the work of party leadership at the regional level'.[100] His own successor as Tuscan regional secretary in 1978, Giulio Quercini, had from 1977 been a member of the Tuscan regional secretariat and before that PCI federation secretary in Catania, Sicily, having previously held posts at the national headquarters in Rome.[101]

There remains the final question of estimating the impact of structural regionalisation on party life as a whole. Since one of the accompanying reasons advanced by PCI leaders in favour of regionalisation of the state has been the need to promote democratic 'participation' in general, the question is pertinent, but so far as internal relationships within the party itself have been concerned the answer must be a sceptical one. The document on party structure approved at the first Tuscan PCI regional congress in spring 1977 dwelt on the need to establish the importance of the regional structures at a deeper level of party activity, for there should develop 'a more direct relationship between regional organisms and the direction of the movement ... in this context it is necessary to reinforce the experience of regional co-ordination of party activity in the factories and places of work'.[102]

The event of the regional congress itself appeared to stimulate wider interest in regionalisation within the party, as the immediate stress placed on the 'fundamental importance' of this by local party leaders in the author's interviews in the autumn of 1977 seemed to suggest. However, the difficulty of projecting the regional structures among the PCI membership at large remained, as one Tuscan party leader noted in the autumn of 1978:

> There is among the groups of leaders in the federations an awareness that the regional committee must become this element of political unification; on the other hand, this sense of necessity has not yet penetrated among the body of the party, that is among the members as a whole. This level of activity has not become a heritage within the depths of the party ... There is in Tuscany a long tradition, whereby the provinces are strongly perceived — also the communes. And this leads to phenomena of *municipalismo*. The regional committee must become a factor in the life of the party, also at the base.[103]

The question of party regionalisation has consequently been conditioned ultimately by the nature of the local and regional environment and the limited form of state decentralisation in Italy as well as by predictable problems of adapting a highly articulated party bureaucracy to such a change. Even for a political party like the PCI, which has a pronounced organisational consciousness and prides itself on being less imbued with provincialism than the other parties, the problems of marrying the practice with the theory of regionalisation have been far from negligible. While attempting to act as a centripetal channel for structural change within the framework of decentralisation, the PCI has itself been largely unable to overcome pre-existing centrifugal tendencies. This is not to decry the significance of this incipient party regionalisation, for the PCI has taken this process far more seriously than any of the other parties, but rather to note that up to the 1980s at least it assumed a purely organisational form rather than one with political impetus.

Whereas any substantial modification of party structures has at best been a slow evolutionary process, though somewhat less so when socio-economic change has been dramatic, the movement of personnel within those structures has, on the other hand, undergone marked innovation in the case of the PCI in the 1970s. The most outstanding development has been a radical rejuvenation of party functionaries, especially at the federation level, involving more than simply the rise of a younger generation of leadership cadres since the new intake has stemmed predominantly from the middle-class intelligentsia. As this development has altered the class balance within the leadership elite, the PCI's traditional working-class identity has been called into question with implications too for the conduct of internal party relationships.

The change in the composition of leadership cadres in the PCI is underlined by a growing preponderance of those who entered the party during the course of the 1970s. This is illustrated, for instance, by the data on the duration of party membership for the 354 delegates (consisting largely of sub-regional party leaders) at the first regional congress of the Tuscan PCI (Table 3.6).

Table 3.6: Duration of Party Membership among Delegates to 1st Regional Congress of Tuscan PCI, March–April 1977

Joined	%
before 1945 (Fascist and Resistance period)	19.49
1946–1956	15.81
1957–1968	19.77
1969–1973	32.22
1974–1977	12.14

Source: PCI Comitato Regionale Toscano, *1° Congresso Regionale dei comunisti toscani: sintesi degli atti e risoluzioni*, 1978, p. 124.

The fact that nearly 45 per cent of the delegates had joined the PCI from 1969 was again reflected in their age structure, where just over 64 per cent were under 40 (Table 3.7).

In areas where the PCI machine had previously been weak and therefore benefited more from the organisational expansion of the 1970s this replacement of old leadership cadres has been quite extraordinary, notably in the Lucca federation where there was an 80 per cent to 85 per cent turnover of such personnel during 1970–1977.[104] But, even where the PCI has been organisationally strong, the rejuvenation process has also been marked especially in the composition of federation organs. The Prato federation saw a virtually complete renewal of its leadership cadres at its 1975 congress. Similarly, the age composition of the Livorno federation committee, elected at its provincial congress in 1976, was as shown in Table 3.8.

Table 3.7: Age Structure of Delegates to 1st Regional Congress of Tuscan PCI, March–April 1977

Age	%
Below 25 years	19.77
26–30	20.05
31–40	24.29
41–50	18.92
51–60	14.97
Over 60	1.98

Source: PCI Comitato Regionale Toscano, *1° Congresso Regionale dei comunisti toscani*, 1978, p. 124.

Table 3.8: Age Composition of Livorno Federal Committee, 1976

Age	%
21–30	28 (35.44)
31–40	18 (22.78)
41–50	18 (22.78)
51–60	14 (17.72)
Over 60	1 (1.26)

Source: PCI Livorno federation, *Il PCI nella provincia di Livorno dal '45 ad oggi: dati statistici ed organizzativi*, 1976, p. 8.

This rejuvenation of leadership cadres is in line with developments in the PCI elsewhere in Italy, where over 50 per cent of the members of federation committees in 1975 had joined the party since 1966 and those under 30 formed the largest single age group.[105] Similarly, there has been a uniformity throughout the country in the growing presence of certain social groups among the leadership cadres, notably students and those employed in the tertiary sector.[106] Workers have continued to provide the largest single element, though in a much dimished form. The social composition of the delegates at the 1977 regional congress reflected this situation (Table 3.9).

The strong representation of white-collar workers is not unusual in a 'Red' region like Tuscany, where the PCI has boasted a long tradition of local government and hence municipal employment. Among the members of the Livorno federation committee white-collar workers

Table 3.9: Social Composition of Delegates to Tuscan PCI Regional Congress, March –April 1977

		%
Workers	148	41.80
Peasants	18	5.08
Employees	64	18.08
Technicians	18	5.08
Artisans	12	3.39
School teachers	32	9.04
Students	41	11.58
Free professions	12	3.39
Pensioners	4	1.13
Housewives	4	1.13
Unemployed	1	0.28

Source: PCI Comitato Regionale Toscano, *1° Congresso Regionale dei comunisti toscani*, 1978, p. 124.

(employees and technicians) provided with 31.64 per cent, a close second to workers (36.71 per cent), followed by school teachers (10.12 per cent) and then students (7.59 per cent).[107] The same federation committee in 1960–1961 had shown out of a membership then of 59: 23 workers, 17 employees but no teachers and only one student.[108]

At the local or *sezione* level, social and generational change have also occurred, though less uniformly and less rapidly because of the influence of local conditions on party development. In the province of Livorno the average age of *sezione* secretaries in 1976 was 34 with some distinct local variations, such as a higher age level on the island of Elba (where party development was relatively backward) and in the city of Livorno itself (because of the traditional stability there of party organisation).[109] Workers provided a marginally stronger element of the leadership at this level in Livorno province and white-collar workers a smaller element compared with the composition of the federation committee there. However, it is clear from the preceding discussion that replacement of leadership cadres among the activist body as a whole was more marked in a generational than a social sense, for at the local level particularly rejuvenation involved the promotion of young working-class activists.

The growing prominence of young middle-class intellectuals is more evident higher up at the intermediary level of the party structure, notably among federation party secretaries. In the four years from 1974 the vast majority of party federation secretaries in Italy — 94 out of 108, as well as 17 of the 20 regional party secretaries — were replaced.[110] The new appointees were invariably much younger and frequently with a student background. As Lanchester has established, the average age of federation secretaries declined even during 1972-1975, with 60 per cent of them under 40 in the latter year.[111] The 1970s have seen an extraordinary rise in the number of students as federation secretaries who had joined the PCI in the later 1960s, accounting for 27.5 per cent of them in 1975, with 42.9 per cent in the south, whereas in the industrial triangle of the north working-class federation secretaries have continued to predominate (45.9 per cent).[112] The 'Red' regions have accorded roughly with the national average with 35.8 per cent working-class federation secretaries and 21.5 per cent students.[113] More specifically, in the Tuscan case, these trends are clear for nearly all of the federation secretaries at the time of interviewing (1977-1978), who were in their late 20s or early/mid-30s, compared with their predecessors who had usually been in their 40s. Their background usually pointed to either involvement in the student movement or a career in the youth organisation, the FGCI.[114]

Before this injection of fresh blood into the intermediary level of PCI functionaries, the situation by the start of the 1970s had become one of stagnation. As Sani noted then in his study of PCI *dirigenti*, there was an under-representation of the young and a clear lack of rotation.[115] Membership of the federal party organs was largely held by those in their 40s, who had maintained their posts through the 1960s, having themselves been promoted as young men as a consequence of the basic renewal of leadership cadres which accompanied the adoption of Togliatti's strategy of the 'Italian road to socialism' in the late 1950s.[116] Since the early 1970s, the renewal of leadership cadres has once again been implemented as a matter of deliberate party policy under Berlinguer, being facilitated by the mechanism of democratic centralism especially where federation-level functionaries have been concerned. The term 'renewal' (*rinnovamento*) has accordingly become a widespread catchword at different levels within the PCI, thus giving legitimacy to this process, but to some extent this policy has made a virtue of necessity for two particular factors prompted a change in leadership cadres. First, the great influx of young members and especially students into the PCI — the 'generation of 1968' — forced the PCI to respond to this politically articulate and active new element in the party, all the more as there were signs of concern among the then party leadership about the PCI's losing touch with the younger generation.^f Secondly, the depletion of PCI leadership cadres in 1975-1976 because of their rapid transfer to administrative posts in local government following the PCI's electoral success necessitated in turn their replacement by new cadres. This occurred on a less massive scale in Tuscany than in most other parts of Italy, as the PCI was already well entrenched there in local government, but nevertheless the cases of Florence, Viareggio and many smaller towns in the region were enough to disrupt the equilibrium within the body of party functionaries. According to the new PCI mayor of Florence, himself a case in point, 'from 15 June 1975, there appeared a new problem of great importance: part of the leadership cadre of the party assumed responsibility in heading many local administrations, and this demanded a quick and almost enforced changing of party cadres'.[117]

Various consequences flowed from this process of leadership rejuvenation in the PCI. First, while attempting to integrate the vast body of younger activists into party life 'renewal' has all the same made generational division more visible. As Emanuele Macaluso, a member of the PCI national Directorate, described in his concluding speech to the Tuscan PCI regional congress in the spring of 1977:

> We have here among the delegates a working-class cadre with strong peasant roots, and an educated cadre that together with these workers matured with the rich experience of the War of Liberation, the great worker and peasant struggles after the War and lived through the events of the Communist international movement.
>   This cadre is still abundantly present in our party, and continues to make an important contribution. Then, we have a cadre that arrived next during the great struggles against the capitalistic reconstruction of the 1950s. This is a cadre that was formed in the struggles against Scelbism, in local government, in the trade-union movement, by means of 'rotation' that was then more common between trade-union work, local administration and the party. Finally, we have a cadre that had its first experiences in the student movement, in the women's and feminist movement, that was formed during the student struggle and that for civil rights. The party has not always known how to accept readily — perhaps because of the weak links with youth and women — the experiences that these comrades have undergone, and has not always known how to deal with outlooks different from our own ... today we see comrades of this generation present, impassioned and active in our party, trying with effort to homogenise themselves with our tradition and our method of

conducting politics.[118]

Macaluso was pointing to a number of interesting conclusions. Generational tensions had been particularly evident in the early 1970s with the rapid promotion of young people to leadership posts, but in time this became largely accepted among older activists. However, there still remained the fact that young *dirigenti* exhibited a different mentality from the older generation, with their different political upbringing and experiences. As the age group which had been politically activated in 1968, many of them had been temporarily involved in the extra-parliamentary Left before entering the PCI. With their predominantly bourgeois background, they revealed a less sectarian social attitude than their elder comrades, who had, for example, followed the practice of choosing Marxist-inspired names for their children and 'felt a sense of shame in going on holiday'.[119] Moreover, the new *dirigenti* had entered a party which was more 'open' and had divested itself of much of the rigid 'trench mentality' of the Cold War. As one young federation secretary in Tuscany himself put it, 'a part at least of this new generation which has come to direct our organisations, entered the party on the basis of a political experience characterised by "many victories and no defeat" '.[120] This has inspired the description of them as 'the generation of the historic compromise'.

Secondly, rejuvenation has brought a different style of party leader at the intermediary level. The term *berlingueriani* has been applied to this new generation of middle-class managerial functionaries, who have risen in the PCI since Berlinguer became party secretary in 1972; although its usage is rather journalistic and interviewees who fitted into this category were themselves reluctant to accept it, seeing it as a label with charismatic implications — 'the position of Communists is not linked to names'. All the same, the term referred to a new type of party functionary even imprecisely. As one Tuscan PCI leader noted, this new type was geared 'not to making propaganda, but to making policy'. A growing specialism in certain policy areas has become a feature among the younger cadres,[121] indeed this is itself a reflection of the PCI's own move away from an oppositional force to one incresingly involved in government. In view of this qualitative change, which has derived from the quantitative inflow of younger generation activists into the PCI, it is not perhaps surprising that some resentments have remained among older cadres. These have taken the form of criticisms that the younger ones with their academic background lack practical experience. According to one regional PCI secretary, these new cadres know all the topography of the DC *correnti* after a meeting of its National Council, but don't know the Christian Democrats in the district; or they discuss the relationship between the factory, society, and the state without knowing what happens in the nearest factory or the district.[122]

Criticisms of *giovanilismo*, or the impatience of youth, were evident in interviews with some older cadres at the local level, especially where there was a prevalence of *sezione* secretaries in their early or mid-20s. In one case, the interviewee argued that 'renewal' had occurred 'too fast', for, while the younger *dirigenti* are 'able, intelligent and speak well', they did not apply themselves easily to routine, practical party work and tended to 'want everything at once'. He stressed that organisational and ideological work went hand in hand but, although the older cadres had tried to train the younger ones, the latter had 'not been inside a factory'.

Thirdly, it is relevant to ask how much the 'renewal' of leadership cadres has affected internal party relationships. It follows from the preceding point that a different perception of popular demands is apparent among the young middle-class intelligentsia, even though it has been claimed that they 'tend to forget their origins' when they work for the party. Conformist pressures do operate through the party career structure, but the different style of conducting politics arising from the generational and social change in leadership cadres has coloured internal relationships. Concern has been expressed about the introduction of the incompatibility rule between trade-union and party posts, which has helped to reduce the number of working-class cadres, so that Giovanni Berlinguer went to the extent of questioning whether there is 'the risk of altering the class identity of the PCI'.[123] There followed a lively discussion in *Rinascita* with many correspondents revealing a mistrust, even hostility, towards 'academic comrades', and a concern that they were losing touch with the PCI's grass-roots.

This question leads us to consider the final aspect of the PCI's development as a mass-structured party during the 1970s; namely, the effect of the various changes in party structure on internal forms of party behaviour and, in particular, the concept and practice of democratic centralism. This problem will be discussed again later with special reference to the PCI's strategy of the 'historic compromise',[g] but it is relevant to this examination of structural relationships to examine here the method of democratic centralism as it reflects on the theme of informal as distinct from statutory forms of internal relationships. Democratic centralism, sometimes re-named by academics 'bureaucratic centralism', is justified officially by the PCI as the process whereby proposals from the leadership are discussed at the party base and then, following their approval, are given full support by the whole membership.[124] According to one Tuscan party leader:

> Democratic centralism is the rejection of the system of organised *correnti* in the party. We are not an academy or a school of philosophy, but a political party. Once having discussed fully, it is necessary that we meet to decide. From the moment in which we have decided, the decision is valid for all Communists ... discipline then intervenes, but after the decision.[125]

The concept of democratic centralism is accepted in an unqualified manner by party activists at all levels, but what is interesting is to observe the implications of it in practice. Two features of party life are worth some attention here: the nature of political discussion in the PCI, and the degree of participation.

Certain 'informal' factors may buttress or modify the imprint of 'constitutional' rules on party life, notably the role of norms of internal party behaviour as well as the social composition of leadership cadres with their advantage in interpreting structural relationships. The nature of political discussion inside a party is a very telling point at which to take some measure of both factors. The very term 'discussion' was so commonly used by party activists in interviews that it could be said to have acquired the status of a 'value'. The idea of discussion at members' meetings does, as noted, fit into the theory of democratic centralism, but in practice it may lead to some flexibility of its interpretation. Attendance at some PCI meetings, as well as questioning of interviewees, did reinforce the picture that very often 'discussion' involved a series of monologues by some party members, often ranging in panoramic fashion over a whole scale of issues, with invariably a winding-up speech by a PCI *dirigente*, who might well be a provincial functionary.

This tendency to produce at worst a 'hierarchical repetition of discussions'[126] does, however, depend to some degree on the outlook of key activists in the *sezioni* as well as the social groups that predominate at party meetings. Soundings on the activity of *sezioni* in the Florence area suggested that debates at party meetings could be lively and even sharp, especially where party leaders were younger and where there was a habit of local debate. In the words of one interviewee, what mattered most was whether internal relationships in the given *sezione* were 'formal' or 'informal'. A crucial point of distinction was the prominence or not of student party members, who pressed for an active role at meetings. In many local cases, this led to students dominating discussion because of their facility in articulating political issues, for, as one correspondent in *Rinascita* noted after the publication of Giovanni Berlinguer's article, 'it seems that the working-class activist has only the task of distributing leaflets and sticking up posters . . . leaving the real and proper business of political leadership to those who can speak better and write better'.[127] Clearly, local personal relationships determined whether this produced any generational or class tension, but the general trend was evident from the Doxa survey of early 1978 on party activism, whereby those who took part almost every week in a party meeting ranged from 32 per cent among young members to 17 per cent among old members.[128]

The influx of young members in the 1970s, especially from the middle of the decade, therefore brought some qualitative change in the nature of party meetings. The implications of this change for internal party relationships were pinpointed by the PCI federation secretary for Arezzo in his speech to the provincial congress in March 1977:

> The contradiction has by now become very evident between what I would call the *verticalizzazione* [concentration at the top] of decisions, whether at the central or federation level, and the pressing demand for participation that comes from the base, from the new comrades who arrive in the party full of intelligence, of energy and the wish to carry on politics. And so, one must bring under discussion one point, that of an organisation that is too pyramidal, where circles which are too restricted elaborate and make decisions . . . I am not saying it is necessary to overthrow this pyramid, but to make more dialectical the relationship between base and leadership, on the one hand decentralising political leadership and on the other finding a [new] method of working and the necessary structures, in order that the party base, the *sezioni*, can make their own contribution to all stages in elaborating political decisions.[129]

Changing forms of internal party debate were most marked in the main urban centres, with their concentration of younger members, but even in the rural areas these new trends have not gone unnoticed. The case of the PCI at Montalcino (Siena) is relevant here, having a rather old membership as a result of depopulation, although some young local *dirigenti*. Prior to the *sezione* congress there in March 1977, the PCI secretary gave an interview to the local party newspaper:

> Q. Renewal doesn't only mean new men, but also different methods of working?
>
> A. In fact, our activity seems to me to need to adapt in line with continuity to the situation that is changing more rapidly than in the past. People today are much more informed than in the past, they know more even if they have undergone and are undergoing the influence of consumer society and all the negative idols this has created. There is therefore less need for assemblies or mass meetings for informing poeple, and more for group meetings and debates for forming opinion . . .
>
> Q. Is the activity of the *sezione* that you lead characterised by this method?
>
> A. I would say that for some time we have faced this problem without coming to a real solution. We have many meetings, but there is not always real debate for shaping decisions, or else this comes very often from our regular comrades who are best-known and most involved, and who take part most in discussions and end up by indicating almost always the decision that is to be taken.
>
> Q. Do you then recognise that there is a need for greater democracy inside the PCI?
>
> A. Certainly, yes. But by this I do not mean absolutely to say that today there is no chance in our party of discussing and being of importance . . .
>
> Q. Do you think the statutory norm of the PCI that regulates its internal life through 'democratic centralism' limits debate and participation?
>
> A. Absolutely not. On the contrary, this principle is safeguarded jealously, because it is the best method of allowing the greatest internal debate for arriving at a decision . . .[130]

While not quarrelling with the idea of democratic centralism, party leaders have frequently touched on the problems of participation among the membership. This has partly been a recognition of the pressures operating from the younger members, all the more as 'participation' has become an 'in' word in Italian politics since 1968, but it also expressed some concern that the leadership might lose touch with its grass-roots, particularly in the new era with the PCI changing its political role from one of a pure oppositional force. Generally, around one-fifth of the membership attended meetings at *sezione* level. A study conducted by Gori in the early 1970s on the Florence federation showed that about 20 per cent tended to be present at these meetings.[131] Evidence from the Tuscan PCI in the later 1970s broadly supported the same level of participation. According to the Pisa federal secretary in 1977, 'even crowded mass-meetings almost never draw more than 20 per cent of the members and rarely reach 30 per cent'.[132] In one industrial centre, it was reckoned that out of 1,400 members in the three *sezioni* only 100-150 turned up at meetings;[133] while in a more isolated rural town the rate of participation was put at 10 per cent to 15 per cent.[134] Even in the PCI stronghold of Sesto Fiorentino on the outskirts of Florence, the data for the *sezione* congresses in 1977 showed that, while the rate of attendance could vary, the number who contributed to discussion was consistently low even in the larger *sezioni* (Table 3.10).

Table 3.10: PCI Sesto Fiorentino: Participation at *Sezione* Congresses, 1977

Sezioni	Members present both evenings	Members who spoke	Membership at time of congress
Sud Ferrovia	85	12	355
Quinto Basso	88	18	264
Quinto Alto	67	9	140
Colonnata	275	14	564
Centro	230	14	631
Campo Sportivo	100	13	302
Campo Zulfanello	141	11	627
Co-op. Italia	40	9	147
Ginori	50	8	65
Dipendenti Comunali	55	11	200

Source: PCI Comitato Comunale, Sesto Fiorentino, *Documentazione Orgànizzativa*, 1977, p. 1.

To some extent this illustrates fairly normal problems encountered by mass-structured parties. Limited participation by the membership as a whole induces the concentration of policy-making among a restricted number. One should add on a specific point that the habit of PCI members to deliver themselves of lengthy speeches does of course reduce the possible total at any given meeting, but in any case speech-making in an Italian context must be treated with caution as a means of estimating party-political influence. In the words of one PCI leader, 'in Italy one discusses much: there is even a sort of "debating mania" (*dibattitomania*), which runs the risk of remaining abstract if it does not leave its mark on decisions and initiatives'.[135] On the other hand, while participation levels have not substantially changed during the 1970s, there has been some evident qualitative change in the patterns of participation. This has led to some greater flexibility in the application of democratic centralism, even if this has not provoked any discussion of its principles, and a less ritualistic form of political discussion. Furthermore, the radical changes in the composition of party functionaries have produced a new style of managerial leadership, which has undoubtedly helped to determine the tone of internal party relationships. While these cadre changes have created some internal tensions, it must be supposed that the new generation of functionaries will settle in their posts as their predecessors did. In short, the PCI is a mass-structured party which has demonstrated a strong awareness of the problems of adapting its various structures to a rapidly changing environment. Even when it may be said that bureaucratic tardiness or convervatism has been evident, the informal organisational values which condition internal party life have helped to lend a certain flexibility to the formal organisational rules.

(d) The 'Party of Government and Struggle': the Internal Dimension

The specific interpretation of democratic centralism within the PCI, its problems of participation and the various patterns of continuity and change in its character as a mass-structured political party, all provide a necessary background to understanding the question of interaction between its external relationships, notably with other political forces, and its own internal life. No political party's evolution in a given period can be completely judged without close consideration of this aspect, as this usually reflects on the effectiveness of internal mechanisms of party discipline, the stability of party solidarity and the imprint of party traditions whether symbolic or ideological. This is, however, a field which is intrinsically ambiguous not only because of the complexities of inter-party relationships, as in the Italian case, but also because parties in general face the problems of both trying to marry strategic with tactical considerations in their alliance with other parties, and of retaining a harmonious balance between their elites involved in this process and their grass-roots.

In the 1970s, the over-riding feature in the PCI's political history has been its presentation and implementation of the strategy of the 'historic compromise', which has required the party to orientate its own organisation and activity less than before to distant and uncertain goals and more to specific political targets with immediate or intermediate prospects. Here, attention will concentrate on the internal dimension of the two-way impact between the party's external and internal relationships, the other dimension being treated later in reference to the PCI's actual formulation of its alliances with the other parties.[h]

So far as party traditions are concerned, any valid starting-point must deal with the continuity between the PCI's strategy from the mid-1970s and its long-term policy of alliances as originally presented by Togliatti in the earlier postwar period. This policy was conceived in terms of alliances between different socio-political forces (rather than specifically individual political parties), whose common denominator was either anti-Fascism or opposition to monopolistic values. According to Cervetti, 'for all the problems of the life of the state and society there should be shown a solution . . . that would guarantee the power of the fullest possible consensus to the work of transformation — this is the character of *government* that Togliatti wanted and knew how to imprint on the party'.[136] Continuity has been stressed at the official party level between this traditionally self-conceived role of a 'party of government and struggle' (*partito di governo e lotta*) and the strategy of the 'historic compromise', but it is interesting to note how the former term — which is also a slogan — is interpreted in the light of the PCI's deeply-rooted sense of its mass character. In the view of a Tuscan regional party leader, the PCI's dual function meant that it was

> a party which is present in the institutions for the purpose of governing, but governing while maintaining a relationship with the citizens; at the same time, a party that is there in the first person, not only among the institutions, but present in society through its direct structures . . . with its members, with its *sezioni*, with the *case del popolo*, with the secretary of the federation, with its regional leaders . . .[137]

It is evident that we have here a variation on the theme of political forces of the Left searching to harmonise their traditional roles as 'parties of protest' with their acquisition of power as parties of governmental responsibility; although this cannot be posed in stark Anglo-Saxon terms of government versus opposition roles because of the many grey shades in between in Italian politics. Furthermore, the unique characteristic of the PCI's approach is that it has from the time of Togliatti seen itself at the conceptual level as a potential governing party; the difference being in the 1970s that this approach has progressively transformed itself *concretely* into greater participation by the party at different horizontal levels of the Italian state structure. The question arises, therefore, whether this advent of the PCI as a governmental force in practice has caused any unprecedented difficulties vertically in its relationship with its own membership base.

In taking the example of Tuscany, naturally the PCI's own postwar record as a municipal governing party must be taken into account as a factor mitigating the impact on the party of its increased governing role in the 1970s. A survey of reactions from the PCI federations throughout Italy to Berlinguer's enunciation of the 'historic compromise' approach in the autumn of 1973 revealed a general acceptance of Berlinguer's line, especially after an internal campaign by leaders in the provinces to emphasise its consistency with Togliatti's approach. There were, however, within this overall acquiescence variations of attitude from region to region. Whereas in the industrial triangle of the north this acceptance was conditional on there not being a trade-union truce as the price for dialogue with the DC, in the south doubts were raised about the PCI's being corrupted by the DC's system of power (notorious for its clientilism in this area) and in the 'White' regions of the north-east there was scepticism about the DC's likely interest in the new advances from the PCI. The 'Red' regions, on the other hand, showed a more confident PCI already practised in the exercise of power, especially in Emilia-Romagna where some collaboration between the PCI and DC had been developing — 'we have been putting the historic compromise into practice for years; we could even say we invented it'.[138] A similar attitude has been met in Tuscany. The PCI mayor of San Gimignano, long a party stronghold, commented:

> In a town like ours, where the party has been in government for 30 years, it is easier to share the line of the historic compromise because we have invented it ourselves . . . we have always had relationships that showed a tendency to receive certain proposals from the minority. Hence, this prepared us for a type of politics of conducting relations with other forces without fear.[139]

These regional variations undoubtedly reflected the different political environments, especially the balance of party strengths, in each case.

Relations with the DC have, however, run less smoothly in Tuscany than in Emilia-Romagna, largely because of the predominance in the past of the anti-Communist *fanfaniani* in the Tuscan DC, and this inevitably coloured early reactions to the Berlinguer's approach. Again, some local variation was evident in the region with a few isolated cases of open dissent, such as in the working-class district of Gavinana in Florence and the neighbouring towns of Scandicci and Sesto Fiorentino, where a handful of youthful activists in the FGCI resigned their membership.[140] Party solidarity reasserted itself overwhelmingly, as elsewhere in Italy, but what was suggested at the time and has become clear since is that perceptions among the PCI membership of the party's acquisition of a governing role and of its *rapprochement* with the DC were notably influenced by events in Rome as well as those in the provinces.

There are various ways ideally of assessing the effect of these developing inter-party relationships on the PCI internally — ideologically, at the level of party activity and in reference to different social groups in the membership. The problem with trying to establish a specific scale of attitudes is that these can inevitably be fluid, an assumption supported by some conflicting responses on the part of interviewees which were not all explained by individual subjective perceptions or varying local situations. Drawing on the earlier discussion of structural relationships inside the PCI and in line with the research approach of this study, it is considered more useful here to focus on a number of pointers and trends apparent in the first half-decade or more since the 'historic compromise' was first launched.

It is a truism that the traditional system of democratic centralism should itself have been an advantage for the leadership in calling on party solidarity to reinforce the line of Berlinguer. Some PCI activists from Siena, writing at the time of negotiations between the PCI and DC for the formation of the second Andreotti Government early in 1978, asserted the conventional rule that it was the task of leaders to conduct 'a whole series of meetings at the grass-roots, in which their essential task is to make pedagogic efforts to win the party in favour of decisions they have taken . . . a position adopted by the central party organs should not take the base by surprise; it should be preceded and accompanied to a large degree by real and proper consultation and by a campaign at the political and conceptual levels'.[141] Broad acceptance of the 'historic compromise' by the membership has furthermore been facilitated by the compelling argument that this party line provided the gateway to legitimacy for the PCI and the means of escape from its 'isolation' in the anti-Communist period since the Cold War.[142] Coupled with this has been a widespread undercurrent of fear among the membership of a possible repetition of the Centre-Left formula of the 1960s, leading to the exclusion once more of the PCI from association with or participation in government. This fear of the consequent division between the two parties of the Left notably surfaced during the polemical debate on Marxist-Leninism provoked by Bettino Craxi, the PSI leader, in the autumn of 1978 causing 'deep anxiety' among the PCI base.[143] This general picture of strong consensus in favour of the proposition that the PCI should enter the national government seemed to be confirmed by the Doxa survey of autumn 1977 on attitudes among the PCI membership. This included evidence on their preferences for a variety of coalition formulas, where the Centre-Left received only 0.2 per cent approval compared with 72.5 per cent who supported variations which all included the direct participation of both the PCI and the DC in the government. Over 80 per cent were happy with the hypothesis of PCI direct involvement in the government, with 18 per cent displeased with this prospect.[144]

While all this evidence appeared to indicate success for democratic centralism and the political factors reinforcing it, it should be remembered that there can be no such thing as pure party solidarity for various influences and developments may intervene to condition its amplitude in any given period. Moreover, while the Doxa survey was based on hypothetical propositions, naturally the ensuing responses could not be divorced from the PCI's actual position of benevolent abstention at the time in favour of the first Andreotti Government. It is when looking more closely at internal reactions to developing political alliances that some differentiation of attitudes becomes evident. In short, although it could be said that democratic centralism seeks to provide a form of dialectical integration within the PCI, the comment of one Tuscan provincial *dirigente* on 'the affirmation of the party line on the principled level, but ambiguities when it comes to concrete choices' seemed more to the point. As expected, PCI *dirigenti* at all levels — and not just the so-called *berlingueriani* — strongly supported the 'historic compromise' strategy, both because their party careers were attached to this but also as they themselves were more versed in the conceptual handling of such broad questions than the membership at large.

The PCI was no doubt helped by the fact that more than half its membership had joined since 1970, and that therefore a sizeable minority has entered since the 'historic compromise' became developed as official party policy. Even so, the question of differing expectations within this context must be borne in mind, and these could vary according to social and generational categories. What is clear is that immediately after the formation of the first Andreotti Government in August 1976, with 'no non-confidence' (*non-sfiducia*) support from the PCI, the party experienced in many parts of Tuscany more than a hint of dissent. This was admitted readily in interviews with both provincial and local *dirigenti*. One federation party secretary interviewed in the autumn of 1977 described the situation as follows:

> We had, when the government of abstention was formed last year, a very hard battle in the party for understanding at the base was rather stretched, and we were involved let's say from August until December of last year, until the congresses, in a continuous discussion internally in the party in the *sezioni*– because after 30 years the party was changing its role, it was fairly explicable to expect this reaction.

Similarly, one local leader in the province of Siena noted that direct contacts with the provincial party organisation had increased since support for the Andreotti Government had created problems of adjustment:

> There was a certain disorientation at the beginning following the change of our party in supporting the Andreotti Government. This created some problems, so that many came from the party federation to clarify and explain the various events and situations that were unfolding at the national level.

There were different signs that the impact on the party of its growing association with national government sensitised PCI leaders all the more to the needs and accompanying problems of carrying the party base. The potential significance of these developments was proffered by one young *sezione* secretary, who remarked that 'there is a constant opening up of the party to others and within itself', which had contributed to a 'maturation' of the party line. Again, towards the end of 1977, a round-table discussion of three PCI federation secretaries in Tuscany dwelt on the internal difficulties of adjustment.[145] Their various replies touched on the argument that the PCI had since 1976 been preoccupied with its new role as 'party of government' without sufficient attention to 'developing the autonomous movement of struggle'. A number of reasons were suggested for this: that the party base, although enthused by the electoral success of 1976, had not been fully aware of the import of developments since, especially as 'inevitable and just compromises' in Rome had only confused members; that the party elites were themselves partly to blame for this as the PCI at the mass base had not been consulted enough; and that the PCI in Tuscany in particular as the party of local government was too involved with 'a series of daily problems, including minute ones, generated by the crisis' so that this everyday routine produced the 'vice of administrativism, which risks losing sight of the great political process and the great objectives'.

After the initial shock produced by the party's indirect support for the DC minority government, the membership seemed to absorb the changed constellation of political parties, although the programmatic agreements concluded in Rome in July 1977 and March 1978 served to draw 'new attention' to this process. There still remained the question whether the PCI could simply overcome the problems of carrying the party base through a programme of continuous activism to sustain party solidarity ('struggle'), or whether certain internal contradictions had appeared with regard to the course being pursued. The question was all the more relevant as the PCI itself linked its organisational activities strongly with its political objectives. The campaign for membership recruitment launched in the autumn of 1977 emphasised as one of its central themes the full application of the July programmatic agreement.[146] Recruitment was regarded by PCI leaders as a thermometer of the internal state of the party, so that a sluggishness in new entrants during 1977 pointed to difficulties in mobilisation. This was attributed by different observers to an awareness among Communists of the gulf between the government programme and political solutions. At the end of 1977, however, this situation reverted itself following the demand from its national Directorate for the PCI's participation in an emergency government, a demand made with at least one eye cast to the party base.[147]

The most serious internal difficulty for the PCI arose from the fact that in the developing situation its projected dual role of 'party of government and struggle' created two allied problems: an impatience with the lack of visible results from PCI governmental support could be matched among the membership by an evident reluctance to swallow the full implications of the actual enveloping relationship with the DC. In both cases, the generational and social categories diverged in their reactions, but did not form any clear-cut overall picture.[148]

With the first problem, the element of gradualism or the 'long haul' in implementing the 'historic compromise' found least acceptance among younger members especially those from an educated middle-class background, among whom the 1976 election had produced too much optimism, for, as a young local party secretary noted, 'many youths were probably accustomed to having victory'. Among this element the PCI's loss of votes in the spring local elections of 1978 had a sobering effect, having in the view of some young activists at Florence a 'positive impact' as the euphoria of two years before was replaced by 'a habit of self-criticism'. So far as older working-class members were concerned, this problem assumed a different form: summarised by a federation secretary as their ability to accept the situation of austerity, but only with the prospect and evidence of change in society.

With the second problem, the main difference of reaction derived from generational experiences. For older members, raised on a diet of anti-clericalism and scalded somewhat by the impact of the Cold War period on Italian domestic politics, the new relationship with the DC required a psychological 'jump' that inhibited full-hearted acceptance of the party line. This outlook expressed itself most commonly in a deep scepticism about the possibilities for a character change in the DC, particularly as this party denied adamantly that its new relationship with the PCI amounted to any first stage in the 'historic compromise'. According to the secretary of one Tuscan party federation:

> These comrades say 'That's fine, the party line is right, the line of the historic compromise, yet we are doing this to change this DC', and unfortunately the events of every day lend reason to this scepticism — when one sees all the compromises of the DC and its lassitude in coming to terms with its own past, its attempt to protect its system of power ... so many comrades say 'is it really possible to make the DC change?'.

On the other hand, some interviewees pointed out a greater patience and philosophical attitude among older members in certain localities, where relations with Christian Democrats were noticeably less 'frontal'. A sense of party solidarity and 'trust' in the PCI was especially strong among the older generation of members, and this included that element labelled 'Stalinists', who in the opinion of a young *sezione* secretary

> are comrades who are engaged in the internal life of the party and

in its outside activities, comrades who follow the party. They don't feel distant from the party because the party is today pursuing democratic unity with the DC.

Younger members again demonstrated a divergent approach to the relationship with the DC. Attitudes here ranged from a greater capacity than older members for assimilating the party line, untouched by direct memories of the polarisation of the 1950s, to a reaction encountered among the more voluble activists of the '1968 generation', who saw in the entente with the DC the ultimate provocation. At the same time, differences were noted on a class scale between young workers who shared something of the mistrust of their elders towards the DC, muted as this was by traditional party solidarity, and the young middle-class intelligentsia in the party who were more articulate and more openly critical of the entente.[149]

This preceding analysis is not intended in any way to suggest that the ranks of the PCI were permeated with dissent or dissatisfaction, but rather to point out that any development of such significance as the 'historic compromise' could hardly transpire without varied forms of critical acceptance or internal tension. Such reactions as have been indicated are difficult to quantify or categorise exactly, as variables such as local party conditions intervened to colour national political perspectives, but also simply as one is dealing here with a subject which is predictably open to subjective interpretations. One conclusion which may, however, be derived from this report on Tuscany is that, if the PCI experienced scepticism, differences of reaction and various problems of acceptance over the concrete application of its strategy among the party base in this traditionally 'Red' region, where its organisational and social roots were significantly stronger and more stable than in most other parts of the country, then its internal difficulties were likely to be greater where its membership was relatively less established and extensive. All this tended to demonstrate that even in a disciplined party like the PCI the leadership were not entirely free to pursue their strategic objectives as they wished, without reference to attitudes within the party base. Indeed, Berlinguer himself admitted later that the leadership had made this very mistake after deciding in 1976 to support the Andreotti Government: 'We did not fully succeed in bringing home to the party the objective situation that had dictated our decision, together with the limitations but also the new possibilities it created for us and for the popular forces in general.' He continued by saying that this was 'our major shortcoming' so that 'the whole party and the broad masses that support us' did not completely understand the different implications of the PCI's role after the 1976 elections.[150]

If the leadership cadres evidenced the strongest commitment to the strategy of the 'historic compromise' both conceptually and in practice, while the party membership hardly disputed it conceptually but was rather sceptical about its concrète application from the mid-1970s, what about the PCI's voters? Their links with the PCI were less intensive than those of its members and they were therefore more distant from internal party debate about the importance of strategic objectives. However, their behaviour had to be judged in the light of general patterns of voting support for the PCI. It is worth noting this briefly as the PCI's electoral advances of 1975-1976 certainly made the application of its strategy more acceptable within the party, just as its loss of some of its gains from 1978 had the reverse effect, even though the PCI was not essentially a voter-oriented party.

In this respect, the PCI was more fortunate in Tuscany than in most other regions because of the strong stability of its electorate there. This was explained by factors relating to the PCI's predominance in this 'Red' region: its traditional bases of support established after the War, reinforced as these were by sub-cultural influences and the party's strong organisational network.[151] As Berlinguer noted in his postelectoral appraisal in July 1979, the party had been much less vulnerable to loss of support in the 'Red' regions compared with notably the south and its record of high electoral volatility: 'We cannot hope to reach everywhere and in a short time levels of party growth that in regions like Emilia and Tuscany are the product of decades of work and also of particular conditions of civil development and democratic organisation of society.'[152] Indeed, from 1946 to the 1970s the PCI in Tuscany had expanded its electorate most in its traditional areas of strength, so that it gradually came to monopolise the voting support for the political Left.[i, 153] For instance, whereas just after the War the PCI gained an absolute majority in 36 communes in Tuscany, this number had risen to 94 in 1972 (national election) and increased further to 125, or 43 per cent of the communes, in 1975 (regional election).[154]

The later 1970s did, however, as elsewhere in Italy, see the first serious electoral losses by the PCI since the War, though to a reduced extent in Tuscany. These started with partial local elections in 19 communes in May 1978 with a small decline in PCI support, but these were limited in that, according to one electoral study, 'the voters, above all because of the Communist Party's role in local government and certainly its strong social presence, have for some time formed an image of the PCI that is more in harmony with the party's official position at the national level',[155] and hence were less alienated by the PCI's entente with the DC in Rome. In the 1979 national elections, the PCI's losses occurred throughout Tuscany (a loss in the region of 1.7 per cent compared with 4 per cent nationally), while in the regional elections of 1980 it managed to retain the level of support gained in 1975 (loss of 0.1 per cent). It is important to note where the PCI's support was most vulnerable. Traditionally, the party was stronger in Tuscany in the industrial and agricultural communes and weaker in the communes with a preponderance of tertiary activity.[156] It was in the last category that the PCI vote began to expand most during the 1970s, that is in areas of growing urban society and especially among middle-class voters, and it was in the same areas that the PCI suffered some losses at the end of the decade. This greater electoral instability related of course to the fact that the PCI's sub-cultural influences were not so deeply rooted among this category of voters and that its organisation had faced the greatest difficulty in establishing or extending its structural links in these areas.

In conclusion, these relative changes in the PCI's electoral base in the 1970s related to the fact that it also encountered problems of integrating new social groups in its membership during the same decade. As shown in this chapter, this transformation in the PCI's own social composition was accompanied by important changes in the age level and class background of its intermediary leadership cadres, not to mention to some extent the nature of its internal political dialogue. All these changes reflected differences in the Italian socio-political environment — the growth of urbanisation, new patterns of political involvement, especially among the younger generation, and the growing volatility of voters in general and the more severe economic climate — but they also derived from the greater political prominence and role of the PCI itself. With its own internal problems in mind, it could be said that the PCI paid a certain price for its success. In other words, the PCI's growing political importance in the Italian state has involved a process of internal adaptation. This has not been easy as the consequent changing balance between the roles of 'government' and 'struggle' has at least in the eyes of many of its own members brought apparent contradictions and more generally a greater gulf between promise and performance. These internal problems came to the fore once the 'historic compromise' no longer remained purely a strategic conception and became more of a concrete reality.

These difficulties of internal adaptation and tension, together with the PCI's electoral losses, did not seem to bode well for the further application of party strategy. In fact, these considerations were paramount in Berlinguer's decision to withdraw support from the DC Government in Rome early in 1979. On the other hand, it was conceivable that with time the party as a whole might accustom itself more to the PCI's fuller participation as a governing force within the Italian state. The party's strategic evolution since the War tended to point in this direction,[157] but much depended on the wider question of whether the political situation in the country and, in particular, the other political parties would favour any continuation of the convergence of the later 1970s.

In view of this uncertainty as of the early 1980s, a more secure indicator is to look at how the various changes listed above had affected the party itself for, as this chapter has confirmed, the PCI's external relationships were very conditioned by its own evolution as a party. It is significant that, on the basis of this regional case-study, the party in Tuscany would still be categorised as an ideological, mass-structured and class party. Subjectively, the PCI remained as such. Its own concern over responding to social change as well as integrating new groups into its membership underlined its self-conception as mass-structured, while its particular interpretation of 'class' in relation to social alliances still held, even though it had experienced some class-conscious friction among its leadership cadres. Again, the PCI remained in its own estimation an ideological force accepting its flexible justification of the continuity represented by the 'historic compromise', as espoused by its leadership; while at the party base the reservations towards the DC which appeared with the application of this strategy may be said to be basically ideological. Certainly, if there were any new electoralistic tendencies in the party, at least in Tuscany, these were contained by the strong element of consistency in the party's self-image.

Objectively, many of these aforementioned subjective considerations overlap and reinforce this same categorisation of the party. It must, however, be added that the various changes noted above in the social composition of its leadership cadres and to some degree of its membership did involve a qualitative development, though not one sufficient to alter the party's categorisation. This conclusion also applied to the growth of more lively internal debate during the course of the 1970s, for the method of democratic centralism could not in any case be taken for granted in directing party activity without reference to other 'informal' modes of internal party behaviour. The PCI had therefore remained essentially the party of integration on the Left in Tuscan politics. So far as this evolution in the party conditioned its political role in the state, it pointed to gradualism rather than any abrupt departure in the application of PCI strategy.

Notes

a. See below, Chapter 3 (b), pp. 64-9.
b. On the latter see below, Chapter 3 (c), pp. 88-95.
c. See p. 54.
d. See Chapter 3 (c), pp. 88ff.
e. See above, Chapter 1 (c), pp. 22-3.
f. E.g. see the comment by the Florentine federation secretary of the PCI in 1972; above p. 54, reference 19.
g. See below, Chapter 3 (d), pp. 103-4.
h. See below, Chapter 5.
i. See above, Table 2.2 on the comparative votes for the PCI and PSI in Tuscany since the War, on p. 37.

References

1. See, for instance, Paolo Farneti, *Il sistema politico italiano* (1973).
2. E.g. see F. Lanchester, 'I dirigenti del PCI: continuità e cambiamenti' in *Il Mulino*, May–June 1978, p. 464.
3. The classic definition of a 'catch-all' party is by Otto Kirchheimer, 'The Transformation of the West European Party Systems' in J. Palombara and M. Weiner (eds.), *Political Parties and Political Development* (1966), pp. pp. 177-200.
4. Interview No. 71.
5. *L'Unità*, 4 July 1979.
6. On this, see Sidney Tarrow, *Peasant Communism in Southern Italy* (1967). Tarrow looks at the problems faced by the postwar PCI in establishing its organisational structure in an environment less conducive than the north to disciplined methods of mobilisation, especially in relation to southern peasants, and more typical of developing societies.
7. Figures quoted by Neri Gori, 'L'Organizzazione del PCI a Firenze, 1945–1971' in *Rassegna Italiana di Sociologia*, 1974, pp. 391, 393.
8. Ibid, p. 393.
9. See Leon Epstein, *Political Parties in Western Democracies* (1967), p. 132 and *passim*.
10. A useful map indicating the prevalence of type of agricultural system for all communes in Tuscany for 1948–1949 is provided in Giacomo Becattini (ed.), *Lo Sviluppo Economico della Toscana* (1975), p. 72. The author confirmed this correlation in interviews in those selected communes visited.
11. Such a case was the town of Volterra (Pisa), where Mario Giustarini, mayor since 1946 (aged 74 as of 1978), had been head of the Committee of National Liberation at Volterra and before the Fascist period an active leader of the Communist youth. Renowned for his skill as an alabaster worker in this famous centre of that industry, he was proudly presented by the local PCI leaders as 'the mayor of all *volterrani*' and as 'the representative figure of our

party, because he has embodied in himself the whole history of the party from 1921 until today'. The 'above-party' appeal of Giustarini, who was also for a time Senator in Rome, seemed to be confirmed by non-Communists at Volterra.

12. See the figures quoted for PCd'I *sezioni* and membership totals by province in R. Martinelli, *Il Partito Comunista d'Italia, 1921-1926: politica e organizzazione* (1977), pp. 123-4, 195. Communist organisation was strongest in the province of Florence with 913 members out of a total of 2,391 in Tuscany as a whole in 1922. At Sesto Fiorentino near Florence, one of the major early local strongholds of the postwar Tuscan PCI, the whole leadership cadre of the PSI passed to the newly created PCd'I in 1921.
13. See David Apter, *The Politics of Modernisation* (1965), Chapter 6.
14. E.g. see the article on Tuscan politics, 'Florence considers itself above extremism' in *The Times*, 24 April 1972.
15. PCI Ufficio Elettorale e di Statistica, *Raccolta di Dati sull'Organizzazione, 1971-1975* (1976), pp. III-IV.
16. For a discussion of these problems in various areas of Tuscany, see the studies of the PCI in the Valdelsa and the Valdarno in *Politica e Società*, September 1977, pp. 21-6 and October 1977, pp. 21-8 respectively.
17. Celso Ghini, 'Vita politica e partecipazione nelle grandi citta' in *Rinascita*, 23 October 1970, pp. 6-8.
18. Ibid.
19. Speech of Piero Pieralli, secretary of PCI Florence federation, at its provincial congress, February 1972, p. 71.
20. Interview No. 87.
21. PCI, *Raccolta di Dati*, pp. 211-14.
22. PCI Siena federation, *Dati Statistici*, 14th provincial congress, March 1977, pp. 5-7.
23. PCI Lucca federation, *Note e riflessioni della commissione organizzazione della Federazione di Lucca*, May 1977, p. 8.
24. PCI, *Raccolta di Dati*, p. 212.
25. Brochures for these campaigns published data on the ratio for every commune in the said province; e.g. PCI Versilia federation, *Dal voto alla tessera: campagna tesseramento e reclutamento 1977.*
26. Article on the Valdarno in *Politica e Società*, (October 1977, p. 25.
27. Angiolo Dionelli and Massimo Baldacci, 'I problemi del partito in fabbrica' in *Rinascita*, 2 September 1977. See also Interviews Nos. 30 and 31.
28. Interview No. 18.
29. Interview No. 37.
30. *Rinascita*, 6 November 1970.
31. PCI, *Raccolta di Dati*, p. 154.
32. Stephen Hellman, 'The PCI's Alliance Strategy and the Case of the Middle Classes' in D. Blackmer and S. Tarrow, *Communism in Italy and France* (1975), p. 406.
33. PCI Livorno federation, *Il PCI nella provincia di Livorno dal '45 ad oggi: dati statistici ed organizzativi*, 16th congress, 1976, p. 11.
34. Ibid., p. 17, and Interview No. 36.
35. Ibid, p. 19.
36. PCI Pisa federation, *Materiale per uno studio statistico sul partito a Pisa*, 1975, pp. 35, 37.
37. Quoted in Paolo Giovannini, 'Il gruppo dirigente comunista' in Luciano Cavalli (ed.), *Classe Dirigente e Sviluppo Regionale* (1973), p. 114
38. PCI Sesto Fiorentino, *Commissione problemi del lavoro*, 6th communal conference, March 1978, pp. 27-8.

39. Ibid., pp. 23-4, detailing the work of the commune in promoting the interests of artisans and small businessmen.
40. Neri Gori, 'Attivismo tradizionale e crisi della partecipazione nel PCI: il caso di Firenze' in *Rassegna Italiana di Sociologia*, 1975, p. 258.
41. *Politica e Società*, September 1977, p. 23.
42. Interview No. 54.
43. Full details of the Doxa survey of PCI membership were published in *L'Espresso*, 30 October 1977.
44. See Togliatti speech at the 1954 national party congress, *VII Congresso del PCI* (1954), p. 33.
45. Stephen Hellman, 'Generational Differences in the Bureaucratic Elite of Italian Communist Party Provincial Federations' in *Canadian Journal of Political Science*, 1975, p. 92. See also the comment of Neri Gori on Florence that 'there was above all a concern over a movement, composed largely of militants of the student movement and groups, that was threatening the Communist monopoly of the poorly mobilised citizens and gave the inhabitants of the *quartieri* the practical example that mass action more incisive than that fostered by the Communist *sezioni* was possible' ('Attivismo tradizionale', p. 286).
46. Interview No. 24.
47. PCI Pontedera, report of 2nd communal conference, June 1977, pp. 10-11.
48. Gori, 'Attivismo tradizionale', p. 287.
49. E.g. see ibid., pp. 275-6.
50. Speech of Marco Marcucci, 8th congress of PCI Lucca federation, March 1977, p. 31.
51. Leonardo Domenici, 'Verso il congresso della FGCI: in bilico tra due modi d'essere' in *Politica e Società*, January–February 1978, p. 46.
52. E.g. the comment of the PCI Sesto Fiorentino 6th communal conference, March 1978, *Documento della FGCI*, p. IV, that 'the desire for participation in debate and political decisions expressed by the new generation is often curbed by rigid plans of the party agreed on the political and organisational levels'.
53. *Politica e Società*, May 1977, p. 12.
54. Ibid., pp. 16-23.
55. PCI Pisa federation, *Materiale per uno studio statistico*, 1975, pp. 29, 42.
56. Ibid., p. 27.
57. Gori, 'Attivismo tradizionale', p. 263.
58. Speech of Vannino Chiti, 11th provincial congress of PCI Pistoia federation, February–March 1975, p. 101.
59. E.g. the report on reactions among female PCI members at Florence to the party's manoeuvres over the abortion bill, *Panorama*, 21 June 1977.
60. For a general discussion of this theme, see G. Galli and A. Prandi, *Patterns of Political Participation in Italy* (1970), Chapter 5.
61. The standard work on the subject is Luigi Brunelli *et al.*, *La presenza sociale del PCI e della DC* (1969), summarised in Chapter 5 of Galli and Prandi, *Patterns of Political Participation*.
62. Interview No. 85.
63. On this see Giorgio Marsiglia, 'I sindicalisti' in L. Cavalli (ed.), *Classe Dirigente e Sviluppo Regionale* (1973).
64. *L'Unità*, 7 April 1977.
65. E.g. see the article on the opening of the *Rinascita* bookshop at Empoli in 1977, in *Politica e Società*, July–August, 1977, p. 70.
66. Interview No. 87.
67. See the historical note on the PCI bookshops in the province of Livorno in

PCI Livorno federation, *Il PCI nella provincia di Livorno dal '45 ad oggi*, p. 13.
68. Interview No. 4.
69. Some earlier studies have emphasised the parochialism of party militants in the 'Red Belt'; e.g. see Alan Stern, 'The Italian CP at the Grass Roots' in *Problems of Communism*, March–April 1974, p. 53.
70. According to a survey of *Unità* festivals in the Rome area young people under 30 and middle-class clerical workers were over-represented among participants, with the former providing 70 per cent of them; see PCI Rome federation, *Chi sono i partecipanti al festival di zona?*, 1975.
71. Report on *Unità* festivals in *Die Welt*, 15 November 1975.
72. PCI Montalcino, *L'Informatore Politico*, 29 July 1977.
73. E.g. the comment 'even the festival in the smallest village, organised by our party, will never resemble a saint's festival: even if there are elements of the saint's festival in it, there is a decisive element of modern culture which is the politics of a great national and democratic party of the working classes' in *Politica e Società*, July–August 1977, p. 71.
74. See *L'Espresso*, 30 October 1977, p. 39. At Montalcino (Siena) the 1978 *Unità* festival was planned by seven different commissions involving many party members. In later thanking party members for their 'involvement and sacrifice', the local party paper hoped the festival would be a spur to further activity (*L'Informatore Politico*, 27 July 1978 and 28 August 1978).
75. According to the Rome survey (see above, ref. 70), 96 per cent of the participants at the festivals voted for parties of the Left – 79 per cent for the PCI, six per cent for the PSI and 11 per cent for Democrazia Proletaria – and only one per cent for the DC.
76. Maurice Duverger, *Political Parties* (1964), p. xvi.
77. R. Michels, *Political Parties* (1962), first published in German in 1911.
78. Gianni Cervetti, *Partito di Governo e Lotta*, speech at Central Committee of PCI, 13 December 1976, p. 17.
79. Ibid, p. 53.
80. E.g. the comment of Orlando Fabbri, secretary of the PCI Prato federation, that 'one of the characteristics of the PCI is this: on the one hand contributing to new institutional and social definitions, and at the same time adapting the organisational structure of the party to this' (Interview No. 69).
81. See PCI Sesto Fiorentino, 6th communal conference, February 1978, *Impegni, ruolo e struttura del partito a Sesto: adeguamento dei livelli di direzione del partito*, pp. 23-4. Interview No. 17.
82. PCI Comitato Regionale Toscano, report of organisation commission, *Proposte per la definizione di un piano triennale di sviluppo del partito in Toscana*, September 1977, p. 2.
83. PCI Sesto Fiorentino, *Impegni, ruolo e struttura*, p. 13.
84. See Raymond Seidelman, 'PCI, decentramento e politica delle alleanze: il caso di Firenze' in *Il Mulino*, May–June 1978, pp. 467-98.
85. PCI Sesto Fiorentino, *Documento del Comitato Comunale in preparazione dei congressi delle sezioni di Sesto Fiorentino*, January 1977, pp. 42-4.
86. See the comment in Salvatore Sechi's critique of democratic centralism, 'L'austero fascino del centralismo democratico' in *Il Mulino*, May–June 1978, p. 432; 'the didactic, simply repetitive character of the language and style of official documents and of speeches – at university meetings the remarks of a Communist are immediately recognised after two sentences'.
87. E.g. the comment in PCI Lucca federation, *Note e riflessioni della commissione organizzazione*, p. 1: 'The data show the effort that still remains to be made not only to reduce the difference existing between our

federation and the rest of Tuscany, but above all to assert in the Lucchesia our party as a mass party ... that is, we must face the problem of PCI members and voters and of members and inhabitants, which means basically that we must strengthen the PCI not only numberically but give it new means, structures and mechanisms so that the *sezioni* ... can express all the appropriate political, cultural and operative powers and functions which are indispensable for a mass party.'

88. Speech by Armando Cossutta in *XIV Congresso del PCI: atti e risoluzioni* (1975), pp. 665-6.
89. *Relazione di Enrico Berlinguer per la preparazione del XIII Congresso nazionale del PCI*, March 1972, pp. 43-4.
90. *Statuto del PCI*, March 1975, p. 15.
91. Ibid, p. 16.
92. Interview No. 91.
93. Based on lists of members of PCI regional organs for 1977 and of regional councillors elected in 1975. This was somewhat below the national average; see F. Lanchester, 'La dirigenza di partito: il caso del PCI' in *Il Politico*, December 1976, p. 697, according to whom 28 per cent of members of PCI regional directive committees were also regional councillors.
94. Interview No. 18 (1978).
95. *Relazione del comitato comunale*, 6th communal conference of PCI Sesto Fiorentino, March 1978, p. 62.
96. See 'Documento di preparazione della conferenza regionale toscano' in *L'Unità*, 4 January 1976; *Politica e Società*, September 1977, pp. 25-6.
97. Notably, the discussion of regional structuralisation of the party in the speeches of Tuscan federal secretaries to provincial congresses in March 1977, prior to the first regional congress of the Tuscan PCI.
98. Interview No. 71 (1978).
99. Interview No. 49.
100. Speech of Alessio Pasquini to Regional Committee of Tuscan PCI, 22 April 1977, p. 8.
101. *L'Unità*, 28 April 1978.
102. PCI Comitato Regionale Toscano, *1˜ Congresso Regionale dei comunisti toscani: sintesi degli atti e risoluzioni* (1978), p. 121.
103. Interview No. 71 (1978).
104. *Politica e Società*, November–December 1977, p. 22.
105. F. Lanchester, *La dirigenza di partito*, December 1976, pp. 699-700.
106. Lanchester, 'I dirigenti del PCI: continuità e cambiamenti', p. 461.
107. PCI Livorno federation, *Il PCI nella provincia di Livorno dal '45 ad oggi*, 1976, p. 8.
108. Ibid., p. 6.
109. Ibid., p. III.
110. *Panorama*, 3 October 1978.
111. Lanchester, *La dirigenza di partito*, p. 704.
112. Ibid, p. 705.
113. Ibid., p. 705.
114. E.g. the PCI federal secretary for Arezzo, 35 years old, had been provincial secretary for Arezzo of the FGCI 1962-1966 and then in charge of FGCI organisational matters in the FGCI national office 1966-1969, Arezzo federal secretary since May 1976; the PCI federal secretary for Lucca, in that position since 1975, 28 years old, had been a provincial and later national functionary of the FGCI, having joined the party in 1967; the PCI federal secretary for Pistoia, in his mid-30s, had joined the PCI in 1968 following activity in the student movement, was a university graduate with

a Catholic family background: the PCI federal secretary for Grosseto, 34 years old, came from a bourgeois family background, joined the PCI in 1970 following a period of extra-parliamentary Left sympathies, studied at Pisa, became mayor of a commune in the province and federal secretary in May 1977; the PCI federal secretary for the Versilia, in that post since 1976, 29 years old and a student at Pisa, had been a member of the federal secretariat since 1970; the PCI federal secretary for Florence, 34 years old and in that post since April 1975, had joined the PCI in 1962, was provincial secretary of the FGCI for Florence 1965-1968; the PCI federal secretary for Pisa, somewhat the exception among these cases, was 52 years old and in that post since 1976, having joined the PCI as late as 1972 after activity in other parties of the Left: a trade-unionist by background, he joined the PSI after the Resistance and left this party in 1964 to join the PSIUP, of which he became provincial secretary for Pisa. (This data is drawn from information supplied in interviews, 1977.)

115. Giacomo Sani, 'Profilo dei dirigenti di partito' in *Rassegna Italiana di Sociologia*, January-March 1972, pp. 121-2, 145, *passim*.
116. Stephen Hellman, 'Generational Differences in the Bureaucratic Elite', pp. 101-4.
117. Interview with Elio Gabbuggiani, PCI mayor of Florence, in *Politica e Società*, September 1977, p. 20.
118. PCI Comitato Regionale Toscano, *1˜ Congresso Regionale dei comunisti toscani*, pp. 100-1.
119. *Corriere della Sera*, 1 September 1975, article on PCI *dirigenti*, 'Un partito in mano ai trentenni'.
120. Marco Marcucci, secretary of PCI Lucca federation, interview in *Politica e Società*, November-December 1977, p. 22.
121. Armando Cossutta, speech to PCI Congress, *XIV Congresso del PCI: atti e risoluzioni* (1975), pp. 666-7; Sechi, 'L'austero fascino del centralismo democratico', pp. 411-12.
122. Bruno Ferrero, PCI regional secretary for Piedmont, in round-table discussion, 'Il partito oggi: il rapporto con le istituzioni e con le masse' in *Rinascita,*, 6 January 1978, p. 11.
123. G. Berlinguer, 'Perche meno quadri operai e contadini?' in *Rinascita*, 10 June 1977, pp. 7-8.
124. For the party explanation, see PCI Statutes 1975, Article 18.
125. Interview No. 71.
126. E.g. the comment of the Sesto Fiorentino PCI on possible improvements in the functioning of local party structures: 'In the first place there should be a greater diversification of roles, avoiding the repetition of discussions in a hierarchical manner which risks "manufacturing" too much the problems and solutions' (PCI Sesto Fiorentino, *Documento del Comitato Comunale*, January 1977, p. 46).
127. *Rinascita*, 22 July 1977.
128. Quoted in *L'Unità*, 19 February 1978.
129. Speech of Vasco Giannotti, *13˜ Congresso Provinciale dei comunisti aretini*, March 1977, p. 3/C.
130. PCI Montalcino, *L'Informatore Politico*, 24 February 1977, pp. 2-3.
131. Gori, *Attivismo tradizionale*, p. 251.
132. Speech of Rolando Armani, *XIII Congresso della Federazione Comunista Pisana*, March 1977, p. 33.
133. Interview No. 30.
134. Interview No. 4.
135. See round-table discussion of Tuscan and national PCI leaders in *Politica*

118 The Tuscan Communists

e Società, January 1977, p. 40.
136. Gianni Cervetti, *Partito di Governo e Lotta*, 1976, pp. 18-19.
137. Interview No. 71.
138. Details of survey published in *Panorama*, 29 November 1973, pp. 50-2.
139. Interview No. 81.
140. *Panorama*, 29 November 1973, pp. 50, 51.
141. Letter in *Rinascita*, 17 February 1978.
142. E.g. the comment of Vannino Chiti, PCI federal secretary for Pistoia: 'to a large degree the old barriers, cunningly constructed, have collapsed, and the coarse criticisms and polemics of visceral anti-Communism have been swept away: the Communist Party has emerged as a great force . . .' (*Relazione all'XI Congresso Provinciale*, February-March 1975, p. 98). One local party activist interviewed emphasised that in his view the party base of the PCI had accepted the 'historic compromise' as a means to a 'kind of survival' to prevent political and social isolation.
143. Interview No. 71.
144. Doxa survey published in *L'Espresso*, 30 October 1977, pp. 38-49.
145. The text of this discussion with the PCI secretaries for Siena, Lucca and Arezzo was published as 'Il nostro dibattito: dal 20 giugno a domani' in *Politica e Società*, November-December 1977, pp. 20-4.
146. See the statement by the PCI Directorate in *L'Unità*, 30 October 1977; also membership campaign brochures issued by the Tuscan party federations in autumn 1977, e.g. that for the Grosseto PCI: 'At the centre of the new campaign for membership should be the following major questions: the new role of the party in national life; the complete fulfilment of the programmatic agreements signed by the parties of the constitutional arc; struggle for more advanced openings at the level of government; themes of our international position and policy.'
147. See the detailed report on the state of the PCI in Tuscany late 1977 in *La Nazione*, 10 February 1978.
148. The following two paragraphs are based on an assessment of the various responses in interviews to this question.
149. Similar conclusions have been drawn by M. Barbagli and P. Corbetta in a regionally-based survey of PCI membership opinion; see their 'Una tattica e due strategie: inchiesta sulla base del PCI' in *Il Mulino*, November-December 1978, pp. 922-67. Based on their survey research on the PCI grass-roots in two party federations in Emilia-Romagna during 1976-1978, they show that the party base is far from compact over the evolving alliance with the DC at this time. While broadly there was little opposition to the principle of the 'historic compromise', the concrete process of applying this in Rome did, however, produce serious tensions within the party. Their results indicate two interesting conclusions. First, a tendency among the base to interpret or rationalise the 'historic compromise' as a tactic or means for coming to power by the PCI leading a Left majority, causing in the process a crisis and collapse in the DC; while the party, leadership cadres differed in accepting the 'historic compromise' as a strategy in itself. Secondly, the main divergence within the membership was generational in that older Communists found greater difficulty in adapting to the process of convergence with the DC, while young Communists (who joined the PCI in the 1970s) found it somewhat, though not markedly, easier to accept the strategic arguments of the 'historic compromise'.
150. Berlinguer's report to the PCI Central Committee, *L'Unità*, 4 July 1979.
151. See M. Barnini, 'La Toscana elettorale in questo dopoguerra' in

Quaderni dell'Osservatorio Elettorale, No. 1, October 1977, pp. 9-55.
152. *L'Unità* 4 July 1979.
153. Regione Toscana/Giunta Regionale, *Il Comportamento elettorale in Toscana: una prima interpretazione* (1975), p. LXVI.
154. Regione Toscana/Giunta Regionale, *Le elezioni del 15-16 giugno 1975 in Toscana* (1975), pp. 9-10.
155. Regione Toscana/Giunta Regionale, *Le elezioni amministrative del 14-15 maggio 1978* (1978), p. 13.
156. Regione Toscana/Giunta Regionale, *Il Comportamento elettorale in Toscana*, pp. XLIX-LII, 196.
157. See S. Tarrow, 'Political Dualism and Italian Communism' in *American Political Science Review*, March 1967.

4 THE TUSCAN CHRISTIAN DEMOCRATS: THE PARTY OF CATHOLIC-CONSERVATIVE MOBILISATION

(a) Party, Movement or Electoral Association?

One of the essential themes of this study is that, in the multi-party setting of Italian politics, the question of alliance strategy or coalitional relationships is inextricably linked to the problems of party identity and evolution. For this reason, the formulation and initiation of new alliances is always a lengthy process. This chapter will therefore follow the same sequence of discussion as the preceding one on the PCI.[a]

This process is most difficult where the parties concerned have very distinct ideological histories arising from traditionally antagonistic schools of political philosophy. The uniqueness and hence 'historical' feature of inter-party relationships in the 1970s has been that, for the first time since the collapse of the postwar all-party coalition under De Gasperi, the two major political forces in Italy have been required to elaborate a direct form of relationship. For the PCI, the 'historic compromise' has been viewed as the gateway to its full legitimacy in Italian politics and presented by its leadership as a logical outcome of its evolving strategy; although, as already seen, this has raised other problems of party identity and caused discomfort among the party base. For the DC, the problems deriving from the new alliance proposition have been substantially different, in particular because this underlined the DC's own decline in political dominance and placed it in a defensive position. Hence, the starting-point for examining the DC's response to the changed political situation in the 1970s, involving the first serious challenge to its identity and role, must be its nature as a political force.

There are several difficulties facing any attempt to classify the DC as a party in a comparative context. Firstly, as Italy's continuous party of national government since 1945 the DC is not easily distinguishable as an autonomous political party in its own right in the sense of having enjoyed an identifiable existence separate from its institutional role in the state. Many of the predictable characteristics of a permanent governing party in liberal democracies — a pronounced electoral orientation, a neglect of party organisation, a reluctance to emphasise party ideology and the over-riding motive of retaining power — are evident in its case. Secondly, the disparity between the formality and reality of its internal structural relationships is vast and considerably greater than in the case of the PCI, thus impeding the definition of its political procedures. Thirdly, generalisations about the DC have to take into account the major qualification posed by significant regional variation in its nature as a political force — predominantly clientilist in some areas (notably in the south), based on a strong Catholic tradition and sub-culture in other areas especially in the north, with considerable variation in the degree of articulated party structures.[1] In Tuscany, all three factors are sufficiently represented despite the region's 'Red' tradition — such as the strong Catholic sub-culture in the Lucchesia, and the background of clientilist practices during Fanfani's period of dominance in the Tuscan DC up to the mid-1970s — to make this case-study feasible. The temptation at first sight is therefore to typify the DC as a *sui generis* form of political party, but that is hardly adequate as a basis of analysis.

The direct bilateral comparison of the DC with the PCI is useful, for as the two mass parties in Italian politics they offer very different examples within that broad category. Whereas the PCI is clearly a mass-structured party, the DC may be regarded as simply a mass party (i.e. primarily in the electoral sense) — a distinction particularly noticeable in Tuscany, where the PCI is more articulated than in most other regions — but again this does not do full justice to the complexities of assessing the DC as a form of political party. Placing the PCI and DC alongside each other as two mass parties based on individual sub-cultures and each with elaborate structural features[2] — the thesis of the institutionalised sub-cultures — is not a satisfactory approach by itself, as it fails to pay ample regard to the 'informal' as well as 'constitutional' patterns of party behaviour. The former may be more readily appreciated through the means of an in-depth case-study, as already shown in looking at the PCI. Referring to the typology used in introducing the PCI, it is evident that the DC in general emerges near the opposite end of the pole from the PCI in being a 'catch-all' rather than mass-structured party,[b] and one which is 'pragmatic' rather than ideological, voter rather than class-oriented and loose-associational in its internal relationships.[c] All the same, such fine distinctions need special qualification in the case of the DC because of its intrinsic complexities as a party. This chapter therefore seeks to consider such questions as: its response to new social pressures in the 1970s and forms of party activity and mobilisation; the changing situation of internal party factions (as a supreme example of 'informal' party procedures); the problems of party reform or revival while remaining a governmental force; and the role of ideology and party identity in relation to new alliance formations.

Much difficulty in categorising the DC as a political force derives from the intricate relationship in its development since the War between the inter-related though distinctly separate entities of 'movement' and 'party', the former comprising the range of different Catholic associations. In the evolution of most democratic mass parties, a process of structuralisation has usually occurred involving an increasing merger between these two entities, with a certain subordination of the 'movement' to the 'party' as its organisational expression. But this has not been the case with the DC. On the one side, it has depended heavily on the state and its facilities; and, on the other side, the Catholic movement has derived its own force from the institution of the Church. Any discussion of the DC as a mass party is incomplete without reference to the autonomous Catholic movement from which it has acquired so much of its strength electorally and politically. Sometimes confusing terminology in this respect was offered by party leaders and activists in interviews, so that the three-point schema of whether the DC was more of an organised party, an autonomous movement or simply an electoral association was employed.

Interesting variations emerged within the region of Tuscany, and to some extent typified patterns elsewhere in Italy. Where there was a strong Catholic sub-culture institutionalised through Catholic associations or supported by DC-allied collateral organisations — such as most importantly in the Lucchesia, but also present in smaller localities (e.g. the mountainous area north of Florence called the Mugello, some districts in the province of Arezzo) — it is possible to speak of a 'movement' as the basis of the DC, though this may be marked by weak party organisation, as in the Lucchesia, because it has been considered unnecessary, with DC control of local government providing an added reason for the absence of organisational stimulus. The city of Florence illustrated a variation on the same theme, with a Catholic movement more intellectual in character than elsewhere and less co-ordinated with the DC as a political force. The DC's expulsion from the city government by the Left in 1975 after 24 years' control, however, forced the DC to develop some new structural features there. The contrasting case to the Lucchesia, which in some respects resembles the Veneto in its Catholic cultural predominance (though not repeating the latter's Catholic presence in financial institutions), was the province of Siena, which as the 'Reddest' in Tuscany has featured no element of Catholic sub-culture and hence no 'movement'.[3] The DC has instead benefited here from its control of the most important financial and economic institution — the Bank of Monte dei Paschi di Siena — with consequent clientilist and electoralistic features. Both the dependence on the bank as the real focus of power control in the province and the very hegemony of the PCI have squeezed out the possible development of a viable organisation by the DC.

Party organisation has tended to develop most of all where the DC has felt acutely the challenge from PCI hegemony in the region and had the activist resources to mobilise. The high point of DC organisation in Tuscany was achieved during the 1950s and 1960s under Amintore Fanfani, who more than any other national party leader revealed a professional sense of the party machine, most notably in his home province of Arezzo and other localities of DC strength in the Arezzo-Grosseto-Siena constituency which he controlled.[4] Behind Fanfani's organisational drive lay the motive of rivalry with the Communist Party structure in a province like Arezzo, where the votes for both parties were fairly evenly balanced during these two decades, and a desire to loosen the DC's dependence on the Church associations. Most significantly, the DC in Arezzo was able to implant its roots among the non-sharecropping peasant class through Fanfani's links with the agricultural syndicates and such agencies as the Corporation for the Development and Irrigation of the Val di Chiana. His contacts with business and industrial circles in Arezzo, whose interests he promoted as a national political figure of influence, further allowed Fanfani the financial resources to promote party organisation to an extent he was unable to achieve elsewhere in Italy in his attempt as national DC secretary in the 1950s to reform the party structure.

With Fanfani's political decline in the 1970s, the state of the DC's organisation has suffered accordingly as part of the DC's general crisis, although, as already noted, the rise of the Left in local administration from 1975 had a stimulating effect on the party especially in the province of Florence. Even this change has often confirmed the interdependent rather than integrated relationship between 'party' and 'movement', for the new mobilisation among Catholic forces in the later 1970s, especially among the young, has operated through the latter to the benefit of the former rather than directly in the form of more regular party activities.

Alternatively, as an electoral association — that is, a party with a loose or spasmodically functioning structure brought into action at election time, and the absence of an institutionalised Catholic subculture — the Tuscan DC has offered the nearest example in the province of Pisa. This is not unrelated to the fact that the Pisan DC has been the stronghold of the Centre-Right *dorotei* faction (led by such national figures as Rumor and Piccoli) with its greater reputation than any other internal DC *corrente* for pure power politics. This has meant that the electoralistic character of the DC has focused on the acquisition and retention of a voting consensus around individual deputies with the tempting prospect of patronage dividends, notable cases being Giuseppe Togni several times national Minister of Posts and of Public Works as well as Edoardo Speranza, *doroteo* deputy from Florence. Such a phenomenon has also drawn on the prestige and consequent deference enjoyed by its national parliamentarians inside the DC. As one younger DC Left leader at Florence commented critically, 'the party has sections of its membership which are in some way connected to a deputy, and therefore their specific task is to guarantee the parliamentary seat for this deputy'. This is of course a special feature of the DC in so many other areas of Italy, notably in the south, while the clear categorisation of the DC as an electoral association is possible in certain parts of Tuscany because of the weakness of the 'party' and 'movement' dimensions.

The example of Tuscany consequently provides more variety than would appear at first sight in looking at a 'Red' area, especially if one examines the sub-regional components of the DC. There nevertheless remains the question of how far the Tuscan party — apart from the structural aspect just considered — may be typical or not of the DC as a whole, ideologically or sociologically. Some brief introductory comments on both features of the Tuscan DC's ideology and sociology seen in an historical context suffice here, as they will be treated at greater length in later sections of this chapter.

Ideologically, while the DC is a difficult party to classify in general comparative terms the definition of 'Centre-Right' is that most applicable. This does, nevertheless, have to take into account two particular qualities of the DC: the apparently wide range of ideological attitudes among its leadership groups, and the ambiguous role that ideology as such plays when considering party behaviour. In Tuscany, the spread of ideological positions as expressed through the *correnti* but also independently of them has been evident, with progressive tendencies among the Florentine Christian Democrats most visible during La Pira's time and again since the fall of Fanfani, and a fundamentalist or 'integralistic' Catholicism especially in Fanfani's bailiwick of Arezzo and to some extent at Florence. Fanfani's long dominance strengthened the conservative image of the Tuscan DC, whose adamant anti-Communism has been an important reference point in the party's development in this 'Red' region. All the same, Tuscany's tradition of anti-clericalism has imposed severe restrictions on the DC's engaging in an ideological battle of an overtly confessional kind, as was very clear from the decisive vote in favour of divorce (nearly 70 per cent) in the 1974 referendum. The party in the region is further noted for its lay Catholic traditions centring on the cities of Florence and Lucca.

Yet, the importance of ideology to the party way of life is often difficult to estimate. This is partly because of the DC's role in government, which has induced a chameleon-like quality in leadership behaviour with a tendency to look to the Right while moving to the Left, and vice versa. Moreover, unlike the PCI, the DC is not noted for its ideology assuming a dialectically integrative role in internal party relationships or providing a firm basis for policy proposals. The very reception of the term 'ideology' revealed highly varied responses in interviews with DC party elites. The most frequent answer was that the DC was guided by 'cultural values', such as in representing the cultural pole in opposition to Marxism or in the attachment to the idea of 'freedom' (the party's conceptual symbol). In similar fashion, others claimed that the DC's insistence on confessional principles as over the issue of abortion meant it was 'more ideological' though at the same time they emphasised that the DC was 'not a prisoner of ideological schemes'. Some were ready to describe their party as 'pragmatic' (notably Christian Democrats of a more conservative orientation), while the majority rejected this term as 'Anglo-Saxon' since it ignored the relevance of the DC's guiding principles despite their acknowledgement that 'politics' in the DC invariably meant the everyday decisions of government action.[5] A conclusion on this aspect would suggest that the DC has more of a 'belief system' than an ideology as its political point of reference.

Sociologically, the Tuscan DC is marginally less representative of the national party. This is a direct reflection of the PCI's social and political predominance and hence the DC's weaker presence in the region — except in the province of Lucca, where the DC has boasted a firm social base among the peasantry and the working class. The key to the DC's inter-class appeal, and therefore its claim to be a *partito popolare*, has traditionally been the presence of the Catholic sub-cultural factor, often reinforced — in Tuscany, as in other parts of Italy — by Resistance experiences in the last years of the War. In the Lucca province the legitimacy of the new DC was promoted by the important role of local priests in the opposition to the Nazi-Fascist occupation (57 of them were executed by the Germans) and the involvement of various DC leaders and activists there (such as Senators Martini and Angelini) in the

Resistance organisation. A similar development occurred at Florence, although Catholic Resistance activity here was confined to certain intellectual and youth circles and was less of a mass event.[6] One related problem for the postwar DC was that its party-political predecessor, the PPI, had failed to establish any significant mass base in Tuscany before the rise of Fascism and had confined its appeal primarily to land proprietors, the urban and rural petty bourgeoisie and some peasant groups.[7] The Tuscan DC has of course, as nationally, created a broader electorate for itself than the PPI, but even so it has emerged in the region, excepting Lucca, as more of a bourgeois party than nationally in the composition of both its membership and electorate, thus reflecting not only the limitations imposed by PCI hegemony but also the social structure of the region.

As indicated, there are many aspects of the DC's development in Tuscany which make this regional case-study sufficiently representative of the major features which have marked the DC as a political force in almost any other area of Italy. In view of its consistent electoral support here of 30 per cent upwards,[d] the DC is clearly a mass party in this basic respect even in such a 'Red' region. The history and role of the Tuscan DC have furthermore been underscored by many prominent national party figures, like Giovanni Gronchi (a Pisan), Giorgio La Pira (a Sicilian by birth and a Florentine by adoption) and Amintore Fanfani (an Aretine). The prominent influence of these figures has illustrated how much the party's political position and identity have been dependent rather more on the personal than the party-bureaucratic factor in contrast with the PCI, so that party tradition and solidarity are less easily identifiable because of the heterogeneous nature of the DC's internal relationships.

(b) The DC's Mass Character: between Socio-political Movement and Clientilist Formation

It has been noted that the DC is essentially a mass party in the electoral sense because of the size and quality of its voting support. Another feature of a simply mass party — as distinct from a mass-structured party like the PCI — is that the relationship between the interdependent 'party' and 'movement' in question is not an integrated one, subject to a degree of discipline fortified by strong organisational links binding the two entities. This relationship is activated most of all during election periods, when the 'movement' sees its political interests being expressed through an energetic supporting role for the 'party'. The autonomy of the Catholic movement *vis-à-vis* the *Democrazia Cristiana* fits into this pattern, but there are additional complicating factors. The 'movement' supporting the DC is not so much a political one proper as a socio-political movement — DC interviewees invariably used the broader and looser term 'Catholic world' rather than 'Catholic movement' — for it is structurally very heterogeneous, including as it must the powerful institutional factor of the Church in addition to the different Catholic associations varying from the overtly political to the cultural (which in the light of the sub-cultural theme are implicitly political). Moreover, as already mentioned, there has been no geographical uniformity about the presence and impact of the Catholic movement and therefore its supporting role for the DC. This section consequently investigates the nature and development of this Catholic movement during the 1970s, and how the DC's relationships with it and with different socio-economic groups have been affected by new political and social pressures.

Historically, the legitimacy of the Catholic movement in most of Tuscany outside the province of Lucca has been weakened by the anti-clerical traditions. Silvano Burgalassi, the historian of religious behaviour in Tuscany, has commented that the Civic Committees as the main electoralistic arm of the Catholic movement after the War encountered basic difficulties facing its 'operation and influence in a political climate, like the Tuscan, generally open to advanced social ideas'.[8] During the 1948 election campaign, at a time of pronounced polarisation between the DC and PCI, Catholic Action in Tuscany found that

> in the cities of Tuscany there exist side by side with the Catholic forces, which are unfortunately very disconnected, sectors of the population (especially the industrial and agricultural proletariat) united by Communism and with an open attitude of hostility towards the Church. This is particularly the case with Livorno, and to a lesser extent Siena, Arezzo and Grosseto. The situation is better at Lucca.[9]

Apart from the predictable contrast between Lucca and the rest of Tuscany, there is a need to differentiate between urban and rural areas. In the former, secularisation and modern trends of thinking have witnessed their greatest impact since the War — the city of Lucca again being an exception — whereas in the countryside the reason for disaffection with the Church lies in the anti-clerical mentality of the sharecropping class.

In this respect, Burgalassi noted an important difference between the DC's relationship with the Church in both areas: while the party has depended rurally on the Catholic associations, and notably the local influence of the parish priest, as a substitute for its own organisation to counter the PCI's presence, in the cities or at the diocesan level the DC has sought a more independent role for itself and accordingly there has been some conflict between 'party' and 'movement'.[10] All the same, Burgalassi calculated on the basis of extensive electoral research up to the mid-1960s that at least seven-tenths of the DC's election results in Tuscany had been attributable to the efforts of parish priests and leaders of the Catholic lay associations and only three-tenths to the electoral machine of the DC.[11] While still operative, this Catholic electoral function has relatively lost influence with secularisation. Hence, the main problem facing the DC in its relationship with the Catholic movement, especially from the mid-1970s, was: how to respond to modern social trends, while being unable to deny its dependence on and semi-organic link with the Catholic associational world. Theoretically, this challenge involved some redefinition by the DC of its Christian 'vocation', but in practical terms the paradox still remained of a party which was at least nominally Christian and yet required to become more appreciative of secular needs.[12] Some DC politicians have preferred to regard their party's religious background as a flexible politico-cultural reference-point,[13] but such a viewpoint cannot avoid the very differences of outlook on this question among DC leaders and activists — some lay Catholic democrats, some Catholic populists and others neo-liberals or conservatives — and erase the fact that at the DC's social base the Catholic connection has remained a factor of reality even though one under challenge. In the DC's crisis of identity in the 1970s, generally recognised as having surfaced with the Divorce Referendum of 1974, the ensuing internal and external confusion of the party arose to a large degree from this historically conditioned ambiguity.

Looking directly at the role of the Catholic associations in this recent period, some significant changes have been occurring, all suggesting that the secularisation process has affected the relationship between 'movement' and 'party'. However, what is important to stress is the difference between confessional and lay Catholic forces, for where the Catholic movement is strongest — in the Lucchesia (particularly the city of Lucca) and the populous Florence area — Catholics and Christian Democrats have evidenced a distinct lay attitude and been most susceptible to new social pressures; by contrast, in the rural province of Siena, where one cannot speak of a viable Catholic movement, the DC has remained directly dependent on the Church itself and therefore more confessional in outlook.

The Catholic movement at Florence has traditionally owed much of its vibrance to the impact of intellectual Catholic circles. One notable example of this phenomenon has been the group whose progressive views on social and political matters has been expressed through the periodical *Testimonianze*, edited by Don Ernesto Balducci. This publication, founded in 1957, became a focus of debate on the importance of the Vatican Council during the 1960s, and in more recent times has been critical of conservative tendencies and the power orientation of the DC. Whereas during La Pira's time of evangelistic and socially-conscious politics in the 1950s and early 1960s — known as the 'Florentine experiment' — there had been a happier rapport between the DC, especially its Left wing, and such influential groups, the estrangement between them in the 1970s undoubtedly contributed to the party's crisis of identity. The 1976 election in Florence saw one of the much publicised examples of independent Catholics standing on the PCI list in Mario Gozzini, who had made a name for himself a decade before with his book, *Il Dialogo all Prova*, promoting open dialogue between Catholics and Communists.

There has over time been a relative decline in the political influence of the confessional Catholic associations. During the early postwar period Catholic Action at Florence played a crucial role in mobilising electoral support for the DC and determining the preferential votes for individual candidates.[14] This form of confessional activity has been far more muted in the 1970s, even though Cardinal Benelli — appointed archbishop of Florence in 1977 — re-introduced an intransigent line in attacking Marxist ideology and defending Catholic interests notably over schools policy. Various Catholic associations in the city of Florence and the surrounding area have become more distant in their relationship with the DC, thus forcing the party to consider developing its own activities. A DC leader from Fiesole, a neighbouring town socially and politically strongly linked to developments in the city, commented on this change:

> The reason lies in the fact that in recent years the connections with those which were the collateral organisations have been lacking. That is, once there was Catholic Action on the side of the Church, the ACLI [Italian Association of Christian Workers] and other

organisations that were very active. There was a sort of identity. With the absence of this relationship, there have developed efforts in the party to initiate its own activity in certain sectors — for example, the GIP [e] have become more prominent with the absence of the link with the ACLI . . . the party as such has acquired more force, more activity.[15]

Some of the Catholic associations, such as the Movement of Christian Workers (MCL), have continued to maintain a regular level of activity, essentially of a political-cultural rather than party-political nature though clearly in sympathy with the DC.[16]

In the Lucchesia similar tendencies of a growing emancipation of 'party' from 'movement' have been visible, even if substantially modified by local traditions, socio-economic conditions and habits of mind. Here, the Catholic associational factor has been a consequence not so much of socially and intellectually active groups as a more widespread subculture throughout the province than in Florence, coupled with Lucca's quiescent political atmosphere. One provincial party organiser of the DC described the loose state of the associations:

> There are so many organisations that assist and unite certain groups, with their small newspapers and local broadsheets. These organisations concern themselves with the interests of women, with public assistance. There is not one factor that unifies them. Many branches, but there is not one tree — only many branches.[17]

There are, however, important exceptions to the weakened role of the DC collaterals. Apart from the Christian trade union, the CISL, which has its heaviest concentration of membership in the Lucchesia,[f] the politically most influential collateral organisation is the Coldiretti (organisation of small farmers) which owes its stronghold here to the traditional dominance of *coltivatori diretti* in the agriculture of the province — the sharecropping system never established itself — especially in the Lucca plain around Capannori and in the Garfagnana in the north. Described by one DC official as virtually 'a *corrente* of the DC', the Coldiretti has remained important for its electoral activity in favour of the DC and in the 1976 election demonstrated its vote-getting ability in the election to the Chamber of Deputies of the director of its provincial federation, Moreno Bambi, with the high number of 26,203 preference votes.[18] The mountainous area of the Garfagnana in particular goes some way to explaining why modern trends have little affected the social equilibrium even with the growth of small industry since the War. The role of the parish priest has still helped to account for the maintenance of DC hegemony. In the words of one DC leader:

> In the countryside of the Garfagnana, which is distant and where the inhabitants live in small *comuni*, there is a strong Catholic tradition. What explains this Catholic presence? Traditionally, what is the point of reference of a small mountain community? It is the pharmacist, and the priest — very often the priest, who is almost the organic centre of the local community, he who practically knows everything, a little about medicine, a little about law, who can sometimes guarantee the rights of the peasants. For these reasons, he has always been an essential point of reference socially speaking.[19]

By contrast, in the overwhelmingly 'Red' province of Siena the DC has lacked this cultural-associational background to depend on. An extreme case illustrating this is Colle Valdelsa, an historical stronghold of the Left, where the DC has been unable to penetrate beyond certain bourgeois circles. As a result, the party was forced here to rely solely on the social and political influence of the Church hierarchy. The Communist mayor of the town described this situation reasonably objectively:

> The DC here is a party which does not have an organisational structure. Therefore, when it needs to mobilise, what has happened as it doesn't have an organisational structure? It is the priest who by means of the organisational structure of the Church contacts those interested in the DC ... the priest, the parochial structure, which are concerned downrightly with showing them how to vote, arranging for bringing sick persons to the polling — because the DC as such is not able to do this here. Then, one finds those occurrences of mutual help. When the Church needs something of a political nature, it generally turns to the DC. For example, if there is a discussion on the schools the DC is disposed to embrace the Catholic ideas on this matter. All those polemics — on the private school, the public school — are the same as conducted by Cardinal Benelli at Florence, and one finds them in all the *sezioni* of the DC.[20]

Very often in the Siena countryside the DC has hardly possessed any semblance of an overt political movement. At Montalcino, another local case of PCI hegemony, the DC cyclostyled news-sheet has contained very little direct party news as such (apart from national events like the Moro kidnapping) and focused more on local events, sporting news, excerpts from radio south Tuscany and reports on Church activities. There is an element of the seemingly non-political in the activities of local Christian Democrats. One relatively active DC collateral in the province was *Libertas*, the sports association, engaged in particular in organising football matches between rival towns or villages, which may be said to act as a socialising agent for Christian Democrats, though party politics was not directly introduced in its activities.[21]

The principal occasion generating the DC's socio-political crisis of identity, linked as this was to the ambiguity of its lay/confessional (or integralistic) dimensions, was the Divorce Referendum of 1974. At the national level, the party was committed to the intransigent line adopted by Fanfani as DC Political Secretary, a position he defended energetically in his tours of provincial Italy.[22] Behind this official stand there lay deep divisions within the DC, expressing the broad lay versus confessional tendencies, so that in many areas of Tuscany the DC *sezioni* felt inhibited in mounting an active campaign and were further discouraged by the pervading pro-divorce outlook in the region. One major exception in Tuscany was Florence, where the DC was very active and a polarised situation developed once the Church there engaged in the propaganda battle. The official line of the party, however, alienated many of its voters and there was a significant margin of difference of nearly ten per cent between the vote of the anti-divorce parties in 1972 (DC plus MSI) and the 'Yes' (i.e. anti-divorce) vote of 1974 in that city. The two other most significant areas of a 'revolt' among DC voters were the traditional DC strongholds of the island of Elba and the province of Lucca. In the former case, voting support for the party was traditionally strong among higher social groups — notably, the wealthy bourgeoisie — for politically conservative rather than Catholic reasons. The predominant lay culture on the island and consequent alienation from Fanfani's fundamentalist Catholic position was underlined by the very high margin of difference compared with 1972: ranging from 10.16 per cent at Portoferraio to 18.11 per cent at Campo nell'Elba.[23]

The case of Lucca is more important because it witnessed not only disaffection among DC voters but also divisions among DC leaders and activists over the divorce issue. Lucca recorded the highest provincial margin of difference in the voting in Tuscany (of 9.28 per cent), the lowest being Siena province with 3.14 per cent. In twelve communes in

Lucca province, this margin rose to within the range of 10-20 per cent, nearly all in the Lucchesia; although in the Garfagnana this tendency was less pronounced (reflecting, as already noted, the more traditional Catholic sub-culture there) with in one commune the margin of difference working in the opposite direction. The basic reason for the reversal by anti-divorce forces in the Lucchesia was the conflict between the area's lay cultural traditions and the DC's official confessional line, a problem already foreseeable when in the pre-campaign period Lucca had been the city in Tuscany with proportionately the lowest number of signatures requesting a referendum.[24]
The anti-divorce campaign occasioned much disquiet among DC leaders in the province. One DC regional councillor from Viareggio declared openly in favour of divorce and campaigned as such. Several others acted more discreetly, following a low-key line supporting the official party position though not out of conviction. In the words of Maria Martini, the Left-wing DC deputy from Lucca:

> When we decided as the DC Left to engage in seeking support against the law on divorce, we informed the bishop of our position, asking him to trust in our political loyalty, rather than taking up intransigent stands. He granted his trust, we conducted a correct campaign, but not in the form of a crusade as one would say ...[25]

This reluctant attitude among DC leaders at Lucca towards the party line on divorce undoubtedly reflected the fact that Fanfani had never found strong support in the province, with the result that the smouldering resentment against his fundamentalist position over this issue provoked strong efforts to 'renew' the DC after the heavy losses in the referendum. This important example illustrated well the tensions caused in the DC by the impact of secularisation.

The experience of the Divorce Referendum — perceived by virtually all DC interviewees as a 'trauma' — represented a crisis for the *Democrazia Cristiana*, since it resulted from a change in the relationship between 'movement' and 'party' to the latter's disadvantage. The basic initiative and momentum during the early 1970s for a referendum to overturn the divorce law of 1970 had come from the 'Catholic world' — militant Catholic groups and the Church itself. In Tuscany, for example, the promoters of a referendum included notably four bishops, who argued in a published letter that divorce would mean more crime, more suicides, more prostitution and more juvenile delinquency.[26] The DC itself, while undeniably 'guided' by pressures from the Catholic movement, comprised within its leadership both lay and confessional outlooks and was aware that the issue could drive a wedge between both tendencies represented in its traditional electorate. However, adamant pressure from Catholic quarters, tactical considerations concerning the other parties and ultimately the fear of alienating its practising Catholic voters forced the DC in a direction opposite to that of the secularist trend of the times.[27] In short, for the first time in its history the DC's ability to appeal to both Catholic and lay voters was seriously in question.

This fundamental threat to its ability to appeal to a heterogeneous electoral base produced an immediate defensiveness by the DC in relation to specific social groups — in particular, women and youth. The fact that there had been a 'revolt' among female voters, a traditional area of strong support for the DC, and especially among younger ones, resulted in the party's rethinking its appeal and consequently adopting a more 'modern' line in its appeal to women in the elections of 1975-1976. A special number of the Poggibonsi (Siena) DC newspaper on 'Women' for the 1976 election stressed the contribution made by the DC to women's role in society since the War, though it was careful to take a middle path between radical demands for change and a conservative approach: 'Rather than Feminism, for a New Condition for Women' was the slogan.[28] The same fear of losing touch with an important group — one recently enlarged by the extension of the suffrage to 18-year-olds — motivated the DC's new emphasis on appealing to young voters. In one local case, the San Gimignano (Siena) DC issued a special election number of its own paper in 1975 for young people. By way of emphasising the real reason for this renewed interest, this issue devoted a whole page to the message: 'Our Future depends also on You — Vote D.C.', and explained the importance and system of voting with the claim that the party had promoted the lowering of the voting age: 'Why has the DC favoured votes for 18 year-olds? Because with the DC the young move from sterile protest to responsible participation; in this way the country will change, and with youth the DC intends to change itself.'[29]

Behind the fears of the DC was the prospect that the party might be reduced to relying for support on the traditional and declining sectors of society. The result of the referendum in Tuscany analysed in socio-economic terms showed that the highest percentage of pro-divorce 'No' votes was located in the communes with a predominance of the tertiary sector (71.64 per cent, with a margin of difference compared with 1972 of + nine per cent and more) and the lowest percentage in the agricultural communes (35.05 per cent with a two per cent margin of difference).[30] Now the DC faced the problem of the urban/rural divide in its base in a more accentuated form, a situation it found itself in as a consequence of the Catholic movement with its active traditionalist elements being the determining force behind the party over the issue of divorce rather than vice versa. For certain important groups at the party base, the DC's concept of 'Libertas' had come to be interpreted as 'personal freedom' rather than to represent the official notion of a defence of democracy or Christian values.

This prospect of an adverse trend against the DC seemed confirmed by the DC's loss of support in the 1975 regional election. However, it failed to materialise as a long-term linear development because of the intervention of new political factors. The period 1975-1976 saw a re-mobilisation of Catholic associations like *Comunione e Liberazione* (CL), MILLE ('Movement for a Free Italy in a Free Europe') and the 'Movement for Life' and their success in attracting younger Catholics.[31] There were various reasons for this further change, but all had one political factor in common: the very shock administered by the Referendum result stimulated various Catholic groups out of their lethargy to recoup their forces; and the rise of the Left, particularly the PCI, in the 1975-1976 elections added substantially to this momentum. One of the Catholic associations benefiting most was the CL, previously confined to Milan as an active force, which now assumed a more energetic role in other larger cities, such as Florence in Tuscany. One Florentine DC leader, sceptical about his party's strategy of *confronto* with the PCI, emphasised the effect of the PCI's demand for more political power in mobilising opinion among Christian Democrats:

> who have warned about the dangers in the line of *confronto*, of the confusion of roles but also of the identity of the DC. They have found support in a movement like the CL, in which we can all rediscover ourselves. If discovering ourselves means not falling to the PCI because we are different, because *we* are not Marxists and so forth ... Therefore, at the point at which the line of *confronto* risked losing some of the DC's identity, or at least making the question of the DC's identity less clear, then the CL became noticed and followed by Christian Democrats.[32]

As a consequence, this new activation of the Catholic movement had a reverse, namely positive, effect on the DC's fortunes, as was noticeable already in the 1976 campaign and thereafter. This development repeated itself, for instance, in the elections to the new school district councils in December 1977 — education being notably in Tuscany a strong focal point of political-cultural conflict — when the Catholic lists were successful, through such associations as the AGE (Association of Catholic Parents), in gaining support for traditional values and exploiting a less intensive interest for the Left among the young.[33] These lists appealed to circles outside the DC's normal electorate — in the 'Red' area of Pisa, for instance, they won half the seats in the district council.[34] While generally this Catholic mobilisation entailed some revival of 'integralistic' ideas — notably in the CL — it owed its origin more to political and social factors than to religious ones, despite some evidence of growing religious sentiment among young people possibly as a reaction to the disintegrating effects of social change. This change, largely urban-based as it was, therefore expressed a more conservative than confessional political outlook, for in reinforcing the DC it in no way reversed the erosion of religious values by secularisation.

Discussion of the party/movement dimension cannot be complete without reference to the DC's role as an economic-financial power rather than simply a political force when considering its mass character. It is here that one is most aware of the difficulty of assessing the DC as an entity separate from its controlling function in the state, a problem also applicable to the region of Tuscany despite the DC's minority status here and limited role in local government, one further reduced in 1975. This feature highlights a further related question, namely the influence of the DC's entrenched positions of economic authority as a consequence of central state patronage in inhibiting its ability to respond readily to new political and social pressures, particularly where the party lacks a supporting Catholic movement, as at Siena.

In Tuscany, as in other regions, the DC has controlled a series of economic or financial agencies including the two main banks which operate throughout the region — the Monte dei Paschi, and the Banca Toscana — the chambers of commerce, the savings banks and a whole series of other public, commercial or agricultural agencies. One study of the Florentine DC in the early 1970s concluded that the party held the presidencies of the following: the Chamber of Commerce, the Innocenti and S. Maria Nuova Hospitals, the Tourism Company, the Agency for Artisan Exhibitions, the transport company ATAF, the Tradesmen's Mutual Fund, the Meat Centre, the Agrarian Union, the Communal Theatre, the Savings Bank, the Banca Toscana and the supermarkets.[35] Among the most important of these positions have been the Chambers of Commerce, where the presidencies and the employee grades have been populated by Christian Democrats and notably by *fanfaniani*. One particular example was Giorgio Gori, DC regional secretary since 1976 and an employee of the Chamber of Commerce at Pistoia. The pattern repeated itself elsewhere, at Pisa and Grosseto where the provincial secretaries of the DC held posts in the Chambers of Commerce there. The Chambers are one of the DC's greatest sources of power, securing its base among the small and medium entrepreneurial class in Tuscany,[36] the presidents being appointed from Rome through a combined decision of the Ministers of Industry and Agriculture.

While tending to support the 'iceberg' thesis of Tamburrano,[37] these powerful footholds of the DC in the economic structure of the region of Tuscany have not amounted to the party here fitting the mass-clientilist model proposed by Caciagli for the DC in the south and specifically for the case of Catania in Sicily.[38] This is not only because clientilism has been a less widespread form of behaviour in Tuscany, but also as the DC has not enjoyed the same extent of local government channels of patronage or mass base. However, the closest version in the Tuscan DC of this clientilist practice developed under Fanfani, the best example still being the Bank of Monte dei Paschi in Siena. As the fifth largest bank in Italy, Monte dei Paschi has enjoyed both much economic power and considerable social prestige in the city and beyond, such as in financing projects throughout the province. It controls the Banca Toscana and the Credito Lombardo as subsidiaries, almost all agricultural trusts in Tuscany, many funds which serve the communes and local institutions, has holdings in transport, tourism and property and promotes a wide range of other activities, particularly cultural.[39] The special feature of the bank is that its administrative council is appointed by the public authorities and hence controlled by political parties: the president and two councillors by an inter-ministerial committee at Rome, four by the commune of Siena and one by the province. Until the 1970s, when the PCI began to change its position of non-involvement and to demand representation, this council had been monopolised by the DC and from the 1960s together with the PSI (as a result of the Centre-Left coalition); and Monte dei Paschi has accordingly for a long time been a battleground for *correnti* politics. One Sienese DC leader explained critically the relationship between the DC and the Bank of Monte dei Paschi:

> In the DC, first of all it is necessary to conquer the party, and then one conquers the bank. Therefore, it is clear that the conquest of

the party means the conquest of the bank ... in the operation of membership enrolment, it is not a question of seeking members who will support a political line as such, but one enrols one's father, mother, brothers, nephews — all the family, not for seeking votes but for prevailing inside the party. He who prevails imposes his options on others with regard to candidacies and inside the bank. This has been the constant mechanism that has now degenerated. This is the negative side of the DC that one must change.

This instrumental attitude towards party membership on the part of DC leaders for reasons of economic power leads one to consider the social structure of the DC's membership *in toto* as a final aspect of its mass character. While the party's economic power positions have had the effect of reinforcing its links with certain of the social groups supporting it — notably public employees — it is important to examine how successful it has been in recruiting different social classes.

There are always possible problems of accuracy in a close examination of a political party's membership, since the only source of detailed information is the party itself, and such problems are expecially likely in the case of the DC both because of its deliberate inflation of membership totals and because of the weaknesses and inefficiencies of party organisation. However, some double-checking with different internal party sources may assist this exercise; and it is proposed therefore to present official party figures since, despite calculated or accidental inaccuracies, they do reflect reasonably the proportion of social groups contained in the membership. First, the geographical distribution of DC membership in Tuscany demonstrates its numerical high points in the populous province of Florence and the Catholic stronghold of Lucca (Table 4.1).

If one compares with the data for PCI membership in the Tuscan provinces in 1975,[g] DC membership surpassed that of the PCI in the province of Lucca and was roughly equal to it in Massa-Carrara, but elsewhere was well behind the PCI totals especially in Florence, Livorno and Siena. This is again illustrated in Table 4.1 here when comparing membership of both parties as a percentage of the population. Clearly, the DC was far less of a mass party quantitatively in this 'Red' region, except where there was no significant Marxist sub-culture.

Secondly, this quantitative inferiority of DC membership in Tuscany should, one would suppose, have affected qualitatively its social composition in the region, but this has not dramatically been the case. As can be seen from the details in Table 4.2 the party is predominantly middle-class (especially of the white-collar variety), but with fair representation among workers.

Table 4.1: Geographical Distribution of DC Membership in Tuscany, 1975

Province	DC members	Members as % voters of DC	DC members as % population (1971)	Cf. PCI members as % population (1971)
Arezzo	7,263	9.90	2.37	7.36
Florence	12,231	5.18	1.07	7.06
Grosseto	5,063	12.37	2.34	7.08
Livorno	4,240	7.57	1.26	9.43
Lucca	11,952	9.93	3.14	2.49
Massa-Carrara	7,416	16.64	3.69	3.90
Pisa	6,233	8.26	0.16	6.12
Pistoia	4,158	7.88	1.63	6.56
Siena	6,135	13.43	2.38	16.36
Tuscany	64,691	8.68	1.86	7.18

Sources: Comitato Regionale della DC, Segretaria Organizzativa for DC membership data; percentage population calculated on basis of 1971 census figures for each province given in Unione Regionale delle Camere di Commercio della Toscana, *Quadri di Economia Toscana* (1974).

Table 4.2: Social Composition of DC Membership in Tuscany, 1975

Sector	Occupation	Totals	% Whole Total
Agriculture	Entrepreneurs	159	0.25
	Direct cultivators	5,479	8.47
	Sharecroppers	816	1.26
	Tenant farmers	21	0.03
	Agricultural labourers	771	1.19
	Miscellaneous	40	0.06
	Total	7,286	11.26
Industry	Entrepreneurs	572	0.89
	Employees	2,929	4.53
	Workers	11,102	17.16
	Miscellaneous	17	0.02
	Total	14,620	22.60
Commerce, Tourism & Transport	Entrepreneurs	2,637	4.08
	Dependents	1,914	2.96
	Miscellaneous	40	0.06
	Total	4,591	7.10

Sector	Occupation	Totals	% Whole Total
Credit & Insurance	Entrepreneurs	56	0.08
	Dependents	1,279	1.98
	Miscellaneous	1	0.00
	Total	1,336	2.06
Artisans	Entrepreneurs	2,381	3.68
	Dependents	1,279	1.98
	Miscellaneous	47	0.07
	Total	3,707	5.73
Free Professions	Professional people	1,084	1.68
	Dependents	184	0.29
	Doctors	21	0.03
	Engineers	9	0.01
	Architects	4	0.01
	Lawyers	9	0.01
	Commercial lawyers	10	0.02
	Veterinary surgeons	2	0.00
	Land-surveyors	15	0.02
	Accountants	4	0.01
	Journalists	1	0.00
	Miscellaneous	2	0.00
	Total	1,345	2.08
Public Employees	State employees	5,693	8.80
	Para-state corporations	1,153	1.78
	Local government dependents	2,748	4.25
	Public insurance	246	0.38
	Hospitals, etc.	876	1.35
	University professors	6	0.01
	Secondary school teachers	53	0.08
	Middle school teachers	72	0.11
	Primary school teachers	88	0.14
	Miscellaneous	70	0.11
	Total	11,005	17.01
Students		4,119	6.37
Pensioners		4,689	7.25
Housewives		9,712	15,01
Others		1,310	2.03
Unemployed		349	0.54
No occupation		622	0.96
	Total	64,691	100.00

Source: DC, Direzione Centrale, Ufficio Organizzazione Interna.

Making a straight comparison with the social structure of DC membership in the whole of Italy, it does seem that the Tuscan party as a whole was less untypical sociologically than one might assume in this 'Red' region. There was a similar proportion of those employed in commerce, credit and insurance, the free professions and artisan work, although all these were relatively small sectors. In Tuscany, there was a marginally higher proportion of public employees and those engaged in industry (including workers), with a smaller proportion in agriculture. Among public employees, there is a clear predominance of those employed by the state and the para-state and local government agencies, thus indicating the party's clientilist roots. The largest difference compared with the national average was the significantly lower proportion of housewives in the DC in Tuscany. They generally provided about a quarter of the party's membership (Table 4.3).

Various brief comments are necessary to put these data into perspective. The apparent reflection in Tuscany of the national structure of membership disguised both regional variations in Italy (e.g. a stronger agricultural base in the south; a stronger working-class base in the north), and also sub-regional variations. A party's membership composition naturally mirrored the particular social environment from which it drew its base, and Tuscany's social structure was, viewed very crudely, closer to the national average than many other regions. However, it is more instructive to examine provincial differences. The basic contrast between Lucca and the rest of Tuscany is once more evident as the DC's stronger base among workers and peasants in the former substantially raised the average for the whole region. The Catholic sub-cultural factor was the main reason, with the additional feature that the DC's stronghold in the agricultural sector among *coltivatori diretti* was accounted for to a large degree by the traditional concentration of this occupational group in the province of Lucca. Another group worth comment are housewives. The lower proportion for Tuscany derived almost certainly from the impact of the 'Red' sub-culture with the socially conformist pressures this created whether through male influence or the environment in general (notably the weak influence of religion). The same feature is suggested by the lower proportion of women members as a whole in Tuscany: 26.84 per cent compared with 37.22 per cent for Italy.[40]

Comparing the DC's membership with that of the PCI in Tuscany, the differences which emerge cause no great surprise: the latter is very much more of a working-class party in its social base, and generally weaker among the bourgeoisie as a whole, in particular among

Table 4.3: Social Composition of DC Membership in Italy, 1972

Sector	Occupation	Totals	% Whole Total
Agriculture	Entrepreneurs	8,056	0.44
	Direct cultivators	189,899	10.39
	Sharecroppers	13,202	0.72
	Tenant farmers	1,902	0.10
	Agricultural labourers	63,753	3.49
	Total	276,812	15.14
Industry	Entrepreneurs	15,007	0.82
	Employees	58,572	3.20
	Workers	236,891	12.96
	Total	310,470	16.98
Commerce & Tourism	Entrepreneurs	70,678	3.87
	Dependents	32,615	1.78
	Total	103,293	5.65
Credit & Insurance	Entrepreneurs	971	0.05
	Dependents	15,996	0.87
	Total	16,967	0.92
Artisans	Entrepreneurs	59,912	3.28
	Dependents	26,983	1.48
	Total	86,895	4.76
Free Professions	Professional people	29,143	1.59
	Dependents	3,327	0.18
	Total	32,470	1.77
Public Employees		227,780	12.46
Students		100,832	5.52
Pensioners		126,435	6.92
Housewives		450,964	24.67
Miscellaneous		94,735	5.18
	Whole total	1,827,653	100.00

Source: Calculations based on figures in PCI, Ufficio Elettorale e di Statistica, *Raccolta di dati sull'Organizzazione 1971-1975*, Vol. II, 1976, originally drawn from DC sources.

white-collar workers.[h] The strength of the Tuscan PCI among the agricultural class also explains the lower proportional representation of the DC here compared with its national average. Nevertheless, despite the middle-class bias among its membership the DC could make some claim to being an inter-class party (*partito popolare*) even in a 'Red' region like Tuscany. This was supported by the evidence of local membership lists where available. At Sesto Fiorentino (Florence) one-third of the DC membership, according to a local party survey of 1970, was working-class, well above the national average though reflecting of course the local economic structure.[41] At Peccioli (Pisa), the membership list revealed the following composition: seven white-collar employees, nine workers, seven in agriculture, five artisans, two housewives, one entrepreneur, one businessman and one student.[42] The level of workers was relatively high in both these cases, but in other communes where DC activists were interviewed the same general pattern of a fair representation of the three elements — white-collar employees, workers and peasants — was evident.[43] Factors confirmed in interviews which tended to support the consistency and stability of DC membership in these sectors were: the strong importance of family tradition outside the cities, and linked to this the persistence of the Catholic tradition whether as an outcome of the (restricted) influence of religion or as an expression of a lay Catholic culture. The effectiveness of party organisation seemed to play an insignificant part; more likely an influence was the role of the DC in economic life, especially the public sector, which explained the high proportion of public employees and other white-collar workers in the party.

In conclusion, it may be said that even in a political environment like Tuscany, which has traditionally not been highly favourable to its operation, the DC emerged as a mass party. The Tuscan DC succeeded in establishing itself as such despite the region's anti-clerical traditions, because it managed to harness substantial support from outside practising Catholic circles, notably among lay Catholics as well as conservative groups. At the same time, its Catholic connection made it more possible for the DC to spread its inter-class appeal, as is evident from its membership structure. Tuscany offers in this respect an interesting case-study in view of its dominant lay culture. The ambiguity of the DC's position in seeking simultaneous support from both Catholic and lay elements created serious problems for the party in the 1970s, when issues like divorce and abortion arose forcing the DC to show its confessional colours. All the same, the problem of responding to the referendum result of 1974 was considerably reduced by the mobilising effect among Catholic and conservative groups caused by the rise of the PCI from the mid-1970s. The DC's subsequent revival owed much to the factor of party-political competition.

Therefore, the challenge facing the party as a socio-political force in the mid- and late-1970s was far from being one-dimensional. There has been a surprising stability of the DC's social base, which phenomenon may be explained partly by the economic roots of the DC, but more important has been its complex relationship with the Catholic movement. This relationship is difficult to analyse and is subject to much variation from area to area, but in general it has had a mutually reinforcing effect on both 'party' and 'movement'. This is primarily because of the socio-political rather than religious influence of the 'Catholic world'.

(c) The DC as a Structured Party: the Formality and Reality

It follows from the earlier discussion that structurally the DC will not easily fit any specific categorisation of political parties, although the description 'loose-associational' is the most relevant. This is both because the DC illustrates in an almost classic way the general assumption that permanent governing parties neglect their own organisation, and a consequence of the peculiarities in its case of the party/movement relationship whereby the former may depend much on the latter for the mobilisation of its supporters and the achievement of other tasks normally allotted to a party organisation. As one Tuscan DC leader commented, 'if everything in Italy had depended on the factor of party organisation, we would have lost'.

The DC is not a mass-structured party, because the organisational bonds which link its mass base to its effective structure are highly informal, generally loose and certainly not subject to any strict bureaucratic framework. The party does possess formally a very articulated structure, one similar in its hierarchical levels to that of the PCI (local *sezioni*, provincial committees as the intermediary unit and the national structure represented by such organs as the Central Directorate and the National Council), but it lacks a party machine.[i] Statutory norms have often been ignored in the history of the DC,[44] a supreme example being the provision that 'it is not permissible to construct within the party organised groups or factions' (Article 22 of DC Statutes, 1976), while the actual existence of the *correnti* is a major individual feature of the DC. In short, Duverger's distinction between statutory and informal procedures in party structural relationships is far more applicable to the

DC than to the PCI.ʲ This section aims to look at both formal and informal procedures in the DC in order to draw some conclusions about its structural relationships and hence its operation as a political party.

Concerning the mechanism of the DC's formal structure, it has been characteristic to note the low level of organisational continuity and the absence of organisational efficiency,[45] which although broadly true fail to explain fully the considerable variation in the DC's structural presence already indicated[k] and to do justice to the complexity of factors which have motivated or induced its organisational life. These factors may be reduced to three essential features: the tradition of the voluntary element, the effects of the party/movement relationship and the DC's governing role and the problems of participation among the membership.

First, while all mass political parties in democracies depend heavily on voluntary effort among their activists the absence of and even aversion to bureaucratic methods in the DC has placed a great onus on the voluntary element. The attachment to voluntary work has drawn strength from a deep-set mentality among party activists, deriving from a traditional bourgeois dislike of the values associated with 'party' (a word omitted from the DC's name) partly because of the Fascist experience but more owing to the belief among many activists that it is a term of the political Left,[46] an aversion significantly less evident among younger DC leaders and activists. Linked to this attitude is the party's conceptual attachment to the value of 'Freedom' (*Libertà*) – as in the words of one middle-aged local *sezione* secretary, in that position for over ten years, 'if I had to be paid party secretary, I would not do it – I am free'. Another older local DC leader, *sezione* secretary for more than 25 years, explained:

> All that we do, we do gratuitously. I as a political secretary have never received any sum. Our organisation is established on this basis, on this point of view. We are all voluntary workers, whether in the youth groups, the women's groups, the GIP organised in the factories especially at the Piaggio works or at the *sezione* level.[47]

This was an obvious point of contrast with the PCI as an organised party.

It is of course a system as well as a mentality. Local party officials are not salaried and are not regarded as 'functionaries', which is also generally true of provincial party leaders, so that their work for the DC is done 'in the afternoon and after supper'. It is therefore usual for them to be employed in a permanent occupation during the day, with provincial secretaries holding such posts as employee of a Chamber of Commerce or teacher, allowing them a certain flexibility of working hours.[48] This part-time unsalaried function of party leadership at the lower and intermediary levels of the DC, combined with their own employment elsewhere, is made possible by the fact that such personnel have come predominantly from the professional classes, where working hours are less rigid,[49] so that they are able to devote their free time and much more to managing the party as was indicated, for instance, by the author's questionnaire with members of the DC's regional committee in Tuscany.[50] This situation naturally has had possible effects regarding the regularity and efficiency of party management. Party offices at the intermediary level furthermore have often had to rely on a minimal number of salaried staff: there were, for example, at the provincial headquarters of the Lucca DC only three full-time officials; while the office of the Tuscan regional committee in Florence employed one full-time and three part-time staff who were paid by Rome.[51] The DC was called by some of its interviewees 'a party of volunteers and dilettantes', but whatever the capabilities of individual leaders it could not claim to have anything like a party machine. As one former provincial party leader emphasised:

> The DC has never had its own *apparato*, it has always had a dilettantish *apparato* in the organisational sense ... the party is composed of a base [i.e. activists] who are incredibly eager, devote their own free time to the party and even give up some of their own work, thus using all that time left over from work.[52]

The DC in Tuscany has nevertheless had more reason to develop effective articulated structures than in many other areas of the country, confonted as it has been by a highly organised Communist Party. The stimulus provided by this party rivalry had the effect after the War of a marked expansion of DC membership, as in other areas of 'Red' dominance,[53] but even here there were problems arising from the voluntaristic mentality. Furthermore, there were practical difficulties relating to the fact that, unlike the PCI, the DC could not outside the province of Lucca draw organisational strength from the experience of Resistance activity. A former postwar DC provincial secretary described vividly his own efforts in founding the party locally at Montieri, a commune in the north of Grosseto province:

The Communists were very organised from the Resistance, they had the men ... We, however, had to improvise. When I founded the DC at Montieri with a group of young men, I did so on my own initiative after following the news on the radio, but nobody gave me directions from Grosseto. When the German army passed north and the Americans came, the Communists suddenly appeared already organised: 'This is the membership card of anti-Fascism' they said to people. We lacked an organisation, so the DC was born on the basis of personal initiative and then grew day by day. At one point, this small group began to obtain use of the public hall. We founded the party in my kitchen, we were 18 young people meeting together. We signed our names on a piece of paper, and then decided to set up a *sezione*, to accept a programme – a very synthetic thing ... we established contacts with people and began to hold meetings, then provincial meetings and congresses. Slowly we developed a structure and organisation – from nothing! It took root and became a plant.[54]

Such voluntaristic approaches countered opposition from Fanfani with his managerial style of party leadership. He achieved a personal dominance over much of the DC in Tuscany (except notably the northwest) from the early 1950s, and in many areas replaced older party personnel, some of whom had been active in the pre-Fascist PPI. Fanfani succeeded in creating some elements of a party machine, although it took the form less of a bureaucratic organisation than of a power structure based more on his personal dynamic energy and his links with economic agencies.[1] Fanfani's indelicate methods of operating also alienated groups in the party, so that with his eventual political decline much of the structural network suffered accordingly. Many of the essential voluntaristic elements had in fact remained in the party, especially at the local level. The case of Fanfani illustrated moreover the importance of the individual effort by party leaders, a necessary precondition for organisational effectiveness in the absence of a bureaucratic tradition, and this was still true of the DC in the 1970s. In this respect, there could be marked differences between provincial secretaries. According to a DC provincial official, 'the good provincial leaders are those who during the week make a tour of the *sezioni*, and therefore speak with the leaders of the *sezioni* trying to understand what are the problems of the local party'; while some provincial secretaries 'never move themselves, simply decide to call a meeting of the committee or directorate, which one must do...'

This dependence of the DC on the individual application of its leadership personnel and the ensuing variability of performance was all the more apparent at the local level. The official of the Lucca DC responsible for party organisation criticised the state of affairs in that province:

> There is organisation at the base, but it is not that it functions. There are *sezioni*, and secretaries of the *sezioni*, but in practice if there is anything to be done now and again it is only the *sezione* secretary who does the work. Around him are another four or five persons, who form the directorate . . . they practically hardly ever see each other. They join the party for reasons of friendship or some other reason . . . the *sezioni* are rarely active, unfortunately — many don't have an office, sometimes they are in the house of a secretary or someone else . . . out of the 153 *sezioni*, there are 23 or 30 on which one can rely in the sense of doing work, because many *sezioni* are rather nominal.[55]

Secondly, the effects of the party/movement relationship and the party's governing role have determined the insufficient state of DC organisation. In other words, it is not just the system of the party structure and the attitudes embodied in it which have worked against the development of a viable party machine, but also the dependence on the Catholic movement which has made it less necessary. The above-described case of Lucca was the best example of this situation in Tuscany, one further reinforced by the DC's continuing control over the vast majority of local administrations in the province even after 1975. A greater awareness of the weak state of party organisation during the course of the 1970s, however, demanded some response from provincial party leaders. One provincial leader of the Lucca DC diagnosed the cause of the problem as the party's stronger concern with its own internal affairs than with its external relations with society:

> The *sezione* has increasingly assumed the character of a structure reduced in efficiency and to some extent detached from the social context, with the consequence that it expresses growing sensitivity to internal problems — election, congresses, appointments and the manoeuvres of different groups — to the detriment of those external factors, that with the changing relations within society offer the party some political opportunity and the chance for an organisational role. The most evident effects are the growing aridness of internal democratic life, the general emergence of the principle of uncontrolled representation, the shortage of alternative leadership

personnel and the degeneration of the structure of *sezioni*, arising from the fact that almost inadvertently the *sezione* has gradually become an element of the power system at the base. Therefore, it is necessary to pay heed to this disease that is undermining the *sezioni*, to give them back the competence to 'carry out politics' . . .[56]

It is relevant to note that this new awareness of the party's structural deficiencies corresponded with the rise from 1976 of a pro-Zaccagnini leadership coalition at Lucca whose declared aim was party 'renewal'. It is often one characteristic of internal DC power struggles that organisational criticism may be a pretext if not a reason for rival political ambitions. 'Outsider' groups within the party, notably from the Left in Tuscany because of traditional *fanfaniani* dominance, have sought to discredit the ruling coalition of *correnti*, and these 'revelations' can provide an interesting reflection on the state of the party. Such a form of behaviour preceded the collapse of Fanfani's dominance in the Siena DC earlier in the 1970s, for here party organisation had suffered from the reliance of the DC on its economic power positions, especially the Bank of Monte dei Paschi, and was in a very moribund state. The document of the list 'Democratic Alternative' presented at the 25th ordinary congress of the Sienese DC in December 1972 drew attention to the fundamental weaknesses of party organisation in the province:

> On the organisational plane, the Sienese DC has shown up to now as having obvious deficiencies. At the provincial level, the executive has always had available no more than very few leaders, who are isolated and not in a position — except on few occasions during a limited period — to pursue a sufficient role in the different sectors of activity. At the local level, the *sezioni* have in the large majority of cases 'struggled along' in an abandoned state, without ensuring for the DC a tolerable political presence in the municipal councils and in local life. At the intermediary (i.e. zonal) level, attempts to co-ordinate the *sezioni* and organise activity have interested only some of the different zones, and in this improvised and discontinuous way have left things almost as they were at the beginning.
>
> The renewal of leadership personnel in the party has proceeded too slowly and marginally. At the local level, this phenomenon is largely accounted for not by the determination of 'older' leaders but rather the objective lack of political opportunity created by the failure of the *sezioni* to interest young people in party activity and political life. At the provincial level, renewal has faced difficulties

and been delayed mainly because of the attachment of the present leaders to their own power positions . . . For some years, the Siena DC has followed a way of conducting politics which has mortified the democratic and Christian characteristics of the party. On the one hand, debate has been weakened and political apathy has grown. On the other hand, the tendency to instrumentalise power and let clientilist and individual interests prevail has been consolidated.[57]

It is evident that political motives have been the predominant factor behind the call for organisational change in the DC, whether of an internal factional or external party nature relating to its general political position. The latter motive became more visible with the rise of the Left in the mid-1970s, and the DC's subsequent loss of power in various localities and need therefore to depend more on its own resources. Very often the party had relied on the prestige and influence of its local mayors, especially in the rural areas, as its integrative force and as a substitute for organisation; while in the cities its political control and support from local bureaucracy had neutralised interest in developing an effective party structure. The DC's loss of the important commune of Florence in 1975 had a profound shock effect on the party there, so that in the following years it was forced to develop its own facilities. New structures were developed to accord with the recently instituted *quartieri* (district units) in the city, while a growing involvement in local issues became apparent, notably among younger members. A Florentine leader from the DC Left explained:

> The role of opposition is very much more difficult, because we lack certain instruments for operating. Holding power in the commune of Florence meant having an *apparato*, and now we must invent one ourselves. Therefore, there is greater care taken with political problems. For example, one used to talk before about some specific problems concerning Florence, such as the railway or the airport, this was studied exclusively at the level of departmental heads in the local government, while the party did not discuss them or very little. Now these matters are by force of circumstances worked out and discussed within the party, and then brought to the attention of the DC group in the municipal council. It is clear that the party has to involve itself more because we have to make decisions in opposition to those taken by the municipal administration . . . So, there is a greater attention to issues especially at Florence, because there are the *quartieri* councils, and we have had to adapt the *sezioni*

in the city to the new political geography. Once we had 25 *sezioni*, which were created according to tradition if only following parish divisions. Today, just as the city is divided into 14 *quartieri* the *sezioni* have been regrouped so that they correspond to this administrative unit.[58]

Thirdly, although the political challenge to and loss of power by the DC clearly stimulated greater party activity in several areas a traditional problem for the DC has been weak membership participation at the grass-roots outside election time. This has reinforced the electoral orientation of the party and the discrepancy between the formal (or theoretical) existence of an articulated structure and its frequently lethargic state in reality. Giuseppe Bartolomei, one of Fanfani's closest colleagues in the Tuscan party, had admitted the problem of a largely passive membership back in 1963:

> The mass of members and the electorate, rather than being entrusted with the autonomous activism of the *sezioni* and the provincial committees, have become the object of a mere propagandistic form of contact that aims simply to obtain that type of passive consensus that is still apparent, in the best cases, in taking out membership, participation in a party or public meeting or only by voting in elections.[59]

A similar picture could be drawn of the level of party activity in the 1970s, outside certain active centres, like Florence, and may be attributed to a variety of factors: the effects of organisational neglect and the lack of interest among the leadership in a systematic membership policy, but also the habits of mind and behaviour of DC members and the reasons why they joined. An official of the Lucca provincial party drew attention to the latter factors:

> People are just not politicised and don't participate in the life of the party. When there are elections they vote for the DC, at least in the Lucchesia. But they don't join the party, for which reason there is a strong difference between members and voters ... many members joined out of habit, not because they felt a duty to participate in something. It is simply a habit ... a member since '50, '48, the older ones — they pay the monthly quota ... even when a *sezione* secretary goes to their homes, notwithstanding his invitations to come to the *sezione*, they don't budge ...[60]

Such attitudes have inevitably reduced the scope for continuous organisational activity by the DC. Attendance at party members' meetings, which are in any case irregular, varied considerably with a level, according to party sources, usually within the range of ten per cent to 20 per cent,[61] although academic research on Italy as a whole has put the average lower at between five per cent and ten per cent.[62]

One further factor which should not be forgotten is the influence of the *correnti* (internal party factions) in filtering membership recruitment of the DC. As one young delegate at a meeting of the Florence DC commented openly: 'When a person asks about joining the DC, then they are anxious at once to know who sent him and to classify him into a *corrente*.'[63] Personalistic reasons for signing up with the DC have meant that membership is regarded as a matter of loyalty to individual leaders rather than an outlet for political activity properly speaking, as one DC source in the province of Lucca noted:

> Unfortunately, organisation is not based on members who come spontaneously to vote or join the party voluntarily – it is the game of power, the game of the *correnti*. You have an *onorevole* [M.P.], a party secretary or some personality, who has friends who contact other friends with a favour, a good turn, a 'recommendation' as is the practice in Italy. A group of friends becomes close to this person and for him they join the party, pay the membership fee. But in practice they don't participate in party life ... therefore, the party depends on certain persons, on power, on certain local figures.

Accordingly, the idea of a membership policy in the sense of a systematic recruitment of new members and the encouragement of their active political involvement has been alien to prevalent attitudes and practices in the DC. An over-riding reason in the past had been the party's stable electoral performance, as one local DC leader from Siena province pointed out with some critical allusions to the PCI:

> So far as recruitment is concerned, the DC does not run after members – because of the electorate of the DC with the 14 million votes it has, with 1,600,000 members. So you understand that many are sympathisers who vote for the DC ... we don't take so many members, we take them when they join, but we don't have to go looking for them, we don't go in for capillary propaganda to make people join the DC. We prefer it that outside the DC there are those who say they are close to us rather than have them as members only

to make up a total.⁶⁴

From the mid-1970s, there were, however, signs of some new patterns emerging, not so much because of deliberate policy on the part of the DC as in reaction to the threat to the party's position from the PCI. In many areas, both urban and rural, local *sezioni* recorded a rise in new membership from the time of the 1975–1976 elections. At Peccioli (Pisa), it was observed that 'there has been a certain revival of the DC, and it seems that behind it is this: many people have approached the party not out of conviction for the DC but as an anti-Communist matter'.⁶⁵ Similarly, at Sesto Fiorentino near Florence there had been some influx of young members after 1975, predominantly from Catholic families as a 'reaction to the emerging possibility of Communist hegemony',⁶⁶ while there was evidence of the DC youth movement becoming more active in recruiting new members particularly in the schools. This growth of more continuous party activity was particularly noticeable at Florence, where it expressed itself in a more deliberate effort to attract new members to the DC. *Circoscrizione 3*, a monthly information bulletin, started in late 1976 for the DC in six *quartieri* of south Florence, included notices urging people to 'Participate personally yourself by joining the DC, which guarantees you freedom and democracy — Join the DC, and you will be a protagonist in your time.'⁶⁷ Another area of new activity in the DC structure has been the growing articulation and impact following the 1975 regional elections of the GIP or *Gruppi di Impegno Politico* (Groups of Political Involvement), the new organisation for Christian Democrats working in factories, such as the Piaggio at Pontedera, and also in public employment. The GIP have been especially active at Florence, Livorno and in the Lucca area, Tuscany being one of the regions with the highest number of such groups.

These new indications of more consistent party activity did not, however, amount to any radical change in the overall approach to organisation in the DC, partly because such developments were localised and not uniform, and also since they were a response to new mobilisation among Catholic and conservative groups allied to the DC rather than any elaborated organisational strategy on the part of the leadership. These new patterns of organisational activity did not essentially alter the picture of the DC as a mass party with minimal bureaucratic procedures.

The limited importance of such organisational changes in the later 1970s as well as the DC's generally weak potential for structural reform becomes clearer on examining a final aspect of formal structures in the DC, namely the dilatory and largely unsuccessful process of party structural regionalisation. A study of the Tuscan DC in the early 1970s concluded on the inability of the party to adapt its own structures to the recently introduced regional level of government in Italy: 'In these last two years of existence, the regional party organs have not developed the role which according to the statutes is within their competence ... for example, the different weight of the various provinces has still prevailed in decision-making, so that provincial interests have continued to be felt very strongly and the regional spirit has been little in evidence.'[68] During the rest of the 1970s, there was no major change in this internal party situation, hence confirming features of the DC's structural relationships already discussed: the low bureaucratic consciousness, the inefficiency of organisational practice and the interlacing of 'informal' power distribution in the DC with the formal party structure, whereby an articulation of the latter is only allowed by consent of the former. The possibility for external stimulation may exist, but it depends on unprecedented political pressure on the DC and even then is likely, as we have seen, to produce improvised rather than systematic modes of organisation.

The creation of the regional level of state structure throughout Italy in 1970 did not act as a powerful agent in initiating any serious structural re-thinking inside the DC. A psychological factor reinforced internal party interests in explaining this reluctance to embark on any regionalisation of the party structure, for throughout most of the postwar period the DC had demonstrated a marked hostility to any idea of introducing regional government as such for anti-Communist and other reasons.[m] A regional structure of the DC has always existed as a formality, essentially as a matter of pure administrative co-operation, and admittedly since 1970 this structure has been given new statutory powers: the regional committee is now elected by the regional congress (instead of its members being chosen by the individual provincial committees as previously) and it has been strengthened in its political role. The DC Statutes (Article 67, 1976) now specify that 'the regional committee expresses and deliberates the general lines of the party's regional policy'. However, by contrast with the PCI the DC has lacked the same political motivation (the association for the PCI with its own legitimacy and growing role in government) and any comparable bureaucratic drive. As already discussed, the PCI in Tuscany also faced problems of overcoming traditional modes of internal party behaviour not to mention the impact of *municipalismo* in this region,[n] so it was not really surprising that these problems were multiplied in the case of the DC because of its more informal pattern of internal structural relationships.

By and large, the same problems have afflicted the regionalisation of the DC's structure in other regions, although the presence in some of them of well-qualified or powerful personalities as regional party secretaries (such as Lombardy and Emilia-Romagna) either encouraged more debate on the question or lent some personal weight to the newly reinforced regional structures. In Tuscany, Ivo Butini (regional secretary, 1973-1976), a long-time protégé and colleague of Fanfani and in his own right having widely recognised dialectical and managerial skills, gave this position some individual weight, but his performance eventually suffered from internal party divisions resulting from his association with Fanfani's decline as a political force in Tuscany. On the basis of his own experience as regional secretary, and previously as provincial secretary for Florence (1963-1969), Butini took a sceptical view about the chances of regionalisation in the DC:

> It has not happened, and probably will not happen, unless we deal with the substance of the powers of the regional committees. The province is a very powerful structure in the psychology of the Italians; while the region has a very weak structure. In this psychological and institutional framework . . . with this quality and quantity of the powers of the provincial committees, the powers of the regional committees are absolutely theoretical. As a matter of fact, they have been exercised at least from the time I was regional secretary in appointments to regional institutions which have regularly been contested by the provinces, also with the votes of regional councillors who had taken a different line in the regional committee. At this moment, this is a structure which is quite formal and does not cut any ice in the smallest way in the process of taking decisions in the provincial committees.[69]

This emphatic judgement was generally supported by the problems in making the regional structure function during the 1970s. The regional committee met only intermittently (e.g. twice in the first nine months of 1978), unlike the regularity of provincial committee meetings (at Lucca normally once every 1½-2 months), and tended not to exert itself. According to the Lucca provincial secretary, himself an active member of the regional committee:

> The persons who count tend to go on the provincial committees which pursue their own political line, have their own weight, while with the regional committee power is extremely small. It is reduced to following activity in the regional council . . . sending political personnel to the regional committee means they are of second rank and not really interested in making this organ work fully. Then, there are difficulties of liaison, of lack of time . . . a combination of political and technical factors which altogether result in considerable immobilism.[70]

The fundamental problem has been vested interests within the party structure (i.e. the dominance of the provincial committees and secretaries at the intermediary level), as well as deeply-rooted political attitudes — one local leader offered the view that 'the regional dimension has not yet entered the mentality of party life'. According to several interviewees, the solution lay in first of all granting the regional structure further statutory powers, such as the right to determine the composition of party lists for regional elections and a degree of self-finance.[71] They stressed it was 'indispensable' to make the regional level independent from the provincial committees, but admitted that without the PCI's centralistic methods and reliance on party discipline this would be a profoundly difficult task, although time could help. Even then, statutory changes alone were not enough, for experience in the later 1970s revealed an ambivalence with a verbal acknowledgement of the need for effective regional structures but an underlying reluctance to implement them. As one younger provincial secretary explained, he had encountered a positive initial response but in practice resistance in putting, for instance, the new zonal structures into effect: 'I met resistance in following up this operation, in setting it in motion — all were in agreement, "Yes, yes, yes" . . . but they were adverse to applying themselves, and there the difficulty arose, especially among the old ones.'[72] This strong *verbal* or *conceptual* support for party regionalisation was also evident in the author's questionnaires conducted with DC regional councillors and members of the regional committee, even though many of them held or had held important positions within the Tuscan party's provincial structures.[73] Such ambivalence could be attributed to a defensiveness in the DC, or more specifically to the effects of external pressures deriving from the operation and legitimacy of regional government but the failure of these actually to overcome internal party interests.

A stronger interest in a more decisive role for the regional party structure in fact arose in the second half of the 1970s with the transfer in 1977 of further administrative powers to the regional governments under Law 382. This combined with internal pressures in the DC for party 'renewal' in general, and the control secured by the Left over the two weightiest provincial parties in the Tuscan DC — those of Lucca and Florence — in the same year. However, prospects for substantial change had to be considered in the light of the complex and sometimes contradictory factors involved in the discussion of party 'renewal', and last but not least of the nature of the DC's informal structural relationships, to which we now turn.

'Informal structural relationships' in the DC principally mean the role of the DC's internal *correnti* or factions as the predominant mechanism in effect directing internal party affairs. The DC as an organisational entity could be described as loose-associational working within a formally articulated structure. The absence of strong bureaucratic procedures in the party has been accompanied by the presence of the *correnti* as important channels at the vertical level of local/national elite communication. While they have operated within the formal structure in the acquisition and retention of leadership positions, the *correnti* have themselves been institutionalised, although varying in their degree of organisational effectiveness — in Tuscany, the *fanfaniani* historically being the strongest in this sense, and some of the Left *correnti* (e.g. the *morotei* and the *Base*) the weakest.

The *correnti* of the DC have been described as representing 'a system of sub-parties'.[74] Indeed, some of them have existed for a long time and have a distinct identity with their own paraphernalia of offices, press organs and financial arrangements and their own recognised leaders, but it is more relevant to discuss their kinetic political behaviour than somewhat statically their institutional character. This may be more easily done by taking a case-study approach and focusing on their operation at the sub-national level.

During the 1970s, the internal party situation of the *correnti* underwent some transformation. There was a certain breakdown of *corrente* discipline with fragmentation and re-grouping of forces and altogether a new fluidity in their positions. This reflected generally the political crisis of the DC in this decade, and in particular the challenge to its role by the PCI. One Florentine DC leader, himself a *fanfaniano* by background, described this transformation:

> Somehow the organisation of the individual *correnti* has become less strict. That is, once they had their own organisation, their own

acknowledged leader, their own executive, their own way of publicising themselves and of meeting, their own rules that led to decisions being taken in the *correnti* before bringing them forward directly in the party — in which situation someone who was not strong in a *corrente* did not count for anything in the party. Something has changed in this sense, because at this moment these firm laws of the *correnti* do not exist any more. There has been a certain increase in the shades and gradation of relationships (*una certa sfumatura di rapporti*), the party organs have begun essentially to follow their own logic somewhat, and they have succeeded sometimes in breaking the over-strict logic of the *correnti*.[75]

Despite this development, the possibility of radical change with the dispersal or collapse of the *correnti* system was unlikely so long as certain procedural and attitudinal practices remained unaltered: the policy motion plus list method of elections to the various party organs; the personalistic element in leader/member relationships; clientilistic forms of behaviour deriving from the DC's power positions, and its continuing command of national office; the strong electoral orientation of party activity, and the preference votes system which encourages factional behaviour; and the very low level of organisational commitment in the DC. Some of these practices were constitutionally-based and therefore theoretically at least open to revision, while others were less easily altered because of the difficulty of changing traditional modes of party behaviour. The combined weight of these factors must be set against the apparently fresh outlook of many younger leaders promoted especially to intermediary positions in the party structure under Zaccagnini's Secretaryship of the DC from 1975. The pro-Zaccagnini forces were in fact themselves based on a loose consensus of Left-wing *correnti* called the 'Zaccagnini line'.

Looking at Tuscany, the party's development in the 1970s illustrated well the changing balance in *correnti* alignments because the DC here was once the main stronghold of Fanfani, whose *corrente* underwent serious fragmentation in the mid-1970s leading to the new dominance of the pro-Zaccagnini Left in the later part of the decade. It is worth examining closely this process to see how much there was any significant metamorphosis in party leadership and management. The Tuscan example further touches on two basic problems concerning differentation between *correnti* in general — the somewhat artificial classification of them into power-oriented *correnti* and policy-oriented *correnti* made in some academic studies, and the difficulty of establishing a clear-cut ideological distinction between them all.

The *fanfaniani* as the dominant group of second-generation party leaders in the DC, who emerged in the 1950s, owed their historical origins to the postwar party Left, but then become part of a widely, based centre grouping and predominantly associated with the exercise of power with their leader's prominence at the national level. In Tuscan, or more specifically Florentine, politics the *fanfaniani* remained, however, as one element in a Leftward grouping — the *Iniziativa di base* — which took control in the party there in 1955. The *fanfaniani* formed an alliance with the Left to support La Pira'a administration in the regional capital, but this broke up in the mid-1960s when they took full control of the Florentine provincial party.[76] By the 1970s, Fanfani and his *corrente* had come to be viewed regionally as well as nationally as ideologically on the fundamentalist Right of the DC. Thus, in ideological terms the *fanfaniani* had moved from Left to Right over twenty years, but the key factor in their behaviour was the acquisition and retention of political power.

It has been a feature of 'outsider' *correnti* in the DC to espouse more of an ideological position, such as with the anti-Fanfani Left in Tuscany during the later 1960s and, it might be added, the *fanfaniani* themselves from the mid-1970s. In this sense, the power and policy orientations of individual *correnti* are interlinked, though the balance between the two may change over time depending on their success in party politics. For example, a group called the 'New Left' presented a document to the provincial congress of the Florence DC in March 1969 stressing the need for an 'open party' and commenting revealingly on the confusing distinction between 'Left' and 'Right' in reference to internal party affairs:

> Too often it happens that members, despite the almost total lack at the party base of internal conflict and even though united on many common demands for renewal, find themselves on opposite sides without any real motives, each one with his label, and reduced to being bearers of votes in support of positions of power that others administer without the possibility of effective control.
>
> At the same time, the *correnti* labels constitute a cover for agreements without serious political content or with contradictory perspectives, in the name of distinctions between Right and Left that with changing times lose most of their meaning.
>
> This rigidity, this way of operating and above all of making members behave for the sake of wasteful schemes has in the course

of time involved all internal party forces ... the most notable case is perhaps the *fanfaniani* who, created as a strongly innovatory group and still consisting at the base of many elements with progressive aspirations, and while maintaining a Left-wing label, now follow a role of immobilism in the national balance of power of the party, in which the only evident political objective seems to be to make their leader president of the Republic.[77]

The document went on to quote from Nicola Pistelli, a prominent leader of the DC Left in Florence until his death in 1964, that 'it is not so that the *correnti* of the Left always contain men of the Left, and that the *correnti* of the Right always contain conservative attitudes'. Indeed, the problem with locating ideological elements in the DC is that the various *correnti* have undulated between different tendencies. When one focuses closely on the internal DC it is like looking into a party-political kaleidoscope, where one slight turn may appear to change the whole ideological spectrum. The relative importance of the policy as against power orientations of the *correnti* was suggested by the attitude and behaviour of the new leadership which replaced the *fanfaniani* dominance in the Siena DC in 1973. One former leader of this new group later associated with the 'Zaccagnini line' commented cynically from his own experience: 'He who adheres to a so-called conservative *corrente*, that of Fanfani, is more progressive than he who adheres to a *corrente* presenting itself as 'renewal', but uses the old methods of clientelism' — a question of new leadership wine in old clientelist bottles!

The *fanfaniani* had in building up their predominance in the Tuscan DC come to control majorities in six of the nine provincial committees, the three exceptions being at Pisa (dominance by the Centre-Right *dorotei*, originally a secessionist group of *fanfaniani*), Livorno (*dorotei* allied with the social-Catholic *basisti* of the Left) and Massa Carrara (control by the *Base corrente*). The *fanfaniani* were unquestionably powerful at Arezzo as Fanfani's own home base, and remained very strong at Florence despite the history of divisions in the party there and the conflicts during the 1960s between Butini as Fanfani's anchor man and the supporters of La Pira. At the Florentine Provincial congress in 1969, the *fanfaniani* had once again reasserted their absolute majority — 25 seats on the provincial committee, compared with eleven for the *dorotei* and six for the *Base* — so that, although Butini retired as provincial secretary to stand for the regional elections the following year, another *fanfaniano* (Sergio Pezzati) had no difficulty in being elected as his successor. Butini remained by far the most powerful figure in the Florentine DC and, because of its political weight, he carried considerable influence in the Tuscan party as a whole, Fanfani himself being preoccupied with national politics. This dominance by the *fanfaniani* was buttressed by the use they made of their control of the party structure in most provinces to promote systematically their adherents to key posts both in the party and in the economic agencies allied to it. One provincial DC secretary explained his own background as a *fanfaniano* opportunistically on grounds of the local political situation 'because Fanfani and his personality influenced everybody somewhat in the electoral district'.

The collapse of Fanfani's position in Tuscany, as nationally, was clearly linked to the distinct failure of his intransigent line over the divorce issue with the referendum of 1974, although it took the direct loss of votes by the DC in the regional elections of 1975 to provoke the contraction and fragmentation of his support within the party. The revolt against Fanfani also drew on a reservoir of disquiet over a longer period regarding his methods of leadership, as was explained by one of his younger DC opponents in provincial politics:

> The loss of power, as one could say, and of consensus for the Fanfani *corrente* did not derive only from that referendum, but this was rather one of the episodes together with many others that led after some necessary deliberation to review the situation. But it was not just this. Principally, it was the elections of 1975 that made the DC realise that effective self-renewal was necessary. This renewal involved the rejection of certain methods of operation of the Fanfani *corrente*, in the management of power . . . In particular, this view gained ground among the young members, but there was also a rejection of the Fanfani *corrente* on the part of some of its older members. But one must be careful not to make this analysis simplistic for one must get to the roots of their motives. Many developments that led to the loss of support for the Fanfani *corrente* involved the readjustment on the part of local bigwigs to the new situation so they could continue to enjoy power . . .

The weakening of Fanfani's party base in Tuscany therefore owed something to factors in local politics as well as to his declining position in national politics. At Siena, the *fanfaniani* had already lost their majority on the provincial committee earlier in the 1970s mainly because of their internal divisions over local power positions in this particularly clientilistic provincial DC. One Sienese Christian Democrat described the process, thereby illustrating the pervading element of opportunism in inter-*correnti* migration, and the consequent ambiguity of ideological labels inside the DC:

> Here up to 1970, so long as Fanfani controlled all political power in the DC in Tuscany, all were *fanfaniani*. The Left was not allowed to delude itself . . . it did not have any weight inside the party. Then, at one point when Fanfani no longer enjoyed absolute hegemony, all those who were *fanfaniani* and had not achieved personal power by means of Fanfani then began to seek it through other *correnti*. Therefore, the movement from the Fanfani *corrente* to the *correnti* of the Left, to the *dorotei*, was an instrumental one because the men remained the same as before. That is, those who controlled the membership cards split in practice over the question of this control, but they were the same men. Therefore, this was symptomatic of the fact that this cleavage occurred not on the basis of political ideas, but for reasons of power. There had been a minimum of cohesion so long as power had been able to satisfy everyone. When this power was reduced and so not all could achieve power, then the DC split. And this is the dramatic feature of the DC at Siena . . . I have always been on the DC Left, but I have viewed critically the attitude of these people, how they 'contrabanded' the Left even though for years they had belonged to the Fanfani *corrente*, which now 'contrabands' the Left but only the instrumental Left . . . the possibility of achieving power with the Left. It is the negative element in this situation.

Although various factors motivated the growing rejection in the party of Fanfani's leadership, the dramatic subsidence of his general position from 1975 underlined the electoralistic nature of the DC now alarmed at its apparently diminished prospects as a political force as a consequence of Fanfani's political misjudgements. At Sesto Fiorentino (Florence), for instance, there followed some 'shuffling of the cards', as it was called, in the local DC after the defeats of 1974 and 1975 with various leaders changing sides from a pro-Fanfani position to one supporting the new DC Secretary, Benigno Zaccagnini. The *fanfaniani* had been stronger there among the older activists, so that an additional factor promoting this change was the pressure from younger ones to give them positions of leadership. What evidently set this process in motion was the election of Zaccagnini to replace Fanfani as national secretary at the end of July 1975.[78] In various other localities, where the DC lost municipal power as in some *comuni* on the island of Elba, there was an immediate outbreak of inter- and intra-*correnti* warfare since the unwelcome role of opposition deprived them of their clientilist channels. The party's electoral shock therefore tipped the scales in the internal balance of *correnti* alignments.

By early 1976, the *fanfaniani* had split into what could be identified as 'orthodox' and 'dissident' streams. This fragmentation of Fanfani's supporters penetrated downwards, as became clear at the beginning of that year in the *sezioni* congresses preparatory to the national DC congress the following March. In the two strongest provincial organisations, the official *fanfaniani* lost dramatically their numerical position of dominance — in the province of Florence sliding from 52 per cent to 40 per cent of the list strength, while in Lucca they were relegated to a minority position: the *fanfaniani* with 20.08 per cent, the pro-Zaccagnini forces 35.76 per cent and a further list called 'Renewal and Party Unity' with 44.16 per cent.[79] The last of these consisted of a mixed group such as *forlaniani* (a group of 'dissident' *fanfaniani*), *andreottiani* and *dorotei*, that is of former supporters of Fanfani who joined with others in proclaiming the tide of party regeneration. The success of the Zaccagnini forces was explained by two factors: support from many prominent DC figures in the province predominantly on the Left (e.g. Senator Pacini, the national deputy Maria Martini and the mayor of Lucca); and the increase of the Left's grass-roots support with the rise of younger local leaders having a background in the Christian trade union movement or one associated with active religious centres.[80] In other Tuscan provinces, there was a multiplication of party lists — seven at Livorno, four at Grosseto (none of whom openly supported Fanfani) and four at Siena with three of them in support of the pro-Zaccagnini provincial secretary. Only in Arezzo province did Fanfani maintain a respectable level of support.[81]

While the abandonment of Fanfani benefited numerically the Centre-Right *dorotei* in a few areas, it was the consolidation and enthusiasm of the different Left groups (the *morotei*, the social-Catholic *Base* and the Christian trade-unionist *Forze Nuove*) which accounted primarily for the decisive emergence of the 'Zaccagnini line'. This was not so much a new *corrente* as a 'tendency' based on a form of confederal co-operation among these various loosely organised factions. The prospect of competition for the local congress electoral lists had made many leadership cadres sensitive or vulnerable to an unprecedented groundswell of sympathy and support in the DC membership for Zaccagnini, who symbolised a 'new face' in the party at a time when it was coming increasingly under public attack for a series of major corruption scandals. In many ways, this mood at the party base represented a demand for change as such rather than necessarily a distinct move to the Left in ideological terms. One Florentine party leader described what happened in his area:

> The Left at Florence had never risen beyond 20% traditionally, even with Pistelli. When we decided to ally with Zaccagnini in 1976, there was an incredible invasion. Numerous people professed publicly their support for Zaccagnini in the *sezioni*, even if before they had been *fanfaniani* and *dorotei*. In this way, we reached almost 40% of the votes. Therefore, I should say it was a great success because up till then there had always been an electoral rigidity in the DC ... With Zac this totally changed.[82]

At the Tuscan DC Regional Congress in April 1976, the new alignment of party forces on its regional committee was consequently as shown in Table 4.4.

Table 4.4: Strength of Party Lists at Tuscan DC Regional Congress, April 1976

List Number	Name of list	Votes	%	Seats
1	'Centralità Democratica' (andreottiani)	6,550	10.1	5
2	'Toscana Meridionale per l'Iniziativa di Periferia' (dissident fanfaniani)	14,600	22.6	11
3	'Toscana Settentrionale per l'Iniziativa di Periferia' (orthodox fanfaniani)	10,400	16.1	8
4	'Con la Linea Politica del Segretario Nazionale Zaccagnini' (Base, Morotei, Forze Nuove)	21,000	32.4	16
5	'Uniti nel Rinnovamento' (dorotei)	12,200	18.8	10
	Total	64,750	100.0	50

Source: Material supplied by the Tuscan DC Regional Committee

For the first time, the *fanfaniani* were in a distinct minority in the DC in Tuscany, although the strong 'dissident' group continued to play an ambiguous balancing role between the supporters of Fanfani and Zaccagnini. However, the new weight of forces was demonstrated in 1977 when pro-Zaccagnini leaders of the Left were elected to the key posts of provincial secretaries at Florence (Enzo Pezzati) and Lucca (Piero Angelini).

The Tuscan DC had undergone a major shift in its internal balance of forces. What distinguished this occurrence in the mid-1970s from earlier intra-*corrente* splits and shifting inter-*correnti* alliances was the greater degree of fragmentation, involving in particular *correnti* which had existed for a long time. In this sense, the violent turn rather than subtle shift of the *correnti* kaleidoscope reflected the DC's political crisis of these years.

All the same, a too one-dimensional explanation of these events should be avoided. Underlying the move to Zaccagnini there was a distinct mood of disillusionment among the party base with the conduct of DC elites. At the time of the author's interviews several years later, this continued to express itself frequently in a regular criticism among local leaders of the 'deteriorating factor' of *correnti* behaviour, sometimes even in the wishful (or defensive) claim that the *correnti* had 'disappeared'. One should also not underrate the factor of sentiment in Italian politics in assessing the grass-roots response to Zaccagnini which did represent a new form of mobilisation in the party. Nevertheless, enthusiasm could always wane unless reinforced by institutional or permanent political factors (e.g. a continuing sense of the party's loss of credibility). One feature which did not essentially change was the low level of membership participation in the party's formal structure. This is important to note since the presence of the *correnti* at the local level has always depended on the personal allegiance of the *sezione* secretary to a certain party figure, a factor which counted in the absence of strong involvement in politics by the membership as a whole.[83] Furthermore, the relative value of *correnti* labels and the ambiguity in translating them ideologically made any internal party consensus based on a coalition among some of them (which the 'Zaccagnini line' essentially was) always potentially unstable. In fact, Zaccagnini's prospective retirement after five years from the DC Secretaryship in 1980 was preceded by some loss of support for his list in *sezioni* congresses in Tuscany at the start of that year, so that altogether the pro-Zaccagnini line obtained 29 per cent rather than over 32 per cent in the regional DC.

The loss of credibility by the *correnti* in the 1970s did give some added force to pro-Zaccagnini support, but even so the 'shift to the

Left' was in many cases a cover for simply careerist opportunism at the local and intermediary levels, especially in the form of a generational change of leadership. For instance, while the official *fanfaniani* maintained their majority at Arezzo there had been a takeover of younger leaders of that *corrente* headed by Tullio Innocenti, who replaced Fanfani's own brother Ameglio as provincial secretary.[84] Finally, it was evident that even with the widely-proclaimed avowal of party 'renewal' old habits of behaviour died hard. One dramatic example of this problem was the extended crisis in the Siena DC during 1977-1978 over appointments to the administrative council of the Monte dei Paschi bank. This resulted from an outbreak of inter-*correnti* conflict with party 'renewal' being interpreted as the replacement of one set of personnel by another, and with the complicating factor of intra-party personal rivalries and the reappearance of clientilistic motives.

This sceptical assessment of the change in the internal balance of *correnti* suggested that their fragmentation did not involve a radically new departure in structural relationships within the DC, nor did the fluidity in their alliances with each other point to any profound reorientation of internal party life. The DC's credibility crisis and external electoral and political pressures meant that the *correnti*, especially those most discredited by their past abuse of power, kept a low profile, but these external pressures lessened somewhat by the end of the 1970s. Any metamorphosis in party leadership and management, as represented by Zaccagnini's tenure of office in the latter half of this decade, was therefore more likely to be temporary than permanent. Indeed, the whole history of the DC internally has shown how much its structural relationships have been dependent on precisely this factor of leadership personality.

This regional study of the Tuscan DC has only looked closely at internal party relations in a restricted time-span, albeit a significant one, but it has underlined nevertheless that structural changes are difficult to implement in the DC because informal procedures are far more influential than formal ones, in contrast with the PCI. Zaccagnini did make efforts to introduce change through internal constitutional rules to reduce *correnti* power — and succeeded, for instance, in abolishing their control over membership registration at the provincial level in 1977 — but this did not erase the fact that the *correnti* derived so much of their strength from traditional attitudes and modes of party behaviour. Characteristically, discussion of 'party reform' in the 1970s tended to focus not on questions of party organisation, but on the vaguer task of renovating the DC's identity as a party. The importance

The Tuscan Christian Democrats

of Zaccagnini's Secretaryship must also be judged by his handling of this problem and his policy approach.

(d) The Question of Party Identity and the Problems of *Rapprochement* with the PCI

The study of inter-party relationships soon leads to the question of how far a coalition, alliance or policy agreement between different political parties assumes an 'organic' character and hence affects their own identity. Broadly speaking, the 'organic' element of an inter-party relationship may be political or based on association. That is, its development may vary according to the degree of intensity in the relationship: it may derive from a *rapprochement* between the parties concerned reinforced by some degree of ideological sympathy, even though not overtly expressed; or it may be the consequence of a harmonisation of programmatic positions sufficient to allow a reasonable partnership in common policy-making; or it may be largely 'pragmatic' in that the 'organic' factor develops from a common association on the basis of necessity or convenience, where this factor is less one of sympathy but nevertheless visible to the party's activists and voters. In Italy, there is a greater flexibility in the definition of inter-party relationships than in many other parliamentary states,[o] but they nearly always involve, especially in the case of the large parties, a long and complicated process of elaborating party positions. With the relationship between the DC and PCI in the 1970s, one principal question has been that in the eyes of the former the latter represented historically its ideological antithesis. This final section will consider both the effects on the DC of its *rapprochement* with the PCI, and those attitudes and developments internal to itself which have conditioned its strategy.

There are several general problems facing parties in a developing relationship with other political forces. First, there is that of marrying the tactical and ideological approaches, required by the need to maintain an autonomous political profile and promote the party interests in a relationship pursued over time in fluctuating political situations. Secondly, there is the problem of maintaining an harmonious balance between the elite and grass-roots of the party concerned with reference to the inter-party relationship. Since compromise at the top elite level is of course central to such a relationship differences may emerge within the party over coalitional approaches and touch off internal rivalries between elites, while at the party base there may be the risk of disaffection over compromises hatched at the top depending on relative expectations as well as the nature and state of wider internal party relationships.

Despite the complexities of the DC's structure as a party, a distinct sense of common 'Christian Democratic' identity was evident among party activists (interviewed by the author) and acted as a constraining force particularly with reference to the party's electorate. One national party leader claimed at this time that 'the DC will automatically lose four-fifths of its support on the day the Christian Democrats come to an agreement with the Communists'.[85] As already seen with the PCI, the pursuit of the 'historic compromise' has by no means been straightforward when taking account of internal party factors.P In the case of the DC, there is both much less tradition of internal discipline and less practice of internal debate at the lower levels of the party structure, so that dissent or disquiet over the party strategy has been expressed differently.

Since the compelling reason for a required change in alliance strategy from 1975-1976 — the electoral rise of the PCI, and its mounting pressure for a *rapprochement* — placed the DC in a defensive position, it was not surprising that its own identity was raised as a central feature in the ensuing discussion of how to respond. Several leaders did so at the regional DC Congress in April 1976, notably Ferdinando Soldati (a former provincial secretary at Lucca and 'dissident' *fanfaniano*), who in reference to the DC's 'crisis of identity and isolation' stressed the need for a new constructive entente (*confronto*) with the PCI, while at the same time 'respecting the precise borders of ideological differentiation' between the two parties and reasserting the DC's 'genuine and competitive popular dimension'.[86] A similar line of thinking marked deliberations in the Tuscan DC during the months and years which followed. A document approved by the regional committee in March 1977 for the party's national organisational conference raised the question of party identity in the context of the DC's move to opposition at the sub-national level: 'it is our conviction that the party must at last undergo careful investigation, a rigorous and responsible search for its own identity and its own role, by formulating immediately a definite modern political programme which shows clearly to everyone its popular, democratic and anti-totalitarian nature'.[87] A further document of November 1977 presented for discussion in the regional committee referred to the 'crisis of relations' between the 'Catholic world' and Italian society which had brought a certain 'isolation' for the party since 1975, but it argued that the necessary rejection of 'integralism' (i.e. Catholic fundamentalism) should not lead to the DC's renouncing its 'traditional culture' which had 'made our movement an original phenomenon in the history of our country'.[88] This latter document did in fact represent the approach of the DC Left (as in rejecting 'integralism'), also showing that party identity could be interpreted with different accents.

These various proposals all represented variations on the theme of the Moro-Zaccagnini strategy of *confronto*, which, while recognising the need for a *rapprochement* with the PCI (and other political forces) distinguished this approach from a political alliance because it should be confined to certain common points of co-operation and not 'confuse the majority and opposition roles'. There was nevertheless an inherent ambiguity in this approach, so that one viable question would be how *confronto*, as largely imposed by necessity, accorded with the DC's political outlook and was received within the party itself. Did it, for instance, create any ideological problems?

It has been noted that the DC is essentially a 'pragmatic' rather than ideological party. This still leaves open the question whether the national leadership's response to the PCI occasioned any conflict with the DC's political values or 'belief system' ('traditional culture' in Christian Democratic language). In the absence of any cohesive party ideology, it is more relevant to speak of certain basic *leitmotivs* in the DC's political outlook, particularly in view of the ideological confusion arising from the role of the *correnti*.[89] Two predominant *leitmotivs* have been germane to the problem of party identity and *rapprochement* with the PCI: anti-Communism as the most over-riding of the DC's ideological motives, and the concept of 'democracy' (essentially meaning the parliamentary form of government) and of *Libertas* (usually interpreted as individual freedom). The latter is linked fundamentally with the former, especially in the eyes of DC leaders and activists who are virtually without exception 'culturally' anti-Communist and with different shades of emphasis see some basic contradiction between PCI ideology and their own attachment to 'freedom' and 'democracy'. This sense of conflicting ideological beliefs has been particularly noticeable in Tuscany, which witnessed more pronounced Left/Right polarisation between the two major parties (the DC in opposition to the PCI/PSI regional government) than in most other regions during the 1970s. It is therefore worth discussing the depth of the DC's anti-Communist commitment, and how this affected the evolution of its relationship with the PCI.

Before looking at attitudes towards the PCI in the party as a whole, it is necessary to begin with the line taken by the individual *correnti*, as they have traditionally determined the course of political discussion inside the DC. It is possible to identify differences of attitude towards a *rapprochement* with the PCI on the part of the various *correnti*, with those of the Left and others supporting Zaccagnini taking a flexible and more 'open' approach, the orthodox *fanfaniani* and others on the Right assuming a position of fundamentalist opposition and in between the *dorotei* with other groups of the Centre-Right with a line combining reservedness and a readiness to compromise where really necessary. However, any clear or absolute definition of their individual positions on this matter is not possible for three reasons.

First, as noted earlier, the ideological stands of the *correnti* have a relative value or play a greater or lesser role according to their political location. The *fanfaniani* have taken an official line of opposition to *confronto* in the party, as is evident from the very negative attitudes predominant in the Arezzo provincial party where they continued to rule.[90] At the same time, there were recognised differences of outlook between the two Left *correnti* with the *Forze Nuove* more negative than the *Base*, the latter showing a more genuine sympathy with the arguments of the *confronto* strategy. On the other hand, all the *correnti* have possessed a certain common denominator in anti-Communism; but what counts is the degree of its intensity and the political use made of anti-Communism. One pro-Zaccagnini local DC leader from the *Base* had this to say on the matter:

> While the majority in the local party support the policy of *confronto* of Zaccagnini, there is a strong component of anti-Communism. Not anti-Communism of a personal kind, but conceptual anti-Communism. Relations with some local Communist leaders are extremely cordial. But I myself have a fear of the PCI – not so much because it is the *Italian* Communist Party as that I know it is very attached to the interests of international Communism. This is always the criticism I make of the PCI.[91]

Secondly, the loss of credibility by the *correnti* system in general from the mid-1970s together with their further fragmentation and changing alliances both reduced the clarity of their positions towards other parties, and facilitated their co-operation behind Zaccagnini whether for opportunistic or policy motives. One *fanfaniano* leader from Florence explained that a more united approach in the party had been helped among other things by the general situation, for in the face of the Communist danger it was no longer meaningful to ask whether someone belonged to this *corrente* or supported another. Above all, it was important to know what the DC wanted in its entente with the PCI. This demand for clarity was made by the electorate and the members of the DC.[92]

Thirdly, as the same interviewee admitted, the *correnti* continued to operate as the guiding factor in the implementation of the party strategy of *confronto*, so that their characteristically subtle methods of manoeuvre tended to confuse rather than enlighten the wider activist body. Several leaders of the DC Left accused the *fanfaniani* of 'opportunistic' behaviour towards the PCI, while one provincial party organiser commented on the confusion among the membership caused by ambiguity at the national level:

> For me it is clear that there is confusion at the national level. The different *correnti* themselves are somewhat in disorder. We have seen *onorevole* Donat-Cattin, who personally used to be for active collaboration with the Socialists and also with the Communists, now becoming anti-Communist. For this reason, the members do not manage to understand. Moreover, those who participate locally in the *correnti* themselves don't manage to understand the attitudes of their *correnti* leaders. Because the *correnti* leaders sometimes make speeches in public saying, 'No to compromise, we do not want this compromise', but in practice we find ourselves so many times on the road to the 'historic compromise', in these small compromises at the provincial level, but public interest is in small things, isn't it? For example, the roads, socio-economic questions, those concerning workers and agriculture — in practice, these are the areas of compromise with the PCI.[93]

The main element in the DC's approach of *confronto* was on the one hand a political-functional role of working out practical agreements with the PCI, and on the other hand a political-cultural position of differentiating between the two parties as ideological forces. Whether the inherent ambiguity here could be solved by the DC's 'pragmatic' character was not certain. Although more possible among the national party elite, this form of behaviour and justification of party strategy was less obvious at the party base. In Tuscany, the pro-Zaccagnini line had gained majority support in the DC from early 1976, but even so the evidence of early reactions to a *rapprochement* with the PCI expressed consternation. In the Siena area, one local DC leader described divided opinions at the party base in the summer of 1977:

> The DC voters and members are a bit confused at this moment. As there are those among the voters who say that the compromise is nevertheless inevitable, and even believe it to be positive. But there are others who say, on the contrary, that the compromise must be avoided as it will do harm not only to the party but also to the whole community.[94]

Members here had begun to perceive this problem of having to respond to the 'historic compromise' from the time of the Divorce Referendum, whereas in the province of Lucca the need for an actual compromise with the PCI in one commune in the autumn of 1975 (one of the few such cases before this process began at Rome the following year) was accompanied, in the words of a local DC leader, by difficulties of 'collaborating with a force that had traditionally been viewed as our opponent'. There was much controversy in the local DC at first and then the agreement with the PCI was absorbed, although 'the mistrust between the parties still remained'.[95]

One of the main problems facing the DC during 1975–1976 was that it had not worked out a strategy in advance of the new political prominence acquired suddenly by the PCI. Hence, there was not sufficient time allowed to foster conviction in favour of the *confronto* approach within the party at large. Typical of this problem was the reaction at the grass-roots in Lucca province, as described by a local DC leader in 1978:

> At the beginning, *confronto* shocked the base of the DC, because it was misunderstood as involving the DC in moving towards the proposition of the PCI. It seems to me now that the base has come to understand the real meaning of *confronto*, even though not fully acquainted with its specific elements. This happened because the DC was unprepared for facing a *confronto* with the PCI on a programmatic basis ... the base was somewhat disorientated.[96]

During the period which followed there emerged a general if reluctant acceptance of *confronto* or an attitude of resignation among the DC membership, at least so far as agreements with the PCI on practical matters were concerned, but party attitudes or feelings about any principled espousal of the 'historic compromise' as enunciated by the PCI remained decisively negative, as became clear from DC interviewees in the representative sample of communes visited in Tuscany during 1977-1978. For example, one local activist at Florence estimated that a formal coalition with the PCI would not be accepted by 70 per cent of the membership and would 'split the party'. Similarly, the mayor of one rural commune answered by saying that only four per cent to five per cent of local members would support the 'historic compromise' with 60 per cent preferring an alliance with the PSI, which had earlier been the practice there. It should be pointed out that these were leaders' interpretations of members' attitudes, but all the same these influenced their own behaviour over this question. Evidence from other areas indicated not much discussion at the party base of the relationship with the PCI, but more often the new political situation had stimulated a renewed electoral awareness among DC supporters and sympathisers and in some cases had motivated people to join the DC.[q]

It was Zaccagnini's main achievement as DC Secretary in encouraging and harnessing the signs of renewed awareness among members in the DC arising from the impact of the party's crisis of 1974 onwards. He did this in such a way that the problems of party identity which began to arise as a consequence of *confronto* were contained, an internal approach which became easier once the DC's electoral decline was checked and even reversed. Although labelled 'renewal' in DC parlance, this change in the mood of activists under Zaccagnini did not amount to party reform of any thoroughgoing kind. There are various ways in which a political party may reinvigorate itself — through organisational or structural readjustment, programmatic renewal or simply refurbishing its image together with a change in leadership. In so far as the last alternative has to acquire some symbolic effect, one may say that Zaccagnini's policy of promoting the DC's identity as a *partito popolare* in the context of the *confronto* strategy involved a largely cosmetic process, even though it did succeed up to a point in producing a new sense of purpose.[r] While this policy therefore had a certain 'superficial' quality, its importance with respect to the DC's own way of handling and accepting the *rapprochement* with the PCI underlined again how much the DC was a different kind of political force from the PCI. Unlike the PCI, whose cadres engaged in a fairly intensive process of self-analytical debate, the DC with the less defined penchant of its activists for dialectical politics could more easily overcome the worst internal repercussions of *confronto* by the simple method of enunciating the values of reform and taking various measures to improve the party image. Some brief references will be made here to the efforts at party regeneration in Tuscany by way of drawing conclusions on the internal dimension of the DC's pursuit of *rapprochement* with the PCI in Italian politics.

One of the principal aspects of the DC's political crisis in the mid-1970s was its loss of credibility among the public: This was in the first instance the main point of concentration of the Zaccagnini policy, as suggested by the interpretation of it by one of his protagonists in Tuscany — Pier Giorgio Licheri, provincial secretary at Lucca and a member of the *Base corrente*. In an official statement, Licheri remarked on the need to 'achieve a different way of managing power, and of establishing relations among the political parties and with society'.[97] Although he stressed the need to restructure the DC as a mass popular party, in fact far less emphasis was placed on organisational means (thus confirming the DC's low level of bureaucratisation) than on 'opening up' the party to its own members with positive repercussions on its electorate. Clearly intended as an antithesis to the leadership style of the now discredited Fanfani, this proposal was not always spelt out clearly, although it did include the establishment of some sense of rapport between the leadership and the party base. In presenting Zaccagnini as a 'new face' representing the 'better tradition' of the DC, the party leadership hoped to erase some of the worse features of its image problem. That this assumption proved remarkably correct illustrated the degree to which DC activists and members were in fact 'externally' motivated. One local leader discussed the galvanising effect of Zaccagnini at the grass-roots:

> Here in Sesto Fiorentino, the presence of a different leader from the visibility point of view, as a different face compared to the old ways of the DC, has been stimulating for the party. This has made it possible for the DC to win over numbers of people who up till then had been outside it, that is, because of the old polemics about the corrupt party which one entered only for reasons of career . . .[98]

Several interviewees pointed out, however, that such a change was more possible where the DC had habitually been in a position of local opposition or where it had lost positions of responsibility in the 1975 municipal elections, and could draw attention to the mistakes of the Left in power.

The Zaccagnini approach carried that much more conviction because it was accompanied by frequent rejuvenation of leadership personnel provincially and locally. This was obviously facilitated by the swing in the Tuscan party from a Fanfani majority to one supporting the new Secretary in 1976, thus introducing younger personnel as party secretaries. Where this happened at the provincial level, the new leaders used their authority to encourage younger promotions as *sezioni* secretaries, although this could sometimes arouse hostile feelings among older activists. One young *sezione* secretary in central Tuscany, aged 29, noted that many younger leaders had been given a preference as a direct result of the 1975 elections. In some areas, the need to accommodate with the PCI had produced a changeover in local government leaders in the DC, some who had administered communes for over 30 years being forced to retire in favour of younger men who were more adaptive to the new political situation. In so many cases, this process involved a necessary but long postponed generational change in party leadership, but making a virtue out of necessity the DC exploited it to enhance the party image of 'renewal'. In the 1976 election, for instance, the Tuscan DC made great play with the 'renewal' of its parliamentary candidates (the lack of which had been a notorious feature of the party in the past). In the Pisa-Lucca constituency, this was noticeable with the replacement of several long-serving parliamentarians (and intermittent ministers) like Togni and Loris Biagioni after a somewhat difficult internal party process of 'persuasion'. This did not always open channels for younger leaders to advance in the party. The emergence of Giorgio La Pira from political retirement in 1976 to head the DC list at Florence at Zaccagnini's behest was clearly an attempt to restore the party's 'Christian' identity in a city where he was still very popular.[99]

Finally, the Zaccagnini policy was effective in so far as it sought to encourage and mobilise a new form of activity at the base, though this tended to be more acclamatory than participatory (in any serious policy-discussion sense). The most immediate response came among young Christian Democrats already activated through the revival of Catholic groups, and for whom the 'idealistic' image of 'Zac' had a special appeal.[100] At a different level, the attempt to promote interest in the party among both members and sympathisers occurred with the initiation in the mid-1970s of the new practice of holding 'Friendship Festivals' annually. These were a direct borrowing from the PCI's *Unità* Festivals with a similar mixture of political speeches and light entertainment with refreshments as a way of demonstrating that the DC too had something to offer the 'man in the street'. In some localities, there developed a rivalry between the different party festivals, but by and large the DC was simply latching on to the ordinary Italian's spontaneous like of open-air socialising especially in the countryside. It was not therefore surprising that, in the province of Florence at least, the *Feste dell'Amicizia* were far more successful in the smaller communes.[101] One local leader, however, claimed a political motive, for, while middle-class circles had previously been inhibited about demonstrating solidarity in this way,

> the bourgeoisie are now frightened by the success of the PCI, for which reason they have begun to come to the festivals of the political alternative. It is a phenomenon of reacting, of self-defence.[102]

This claim pointed again to the DC's function as the main, if not exclusive, channel for anti-Communist mobilisation. Here was the chief reason for its own political revival in the later 1970s rather than this arising from intrinsic factors in the party. This function was notably evident in the region of Tuscany, where the DC acted as the political pole in opposition to both the predominant PCI and its alliance partner here, the PSI. It is therefore worth referring briefly to its electoral support in the region.

The DC has maintained a consistent level of voting strength of around 30 per cent to 31 per cent in Tuscany since the 1950s, when its level of support was somewhat higher — in fact, the DC became in 1958 the strongest party in the region though only just ahead of the PCI.[s] Sub-regional variation in electoral strength shows that the Catholic sub-cultural factor has been one important determinant of DC support, as is indicated by its superior vote in the province of Lucca.[t] While tradition has therefore been as influential as in explaining the PCI's electoral composition in its own areas of predominance, it is crucial in estimating the DC's quality as a mass party to look at its ability to aggregate the secular Centre-Right or conservative sectors of society and to adapt to socio-economic change in the region. Here, the record of the DC has indicated serious weaknesses in the party's electoral base, for the decline in its level of support since the 1950s has been due to its lack of appeal in the developing areas of Tuscany, where especially industrialisation but also to some extent the growth of the tertiary sector have occurred.[103] A closer examination of the DC's electorate shows it to be the antithesis of that of the PCI in the region, thus underlining their respective monopoly of the Right and Left poles. This antithesis is evident when taking account of the PCI's electoral benefit from industrialisation and also generally in that the DC has throughout the region been stronger where the PCI has been weaker.[104] In the latter instance, the DC has, according to the classification of Tuscan communes by economic activity, been strongest in rural areas, especially in smaller communities and where small farmers (*coltivatori diretti*) have predominated.[105] This has inevitably overlapped with the sub-cultural factor, as was illustrated in the 1975 Divorce Referendum when the anti-divorce 'Yes' vote was higher in the rural communes than in any of the others.[u]

The general picture of the DC's electoral support in the region is not, however, entirely negative. This relates to its success in attracting groups of non-Catholic (i.e. conservative) voters notably from the middle classes, as it has done in Italy as a whole. There has been some evidence in this respect of the DC benefiting from socio-economic change, specifically among the growing urban bourgeoisie in some branches of the tertiary sector in the main cities (in particular those employed in public administration and in the public services such as the hospitals). It is significant that it is in the main cities in Tuscany where the Marxist sub-culture is less intensive, and that accordingly the DC has in most cases in the region enjoyed a higher vote in the provincial capitals than in the provinces as a whole – including the city of Siena (with its strong tertiary activity), though not Livorno because of its pronounced Left tradition.[106] This urban vote for the DC became that much more visible from the mid-1970s, when the PCI's electoral advance provoked a counter-response among supporters of the small Centre-Right parties who flocked to the DC as the main anti-Communist force and balanced its losses to the Left.[107] These various features were in line with trends in electoral behaviour elsewhere in Italy, although clearly the DC was comparatively that much less of an inter-class party in this 'Red' region.

In conclusion, this regional study of the DC in the 1970s has emphasised how much the party has remained essentially voter-oriented. This quality provided the key to both the DC's perception of and response to its own political crisis in the middle of that decade, not to mention that the reduction in electoral pressures allowed it to regain its internal morale by the end of it. Hence, it was, above all, party competition, viewed by the DC in strongly electoral terms, which accounted for its continuing strength as a political force.

This voter-orientation of the DC also provided the link between change and continuity in its evolution as a party during the period under discussion. It was therefore no surprise that the DC should also still be classified as a 'catch-all' rather than mass-structured party which was loose-associational in its internal relationships. The DC's electoralistic outlook meant that the need for 'party reform', as the solution to its political crisis, was interpreted first and foremost as a matter of image renovation rather than programmatic renewal or organisational readjustment. However, all such classificatory definitions as above are relative in that they express a basic orientation and not an absolute state in a political party. It is the virtue of a case-study approach in particular to be able to focus more closely on the degree of a party's various characteristics, and in taking a relevant period of time to assess how it might change or adapt.

In considering new elements in the Italian socio-political environment — changes in political involvement and electoral behaviour, greater socio-economic pressures — the DC revealed a certain adaptability, even though more under duress than through any political foresight. Its adaptability was significantly assisted by some of its own particular features. The complex relationship between the Christian Democratic party and the Catholic movement was such that the autonomous role of the 'movement' allowed it to help recharge the energies of the 'party'. This occurred for political reasons, arising from party competition, so that the DC was able to neutralise at least for the time being the translation of secularist trends into adverse electoral tendencies. Furthermore, the discredited mechanism of the *correnti* as the dominant arteries for internal party relationships contributed nevertheless to the DC's limited form of regeneration. Their existence as competing channels for political promotion in the party meant that the alteration in their balance of alignments from the mid-1970s — in Tuscany, favouring the Left *correnti* as against the previously dominant Right ones — resulted in the emergence of alternative leaders and to some extent a generational change in their composition locally and provincially. Characteristically, it took intense electoral pressures for this transformation finally to occur.

Finally, this chapter has demonstrated how different a kind of political party the DC is from the PCI, whose evolution was examined in the preceding chapter. This basic contrast is evident both when considering the general classifications into which the two parties fall, and in looking at their operation in more depth and detail as in the region of Tuscany. There are of course problems in extending this comparison to the whole of Italy, bearing in mind that Tuscany is a 'Red' region, but all the same the DC has evidenced here much of the structural and ideological variation it has displayed across the country. In view of this contrast between the DC and PCI and the close interlinkage between their internal and external relationships, the question of their strategies towards each other acquire a rather more demanding and interesting context.

Notes

a. See general points made at the beginning of Chapter 3 above, pp. 45-6.
b. See above, Chapter 3 (a), pp. 46-7.
c. See above, Chapter 3 (a), p. 46.
d. See above, Table 2.2, p. 37.
e. Gruppi di Impegno Politico (Groups of Political Involvement), a new organisation of the DC in the factories allowing sympathisers to establish a connection with the party at their work-place without becoming formal members.
f. See above, Chapter 3 (b), p. 71.
g. See above, Table 3.3, p. 57.
h. See above, Tables 3.1 and 3.2, pp. 51, 52.
i. This contrast in practice between the DC and PCI was illustrated by the author's own acquisition of documentary material. Whereas this was in abundant supply in the case of the PCI, often very detailed and statistical in nature, such documentation either did not exist with the DC or was not readily accessible on a formal basis. What existed either tended to be sparse on information, reflecting the fact that real politics in the DC is conducted 'informally' and not bureaucratically, or it spelt out one particular *corrente* line of approach inside the party.
j. See above, Chapter 3 (c), p. 77.
k. See above, Chapter 4 (a), pp. 122-4.
l. See above, Chapter 4 (a), p. 123.
m. See above, Chapter 1 (c), pp. 20-2.
n. See above, Chapter 3 (c), pp. 79-80.
o. See below, Chapter 5 (a), p. 187.
p. See above, Chapter 3 (d).
q. See above, Chapter 4 (c), p.153.
r. For a fuller discussion of Zaccagnini's policy of 'renewal' as DC Secretary, see the author's article 'The Italian Christian Democrats after Moro: Crisis or Compromise?' in *West European Politics*, January 1979, especially pp. 75-80.
s. See Table 2.2 above, p. 37.
t. See Table 2.1 above, p. 37. In the 1979 national election, for instance, the DC obtained absolute majorities in 20 of the 35 communes in Lucca province, virtually all of these in the Catholic Lucchesia. They included the city of Lucca (50.3 per cent), and in six of them the DC gained a vote of between 60 per cent and 70 per cent.
u. See above, Chapter 4 (b), pp. 132-4 for a discussion of the DC and voting in the Divorce Referendum in Tuscany.

References

1. Giorgio Galli, *Storia della DC* (1978), pp. 296-7. See also Mario Caciagli, *DC e Potere nel Mezzogiorno* (1977), pp. 113-14, 501, on the DC as a mass clientilist party in Catania.
2. Notably in G. Galli and A. Prandi, *Patterns of Political Participation in Italy* (1970)
3. There are of course minor exceptions; e.g. the small commune of Gaiole in Chianti noted for its local religious tradition.
4. Fanfani was assiduous in his visits to local party branches; e.g. one DC mayor of a locailty in Siena province: 'the majority of the party has always been the

fanfaniani here; Fanfani really put in a personal appearance here — he often visited me, stopped to call on our *sezioni* in the area to speak and discuss'.

5. In written questionnaires with members of the DC regional committee, 7 out of the 17 who responded considered the DC 'relatively more pragmatic' and 9 thought it 'relatively more ideological'. One considered the DC more ideological compared with the lay parties and more pragmatic compared with the PCI.
6. Mario Rossi, 'La Chiesa e le organizzazioni religiose' in Unione Regionale delle Province Toscane, *La Toscana nel regime fascista* (1971), pp. 370-1.
7. Ibid., p. 346.
8. S. Burgalassi, *Il comportamento religioso degli italiani* (1968), p. 151.
9. Report on the 1948 election campaign from the Tuscan regional delegation of Catholic Action to the general presidency in Rome, Florence, 30 April 1948.
10. Burgalassi, *Il comportamento religioso*, p. 151.
11. Ibid, p. 152.
12. See G. Tassani, 'Laicità della DC e "ricomposizione" cattolica' in *Il Mulino*, September–October 1978.
13. E.g. Aldo Moro: 'in characterising the party as Christian, there is no pretence of applying any inadmissible confessional discipline . . . instead, reference is made to values which inspire our political involvement and offer a reason for its being included with its own spiritual and cultural heritage among the political movements, among the popular forces', quoted in ibid., p. 707.
14. Giovanni Spinoso, *Il Ruolo di 'Potere' della A.C. nella comunità fiorentina, 1946-1966*, thesis for Florence University.
15. Interview No. 93.
16. The MCL has claimed to have more than 15,000 members in the province of Florence and operates via five sub-associations concerned with occupational illness, occupational qualifications, leisure-time activities, technical assistance in agriculture and workers' co-operation. Its activities are regularly advertised and reported on in its monthly publication, *Orientamenti Sociali*.
17. Interview No. 8.
18. Moreno Bambi, DC member since 1952, was chairman of the DC group in the municipal council of Empoli, a member of the executive board of the chamber of commerce at Pistoia and president there of the provincial mutual fund for direct cultivators.
19. Interview No. 90.
20. Interview No. 54. This portrayal was supported by discussions with DC leaders active in the Siena area.
21. One local leader claimed that *Libertas* 'does not go in for political argumentation, but rather engages in cultural preparation'. For reports on its activities in the province of Siena, see its monthly publication *Siena Sport*.
22. See report on Fanfani's campaign in Tuscany in *Panorama*, 14 February 1974.
23. Regione Toscana, *Il Referendum del 12 maggio 1974 in Toscana* (1974), p. 32.
24. Interview No. 95.
25. Interview with Maria Martini in *Politica e Società*, May 1978, p. 56. One DC mayor in Lucca province dissented by voting in favour of divorce as he was 'embittered' by the party position on this question. Such dissenters came from the Left of the DC.
26. Quoted in *The Guardian*, 25 June 1971.
27. See M. Clark, D. Hine and R. Irving, 'Divorce – Italian Style' in *Parliamentary Affairs*, Autumn 1974, pp. 344-5, 347-8.
28. *Il Taglio*, June 1976.

29. *Il Corvo delle Torri*, DC San Gimignano, 5 June 1975.
30. Regione Toscana, *Il Referendum*, p. 13.
31. See the report in *Panorama*, 31 January 1978.
32. Interview No. 84.
33. See Pippa Pridham, 'The problems of educational reform in Italy: the case of the *decreti delegati*' in *Comparative Education*, October 1978, pp. 232-5, which draws examples from Tuscany.
34. For the full results in Tuscany, see *Politica e Società*, November–December 1977, pp. 56-61.
35. From material provided by Professor Paolo Giovannini of Florence University. See also article on the Florentine DC in *Corriere della Sera*, 26 October 1975; and *Città e Regione*, April 1975, p. 34.
36. Fiora Imberciadori, 'Il gruppo dirigente democristiano' in L. Cavalli (ed.), *Classe dirigente e sviluppo regionale* (1973), p. 142.
37. 'The party is like an iceberg – the biggest and most important part is invisible underneath the surface' (G. Tamburrano, *L'Iceberg democristiano*, 1974).
38. Caciagli, *DC e Potere nel Mezzogiorno*.
39. See article on Monte dei Paschi in *The Times*, 27 October 1975.
40. PCI, *Raccolta di dati sull'organizzazione, 1971-1975*, pp. 445, 448.
41. Based on membership figures for 1968 (Interview No. 92).
42. DC membership list, Peccioli. Of these 33, ten were described as new members including four workers.
43. E.g. the DC membership for Radicofani (Siena) included roughly ten white-collar workers, 15 wood-workers, 20 direct cultivators, 20 women and some students (Interview No. 7). For the province of Siena white-collar workers, peasants and workers provided about 70 per cent of the DC membership (Interview No. 2, 1977).
44. E.g. the criticism of the 'New Left' list at the 1969 provincial congress of the Florence DC that concerning the party structure 'the present statutory norms and the organisation have often been disregarded and overtaken by time, and internal party democracy is rarely as described' (*Contributo della Nuova Sinistra al XIX Congresso Provinciale Ordinario della DC*, Florence, 29-30 March 1969).
45. E.g. S.G. Cappello and G. Sani, 'La DC come sistema organizzativo' in *Il Mulino*, No. 3, 1969.
46. Interview No. 2.
47. Interview No. 32.
48. E.g. the DC provincial secretary of Grosseto, employed in the Chamber of Commerce, was able to spend about 30 per cent of his time on party work (Interview No. 39); the DC secretary at Lucca was a university professor as well as being an active member of the regional council; the DC provincial secretary at Arezzo was a teacher; and the Florence provincial secretary was the president of a hospital.
49. E.g. in 1968 the members of the DC provincial council for Florence included 53.8 per cent white-collar workers, 20.5 per cent from the free professions and 12.9 per cent teachers; only 5.1 per cent were full-time party officials (quoted in *Città e Regione*, April 1975, p. 30).
50. Of the 17 members of the DC regional committee who responded, nine devoted 'much time' to party work, only two 'only one's free time' and six gave themselves full-time to the party (of these six there were three national members of Parliament and one party official).
51. Interviews Nos. 11 and 27.
52. Interview No. 2.
53. Giordano Sivini, 'Gli iscritti alla DC e al PCI' in *Rassegna Italiana di*

Sociologia, 1967, p. 437.
54. Interview No. 78.
55. Interview No. 8 (1978).
56. Report by Baldo Ghilardi, member of DC Lucca provincial committee, on the organisational state of the DC in the province of Lucca, late 1976, from material supplied by the DC provincial office at Lucca.
57. *Documento Politico della Lista 'Alternativa Democratica'*, XXV Congresso Provinciale Ordinario della DC, Siena, 16-17 December 1972.
58. Interview No. 89.
59. Comitato Regionale Toscano DC, *Quaderni di Toscana Più 3: Il Partito*, p. 22.
60. Interview No. 8.
61. Based on the author's investigations in the communes visited. Mario Signorini's own researches for the province of Florence indicated a level of 15 per cent to 20 per cent. (Interview No. 84). Party activists elsewhere in Tuscany estimated the level usually at 10 per cent to 20 per cent.
62. See D. Wertman, 'La partecipazione intermittente, gli iscritti e la vita di partito' in A. Parisi (ed.), *Democristiani* (1979), pp. 61-84. The average level of attendance is, however, higher in the north and central regions, and lower in the south.
63. Quoted in *La Nazione*, 28 November 1977.
64. Interview No. 3.
65. Interview No. 20.
66. Interview No. 92.
67. *Circoscrizione 3*, July 1977.
68. F. Imberciadori, 'Il gruppo dirigente democristiano', p. 140.
69. Interview No. 13 (1978).
70. Interview No. 27 (1978).
71. Cf. Document of the Tuscan DC regional committee, *Contributo della DC toscana alla conferenza nazionale organizzativa per i problemi dello statuto: proposte*, 28 March 1977, whose suggestions for changes in the DC statutes included a role in choosing candidates for the national and European parliaments and control over membership recruitment.
72. Interview No. 56.
73. Nine of the 15 DC regional councillors replied to detailed written questionnaires. Of these seven considered the possible regionalisation of the DC's structure 'very important', two thought it 'important' and none thought it 'not very important'. In reply to the question 'Should the provincial structure of the party remain much more important than its regional structure in the future?', eight replied 'no' and only one 'yes'. 17 of the 50 members of the regional committee replied to similar questionnaires: in reply to the question 'Do you consider the regional level of the party structure . . .', eleven considered it 'very important', four thought it 'important' and only two 'not very important'. All respondents thought the regional structure should be strengthened to accord with the acquisition of new powers by the regional governments (none replied with 'no'), and all but two thought the provincial committees should not remain much more important than the regional party structure in the future.
74. Giovanni Sartori, 'Proporzionalismo, frazionismo e crisi dei partiti' in *Rivista Italiana di Scienza Politica*, December 1971.
75. Interview No. 84.
76. Imberciadori, 'Il gruppo dirigente democristiano', pp. 132-4.
77. *Contributo della Nuova Sinistra al XIX Congresso Provinciale Ordinario della DC*, 1969.

78. Interview No. 92.
79. See detailed report on DC Lucca *sezioni* congresses in *L'Unità*, 10 February, 1976.
80. Ibid.
81. Report in *L'Unità*, 14 January 1976.
82. Interview No. 89.
83. One regional party leader commented on 'the self-identification of certain persons around whom the members revolve, and these can be relations of political affinity or of a clientilist nature . . . For example, in one area a person number one is important. This number one says "I am with Zac", so all those who are his friends go with Zac . . . this phenomenon is normally connected with the *sezioni*. Individual members don't follow politics in a very refined way. Changes occur at the intermediary level. It is the local leaders, normally of the *sezioni*, who change direction and hence change the relations between the *correnti*. Therefore, we are talking about a minority influence within the party.'
84. *La Nazione*, 3 June 1976. This was accompanied by the appointment of several young *sezione* secretaries. Innocenti maintained that among the young *fanfaniani* there was 'a great admiration for Zac' (Interview No. 56).
85. Carlo Donat-Cattin, quoted in *The Economist*, 26 June 1976.
86. *Il Popolo*, 13 April 1976.
87. See ref. 71.
88. *Appunti per il dibattito in comitato regionale DC*, 25 November 1977, p. 3.
89. Geoffrey Pridham, 'Christian Democracy in Italy and West Germany: a comparative analysis' in M. Kolinsky and W.E. Paterson, *Social and Political Movements in Western Europe* (1976), pp. 149-53.
90. Interview No. 56.
91. Interview No. 92.
92. Interview No. 84.
93. Interview No. 8 (1977).
94. Interview No. 3 (1977).
95. Interview No. 26. The commune was Barga (Lucca).
96. Interview No. 97.
97. Published in *La Nazione*, 3 January 1976.
98. Interview No. 92.
99. Zaccagnini's letter to La Pira, *La Nazione*, 11 June 1976. See La Pira's electoral advertisement in *La Nazione*, 19 June 1976, in reference to his selection: 'With this choice, the DC wanted to recall the human and Christian values that are at the basis of its political action.'
100. See statement of Florentine young Christian Democrats in favour of the 'Zaccagnini line' in *Avvenire*, 6 February 1976.
101. Interview No. 89.
102. Interview No. 92.
103. M. Barnini, 'La Toscana elettorale in questo dopoguerra' in *Quaderni dell'Osservatore Elettorale*, No. 1, October 1977, pp. 39-40.
104. B. Bartolini, 'Analisi ecologica del voto '76 in Toscana' in ibid., No. 2, February 1978, pp. 69-76.
105. Ibid., pp. 69-70.
106. Ibid., pp. 71, 74.
107. Barnini, 'La Toscana elettorale in questo dopoguerra', p. 45. In 1976, the PLI vote in Tuscany was decimated and that of the PSDI reduced by half.

5 INTER-PARTY RELATIONSHIPS AND THE POLITICS OF CONVERGENCE: THE TUSCAN EXPERIENCE

Following the preceding discussion of the integrative and adaptive capacity of the two major political parties as separate entities, it is essential now to consider relationships between them themselves and with third or small parties in order to complete this analysis of their overall role in the changing political and socio-economic environment of Italy in the 1970s — such as the growing importance of the PCI's role in Italy's political system, decentralisation in the state structure, the critical state of the country's economy and various social pressures including demands for social reform or modernisation. Inter-party relationships provide a crucial key to broader questions introduced at the outset of this study: have these changes had any de-legitimising or the opposite effect on the political system; related to this, to what extent have the respective major parties succeeded in channelling or controlling these changes and pressures; and what role, if any, have the smaller parties played in this context?

Inter-party relationships are crucial to answering such problems for two important reasons. First, political parties have been the over-riding and pervasive factor in the operation of the Italian political system even to the extent of supplanting the inefficient bureaucracy in vertical relations between centre and periphery, as Tarrow has shown.[1] Secondly, the form of Italy's party system — multi-party with predominant elements (i.e. DC and PCI) — has meant that political consensus and action has to be built on accommodation between different parties. The importance of inter-party relationships is obvious from an examination of representative speeches by politicians in Italy with often considerable attention being paid to the problem of how to formulate alliances. Even though accommodation between parties may take on the outward appearance of crude bargaining between political elites in Rome, this process is not conducted without reference to and indeed is conditioned by wider factors — summarised by the three-part relationship of parties mentioned earlier, with the state and the community as well as between themselves.[a] That is, considerations of the stability of the state and society enter into the formulation of relationships between parties, alongside the motive of political power.

It is no surprise, therefore, that the problems arising from the changing environment of the 1970s and the consequently less 'static' condition of the party system have focused so much on inter-party relationships. Politically, this has occurred directly because of the DC's decline in dominance and the exhaustion of previously attempted alliances (notably the disintegration of the Centre-Left from the early 1970s), together with the PCI's advance in electoral strength and hence compelling demand for a greater presence in the institutions of the state; while, at the same time, it has been argued (most forcibly by the PCI) that the crisis in the economy and Italy's serious social tensions require broad co-operation among the different political forces.

Before turning to a discussion of the politics of convergence, whereby the PCI has as the alternative predominant element in Italy's multi-party system been included more and more during the 1970s in the process of consensus formation, it is important to note the principal relevant characteristics of Italian inter-party relationships. There is not much systematic literature and hardly any empirical theory about coalition or alliance behaviour with regard to the Italian example. In the study of Italian politics, political parties are usually treated individually and separately which, although a valuable approach in itself, does have the disadvantage that inter-relationships receive little more than spasmodic or passing mention.[2] This is a serious omission for political parties and their behaviour are to a large degree a product of their environment, within which the factor of party competition as well as accommodation must rank high.[3]

Inter-party relationships are conditioned by both internal and external determinants with respect to the parties concerned. As Chapters 3 and 4 have shown[b] there is a strong inter-connection between a party's alliance strategy and such internal aspects as party ideology especially with the PCI or identity as in the DC, differences of outlook among leaders and activists over inter-party relationships (notably among the DC's *correnti*, but less evidently within the PCI's leadership cadres with their solidarity behind the 'historic compromise') and the degree of internal party participation (less of a problem in the DC, but considered a vital factor in the PCI with its emphasis on maintaining support for its strategy within the party base). External determinants of inter-party relationships include the balance of political forces (especially the relative strength of the DC and PCI) and their different strategies, as favouring one alliance partner over another, where electoral motives may feature strongly; the nature of and opportunities created by the instruments of state power — notably, the DC's dominance in postwar Italy cannot be explained without noting the advantages for it accruing from the country's centralised political system, while the establishment of the 'ordinary' regions in 1970 offered a major new chance to the PCI to exercise power; and the incidence of political or socio-economic problems which, as noted above, might require new alliance formulas. This chapter will concentrate on these external determinants, the internal ones already having been examined in the major parties.

It emerges from this schema of determinants that inter-party relationships are subject to multifarious influences or motives. This approach affords a more objective context in which to assess the Italian version of inter-party relationships than that often adopted by outside observers of Italy's politics who focus on the ideological factor to the exclusion or neglect of others and, failing to interpret events, fall back on ritualistic comments about Italy's 'complex' party behaviour. It is indeed a complex subject but not beyond explanation, if only the starting-point chosen is that ideology in Italian politics is an important but relative factor,[c] and indeed in any country should always be evaluated not in isolation but in relation to other possible forms of motivation.

This chapter aims at helping to interpret Italian inter-party relationships, taking the regional case-study, during a period when — reflecting the less 'static' condition of the party system — these became more fluid than at any preceding time since the onset of the Cold War. Tuscany is in some respects untypical of the country as a whole — notably, the dominant party here is the PCI and not the DC — but this does, on the other hand, provide a useful example for estimating how much the PCI with greater electoral support behind it is in any better position to impose its strategic preferences on other parties, and if not why not. The establishment of regional government did of course introduce a new level for party competition and the operation of alliance strategies and it is interesting to see how these factors came to rule over regional as much as national politics, thus confirming the dominance of the party dimension in the Italian political system. There is another special angle to this study, namely the extent to which party strategies enunciated and pursued in Rome are replicated throughout the country at the different sub-national levels, and whether alliances concluded at Rome pre-judge or condition those formulated locally and regionally or even vice versa; e.g. the Centre-Left was first experimented with in various major provincial capitals such as Genoa, Florence and Milan in the early 1960s before it was attempted in national government.

This regional and local approach to the study of inter-party relationships therefore offers a certain depth to a subject which cannot be fully appreciated by concentrating purely on the national level of political developments. This chapter will consider the evolution of inter-party relationships and the relationship of the individual parties with the state structure rather than, say, the content of their policies *per se* which will only be included when relevant to the central theme. Inter-party relationships will be examined both in the longer-standing domain of local government and the new arena of regional politics, but first it is helpful to look more fully at the orientation and priorities of the different party strategies in general, and how far these have promoted or hindered the politics of convergence.

(a) The Evolution of Party Strategies: Converging in the Same Direction?

It follows from the foregoing discussion that party strategies, however much they are directed to structural or social reform or motivated by the preservation or acquisition of political power, focus considerably on the question of alliance partners. The term 'party strategy', one very much employed in Italian politics, has virtually become a synonym for preferences in inter-party relationships.

Alliances range widely in Italy from formal coalitions, through the inclusion of partner-parties 'in the majority' (where the allied party does not enter the government, but guarantees parliamentary voting support) and programmatic agreements or 'pacts' to looser arrangements where the party or parties in question may assure their abstention (often in the case of minority administrations). These variations in gradation of alliances, sometimes confusing to the Anglo-Saxon observer accustomed to more clear-cut options, all require an element of deliberate or opportunistic 'convergence' between parties involved, but this very multiformity of alliances allows for some flexibility in the application of party strategy. Such flexibility may be necessary when ideological or electoral considerations inhibit a party's engagement in a full alliance or coalition, as expressed, for instance, in its concern for its 'autonomy' (often by the PSI) or 'identity' (the DC *vis-à-vis* the PCI). There can also be much ambiguity or convolution in Italian political rhetoric about alliances for tactical reasons, where different parties may appear to be speaking the same language but in fact their verbal smoke shrouds divergent intentions, or indeed vice versa.

These general remarks facilitate understanding of the period from the mid-1970s, when the PCI's proposed 'historic compromise' entered a new stage with its concrete application and became the dominant theme of strategic discussion between the parties. The central debate in Italian politics about the 'historic compromise' has inevitably concentrated largely, so far as prospective alliance partners are concerned, on the direct relationship between the PCI and DC because of their combined dominance of the multi-party stage, their historical antagonism and the relative novelty of the PCI's quasi-involvement in government and policy-making. What emerges from their closer inter-relationship, as illustrated by the Tuscan experience, is their different and often contrasting concepts of the meaning of alliances — the PCI advocating a form of consociative democracy,[d] while the DC has taken a position more analogous to the Anglo-Saxon practice of a separation between government and opposition roles — and different approaches to programmatic formulation, in addition to their own rival interests as parties. Perhaps this reflects their different characters as political parties, as discussed in Chapters 3 and 4, but all the same the Italian political situation in the 1970s has required a new approach to alliances in both cases. Moreover, strategic discussion cannot be conducted without defining their respective positions towards the PSI as the third party or even the small parties, either for the purpose of political majority-building or reinforcing broad social alliances. What has the fluidity in inter-party relationships from the mid-1970s therefore produced? Individual party strategies will first be considered in turn, and then comparatively.

The general strategy of the PCI known as the 'historic compromise' has been outlined elsewhere,[4] so that it is not the intention here to discuss this comprehensively. This strategy's main priorities do, however, need emphasising briefly to show what the PCI means by its idea of structural or socialist change within a democratic institutional framework and these may be verified by reference to the party in Tuscany.

First, the PCI has traditionally stressed more than the other parties the social dimension to political alliances, that is the importance of parties as representatives of different social forces in Italian society. This was seen historically as necessary because of Italy's fragmented social and economic structure, but it was viewed as a matter of urgent concern in the light of the country's economic weaknesses and pronounced social tensions in the 1970s.

Secondly, while continuing to stress the social dimension of its strategy the PCI has with the 'historic compromise' paid increasing attention to the political dimension of alliances with other parties, especially with the DC. Again, historically, this was reasoned on the basis of Italy's having a relatively young and hence possibly fragile democratic system, a consideration related to Berlinguer's concern over the significance of the military putsch in Chile in 1973. This line of thinking was shown by the PCI's renewed reference to the anti-Fascist motif as the common postwar starting-point for the various parties. As the Tuscan regional party secretary underlined in his speech to the regional congress in 1977, the debate between social and political forces was 'linked to the inheritance of the idea of anti-Fascism which has united and still unites different social classes and political forces . . . and the various articulated forms of Tuscan society'.[5]

The general outline of the PCI's proposed broad alliance with other parties was manifest, but, when it came to specific forms this should take, the presentation of the party line seemed ambiguous. This was illustrated by the speeches of federation secretaries, as careful exponents of party strategy, to provincial party congresses in Tuscany, insisting that the 'historic compromise' could not be identified as a conventional coalition formula, but was 'above all a constant way of maintaining relations and solidarity between the parties of the constitutional arc on some major questions'.[6] One other federation secretary defined the necessary unity between different parties for the 'renewal' of society as a flexible arrangement whereby they could 'unite and dissolve' on the basis of policy agreements while maintaining free competition between themselves.[7] There were several probable reasons for this apparent lack of clarity: a continuing insistence that the social importance of political alliances was more important than their precise institutional labels; an element of tactical caution, the PCI being desirous not to arouse any underlying hostility among the party base at too blatant an espousal of a coalition with the DC; but whatever the balance of motives it is clear that such a presentation of the party position was a further illustration of the flexible formulation of alliances in Italian politics mentioned above. In effect, however, the PCI came to press for a direct alliance with the DC during the course of the 1970s.

Thirdly, the launching of the 'historic compromise', whereby the PCI took a major step in coming in from 'out of the cold' of relative isolation in opposition, involved a clearer definition of its relationship towards and concept of the state because of its consequently enlarged governing role. This definition led to a growing emphasis on more participatory forms of democratic practice, a line strengthened all the more by the experience and memories of the protest movements of 1968-1969, some of whose demands the PCI sought to harness. The Tuscan regional secretary expounded his party's view when he wrote of the need for completely overcoming that obsolete separation between institutions and society, which had left so much room for corporatism and misgovernment to proliferate and that the principle of mass participation should be applied not merely to parliamentary organs, but 'all centres of participation and democratic life involved in society, from the productive world to the cultural world'.[8]

So far as parliamentary assemblies were concerned, the PCI explicitly criticised the DC for adhering to the traditional concept of the division between government and opposition, and in doing so argued the case for a pluralism whereby 'the majority appeals clearly to all democratic political forces present in the [regional] assembly and in Tuscan society because, respecting fully each one's role, it is desirable to draw them close in a common effort to protect the interests of the population'.[9] Applied to the area of local government, this principle emphasised the importance of this level as an expression of popular sovereignty in contradiction to the traditional distinction between the powerful central government on the one hand and dependent local administration on the other, the idea of pluralism being used here to oppose the centralised and hierarchical state.[10] The PCI advocated, for instance, that municipal councils should be strengthened in their role in relation to local administrations.[11] In short, the party's approach was analogous to the idea of assembly government, but as part of its general support for 'reform of the state' in the context of granting powers to the new regional authorities.[e] What is interesting to note is that the PCI chose to elaborate its concept of the state all the more because of its growing role in government, especially at the sub-national level.

These three features represented the main lines of the PCI's strategy, although each was accorded differing emphases according to the practical application of this strategy during the period under discussion. Perhaps the most significant consideration surrounding Berlinguer's proposal of the 'historic compromise' was that, combined with the favourable turn of political and electoral events soon after it was formally launched, it allowed the party finally to break with a position of strategic inferiority and seize the initiative in inter-party debate, putting the other parties somewhat on the defensive. Undoubtedly, while the 'historic compromise' involved a strong continuity with party strategy from Togliatti,[f] the new political situation in which it was reinterpreted in the 1970s posed strong potential benefits for the PCI's own legitimacy as a political force in Italian politics. More than any other of the parties during this decade it was intensively concerned with the importance and priorities of strategy and inter-party relationships, as becomes very clear when looking at the approaches of the other parties.

As the other principal political force, the DC above all was required to respond to the PCI's 'historic compromise' initiative and develop an alternative or complementary strategy. In recent years, the DC had, despite the collapse of the Centre-Left alliance, shown no signs of new strategic thinking apart from its predictable aim of preserving political power. The line adopted belatedly by the Moro/Zaccagnini leadership and called *confronto*[g] did involve some break with continuity with its more positive attitude towards the PCI, although there are several grounds for questioning that it was a strategy at all or if, in the context of flexibly formulated inter-party relationships in Italian politics, it could be recognised as such, it was one neither decisive nor systematic nor long-term.

First, the weakness of the DC response to the PCI's initiative stemmed from the fact that the party's position was essentially defensive. As indicated in Chapter 4, this was because the DC had not thought out any systematic position for itself in advance of the PCI's political rise in the mid-1970s, and that thereafter the DC was fundamentally opposed within its membership to any principled espousal of the 'historic compromise' on ideological grounds.[h] This same defensive attitude was also strongly represented within the leadership of the party, if only because generally it reflected on the DC's loss of dominance at this time. On the eve of the PCI's electoral successes of 1975-1976, the line of the DC as presented by its national secretary, Fanfani, was unequivocally 'the rejection of the Communist proposal of historic compromise, both gradual and immediate, at the national level and locally'.[12]

With the PCI's acquisition of a greater role in local and regional government throughout the country from 1975, and the confirmation of its new electoral strength in the national election of 1976, the DC, having abandoned the discredited Fanfani, began to adapt to the new political situation. The attitudes of Tuscan party leaders typified this changed approach, particularly in a region where PCI/DC relations had been polarised (since much of the Tuscan DC had been a stronghold of Fanfani). There was greater recognition of the need for some (unspecified) political accommodation with the PCI, but there remained a reluctance to accede to PCI pressure for a formal or 'organic' alliance which was common to both Left and Right within the DC, although with differing moods of attitude towards the PCI as a party. One local DC leader from a Left *corrente* argued that his party would not accept the 'historic compromise' for ideological reasons, because of its attachment to the concept of 'freedom' and opposition to dictatorships, but acknowledged fully that socio-political and international environmental factors (e.g. the PCI's own evolution, the more open attitude of the Church towards it, the growth of detente) all favoured 'a more civil atmosphere of political debate, but to say that there is an evolution that will lead to the historic compromise is to make a fundamental mistake'.[13] On the Left of the DC, the view was most strongly represented that the DC's former ostracism of the PCI would have to cease: 'It is clear that in the present political circumstances the idea of opposing the hegemony of the PCI with the levers of the central state is less and less valid, and that the required strategy is that of increasing those forces in society disposed towards our side of the political conflict.'[14]

On the Right of the party — in Tuscany, the *fanfaniani* chiefly and to a lesser extent the *dorotei* — the tendency was one of greater ideological reservation and cynicism towards the PCI. One Florentine *fanfaniano* leader formally supported the party line of *confronto*, but stressed that it was 'basically a tactic, a strategy that aimed at exposing the contradictions that exist within the PCI', as over its relationship with Moscow.[15] The response of Ivo Butini, former DC regional secretary and once Fanfani's second-in-command in Tuscan politics, was more interesting for it touched on the fact that, while traditional ideological divisions separated the two parties, there was some *de facto rapprochement* between them, not least because of PCI strategy. Referring to the PCI's cautious line earlier over the divorce question in contrast with the radical line of the lay parties, together with the attempt by 'anti-Communists' in the DC to reach agreement with the PCI to prevent divorce being legalised, Butini commented in 1977:

> If you go into the local offices of the DC, the party most hated is the Radical Party, after the Radicals the Socialists are hated next, after the Socialists then the Republicans, after the Republicans then the Social Democrats — and *after* them then come the Communists![16]

The issue of divorce certainly drove a deep wedge between the DC and all the lay parties, who were adamant proponents of legalisation, but, while individual issues affected inter-relationships between these particular parties, traditional ideological reservation, if not hostility, continued to hinder any radical change by the DC leadership in their line towards the PCI. As a result, the DC's policy of *confronto* was inherently contradictory in that it accepted a form of empirical compromise with the PCI, but denied this had any formal significance.

Secondly, the line adopted by the DC towards the 'historic compromise' was conditioned strongly by electoral considerations, particularly as it was such a voter-oriented party.[i] Even if DC leaders were less considerate than their PCI counterparts of the problems of internal party participation among the membership[j] and indicated a certain latitude in being able to mould the opinions of members on political questions,[17] they consistently felt constrained by the likely negative repercussions among DC voters towards a formal alliance with the PCI. This motive was regularly mentioned or it emerged indirectly in the author's interviews with DC personnel, and whether or not party leaders were exactly correct in this assumption about their voters[18] — some of them suggested DC voters would be more 'confused' or 'divided' rather than purely negative — the fact they made it is the operative factor. Historically, this electoral consideration was no new occurrence, for in the past the choice of coalition partners had been commonly linked with the question of electoral appeals by the DC.[19] Thus, in Tuscany the DC leadership rejected PCI overtures after its 1975 election success for co-option by the PCI/PSI regional government because this would be a 'betrayal' of DC voters.[20] One DC leader stated more calculatedly that 'the relationship between the DC and PCI should be conducted by means of precise options undertaken in order that we are free in this way to win, at the electoral level, *confronto* with the Communists'.[21] This assertion of the electoral motive was invariably coupled in speeches by Tuscan DC leaders with the need to maintain the government/opposition divide between the two main parties. Hence, the electoral motive (the use of anti-Communist appeals to mobilise the DC electorate) may be added to what was a strong conceptual belief among DC leaders about the separation of government/opposition roles in a democratic political system.[22] This concept helped to shape the DC approach towards the PCI.

Thirdly, a coherent response to the 'historic compromise' by the DC was prevented by its own internal divisions when it came to the specifics of relations with the PCI. These divisions have already been treated in preceding discussion about differing interpretations of *confronto* between the DC Left and Right; and, moreover, as shown above,[k] the *correnti* continued despite their loss of credibility to channel internal discussion over party strategy. The resulting picture was invariably one of confusion about the practical application of DC strategy, especially when looking at different areas of the country where the presence of different *correnti* might vary. For this reason in particular the DC proved to be a frustrating partner in dialogue with other parties. The most frequent complaint expressed by PCI leaders about their experience with the DC's line of *confronto* was not so much the latter's continued attitudes of anti-Communism as 'incoherence' and 'contradictions' in its approach and strategy. One PCI federation secretary attacked the DC for lacking a strategy that was 'scientific' (i.e. systematic), and for operating virtually on a 'day-to-day' basis;[23] while similar criticisms were voiced by PCI federation secretaries in other provinces of Tuscany. It might also be pointed out that this lack of coherence gave the DC certain tactical advantages of procrastination in dealing with the PCI. In short, while the PCI possessed a long-term strategy whose ambiguities were highlighted by its concrete application, the DC lacked any such strategy (beyond a desire to maintain power and keep the PCI if possible at arm's length) for its position was attuned more to the dictates of everyday politics. All the same, the DC could not avoid the question of having to make alliance preferences.

The strategy of the PSI is interesting as an example of a third-party situation, this role being made possible particularly by the proportional representation electoral system but also by the PSI's having a mass organisation and electoral strength weaker than those of the DC and PCI but distinctly superior in both respects to the other lay parties. The PSI has suffered from the strategic dilemma common to third parties in having to choose an alliance with one or other of the two major parties (and being internally divided over these alternative possibilities), while trying to maintain its identity and credibility, especially among its actual and potential voters, and counter any impression of vacillation.[24] Claudio Signorile, the national PSI leader, described this need for a strategic choice by saying that 'equidistance may be an element of geometry, but it is not of politics', for political pressures external and internal to the party (e.g. the alliance opportunities created by the main parties, the need for some orientation to guide party activity) mean that the abstract notion of complete independence is not practically feasible. In reality, however, the PSI's desire to avoid being both a 'pendulum party' (oscillating regularly between alliance partners) and a 'bloc party' (in semi-permanent alliance with one major party against the other) has created for it a position of inherent ambiguity in Italian politics.

This pivotal position of the PSI as intermediary party, required by both the DC and PCI as an alliance partner for the purpose of majority-building, and its own strategic ambiguity have been highlighted particularly in the 1970s by changes and the greater state of fluidity in the Italian party system with the advance of the PCI and its greater legitimacy as a political force and hence alliance partner in competition with the DC, not to mention the stronger controversy lent to inter-relationships at the sub-national level with the introduction of regional government. The decade opened with the gradual disintegration of the Centre-Left, motivated on the PSI's part by its disillusionment with the DC over the failure to implement agreed reform policies and its own lack of electoral dividends, and the PSI's move in the direction of the PCI. This process took place first of all locally and regionally, when from the early 1970s new PCI/PSI alliances were formed, a trend strengthened by the electoral shift to the Left in 1975. Nationally, the PSI strategy from 1976 known as the 'Left Alternative' favoured an alliance with the PCI to replace the DC in government.

This closer relationship between the PSI and PCI was not, however, free from internal conflicts, which in the PSI's case were instigated by two major concerns: an uneasiness over the PCI's substantial electoral success without any corresponding gains by itself; and a growing apprehension at the start of *rapprochement* between the two main parties to the likely exclusion of the PSI's pivotal influence. The PSI's objections to the 'historic compromise' were expressed most commonly in criticism of the PCI's 'optimism' about stimulating a change in the DC and dismissal of it as a recipe for political stagnation,[25] but underlying this was a deep fear over its own impotence in terms of wielding political power and influence. Some insight into the PSI's dilemma was provided in an interview with the party's regional secretary in Tuscany, Paolo Benelli, in the spring of 1978. Commenting on the value of continuing the Left alliance with the PCI in this region, Benelli nevertheless emphasised the strategic divergences between the two parties:

> The principal one is this: the Communists want to transfer to the local level the policy of broad ententes, while we want to reconcile the policy of national unity with strengthening our autonomous role. In other words, we want to maintain the function of majorities and minorities allowing for a contribution by each democratic force, beginning with the DC, but without impairing their different roles ... there exists a concrete basis for a clear and open relationship between majority and minority and for some co-operation on specific matters. This we have advocated for years, but with a difference: for us, this is an aim in itself, for the Communists it is only a stage.[26]

This was a fair statement of the new PSI strategy as a long-term proposition, whereby it rejected the PCI's concept of a consociative democracy, only when it came to its application in the current situation the PSI was unable to free itself from its traditional dilemma. While from 1976 the PSI played a crucial role in the formation of a national government of emergency, bringing the PCI for the first time for three decades into the ruling majority, a glance across the country showed that by no means were all Centre-Left alliances unscrambled (as in areas of the south). The party justification of this inconsistency was that it opposed the 'mechanical transposal' of national alliances to the local level, and that a key factor was the need to form majorities which could vary according to the different balance of party strengths in different areas. As Benelli asserted, the PSI considered the Centre-Left formula 'dead and buried', but added this did not involve 'haughtily cutting all relations with the DC; rather we want a new relationship with the DC'.[27] The end of the decade in fact saw some *rapprochement* between the PSI and DC, combined with the former's adoption of a more aggressive line towards the PCI beginning with Craxi's polemical attack on Leninism in 1978,[28] followed in 1980 by the formation nationally of a *de facto* Centre-Left government while denying its formal birthright. Thus, during the decade the PSI had as a trend (though not uniformly so in practice) swung from one major party to the other and back again in its choice of alliance partners, in the hope that by stressing its own 'autonomous' identity it could avoid both labels of 'pendulum party' and 'bloc party'.

Even though the DC, PCI and PSI and their inter-relationship have dominated Italian politics, the role of the remaining small parties cannot pass without some mention. This is because, although subordinate, such traditional small parties as the Republicans (PRI), Social Democrats (PSDI) and Liberals (PLI) are recognised according to their additional numerical strength and individual political weight as necessary partners in majority formation. Their own political presence has been assured by a combination of their historical ideological traditions, localised strongholds of voting support and the prestige of their individual leaders. Indeed, the PCI persistent in its search for broad alliances has courted several of these parties, which — particularly the PRI and PSDI — played some secondary part in the formation of new PCI-led coalitions in local politics from 1975 and supported the national emergency government from 1976. These parties are, on the other hand, too minor to develop their own strategies, being essentially dependent on the strategic options presented by the two main parties. For example, the PRI and PSDI were motivated in their convergence with the PCI by its strategic evolution and growing legitimacy (as shown by the 1975–1976 elections) together with consideration of Italy's socio-economic crisis, although at the same time their continuing ideological reservations towards the PCI led to their rejection of the principle of the 'historic compromise'. It was of course above all its anti-Communist ideology which led the right-wing PLI to refuse any co-operation with the PCI at all, *de facto* as well as principled. The other traditional force, the neo-Fascist MSI, remained as a party-political outcast from the 'constitutional arc' for historical and ideological reasons.

A combined assessment of the different party strategies identifies some convergence, or rather differently motivated forms of convergence, between the various political forces. This did not, however, amount to the consociative arrangement sought after by the PCI. The different co-operative arrangements established from the mid-1970s between the two main parties and involving the third and the other small parties — external support for the DC-led government and then the programmatic agreement in Rome, coupled with variations on this theme in the regions and municipalities (also where the PCI was the strongest party) — all fell short of an 'organic' or formal alliance and were subject to differing, if not conflicting, interpretations by the parties concerned. The distinction made by the DC, PRI and PSDI between *de facto* and principled co-operation with the PCI seemed at first sight somewhat artificial until it is remembered that the conceptual starting-points of both sides with regard to inter-party relationships were dissimilar, not to mention that tactical and ideological considerations coloured their approaches. The PSI did not have objections for historical reasons to a formal alliance with the PCI, although tactical motives and concern not to lose its identity inevitably clashed with the PCI's aim of converting alliances on the Left into a broader coalition including the DC.

In short, the PCI differed from its actual or prospective alliance partners in viewing *de facto* co-operation from a principled standpoint as representing progress towards the 'historic compromise'. To be more specific, there were three main factors promoting convergence between the different Italian parties during the 1970s: the PCI's strategy itself and its own growing semi-independence in relation to the international Communist movement, so far as this helped to make it a more legitimate partner for the other parties; the PCI's electoral success of 1975–1976 with a consequent change in the balance of forces and a greater role for the PCI in the state institutions at different levels, which obliged the other parties to accept its viability in policy-making; and the sense of compelling national problems which provided a strong argument for an emergency government unifying all forces. The preceding discussion of party strategies reveals that, while the PCI was first and foremost motivated by its own strategic considerations but also by the third factor (for Italy's socio-economic crisis was seen as a potential threat to democratic stability), the other parties responded first and foremost to the second factor, though not to the exclusion of the other two motives (at least among some groups of leaders within them).

This general discussion of motives behind party strategies does, nevertheless, leave several follow-up questions. What constraints does the complex and time-consuming exercise of inter-party relationships impose on the essential task of policy-making? Italian politicians are often natural conceptualisers, but when it comes to the practical business of everyday politics how much do party strategies condition or determine party alliance behaviour at the various levels of the party structures? Finally, does the evidence so far suggest that convergence, albeit deriving from varying motives, is based on some permanent or long-term features of change, or is more likely to be a temporary phenomenon?

Here, a case-study approach provides a useful concrete illustration of party strategies in operation and inter-acting and, even though the balance of party strengths will vary from region to region and inter-party relationships might be affected by particular local situations, there is sufficient evidence to elucidate general problems relating to the above questions. The case of Tuscany does differ from most other Italian regions in that the PCI's dominant strength in this 'Red' region has lent it an added legitimacy as a political force, in contrast with 'White' regions where it has suffered from a weakness in this respect;[29] on the other hand, this very strength of the party in Tuscany has been regarded by the PCI as a key factor in the promotion of its own national strategy. Giorgio Amendola, writing in the party weekly *Rinascita* at the time of the introduction of the new regions in 1970, stated:

> Tuscany is as a region disposed by its history to perform an avant-garde function in the democratic development of the country . . . a majority of the Left, open to new relations with the democratic and popular forces of Catholic inspiration, can by overcoming obsolete forms of mistrust and discrimination usefully help to enlarge and strengthen the union of the popular masses. Such a process will offer other regions a civil example of new political relationships and promote the formation at the national level of a new majority, of a government alternative to the Centre-Left.[30]

Amendola's statement represented the strategic importance given to Tuscany before the regional structures began to function, but before looking at the first decade of regional government which followed it is necessary to put this new institutional experiment in context by assessing first the success or failure of party strategies in local politics during the same decade of the 1970s.

(b) Inter-party Relationships: the Case of Local Government

There are three relevant approaches to the importance of local politics in the context of party strategies: the direct impact of nationally determined strategies on the local level, and how far the respective parties attempt to co-ordinate the alliance behaviour of their grass-roots activists; the actual process of local alliance formation, to what extent particular local factors modify the application of party strategies and generally whether local politics is less politicised; and the results of local alliance formation and, in particular, of the PCI's stronger role in local government by way of influencing or acting as a precursor to inter-party relationships at the national level.

All evidence from Tuscany during the 1970s has underlined that national party strategies *and* their application nationally have been the primary if not over-riding factor conditioning local alliance formation, though not always exclusively so, for local situations may play a sub-ordinate role. This tends to accord with what little research there has been on other areas of Italy.[31] The consensus among interviewed leaders and activists of both main parties at the sub-national level in Tuscany was that national strategic objectives were the prior consideration in their own alliance behaviour. Thus, one DC leader with experience in both local as well as regional politics in Tuscany commented that 'the large mass parties have very precise national points of reference; therefore, all that occurs at the national level certainly is strongly reflected in regional and provincial situations';[32] while a local DC leader at Florence agreed that normally local alliances are determined by national politics with local factors in second place, the only small exception being in small mountainous localities where the latter were possibly more influential. On the PCI side, the common view was expressed by one federation secretary, who remarked that provincial and local developments could not be isolated from those at the national level and asserted: 'The debate developing at the national level is strongly present at the provincial level; therefore, its influential, objective developments are much perceived and are reflected strongly at the provincial level.'[33] One local PCI leader in the countryside outside Siena agreed that, although local motives could be important, alliances were formed 'on the basis of precise regional and national lines of direction; it is sufficient to think of what is happening in the commune of Siena, at the regional level in Tuscany and of the behaviour of, for example, the Socialists in Italy'.[34]

If there were possibly an element of party self-justification in these statements, the fact that local leaders (who were those directly responsible for implementing party strategies) thought in these uniform terms was itself significant. The uniformity of strategic approach was above all promoted by general structural factors in Italian politics, notably the centralised state and the centralised formal party structures. It was furthermore the deliberate policy of the leadership of the main parties at the national level to determine the course of alliance formation locally as much as at other levels of the state structure.

This co-ordination of alliance strategy was particularly evident in the case of the PCI, which has possessed the organisational machine to control this activity by its local leaders, all the more so in a 'Red' region like Tuscany where this machine was strongly articulated. It was the intention of national PCI leaders to stress the overall significance of local alliance formations as representing progress towards the implementation of the 'historic compromise'. This integrated approach was illustrated by Gerardo Chiaromonte, who in a speech to the party central committee in July 1977 commented on how DC-PCI *rapprochement* in Rome should facilitate broad alliances in local politics:

> We are advancing towards the attainment of our objectives, striving for the full implementation of the programmatic agreement – in the Parliament, in the regional, provincial and local councils, in the whole of society ... The unitarian process must advance – and this is the direction in which we are working – in the relations between the groups in the Parliament and in all the elected local assemblies ...[35]

Local government was therefore seen as an important channel for the application of party strategy, just as the PCI tended to regard and publicly interpret local elections (in official Italian terminology called 'administrative' elections as distinct from 'political', i.e. national elections) as significant indicators of the success of national party strategy.[36]

This policy outlook determined by the national party leadership has been the primary factor in the PCI's local alliance formation, although the extent to which newly established municipal administrations were in practice directly discussed at Rome depended on the cases concerned. The major cities or notably difficult cases invariably involved national party personnel in the negotiations, while the question of smaller communes was usually left to direction from the provincial party leaders.[37] In the latter instance, the party has claimed that it has not sought to 'superimpose' its strategy on local situations[38] and has admitted that a 'global assessment' of varying local cases is not always possible;[39] however, direct guidance by the party federation is always provided, though this does not necessarily have the required results. For instance, after the PCI's election success in 1975 the party provincial office in Siena directed the *sezioni* to contact DC groups on local councils 'with a view to overall co-operation in administrative tasks'. Many PCI *sezioni* did not like carrying out this directive, as the DC was especially 'Right-wing' in this area, but generally the latter refused this offer in any case, although there occurred some practical co-operation in a few communes.[40] Generally, as shown above,[1] internal party dissent towards the 'historic compromise' was more evident among certain groups of members and least likely among leadership cadres, even local ones, although the latter could be influenced by the former.

The DC has similarly sought to determine a uniform approach in party strategy at the local level, although its less bureaucratic internal structure has meant that co-ordination has been managed less efficiently. While not so emphatic as the PCI about local alliances being indicators of national developments, its leaders have implicitly acknowledged the significance of the former for the latter. Thus, the line adopted by Tuscan DC leaders in the early 1970s with the approval of the national party was to press for 'coherence' in local alliances with respect to the national coalition (i.e. the maintenance of the Centre-Left), and that municipal politics should not be considered 'an area for experimenting with new and opposed majorities' (i.e. of the Left). The DC provincial secretary for Florence justified this: 'The autonomy of local authorities cannot be measured according to their ability to form majorities which are different from or contrary to those operating nationally: this is a mistaken concept of autonomy ... the idea of local autonomy is not concerned with the formation of local administrations and majorities, for this should maintain the structure of the power in the state.'[41]

This was of course a defensive doctrine aimed at preserving the DC's dominant role in the government of the country at different levels in the face of growing pressure from the PCI for a greater role here, but its implementation depended not least on the (declining) willingness of the Tuscan PSI to keep to the Centre-Left formula. In fact, it was in the 'Red' regions of Umbria and Tuscany that Centre-Left administrations first began to be terminated by the PSI following the 1970 local elections. The DC adjusted and rationalised its position in the light of this change with the 'Forlani preamble' (named after the party's national secretary), whereby PCI/PSI alliances were only acknowledged by it when numerically necessary with the PSI completing the majority. The DC continued to try to maintain the Centre-Left wherever possible, but this became progressively less feasible once the national coalition in that name ceased operating from 1972. Florence was the last major bastion of the Centre-Left in Tuscany which, because of its influence and prestige, was regarded as an important counter-balance to PCI dominance in regional politics.[42]

Following the loss of Florence to the Left and the general PCI advance in 1975, the DC took a more defensive stand, though the national party formula of *confronto* was slow in being formulated with regard to local politics. One Tuscan party leader, Tommaso Bisagno, warned the DC in 1977 that, while the 'creeping historic compromise' had to be watched guardedly at Rome, 'the historic compromise which is dangerous is that conducted at the grass-roots, at intermediary levels, because this creates a close network of interests that would later be very difficult to disengage from'.[43] Eventually, the elaboration of the party line of *confronto* gave an official blessing to dialogue with the PCI, which was interpreted as excluding formal co-operation locally between the two parties. Following the programmatic agreement at Rome in the summer of 1977, involving the DC, PCI and four other parties, Zaccagnini as national DC secretary made it clear that this should not be viewed 'as a signal in the regional and local administrations for a move towards forms of common management of political responsibilities'.[44]

This guidance was generally followed by provincial party leaders. For instance, in the case of one commune (Forte dei Marmi) in the province of Lucca a DC administration was formed early in 1978 with the supporting votes of the PCI, two of whose councillors were given administrative responsibility but not formally as part of the municipal executive. This compromise arrangement, following a period since 1975 in which the local PCI had informally supported the DC, was only reached after approval was given in person by Zaccagnini.[45] The rejection by the provincial party office at Lucca of an 'emergency administration' at Forte dei Marmi was justified with reference to the general party line: 'The DC considers that the leadership of Forte dei Marmi and the group of councillors ... can keep the experiment of Forte dei Marmi within the limits established by the provincial committee which, according to the line of the national secretary, has excluded in our province a common presence of the DC and PCI within the local administrations, but has not excluded, rather has urged, as much *confronto* as possible with the parties of the constitutional arc.'[46] The head of the DC local group at Fiesole, near Florence, similarly agreed that relations with the PCI 'depend to a certain extent on Rome, because a party position at the national level undoubtedly debars different political lines locally'.[47]

These two examples were, however, taken from areas where the 'Zaccagnini line' was strongly supported because of the dominance internally of Left *correnti*. In the province of Arezzo, on the other hand, the continuing control by *fanfaniani* over the provincial party meant that *confronto* was regarded with little enthusiasm and dialogue with the PCI hardly existed here. According to the DC provincial secretary, the programmatic agreement at Rome in 1977 produced strong reactions in the Arezzo party which viewed the event 'extremely negatively' and had despatched memoranda to the national party office expressing its opposition to the agreement as 'extremely dangerous'.[48]

It has already been shown that in general the *correnti* were the real channel for political, and hence strategic, discussion inside the party; and this affected local politics because the *correnti* were present at the local level according to the personal allegiance of local party secretaries to a certain party leader.[m] Vertical relationships through the *correnti* have more often than not conditioned the formation of local alliances on the DC side or, as one Tuscan DC leader explained, 'the national situation carried weight, because it operates via local leaders who have their national allegiances'.[49] The pull of *correnti* membership has been invariably the principal factor behind the incongruity of DC strategy, as it has appeared in different shapes and forms when comparing various localities where different *correnti* might control the party. There was also the allied problem where local DC leaders revealed a lack of initiative in relations with other parties, depending as they did on direction from their respective DC leaders above. The PCI federation secretary for Pistoia commented in 1975 on his experience in dealing with the DC in different communes of the province:

> I refer to a sort of waiting on events, even among the most forward-looking groups in that party, a considerable reluctance to involve

themselves in general issues of politics which are delegated only to decisions at the national level, attitudes which reveal ... the decline of political action in the DC to the level of modest provincial pragmatism.[50]

This was written at the time of Fanfani's national Secretaryship and before the advent of the DC line of *confronto*, when the prospect of a changed relationship with the PCI had some stimulating, divisive and often negative effect on local party activists, but the above comment nevertheless pinpointed one feature in the DC locally which by default invariably allowed the party hierarchy to impose its will — a certain lack of political involvement and a deference to party authority.

With the remaining political parties, the national determination of local alliance formation was less clear. In the case of the PSI, a uniform national approach was inhibited by its very strategic ambiguity discussed in the preceding section. As the third party, a position it also invariably held both regionally and locally throughout Italy, the PSI was compelled to take account of the balance of strength of the DC and PCI which varied between different areas. This meant that regionally, but also locally, the PSI was faced with different alliance prospects. There was also the fact that somewhat like the DC the influence of internal *correnti* determined the application of party strategy. In Tuscany, the balance of *correnti* accorded with the internal coalition between the younger-generational Left and Right (the 'autonomists') which in revolt against the older-generational Centre groups around De Martino had brought Craxi to the national Secretaryship in 1976 — indeed, the Craxi-Signorile axis was somewhat stronger in the region than nationally.[51] This acted as a guarantee for local adherence to the Craxi strategy of the 'Left Alternative' for, as with the DC, local *correnti* allegiance was transmitted via the provincial party federations — this being all the more likely as in Tuscany the Left and Right factions had a strong background of internal collaboration. In effect, the 'Left Alternative' had operated in Tuscan communes increasingly from 1970, though not uniformly until the 1975 elections allowed the PSI to make a final break with the DC in the Centre-Left, until when it remained in coalition with the DC in several major cities (notably Florence, but also Viareggio and Massa).

Because of its strategic ambiguity, a certain autonomy was often left to the PSI at the grass-roots with respect to local alliances. As one local Socialist leader noted, the party has made a virtue out of 'freedom of action' in this respect as when, for instance, 'during the Centre-Left period the PSI did not bind the party at the local level automatically to this formula',[52] for in many cases in Tuscany the Centre-Left was numerically impossible because of PCI predominance. However, when it was a matter of formalising or reinforcing a new trend in local alliances the decision was taken at the national level of the party. This occurred both in 1970, when new Left alliances were inaugurated in the 'Red' regions, and in 1975 when this coalitional preference was applied generally in much of Italy, in both cases the PSI leaving the strategic option open until after the elections revealed whether the relative electoral positions of the PCI and DC made this possible.[53] In the case of the other small parties, their localised strength made them even more dependent on the alternate dominance of the PCI or DC and their own alliance preferences, although the fact that the former did not hold a pivotal position (with a few local exceptions) allowed them a greater freedom than the PSI to opt out of taking sides. Even so, some trends were apparent in their local alliance behaviour which was influenced by their national relationships with the two main parties. This was shown in the greater readiness of the PSDI and PRI to support externally or enter some Left administrations following the 1975 elections in Tuscany.

This consideration of local conditions now leads the discussion of inter-party relationships to the second aspect of the actual process of local alliance formation and to what extent particular local factors might modify the application of broad party strategies. It is clear from the preceding examination of the sub-national co-ordination of party strategies that there was only limited scope for local factors to emerge, particularly with the main parties. All the same, the influence of local conditions cannot be excluded, and these will now be discussed.

In an interesting essay on the application of PCI strategy in the province of Milan, Peter Lange has emphasised its need to adapt strategy to different local contexts and illustrated how much responsibility for this lay with local leaders, who were often more conditioned by concrete situations and inter-relationships in their localities than by the concepts of national strategic goals.[54] Looking at different socio-economic areas within the province, he rightly noted that party inter-relationships, as between the PCI and PSI, varied in intensity, but he failed to provide and evaluate any overall categorisation of different (including other) local factors and omitted relevant discussion of internal party mechanisms of control in implementing party strategies. His investigation was in fact conducted before the political situation in Italy began to become more favourable towards the PCI's strategy. This last development, as already seen, made some difference above all with the PCI's electoral breakthrough in acting as a pressure on the other parties to respond to the challenge of the 'historic compromise'. While this general turn of events undoubtedly had its impact on the local dimension of Italian politics, it is still necessary to estimate the influence of specific local determinants of party alliance formation. These may be treated according to the following categories: local political tradition affecting the respective parties; the socio-economic structure of localities; the local balance of party strengths; and, very significantly, the extent to which local politics is dominated by partisan allegiances.

The question of local political tradition has derived force from the continuation of local loyalties and, in particular, of localised historical experience and political identification in Tuscan society.[n] With regard to party-political development and alliance preferences, this factor has been especially noticeable on the political Left, which has traditionally been dominant in much of Tuscan local politics notably through the strong role played by the PCI in local administrations. This firm tradition of the PCI as ruling party in so many Tuscan localities gave an added stability and credibility to its strategy of the 'historic compromise' and active claim to be a governing party launched in the 1970s. The PCI's partial involvement in national government at Rome during 1976–1979 therefore seemed more in accord with party's precedent in Tuscany than in most other regions in the country. In the case of the Tuscan PSI, local tradition was even more evident in that this was expressed in a distinct alliance preference for the Left — that is, coalitions with the PCI in municipal politics. This solid unitarian tradition, readily acknowledged by leaders of both parties in the region, had its roots in local socio-cultural traditions of working-class solidarity, was a fact of life accepted by the local party bases and was most apparent in areas where the combined Left dominance was overwhelming. The PSI vice-mayor at Volterra, one such case in point, commented on this:

> The factors which unite the Communists and Socialists in the government of the town originate somewhat in the Socialist tradition of this town — it has a tradition of the Left, a lay and democratic tradition, which goes back to the fact that the working-class movement in our town grew up with the Socialist Party, was reinvigorated, strengthened and enlarged with the birth of the PCI. This is a constant tradition found above all in Tuscany and Emilia.[55]

It was for reasons of this local unitarian tradition, which naturally coloured the Tuscan PSI's Leftward orientation, that the experience of the Centre-Left in the 1960s proved painful, both inside the PSI and in the party's relations with the PCI.[56] In local cases of such DC/PSI coalitions, affective links between local Socialists and Communists were ruptured for national strategic purposes, despite the principle of local autonomy in the PSI (a principle often exploited more to justify the contradiction between a local alliance and that followed nationally). Apart from the unique case of Florence, Centre-Left administrations began to appear regularly in Tuscany from 1964, that is once it had been formalised in national politics, and were regarded by the Tuscan PCI with a sense of class and political betrayal or, in the words of Amendola, who maintained close relations with the party in that region, as representing 'a policy imported from outside and not corresponding to the traditions and requirements of the region'.[57] Not counting the important exception of Florence, which inaugurated one of the first Centre-Left local administrations in Italy under La Pira in late 1960 — this owed much to his own progressive influence, and was not as elsewhere motivated by anti-Communist considerations — most of these local cases lasted less than half a decade and few survived the local elections of 1970.

If the pull of local tradition was one factor in the return of the PSI to Left alliances in Tuscany, reinforcing its national disillusionment with the Centre-Left, it was still secondary. This was because, notwithstanding the background of unitarian co-operation, relations between the PCI and PSI were strongly affected by their own differences of national strategy. The Tuscan PSI, for instance, opposed the other's desire from the mid-1970s that the Left alliances should be broadened to include an 'entente' with the DC. In fact, the PSI reacted by insisting on its own autonomous identity and this affected their collaboration in local government, especially where new Left administrations were established in the mid-1970s. Negotiations between the two parties after the 1975 elections were not always easy, one issue being the PSI's demand for strong representation including in many cases the post of mayor — of 146 PCI/PSI administrations formed then, 100 were headed by PCI mayors and 46 by PSI mayors, despite the fact that the PCI was invariably the much larger of the two parties. One Tuscan PSI leader detected an attitude of 'intolerance' in his party towards the PCI, even though the party strategy of the 'Left Alternative' was basically accepted in the region:

This intolerance derives from the fact that in a society like Tuscany, in which the PCI is the prevalent force, this type of agreement [the programmatic agreement at Rome, 1977] brings to the fore locally the difficult situation facing the PSI nationally. The PCI is completely oriented towards the policy of the historic compromise, while the majority that has been formed in the PSI finds itself somewhat squeezed by this policy. There is continuous criticism, but in practice there is compromise.[58]

Any contradiction between local unitarian traditions and this tension in PCI/PSI relations was therefore itself a cause locally of the PSI's being torn between divergent loyalties.

Turning to the second factor, Lange's study of the Milanese PCI was based largely on a categorisation of localities according to socio-economic factors. According to him, different environmental conditions when comparing urban areas (where party *sezioni* may be isolated and contacts with those of other parties may be poor), dynamic suburban areas (where social problems are more pressing and accordingly political parties interact more) and static rural areas (where political initiatives are less likely) may affect the prospects for party alliances.[59] In Tuscany, there is an absence of any major conurbation comparable to Milan, while any clear divide between urban and rural areas is complicated by the region's diffuse economic development after the War,º so that other corresponding criteria have to be taken. A broad distinction may be applied in the first instance demographically between communes below and above a population of 5,000 and then among the larger communes to distinguish from others those centres which have featured dynamic change since the War, namely where population growth and/or industrialisation has occurred. In Tuscany, these are not always identified with the main city areas.

The first distinction is a direct result of the fact that, while the proportional electoral system operates in communes above 5,000, in those below that figure seats in municipal councils are allotted according to a majoritarian system so that the strongest individual party gains an overall majority. This means that viable oppositions and hence more competitive situations may exist in the former case, but not in the latter where the party controlling the administration may well totally dominate the municipal council, with different consequences in each case for inter-party relationships.

The further point of distinction is that in centres of socio-economic change, as Lange pointed out, political parties are usually required to respond to inevitable social problems with a stimulating effect on political debate and dialogue. Cities like Livorno, Pisa and the Versilia area — more so than the more provincially-minded and quiescent cities like Lucca and Siena — come to mind, but a good example in this respect is the city and area of Florence. One much-quoted event in recent Florentine experience was the city floods of November 1966, which had an important effect in mobilising the public, an episode which eventually contributed to the formation in the city of self-help neighbourhood councils (*consigli di quartiere*).[60] The political parties, the PCI the most conscientiously, attempted to direct this new form of mobilisation; while among the Christian Democrats it was the parishes, the Catholic assistance organisations and certain progressive Catholics located on the DC Left rather than the party as such which tried to channel this new activity in the aftermath of the floods. It is significant in this context that Florence was one of the earliest centres of dialogue between the PCI and Catholic groups, an opening mainly at an intellectual level which received some encouragement from La Pira during his second term as mayor (1961–1964) and became well-known through the publication in 1964 of the book, *Il Dialogo alla prova*, edited by Mario Gozzini, a Left-wing Catholic.[61]

This kind of dialogue occurred primarily among cosmopolitan, intellectual and progressive circles on the Catholic side, while in the countryside attitudes towards the PCI remained suspicious and certainly not willing to initiate new ideas.[62] The DC itself, controlled at Florence by the *fanfaniani* from the mid-1960s following their overthrow of La Pira, reacted negatively to this dialogue, although this caused an internal rift between these DC leaders and progressive Christian Democrats which later contributed by the early 1970s to the party's decline in the city. Such a development with Catholic groups acting as an avant-garde and a pressure on the DC was very unlikely in the purely rural areas, for there was a vast difference of environment between, notably, the city of Florence and the geographically isolated smaller communes as in the Chianti, the Apennines north of Florence or the depopulated area to the south of Siena. Commenting on his own experience as a former mayor of a small commune compared with urban politics, the PCI federation secretary for Grosseto noted:

> At the provincial level, it is easy to succeed in opening up new relations between one political force and the other. At the communal level, things are much more difficult . . . because here we encounter a closed attitude among the other parties. Relations with

the PSI are good, but we have a notorious difficulty in opening up contacts of unitarian collaboration with the *sezioni* of the DC.[63]

Although this factor was strongly overlaid by the geographical balance of local *correnti* dominance (i.e. a more intransigent attitude towards the PCI where the DC was controlled by the *fanfaniani* or the Right) the socio-economic structure of the DC in a given area appeared to have some influence, for, as already shown, the DC was in this respect very differentiated throughout the region.[p] Where its social base was specifically geared to the promotion and defence of certain economic and financial interests and as a distinct minority force it lacked any supporting movement (as in the province of Siena), it proved less available for new relations with the PCI; while in other areas its mass character made it more susceptible to the changing political situation, notably to electoral pressures,[q] though so far as this availability to dialogue with the PCI was influenced by the DC's Catholic links there was some difference between the more urban and the purely rural areas.

The third factor of the local balance of party strengths is more straightforward and may be discussed briefly. Essentially, it involved what may be called the numerical determinant (i.e. the need to form a majority) in relation to the political determinant. The latter represented the influence of party strategy — that is, its implementation locally depended on political solidarity among preferred alliance partners going beyond the function of majority-building. As already seen, the numerical determinant was used by the PSI to justify or explain its local variation in alliance formation according to which major party predominated, and indeed its Centre-Left alliances with the DC in Tuscany in the 1960s were only found in those communes where such majorities were possible. Local instances may therefore be categorised according to whether the PCI or the DC was dominant (notably in communes under 5,000 because of their electoral system, but also some larger cities where either party was intrinsically strong like Lucca for the DC and Livorno for the PCI), and otherwise cases where the balance of parties was more even. The same factor operated in 1975, when with the PCI's electoral advance a combined majority emerged in many additional communes for the formation of new Left administrations.

Sometimes, this numerical determinant was difficult to gauge statistically for there were instances too where minority administrations were shored up by external support from other parties (as in national politics). This device was the one most commonly used to establish PCI/DC collaboration in local politics, for formal coalitions between the two parties were virtually unknown in Tuscany, although isolated and often controversial and transient examples occurred elsewhere in Italy, such as the Veneto and parts of the Mezzogiorno (where dire social conditions provided a compelling argument). In the DC's case such informal arrangements clearly allowed it to reconcile PCI collaboration with its own ideological reservations and concern about electoral repercussions among its voting support. These were almost always where the DC was in control of local administrations, and wished to maintain office even at the cost of compromise with the PCI. In the province of Lucca, where the DC had because of its strength traditionally controlled most communes, several instances occurred following the 1975 elections. At Barga, the DC lost its absolute majority then and in September of that year formed a programmatic agreement with the PCI as one local example of this before that arrangement occurred nationally at Rome. Similarly, the DC administration at Lucca engaged in discussions with the PCI and other parties as a result of the political impact of the 1976 national election leading to a programmatic agreement a year later.[64] This occurred despite the DC's having a small majority in the city council, but the move to the Left and the DC's national entente with the PCI created pressures which the local DC found hard to resist. The political determinant, however, operated most of all in the line taken by the PCI, which sought the broadest possible alliances even when support from other parties (e.g. the small lay parties) was not necessary for majority reasons. This was in effect a reflection of the party's pursuit of a consociative democracy.

Finally, the question of the intensity of partisan allegiance in local politics is relevant to our discussion because it illustrates the degree to which party strategy is perceived locally and therefore conditions relationships between leaders and activists of different parties. Local mayors and party leaders, from all three main parties, invariably made the point in interviews that personal contact between political adversaries was always good and that, even though their partisan allegiances were recognised, these were not a barrier to socialisation. Thus, a typical answer came from the leader of the DC council group at San Gimignano: 'At the personal level, at the human level, we are a small town, we all know each other, we even stand at the same bar together — relations are good, extremely correct.'[65] In other localities, it has been perhaps more common for Communists and Christian Democrats to frequent different bars (not to talk politics necessarily, but largely to play cards and just chat with friends). But, even if this practice continued, party activists generally indicated a disappearance of the rigid polarisation at the societal level, as was experienced in the period of the Cold War and even after. In the view of one PCI mayor, 'in the past there was a rupture in relations, but with the years there has been more movement here', while a local DC leader agreed that 'the period of very dramatic diametrical opposition politically is finished, but there is no possibility of an entente on major local problems'. Invariably, the latter meant that in communes run by the Left the DC opposed the budget (the key to local policy prospects and therefore symbolic), but there could be agreement between both sides on small local matters.

What did this situation mean and what consequences did it have for inter-party relationships in the 1970s? While there had taken place a change in political atmosphere affecting local politics, this did not automatically lead to any significant or concrete reduction in the DC's reluctance to accept the overtures from the PCI. This was partly because of traditional ideological reservations held by local DC leaders and their deference to the party hierarchy over strategic questions, but also because the emphasis by PCI activists on the symbolic importance of co-operation (as justifying the 'historic compromise') tended to alienate the local DC.[66] Furthermore, the defensive position of the DC at this time, the hesitation and delay of the party hierarchy in developing a strategy in response to the PCI and the fact that involvement in the application of a party strategy required some conceptual grasp of wider political issues, all tended to inhibit local DC activists. Local instances of pragmatic co-operation therefore occurred, but these stopped short when strategic considerations were introduced. Ultimately, these conditions related to the different characters of the two main parties, especially the fact that the PCI was self-consciously an ideological party and the DC not so. Furthermore, regular human contact and the more relaxed social atmosphere applied far more to the small communes than to the larger urban areas where partisan involvement was usually more intensive and the party situation more competitive,[67] but this point brings the discussion to the third and final aspect of inter-party relationships in local government.

Attention will now focus on the consequences of local alliance formation, with particular reference to the stronger presence of the PCI in municipal government, for the general standing of the parties and for national politics. This study has so far shown that competitive rather than intransigent or polarised politics came to mark the inter-party relationships at the local level in the 1970s, but that the strategic objectives of the various parties and especially the PCI's 'historic compromise' failed to materialise to any great degree because of a situation of stalemate. This was because 'convergence', widely acknowledged verbally by the different parties as necessary on grounds of the country's serious economic and social problems (the 'Italian crisis'), was differently motivated and differently interpreted in each party's case. Undoubtedly, diverse and sometimes conflicting party interests — the DC's maintenance of its power positions, the PCI's aim to be accepted as co-partner in government and the PSI's determination to preserve its independent identity as a third force — lay behind this problem. Nevertheless, the need in Italian politics for political consensus and action to be based on accommodation between different parties and electoral pressures resulting from the PCI's advance in the mid-70s and its increasing executive role at the local level did dictate a changed political situation from this time.

The PCI justifiably emphasised the importance of its unprecedented electoral successes in the local and regional elections of 1975, although in doing so it ran the risk of arousing too high expectations and was later to admit this as a tactical mistake. To some extent, this derived from its own reading of the meaning of the election outcome. The PCI had campaigned strongly with the argument that its electorate should be increased in order to defeat the DC — that is, hit the DC where it was most vulnerable, at its electoral base, and allow progressive elements in it to replace its then discredited conservative leaders (notably Fanfani) — and hence reinforce the 'historic compromise'.[68] Following its subsequent success, the PCI tended to project its own strategic objectives into the result. The outcome was widely hailed as the destruction of 'anti-Communist prejudgements' in the DC, and as inaugurating 'a new and intense period of unitarian collaboration between all forces in the institutions'. In a sense, the PCI proved to be correct in that the DC's conservative leadership — in Tuscany, the *fanfaniani* — lost power and authority in the party, but the PCI's other assumption proved to be over-optimistic. The DC was forced to respond to the rise of the PCI and in many cases change of power in favour of the Left, but it acted rather more out of necessity than out of any conviction that inter-party relationships had entered a new historic stage. Furthermore, the PCI's 'hard line' of aiming to weaken the DC was tempered in the later 1970s by the dictates of party strategy, which now chose to emphasise instead the need for direct co-operation with the DC as a whole.

The evidence of the PCI's advance was substantiated by its increase in administrative posts after the elections of 1975. Nationally, it took over control with Left administrations in most major cities in the country, including Milan, Turin, Rome, Naples, Florence and Venice. Altogether, it became the major governing party in 2,778 out of 8,068 communes, including 39 out of 95 provincial capitals, while holding the position of mayor in 1,362 and 21 cases respectively.[69] This compared with the situation before 1975, when the PCI was major governing party in 2,441 communes, including 24 provincial capitals, while holding the mayor's position altogether in 1,107 cases.[70]

In Tuscany, the shift to control by the Left was less dramatic as the PCI already held a majority of administrative posts throughout the region. Taking the post of mayor (with figures for pre-1975 in brackets), the PCI now held 156 (142), the PSI 61 (41), the DC 54 (90), the PRI 2 (2), the PSDI none (3), Left independents 10 (9) while the extreme Left PdUP now held one such post and Centre independents 3.[71] In total, the Left now held four-fifths of the local administrations in Tuscany, with the DC largely confined to its governing role in its traditional stronghold of the province of Lucca. Perhaps more significant than purely this statistical evidence of PCI strength was the shift in party allegiances following the election. As Table 5.1 shows, there remained a mixture of different combinations, but all the same distinct trends were visible. There was above all a consolidation of PCI/PSI alliances, also where the PSI was not required numerically to complete a majority, and connected with this was the PCI's aim of coalescing even when it had previously governed alone and was still able to do so. In fact, the number of administrations in which the PCI governed by itself fell from 55 before 1975 to 24 after the elections. Also evident was a decline in Centre-Left administrations (now confined to eight largely small and isolated communes – six of them had a population of less than 5,000), as well as a limited growth in coalitions between the Left, including the PCI, and small Centre parties.

Except for the small mountainous commune of Sorano (Grosseto) and the tiny commune on the island of Capraia (Livorno), there were otherwise no instances of formal DC/PCI alliances and in these cases particular local factors, such as disaffection by DC councillors with their own party, accounted for such exceptions. This, however, did not include the quiet but growing trend of *de facto* co-operation between the two main parties (with others) in less formal ways, such as programmatic agreements (i.e. a consensus on a policy document for the period until the next local elections in 1980) and agreements over appointments to such public agencies as hospital presidencies and boards, health syndicates, charitable associations, transport bodies and miscellaneous commissions that formed the patronage of

Table 5.1: Coalitions in Tuscan Local Politics, Before and After 1975 Elections

	Up to 1975	From 1975
1. Left Administrations		
PCI	55	24
PCI + PSI	52	146
PCI + PSI + PSIUP	17	-
PCI + PSI + Ind. Left[a]	7	32
PCI + PSI + PSIUP + Ind. Left	3	-
PCI + PSI + PdUP	6	2
PCI + PSIUP	2	-
PCI + PSIUP + Ind. Left	2	-
PCI + PdUP	7	-
PCI + Ind. Left	13	6
PSI + Ind. Left	1	1
Total	165	211
2. Left Administrations with Participation of Small Centre Parties		
PCI + PSI + PRI	3	2
PCI + PSI + PdUP + PSDI	1	-
PCI + PSI + PSIUP + ex-DC[b]	1	-
PCI + PSI + PSDI + Ind. Left	-	1
PCI + PSI + PRI + Ind. Left	-	1
PCI + PSI + PSDI	-	4
PCI + PSI + PRI	-	1
PCI + PSI + MUIS[c]	-	2
PCI + PSI + MUIS + Ind. Left	-	1
PCI + PSI + PRI + Ind. Centre[d]	-	1
PCI + Alt. Dem.[e] + PdUP	-	1
Total	5	14
3. 'Historic Compromise'		
DC + PCI	1	-
PCI + PSI + DC	-	1
Total	1	1
4. Centre-Left Administrations		
DC + PSI	7	2
DC + PSI + PSDI	7	1
DC + PSI + Ind. Centre	1	-
DC + PSI + PSDI + PRI	5	3
DC + PSI + Ind. Left	1	1
DC + Ind. Left	1	1
Total	22	8

	Up to 1975	From 1975
5. Centre-Right Administrations		
DC[f]	43	47
DC + PSDI	8	4
DC + Ind. Centre	7	5
DC + PSDI + Ind. Centre	5	2
DC + PRI	1	-
DC + PSDI + PRI + Ind. Centre	1	1
DC + PSDI + PRI	1	1
PSDI	1	-
PRI	-	1
Ind. Centre	-	1
Total	67	62

Notes:

a. Ind. Left = Independent Left or those on the PCI list without party membership.

b. ex-DC = This was the case of Pisa, where in 1971 two DC councillors including the mayor broke with their party and changed sides to the Left. This led to the collapse there of the Centre-Left administration and the formation of a new Left administration under the same mayor, who headed the PCI list in the 1975 elections as a Left independent.

c. MUIS = The label adopted by dissident PSDI councillors in three communes in the province of Massa Carrara who after the 1975 elections supported a formal alliance with the PCI and PSI contrary to their party's provincial leadership.

d. Ind. Centre = Independent Centre, non-party affiliated but belonging to political Centre-Right or Centre.

e. Alt. Dem. = Democratic Alternative, label adopted by three councillors in one commune on the island of Elba who before the 1975 elections split from the local DC over the issue of an alliance with the PCI. One of them became mayor in the new Left administration with the PCI.

f. This increase in DC administrations in 1975, despite the swing to the Left, occurred because while the DC lost power everywhere else in Tuscany it gained several administrations in its stronghold of the province of Lucca. In fact, with one exception of a very small mountainous commune (where the DC replaced the PSI + Ind. Left) it was a question of the DC by itself succeeding an alliance with the Independent Centre.

Source: This data is based on information provided in Regione Toscana/Giunta Regionale, SEDD, *Mappa Politico-Amministrativa della Toscana,* October 1975.

local government. In this sphere, there has been greater accommodation between local Christian Democrats and Communists since the shift to the Left in 1975, although two points should be made about the DC's response here. Unlike the PCI, the DC has not viewed this area of accommodation as 'political' (where 'political' = political/institutional, i.e. it refers to relations between parties in municipal councils); and it does seem to reflect on the DC's strong instinct for patronage positions even when attaining these involved dealings with the PCI.

Within the local councils in Tuscany, as already seen, the DC only went so far as *de facto* co-operation when necessary rather than formal alliances with the PCI. Its insistence on maintaining the government/ opposition divide was particularly noticeable in those communes where it had lost power to the Left in 1975. The immediate reaction of the DC to its expulsion from office was often traumatic and bitter with the latter feeling directed outwardly towards the PSI for breaking up the Centre-Left, although it also turned inwards leading to sharp controversy between different *correnti* and age groups among Christian Democrats. This was seen, for instance, in the province of Massa Carrara, where in several cases the PCI acquired a role in local government for the first time, but nowhere was this reaction by the DC more evident than in Florence, which it had ruled continuously since 1951. Butini, the DC regional secretary, described the sense of loss of this city as if the West Germans had lost West Berlin in the 1950s, for Florence was 'the show-case of the West in the red sea of Tuscany'.[72] Some of his younger party colleagues disagreed, arguing that opposition could well be a 'purgative' for the DC, a view which provoked Butini to anger in an interview:

> One cannot do things in politics without power. This foolishness in the Florentine and Tuscan DC! It is an example of mental confusion, and something which worries me most of all. When we were in power some of us made a moralism out of power, and now that we are out of it everybody has gone mad! But, as for me, I haven't lost my head. We have carried on politics with power, and now we will do so without power.[73]

Eventually, the energies of the DC were channelled into an oppositional line criticising and exposing the Left's deficiencies and policy lines in local government, publicising any tensions between the PCI and PSI and seeking to exploit any apparent failures by the PCI in particular to live up to its campaign promise of a new approach in municipal administration. Consequently, there developed a more competitive political situation after 1975, especially as the party-political orientation of local administrations became a controversial subject throughout Italy,[74] promoted on the PCI's part by contrasting its role with the DC's 'corrupt' record in municipal government. It hardly needs saying that this controversy made the PCI's aim of collaboration with the DC that much more difficult to achieve.

The dominance *per se* of the PCI in local politics, as in Tuscany, did not therefore further significantly the process towards a formal alliance with the DC; in fact, there were indications that the DC proved more amenable to accommodation with the PCI in areas where it was stronger (as in the Veneto and the south), because of its readiness to compromise for the uppermost aim of maintaining power. However, the growth of *de facto* co-operation on the part of the DC did reflect the changed political atmosphere of the 1970s and recognition by it of the PCI as a viable party of government. But what wider implications did this change have for the general standing of the parties and for national politics? This is a valid question, not least because the PCI itself saw, in the words of one of its Tuscan leaders, 'a national incentive in our action of government and struggle at the grass-roots'.[75]

One distinction between the 1970s and earlier decades, especially the 1950s, was that centre-peripheral relations between the DC as the party of national government and the PCI ruling at the local level had improved qualitatively. Until the early 1960s, there had been frequent accusations by the PCI of discrimination against Left administrations by the central government, particularly over the distribution of resources. While there was some evidence of DC administrations being given favoured treatment, it is equally likely that polemics on this issue derived from the polarised state of Italian politics in the period of the Cold War and immediately afterwards.[76] By the 1970s, this form of controversy had virtually disappeared completely. As one local PCI report of 1978 on the party's role in municipal politics noted in comparison with the past:

> The most significant change is clearly political. That is, the forces of the Left and also therefore our own party have tended towards overcoming their idea of antagonism between the local administrations and the central government. For them this was at one time a sort of counter-power, but nowadays this idea has been abandoned.[77]

This was an admission that the controversy had, at least in part, been deliberately promoted by the PCI itself, for it was obvious that the PCI's own changed attitude in the 1970s was a consequence of its strategy of co-operation with other parties. On the DC side, the increasing role of the PCI in sub-national levels of the state structure, beginning with the inauguration of the regions in the 1970s but more particularly with the growth of the PCI's local government control from 1975, made any discriminatory approach no longer feasible. The PCI's own support for the DC national government during 1976-1979 reinforced this change.

If the PCI no longer evidenced a 'fortress' mentality over its role in local government, what effects did the changed state of centre-peripheral relations have on PCI policy? This question must be seen in a broader context, for by the 1970s the PCI's purpose in local government had undergone a profound change as part of its overall strategy. In place of its earlier emphasis on scrupulous 'good administration' of efficiency and parsimony, a model symbolised by the case of Bologna, the PCI underwent in the course of the 1960s an internal debate calling into question its 'neutral' line and adopted a more activist policy.[78] Growing social tensions in Italian cities related to the country's slower economic development helped to overcome the party's cautious approach, which had been influenced by the generally restricted idea in Italy of local government over social affairs but above all dictated by the PCI's desire to establish a reputation for reliable administration, and it now paid greater attention notably to the role of social services.[79] By the 1970s, when Italy's socio-economic state had worsened and the PCI came to acquire greater responsibility in local (and the new regional) administration, the party had formulated a view of local government as an instrument for responding to social needs and for promoting social change.[80] Unlike earlier decades, the PCI administrations during the 1970s featured on average a stronger propensity for spending programmes than those of the political Right, and generally acquired a positive record on social services.[81] Furthermore, whereas previously the PCI had given little thought to co-ordination between local administrations, it now strongly advocated new structures to facilitate such co-ordination, especially as the advent of the regions opened up the prospects for policy activity at the sub-national level.

Altogether, this change of approach by the PCI towards an activist line became known in its own words as 'the new method' of local government. This term, which became a slogan of the party in the 1975 local elections, encompassed the PCI's offer of more open and honest government aimed as a response to public demands for 'participation' and evidence of disaffection with traditional institutional procedures. As was clear, this new approach by the PCI to local government related integrally to party strategy:

This objective — the unity and involvement of different political forces and social groups — is one of the principal aims we have preferred for years, and which characterises 'the new method of governing'. This objective is all the more valid today in the face of the basic crisis affecting local administration. Around this and in conjunction with this is the achievement of all other aspects of the 'new method of governing': (1) decentralisation and participation; (2) moral and political rigour and immaculateness; (3) rigorous decisions on policy content — all the more urgent and necessary because of the crisis of local financing — and their co-ordination at the district and regional level.[82]

This approach was upheld as a contrast to the DC's reputation for 'misgovernment' and 'clientelism' in local administration; and the PCI was aware that its own credibility depended heavily on its ability to meet this challenge.

The last aspect of the PCI's role in local government and its implications for both its own standing and its relationships with other parties is therefore its record in implementing this changed approach, specifically during the period 1975–1980. In short, did its performance here strengthen or weaken its legitimacy as a political force and governing party, and consequently further or detract from the prospects for the strategy of the 'historic compromise'?

The first and obvious point that has to be made is that the very socio-economic problems, which had prompted the PCI's change of approach and indeed contributed to its electoral advance with the DC's loss of credibility in the mid-1970s, themselves acted as a severe constraint on Communist policy implementation in local government. While the institutional link with the centre had improved, in practice its usefulness depended not least on the entrepreneurial skill of individual mayors in negotiating subsidies through personal and political contacts. But overall the chronic and worsened state of municipal indebtedness and declining available resources imposed enormous limitations on the communes. The Left administrations felt this restriction most painfully, because the large-scale social spending they envisaged was simply not possible to implement in full. This major problem — referred to by the new PCI mayor of Turin as 'the financial *via crucis* of administrators in local government' — was a common point of complaint and frustration by the PCI, which seemed possibly to have underestimated its constraining influence in many areas. This was especially so where its leaders, taken by surprise by the party's unprecedented electoral gains in 1975, found themselves propelled into positions of local authority without the necessary preparatory experience. This deficiency was only partly mitigated by the PCI's crash courses in local government training instituted at party schools after the 1975 election.[83]

The lack of necessary resources was regarded by the PCI with the greatest despair in the south, where social problems were most acute and where disappointment with its performance was greatest, as became evident in PCI losses in local elections there from 1978. In the north, the party faced its most awesome challenges in the metropolitan centres such as Milan and Turin, while in Tuscany this general problem of the gulf between promise and performance was reduced, though by no means erased, by two mitigating conditions. First, there was the fact that urban society in Tuscany, although ravaged by precipitous postwar development, did not present the same social disharmony as encountered in the south and the northern conurbations. Secondly, the PCI's already long practice and firmly-rooted tradition of municipal administration, together with its electoral dominance, acted as a stabilising factor. This strong control throughout the region allowed the PCI, for instance, to be the motive force behind Tuscany being one of the most advanced regions in introducing new co-ordinative structures into local government. These were the *comprensori* (district councils) and *comunità montane* ('mountain communities'), which, consisting of nominated representatives from different communes in a certain area, were intended to promote their co-operation over common problems. It is significant that these new structures provided a channel which evidenced much *de facto* co-operation between the DC and PCI, largely because they were consultative rather than executive bodies and also that much more removed than municipal councils from electoral politics.[84]

Nevertheless, the Tuscan communes also experienced many of the same problems encountered elsewhere even if less intensively. The complaint and fear was expressed by one PCI federation secretary that there was a danger of the communes ceasing to be the 'fundamental point of reference' as the institutional structure closest to the public, for with the possibility of having to cut social services 'woe betide us if we confine ourselves to administering destitution'.[85] This lack of finance was particularly inhibiting to Left administrations because of the PCI's definite idea of policy initiative at this level, involving the transformation of a system of private commodities into social ones with consequent effects on the structure of production favouring small and medium enterprises over monopolies.[86] As one Tuscan PCI leader put it: 'With our policy programmes we aim at the co-ordinated intervention by public authorities, not only to stimulate the market by means of enlarging public spending, but also to intervene in the economic and productive structures, in the process of accumulation and therefore in the forms of consumption and the organisation of needs'.[87] But, despite these definite intentions, the policy results in this general situation of economic constraint hardly amounted to a radical new departure in local government. Inevitably, there arose some disillusionment with the PCI record especially among its new voters.

So far as the effects on the PCI's standing were concerned, a necessary distinction must be made between those communes it had long administered and those where it assumed power in 1975. In the latter case, expectations of the PCI's performance were higher because of the impact of the change of power for, as one PCI mayor of a traditional Communist commune in Tuscany commented:

> It is a great opportunity to administer a commune previously administered by the Christian Democrats, because it provides the opportunity to demonstrate the differences that exist between administration by the DC and administration by the PCI. In our case, on the other hand, since the citizens here have never been administered by the Christian Democrats, we don't therefore have to over-emphasise their shortcomings and our own ability to respond to the needs of the people. In this sense, alternation in power can be negative ...[88]

There was also the fact that coming to power in 1975 coincided with the height of the financial crisis and that local problems were invariably more pronounced in those communes acquired by the Left in 1975 (as one factor in the DC's loss of popularity), not to mention that in these cases the local PCI and PSI did not have the same background of solid co-operation in administration as in the traditional 'Red' communes. It was no surprise that many of the local examples of friction between the two parties over policy issues occurred precisely where they had come to power in 1975. Tuscany offered in addition to the traditional 'Red' communes many instances of new Left administrations, but none better than the city of Florence.

The case of Florence is worth some mention because of its prestige and weight — culturally, socially, demographically and also economically — within the region. The PCI's record in local government during the later 1970s was inevitably measured to some extent by this prominent example. Despite the PCI's presentation of an 'organic plan' for city development, its concrete achievements during the five years which followed the election of the Left administration in 1975 were limited and, seeing that many of the problems required not only adequate financial backing but also a long-term solution, it was perhaps no surprise that performance fell well short of promise. This was particularly the case with housing, an area urgently needing attention in an expanding city and a major tourist centre. In addition, the PCI had emphasised this problem in its criticism of previous DC administrations and in its own projects for mass tourism. One individual plan was implemented promptly, namely the creation of city district councils (*consigli di quartieri*), an innovation regarded by the PCI with great importance as its method of making local government open to 'participation' by the public. In fact, Florence was the first city in Italy to hold elections to these new bodies, in the autumn of 1976. Otherwise, the Left administration's most active area was its cultural policy, for which much potential existed at Florence. The city offered many opportunities as a conference centre, and much attention was given to sponsoring individual artistic projects and promoting new ideas in cinema, drama and music. In this respect, the administration benefited from co-operation with the Left government of the region, which assisted with welcome funds.

Despite the PCI's basic aim of social structural change, it does seem that strategic considerations dictated a certain caution over not causing concern to the party's new middle-class voters and a preference for unadventurous administration. This approach was personified by the reassuring role played by the mayor at the Palazzo Vecchio. Elio Gabbuggiani, 50 years old, had a background as a party functionary and was a member of the PCI Central Committee, but he had already become publicly known as president of the new Tuscan Regional Assembly during its first legislature (1970-1975). A common judgement of him, not confined to non-Communist circles, was that he excelled at the visible or representational role but not the administrative side of local politics, a view which must be set alongside the limited dividends arising from administrative work because of above-mentioned constraints. As a public figure Gabbuggiani acquired something of an 'elegant' image, even being described by *La Nazione*, hardly a newspaper friendly to the PCI, as 'the flower in the buttonhole of Florentine Communism', and once mayor became an active spokesman for the city at home and abroad. He promoted its cultural links with cities in other countries, both East and West. Rivalling La Pira, who as mayor of Florence had become a minor international figure for his individual efforts to further East-West contacts, Gabbuggiani travelled widely abroad and created a record as the first PCI mayor to visit the USA in 1977. This was in connection with Florence's town-twinning with Detroit, but it had a wider aim, for the previous year he had strongly supported US bicentenary celebrations at Florence and had sought various other opportunities to further American contacts. In short, Gabbuggiani became virtually an ambassador for Florence and by implication for the PCI with its strategic aim of acquiring international legitimacy.

His symbolic importance was well appreciated by the party in the region, where several other PCI mayors commented on his role as a 'flag' for the PCI and as a convincing exponent of the party strategy. Internally, his particular diplomatic skills as a mediator were put to good effect notably in managing the PSI as a coalition partner in city politics, despite its differences with the PCI over various issues (including a controversy over a public conference on dissent in the USSR), and indeed he was acknowledged by a prominent Socialist leader as 'the right man for the PCI's policy of alliances, respectful of adversaries and one who creates fellow-feeling'. As to the DC, however, relations with the Left administration remained competitive along government/ opposition lines, where the DC mounted regular criticisms of the administration's 'failures' and rejected PCI offers to co-operate, as for instance in forming common lists for the *quartieri* elections in 1976.[89]

Despite its limited achievements, compared with the expectations of 1975, and the DC's exploitation of this with its slogan '5 Years Ago the Red administrations promised miracles – who has seen them?', the Left managed to hold on to their newly acquired gains in the 1980 local elections in Tuscany. PSI extra voting support balanced some losses by the PCI, while in Florence the popularity of Gabbuggiani (who won here the largest number of preference votes) contributed to this result. The Tuscan PCI had gone out of its way to explain and publicise its record for the previous five years, as in regular articles on its local administrations in the party regional review *Politica e Società*, and took these elections very seriously.

Any general assessment of the PCI's success in furthering its strategic aims through its local government role must be differentiating. Judging by the 1980 election outcome, it had avoided the worst predictions about disappointment with its performance among its voters of 1975. Inter-party relationships had in Tuscany undergone some change with a reinforcement of Left alliances between the PCI and PSI, building on this tradition in the region, and there developed more flexible relations between the PCI and DC. The DC's electoral setbacks of the mid-1970s, together with the collapse of the Fanfani leadership, resulted in less intense antagonism between the two parties, marked by some growth of *de facto* co-operation in local politics, but any significant move towards the 'historic compromise' concept of broad alliances failed to materialise. The main reason for this was that local alliance formation was first and foremost dictated by national strategy. Even though particular local conditions could occasion some secondary variation in the actual process of alliance formation, there was no movement in inter-party relationships which could have acted as a precursor to new alliances at the national level. It seemed, therefore, that the PCI had been too optimistic in its view that the electoral blessing apparently given its new approach in Italian politics and the major problems facing the country would bring about a qualitative change in relations between the main parties. Party politics had remained competitive, not least because the DC had seen a challenge in the rise of the Left in the mid-1970s, but the fact that it was competitive rather than polarised indicated how much the political atmosphere had changed from earlier decades. As to whether the PCI had acquired much greater legitimacy as a political force, this question must be answered by looking also at its role within the new regional structure of the state.

(c) Inter-party Relationships and the New Regional State Structure

Tuscany was one of the 15 ordinary regions inaugurated as a new intermediary level in the state institutional structure throughout Italy in 1970, Florence being its capital and therefore the seat of the new regional executive and parliamentary assembly. A decade later is a suitable juncture at which to make a valid, though obviously somewhat interim, assessment of the importance of regional government for inter-party relationships and the success or otherwise of the respective parties in promoting their strategic objectives. Sufficient time has at least elapsed for patterns in this respect to have emerged.

One definite conclusion is now offered, and will be generally evident from the following discussion, namely that the political parties very rapidly came to dominate the operation of the new regional structures, just as their various positions had determined the original delay and eventual introduction of them.[1] This is perhaps no surprise considering how much the parties had since the Second World War permeated the functioning of the political system, both at the national level and also locally, as we have seen. What is more specifically interesting, and relevant to the present theme, is that the introduction of the regional structures had a stimulating effect on party competition and of course presented a new area for the application of party alliance strategy. This occurred even though regional politics delayed in actively concerning itself with policy matters until the regional statute (i.e. constitution) had been formulated, and then was very limited in its scope for policy action until the enlargement of regional powers in 1977.[s]

It may also be noted that the new regional structures introduced a factor of complexity with regard to the uniformity of party alliances in Italian politics, for the balance of party strength varied from region to region. The PCI chose in 1970 to exercise its dominance in the 'Red' regions, of which Tuscany was here an important example, to drive a wedge between the two main components of the Centre-Left by winning the PSI as a coalition partner in the Tuscan regional government (as well as in Umbria, while in Emilia-Romagna the PCI ruled alone) and provoking a defensive reaction from the DC. Did it therefore follow that the PCI's entrenched position in the potentially important regional level of the sub-national structure of the Italian political system — enlarged by its entry to three more regional governments in 1975 (Lazio, Piedmont and Liguria) — gave it a new opportunity and advantage in its more activist strategy in the 1970s, and what influence did this have on the strategic considerations of the other political parties? Did the regional experience differ in any way from that in local politics?

It was certain that national strategic motives would dominate party behaviour in regional politics, seeing that, as already shown, they did so over the question of local alliance formation, only more so. Regional politics being at a higher level was perceived with greater political intensity than municipal politics, or, if there were any comparison, it was with the politics of the larger cities such as Florence rather than the smaller communes. Comparative research by Riccamboni has shown that the new regions were regarded 'not only as an articulated structure of the state, but as a new potential level for the aggregation of political demands and the management of the country's resources',[90] and the evidence of the Tuscan case since his work was conducted would tend to reinforce that conclusion.

One principal reason for the difference of intensity between regional and local politics is that at the former level politicians are a professional class unlike in the communes (except for the larger cities), where mayors and administrators are part-time unsalaried personnel who spend their non-working hours on municipal business. This feature was emphasised by Riccamboni in his study of regional councillors which showed that 'the regional political class represent an element in the Italian political machinery which is not secondary'.[91] Less than one-quarter of regional councillors had no party career, with a particularly high correlation in the 'Red' regions because this party career background of regional councillors was that much more pronounced in the PCI.[92] In Tuscany, the body of regional councillors elected in 1975 incorporated a very high proportion of political professionals with many of the highest-ranking party or municipal leaders in the region, including many party provincial secretaries, a few regional party secretaries, many mayors of the major Tuscan cities and in a few cases former national parliamentary deputies. This was especially notable in the case of the PCI, which of course in this 'Red' region had many more municipal leaders on offer, among whose regional councillors of 1975 were the Tuscan regional party secretary, two former national parliamentarians, the ex-mayors of Livorno, Grosseto and Prato and the former regional secretary of the CGIL, the Communist-allied trade union federation. The DC group in the Regional Council included five former party provincial secretaries, one of whom was also formerly regional party secretary, and two current DC provincial secretaries. Furthermore, it hardly needs saying that regional elections enjoyed a greater political significance than local ones, although, as the three occasions of 1970, 1975 and 1980 showed, the coincidence of both events made it difficult to separate strictly their individual political impact.

The existence at the regional level of a professional class of politicians raises the question of whether they might develop some political autonomy over alliance formation, since they had more political weight than local politicians. It has been suggested that regional politics is a freer terrain in which to explore new alliance possibilities as between the DC and PCI, because unlike national politics it is not subject to international constraints (especially counter-pressure from the USA in particular).[93] This last point is true, but on the other hand the main constraint as to a formal alliance by the DC with the PCI has derived intrinsically from the former's own strategic priorities, identity and political ambitions, as the Tuscan experience has confirmed. So far as regional politics is directly concerned, this factor has been reinforced by the close relationship between the political groups in the Regional Council and their respective party structures. In the PCI's case, this follows the traditional pattern of close personnel interlinkage between parliamentarians and party leadership cadres as well as bureaucratic mechanisms for consultation, consensus formation and control.[94]

With the DC, this relationship is less formally regulated but nevertheless assured by the mutual participation of regional group leader and regional party secretary in each other's executive organs,[95] and is of course subject to internal *correnti* procedures.

Ultimately, this possiblity for autonomy over alliance formation relates to the regionalisation of party structures but, as already shown, the PCI as the most advanced case in this respect had developed this change in organisational rather than political terms. Its regional leadership was well-integrated within the overall party structure, while for the DC regionalisation at least during the 1970s did not acquire any serious political meaning and was in any case overlaid as usual by *correnti* patterns.[t] Looking at the regionalisation of the smaller parties, with their weaker organisational articulation, it was no surprise that this process had hardly started by the end of the decade. With the minor parties, regional structures existed formally, as in the case of the PRI and PSDI, but they had no political importance. The PSI as the third party had shown more consciousness of the need to adapt its party structure to the new regional level of government and had granted new powers to its regional organs at the 1976 national congress, such as over membership recruitment, with regional congresses being upgraded in political status.[96] In Tuscany, this change had by the late 1970s progressed more than in most other regions as the PSI was organisationally stronger here, but all the same it encountered the same problems of resistance of traditional structural interests as within the main parties and at best had to be viewed as a gradual process.

While in local politics the PSI had allowed its local leaders a certain autonomy over alliance formation, as already shown, this approach was less likely to be applied to regional politics because of its greater visibility — that is, alliance formation at this level had to be better coordinated with national strategic concerns, so far as possible, rather than treated somewhat loosely as had sometimes occurred in local politics. The Tuscan PSI admittedly possessed in Lelio Lagorio, president of the regional administration in 1970-1978, one of the early strong proponents of regional government in Italy in the 1970s, with his active advocacy of further devolution of institutional powers and policy areas,[97] but his closeness to Bettino Craxi as national party leader affirmed that his regionalism would not lead to any independent line over party strategy in Tuscany. Indeed, his promotion to a national party post in 1978 and appointment as national Minister of Defence in 1980, while illustrating as a notable first example how a regional could lead to a national political career, also indicated how much the two levels of activity were closely interlinked.

In short, national strategic considerations were for political and structural reasons able to predominate in alliance formation at the new regional level. It was therefore to be expected that the general factors conditioning party strategies already discussed and seen in operation at the local level — such as the different conceptual approaches to alliance formation comparing the PCI with the other parties, their differently motivated behaviour in the growth of convergence from the mid-1970s — would be reflected in regional politics. Nevertheless, it is worthwhile seeing how party strategies evolved regionally in Tuscany in view of the PCI's role as a regional party of government, and again to ask whether developments at this level in any way created a pressure on alliance formation nationally.

It emerged very clearly that the PCI saw in the regions from 1970 a central forum for the application and promotion of its strategy, and that many of the ideas it elaborated during the decade were already in evidence in the 'Red' regions where it assumed control before the 'historic compromise' was formally enunciated late in 1973. In Umbria, the party produced in 1970 a document on the PCI's prospective role in the region emphasising that

> the region is not merely an addition, a kind of super-commune that does not modify the old centralised state and its conservative policies: it is instead the instrument for transforming the old state structure, and for creating a modern democratic state based on local autonomy, decentralisation of power and therefore on popular participation. With the regions there should set in motion the process of radical transformation of the state, of its real political reform.[98]

In Tuscany, the party followed the same approach which, as the decade progressed, became know conceptually as 'the reform of the state', a catchword which described the PCI's activist line in utilising its sub-national power positions to promote its own policy solutions in conjunction with the other political parties.

As indicated by the preceding statement, the 'reform of the state' embraced inter-related themes. First, following its long-term advocacy of regional government the PCI pressed strongly for a politically meaningful devolution of authority to the sub-national level. This proposed structural reform was not exclusively confined to the role of the new regional governments, for, as discussed above, it included the dovetailing of the communes and new inter-communal consultative structures into the overall plan of a greater role for the different sub-national levels of the state structure in the government of the country.[u] A key element in this integration of policy activity was co-ordination between the regional and municipal authorities by way of strengthening, as the PCI saw it, the relationship between the state institutional structure and society and hence 'participation'. There indeed developed in Tuscany a practice of regular consultation between regional and communal levels over prospective regional legislation, a process which became more relevant once the municipalities as well as the regions were granted new powers under Law 382 in 1977. One PCI mayor expressed not merely the party standpoint but also drew on his own experience when comparing this significant though embryonic change with the problems of contacts in Rome:

> When one went to a national minister, there was a bureaucratic filtering process that never ended. In short, one finally arrived before the minister feeling enormously weakened on the psychological level ... while with the region this differed not because there they are my party comrades ... they are all persons, we all know each other, the relationship is direct and power closer ...[99]

This was true, although it undoubtedly helped that during this first decade the Tuscan regional bureaucracy was new, relatively young in its personnel, not yet subject to the tendencies of Parkinson's Law and largely staffed by sympathisers of the political Left.[100] Furthermore, while common membership of the PCI or PSI obviously smoothed communal/regional relations, DC mayors were not necessarily disadvantaged — on the contrary, it was the PCI's strategic aim to use its regional authority to promote co-operation with Christian Democrats. This of course acted as a pressure on the DC, which more often responded negatively than positively as the tense relations between the DC-led commune of Florence and the new Left regional administration during 1970–1975 illustrated. However, the DC mayor of one small commune pointed out in 1977 that the new institutional framework had also promoted inter-party contacts and even boasted that he had helped to lubricate the Tuscan region's efforts to carry influence in Rome:

> Many regional ministers (*assessori*) are friends of mine. On occasions when the region has had need of a hand in dealing with the state, I have always gone with the regional vice-president Bartolini to Rome to see the minister, when I was president of the district council. I

have always been available when the region needed help. Of course, this has conditioned relations with it, but these have been of an administrative nature.[101]

By the late 1970s, while routine procedures governed relations between administrative leaders of both main parties, general political relations between the parties themselves were marked more by their competitiveness.

Secondly, the 'reform of the state' approach demanded that the new institutional framework at the sub-national level, with the regions as the spearhead, be given an important part in the formulation of the country's policy (*programmazione*). What emerges from PCI thinking on this matter is the stress placed on furthering regional development within the national context.[102] This led to a change of line in the PCI compared with the past, when the 'Red' regions, although not then institutional structures, had been regarded by the party as 'islands' which stood apart from the rest of the country. Now they as much as other regions were to be considered as an integral element in the working of the state structure, and above all in a position to make a valid contribution to the solution of national problems.[103] This ambitious idea of the policy-making role for the regions was defined by the party as the doctrine of the 'open region' (*regione aperta*), or one which acted 'non-bureaucratically' as an important aggregative force. According to Gabbuggiani, the Florentine PCI leader, the 'open region' had three characteristics: it should be constructed in such a way as to favour 'a fruitful political dialectic' between assembly and executive and between the region and social forces; its institutional framework should be given 'real power' which would allow it to act as an agent for popular 'participation'; and, its institutional and financial powers should allow it to contribute fully to the political direction of the country.[104] This programmatic theme explained the insistence with which the PCI pressed for the granting of new powers to the regions in 1977, a decision certainly helped by the PCI's influence at Rome through its support of the national government.

Once again, the pressure emanating from the PCI through this change and hence the PCI's enhanced governing role at the regional level forced the other parties, and particularly the DC, to respond. The doctrine of the 'open region' involved particularly 'a relationship which is not closed between the political forces represented in the region and in society ... if it is the Council [i.e. its majority] which decides, proposals should come from all forces present, all equally privileged and corresponsible'.[105] This was of course another rendering of the PCI's concept of 'consociative democracy'; and, as we shall see, the Tuscan DC true to its different idea of inter-party relationships reacted negatively to the PCI's approach. In practice, however, the new institutional framework of the regional council required the DC to assume concrete positions over different policy areas following initiatives taken by the PCI/PSI regional government. The process of policy-making was, however, very slow in evolving because the national government was tardy in providing the regions with funds and because the regions themselves possessed rather limited powers until 1977.

Nevertheless, some patterns of PCI policy did emerge with its special consideration for agriculture, favouring small over large holdings on the principle of transferring ownership to those who work the land, and opposing the neglect of the countryside as a result of industrialisation for socio-economic reasons. Industrial policy aimed at controlled and balanced development with a priority accorded the interests of small and medium enterprises, notably such as artisans. These different priorities reflected the PCI's particular social base in Tuscany. This consideration lay behind the differences and conflicts between the various parties in the region, including those over agriculture between the two Left-wing parties in the regional administration, for the PSI with its more urban electorate was less enthusiastic than the PCI in this area. Perhaps, the most polemical issue that emerged between the Left as a whole and the DC was over the role of private as against public schools, although as the constitutional role of the regions here was extremely peripheral this did not focus much on concrete policy proposals. The regional government was, despite its various institutional and political restrictions, quite active in producing a variety of different programmes, notably the comprehensive programme on regional development in 1977 as well as special projects for agriculture, transport and the draining of the Arno and other rivers in Tuscany.

There is unfortunately not the space here to consider regional policies in depth and detail,[106] for our main point of reference is inter-party relationships. It is, however, worth noting in this context at least that the PCI's position of authority in Tuscany and other regions did advance its acceptance as a viable governing party, both by other political parties and more broadly.[v] Internally within Tuscany, this was noticeable in that different economic interests — some of which like the banks and industrialists had traditionally been allied to the DC — took note of the new regional authority and accepted it as a focus for pressure-group activity. Industrial circles, for instance, responded fairly readily after the establishment of the Tuscan region in offering specialist advice on policy matters and in being generally available for dialogue with the regional administration,[107] a tendency which of course increased after the granting of further regional powers in 1977. This process of involvement in regional politics certainly had some effect on the attitude of other parties for, as one prominent DC regional leader admitted in reference to agriculture: 'Today, the peasants have to deal with the region; yesterday they were dealing with the Ministry of Agriculture — therefore, he who possesses power at the regional level today influences the peasants more than was the case before the region was set up, and this alters [socio-political] relationships'.[108] Externally, the legitimacy of the PCI as a party of government benefited from the fact that there developed during the course of the 1970s some degree of inter-regional co-operation or consultation over matters of joint interest, even where regional administrations were led by both the DC and PCI, for the purpose of strengthening their common pressure on Rome for the granting of financial resources.[109]

So far as inter-party relationships in Tuscany were concerned, the PCI, while in a greater position to take the initiative in furthering its strategic objectives, was all the same dependent somewhat on the other political parties for their co-operation. In general, this reflected on the practicability of the PCI's preference for broad alliances; while, specifically in Tuscany, it referred to its coalition with the PSI. The same problems and patterns of differently motivated strategies and preferences over forms of convergence were apparent, as already discussed in this chapter.

On the one had, the tradition of Left co-operation with the PCI in Tuscany and other 'Red' regions was one important factor leading to the formation of their regional coalition in 1970, and it helped that both parties were strong advocates of regionalism. There was also the PSI's national strategic motive in wanting to distance itself by this time from the Centre-Left. The party chose, once the regional election outcome was clear in 1970, to make a *casus belli* of the formation of Left regional administrations in Tuscany and Umbria for the start of its break with its general alliance with the DC, coupled with the fact that its holding the balance in these regions encouraged its desire for office at this level.[110] This move by the PSI could be seen as a partial victory for the PCI, which had used the regional elections to campaign against the Centre-Left formation. This strategic decision by the PSI was taken with the full involvement of its national leadership, all the more as the allotment of regional posts entailed the establishment of an intricate balance between the two parties of the Left. For instance, while there was a PCI president of the regional government and PSI president of the regional assembly in Umbria, these party appointments were deliberately reversed in Tuscany with Lagorio (PSI) as government head and Gabbuggiani (PCI) as assembly president. Furthermore, within the Tuscan region itself a balance was established between regional, provincial and important municipal posts. After 1975, when the city of Florence was won by the Left and a PCI mayor was appointed, it became necessary for a PSI nominee to replace the PCI president of the province of Florence, so that a balance was maintained with the division of the two regional posts between these parties remaining the same. Commenting on this 'game of equilibria', a Tuscan PCI leader noted how each region was not autonomous in this respect for here they 'entered into the national framework'.[111] It was for this reason of balance that, following Lagorio's retirement in 1978, the new president of the regional government automatically came from the PSI (Mario Leone) and that this was not questioned by the PCI.[112]

On the other hand, this alliance with the PCI in the Tuscan regional government did not imply necessarily that the PSI found a harmonious convergence with its senior partner over strategic aims. Indeed, the Tuscan PSI tended through the 1970s to accentuate its own individual role in the regional administration, which it was able to do with some effect because of its holding the presidency.[113] Even following its decision in 1970 to join the Tuscan coalition, the PSI went out of its way to reject the label of being *frontista* (of belonging to a 'popular front'), which of course was given it by the DC opposition. For instance, speaking in the first session of the new regional assembly elected in 1975 Mario Leone insisted that during the past five years the PSI had not been 'in the shadow of the PCI' and had shown its own original contributions to regional policy-making, for the two parties while co-operating in government as their 'meeting point' nevertheless had their divergent strategies to follow.[114] This divergence became clearer once the PCI actively pursued the 'historic compromise' in regional politics, when the Tuscan PSI revealed its opposition to programmatic agreements with the DC and, in a much publicised controversy in 1977, violently rejected the idea proposed by the PCI that the DC should be given the post of president of the regional assembly. Lagorio went on record at this time as saying that the Tuscan situation was not comparable to Rome, because the regional government had a firm majority, and that he was motivated by the British model of government/opposition relationships.[115] PSI resistance was therefore one factor in restricting the PCI's scope for convergence with the DC in Tuscany, but the main opposition to this came from the DC itself.

The establishment of the Tuscan region and election of the PCI/PSI government produced a defensive reaction from the DC, which feared that its power position would be weakened by the threat to its alliance with the PSI which nationally had operated since 1963. This negative response was all the greater because of the DC's own reluctance to establish the regional structures, since it rightly foresaw these would provide the PCI with a new power basis.[w] This concern was voiced yet again shortly before the regional elections in 1970 by Sergio Pezzati, DC provincial secretary for Florence, who feared not only the PCI wish to disrupt the Centre-Left but also its 'instrumental' use of the regions as both evidence of a 'class conquest' and as a basis for promoting its own policies.[116] In a further speech he made later in the year, Pezzati predictably denounced the PCI's doctrine of the 'open region' as a device for its 'assault on power'.[117] He asserted that this line in Tuscany had a national importance; in fact, the DC here had campaigned strongly in its appeal to those who feared 'a regional government in the hands of the PCI', arguing that the designs of the Communists had to be checked in the 'Red' regions.[118]

So far as the DC line of rearguard action expressed an alliance preference, this was directed towards a Centre-Left coalition in Tuscany. It was able to maintain this position during the election because the PSI did not finally decide on a Left administration until after the result and publicly refused to commit itself beforehand. The decision by the PSI to opt for the Left alliance in Tuscany sparked off bitter polemics on the part of the DC, which denounced this decision as 'a subversion of the electoral will' and as a 'contradiction' with the Centre-Left at the national level.[119] In the course of these summer weeks, the Tuscan DC developed its strategy of intransigent opposition which became known provocatively as the 'Battle of Tuscany'. The arch exponent of this was Ivo Butini, the leading *fanfaniano* in Tuscan regional politics and now chairman of the DC group in the new regional assembly. Originally aimed at preventing the PSI from allying with the PCI, in which it failed, the 'Battle of Tuscany' continued as the motto of the DC opposition which pursued its intransigent line towards not only the regional government but also where possible Left-administered communes. Through the 'Battle of Tuscany', the *fanfaniani* who largely controlled the DC were calling into question the legitimacy of the PCI to govern.

It was significant, however, that Butini's intransigent line towards the political Left in Tuscany met with internal DC reservations, thereby reflecting on the party's divisions over strategy in its increasingly defensive position. In fact, there was intervention from the national party leadership concerned that Butini's line, which at one time threatened to end the Centre-Left in the city of Florence if the PSI entered the regional government with the PCI, might damage the DC's general relations with the Socialists.[120] Butini himself later commented that this lack of support from the national DC had two motives: 'because they did not want to sour relations with the Socialists, and, secondly, because they preferred an anti-Communist campaign on the ideological level than on the level of dispute about political issues and administration'.[121] There was also internal disagreement inside the Tuscan DC over the 'Battle of Tuscany' reflecting *correnti* divisions. It soon became clear that this intransigent line was spearheaded mainly by the *fanfaniani*, and that wherever they held a majority in provincial party executives (as at Florence and Arezzo) this line was supported. But otherwise it was received lukewarmly or even opposed (as at Lucca), in Tuscany above all by the party Left and also the Centre-Right *dorotei*, both of whom preferred an alliance with the PSI but were not prepared to make a fundamental issue out of its coalition with the PCI regionally and locally.[122] The intransigent line was, however, never absolute, for it concentrated on certain major policy areas where party differences were obviously great and, typical of cases of polarisation in national parliaments, was accompanied by much legislative co-operation over other especially routine matters.

Ultimately, the line of intransigent opposition to the PCI/PSI regional government was discredited by the swing to the Left in the 1975 regional election, followed as this was in Tuscany by the collapse of the *fanfaniani* dominance there, notably with the fall of Butini.[x] It was significant how much the DC felt vulnerable to these new electoral pressures, and that its change of regional line was affected by the national political context. Butini later commented on thinking in the party at this time, when he said that the 1975 election confirmed the unity of the Left and that the national situation after the PCI success in the 1976 elections, with that party's gradual involvement in support for the DC Government at Rome, meant that the party line in Tuscany had to be modified.[123] In fact, while the tone of intransigence on the part of the DC group in the regional council disappeared, a revised party line was slow in emerging and depended as a precondition on a clarification of the internal balance of strength among the *correnti*. For instance, the main initiative for establishing a new approach (which accorded with the national strategy of *confronto* now being promoted by Moro and Zaccagnini) came from the Lucca provincial DC which emerged as the focus of anti-*fanfaniani* activity once the latter's collapse created a vacuum and was able to carry weight because of Lucca's being the main geographical stronghold of the party in the region. Late in 1976, the Lucca DC presented its own agreed document on party strategy (in fact, discussed at *sezioni* meetings within the province, a new development in internal party consultation) to the DC regional committee, setting out the reasons why the party line should be changed. It argued that the 1976 national election created 'a changed political context' and the need for 'broad programmatic convergences'. This meant that dialogue had to be opened at the institutional level (i.e. within the regional council), although the party should remain firmly against a formal coalition with the PCI for these two parties should keep their position as a 'natural alternative' to each other. The Lucca DC advocated that the line of *confronto* be applied generally at all levels — national, regional and local — and that so far as the regional level was concerned it was essential that the DC took the initiative to emerge from its role of isolation'.[124]

It took until the autumn of 1978 for the Tuscan DC to commit itself formally to the line of *confronto*, essentially because this required the formation of a strong enough internal coalition between the *correnti* including dissident *fanfaniani*. The delay in formulating a national party strategy did not help, although the Tuscan DC tended to lag behind most other regional Christian Democrats because the orthodox *fanfaniani*, although discredited and weakened, were still relatively strong numerically and were thereby able to play a delaying game. In any case, typical of the DC's internal methods of procedure, this process of a strategy change involved not merely filibustering debate as well as moves and counter-moves, but also a long and tortuous series of discussions, almost by way of the party talking itself into or acclimatising itself to the possibility of closer co-operation with the PCI.

The line eventually agreed within the Tuscan DC was analogous to the national strategy of *confronto*, except of course that the roles of the two main parties were reversed with the DC having regionally to apply this line to its position of opposition. As defined by various party leaders of the Left — Nello Balestracci, Butini's successor as leader of the DC group in the regional council, and Enzo Pezzati, the new DC provincial secretary for Florence — *confronto* in Tuscany entailed on the one hand a continued insistence on the separation of government versus opposition roles, but on the other a readiness to engage in regular and more 'open' consultation with the regional government, including the PCI, over policy matters. According to Pezzati, this line meant there was 'more empiricism' in the DC's approach,[125] or as Balestracci put it more explicitly:

> In order to involve the different forces in the process of consensus, it is necessary to have a minimum of homogeneity as to general objectives. If the [regional government's] programme is aimed at correcting the most questionable elements of our capitalist structure, we are in agreement; but if it is a question of opening the road to socialism, not knowing what form this takes, probably we would not be in agreement.[126]

So far as relations with the PCI in the regional council were specifically concerned, the DC was prepared to consider an 'institutional agreement' — that is, the DC as opposition could head some council committees or even have the council presidency, although, as Balestracci emphasised, such an agreement could only be concluded if it were not treated as a stage towards the 'historic compromise'.[127] The DC in Tuscany as well as generally made a principled distinction between 'institutional' or even 'programmatic' agreements and a formal alliance with the PCI.

Combined with the DC's new flexible approach was an element of studied ambiguity, for which there were various reasons. First, there was tactics. *Confronto* was adopted by the DC, under strong electoral and political pressure, but this did not reduce its position as principal party-political rival to the PCI. The ambiguity in *confronto* allowed it to present its convergence with the PCI in a different light from the latter and maintain its free identity as electoral competitor. Secondly, this ambiguity derived of course from the fact that the DC's public positions invariably resulted from some inter-*correnti* compromises. This showed later in that *correnti* leaders enterpreted *confronto* somewhat differently, though this was often expressed in more subtle than blatant terms. Butini, who by 1978 had come round to allying himself with *confronto* officially, nevertheless stated revealingly in an interview on the new strategy: 'The objective is the same as that of the Battle of Tuscany, of separating the Socialists from the Communists, but the means are different.'[128] When pressed on this point, Butini described the difference of means:

> I have considered that the party should take a step forward in trying

to debate not so much with the Left majority as a united bloc, but
with the two parties separately according to circumstances. Even if
they remain together in the regional government, their ways of
acting and operating *vis-à-vis* the DC are not the same.[129]

Though Butini's approach to *confronto* was from a different direction
from that of other party leaders, his thinking overlapped considerably
with theirs. Indeed, his statement alluded to the difference of strategy
between the PSI and PCI, which by 1978 had begun to become visible
because of Craxi's more aggressive line towards the PCI in national
politics. Thirdly, the strategy of *confronto*'s ambiguity illustrated the
flexible variations in inter-party relationships. Indeed, 'institutional' or
sometimes 'programmatic' agreements became a trend in DC/PCI
relations in the Italian regions during the latter half of the 1970s. This
did not of course mean that the DC ceased viewing this convergence
differently from the PCI as *not* leading to the 'historic compromise'.

This confirmation of the different motives behind as well as
different concepts of party-political convergence in looking at the PCI,
the DC and also the PSI — which had become evident in its application
in practice from the mid-1970s — suggested a sceptical conclusion
about the course and direction of inter-party relationships in Italy, and
how far they were undergoing substantial change. The Tuscan experience
of inter-party relationships during the 1970s has shown that the PCI's
regional dominance *per se* did not coerce the DC into any greater
acquiescence in, or convince it of the merit of, the PCI's strategic aims.
In fact, this very dominance as underlined by the creation and operation
of the new regional institutional structures — in enlarging the PCI's
scope for its governing role at the sub-national level — had a stimulating
effect on the DC. There was also a certain transitoriness about Italian
party alliances, all the more so in the 1970s when inter-party relationships had entered a more fluid state than in previous periods. This was
demonstrated by the fact that the DC's gradual and reluctant movement towards *de facto* co-operation with the PCI, as in local and
regional but also national politics, was above all an unavoidable response
to unprecedented electoral pressure resulting from the advance of the
PCI in 1975–1976.

Reading between the lines of internal DC debate over strategy, and
also to some extent the party's public justifications of its changed
approach, one evident consideration looked to the eventual possibility
of a decline or reversal in the PCI's electoral growth so that this constraint on the DC would slacken. Evidence of this came sooner than

expected, in local elections especially in the south from 1978 and then generally in the national election of 1979; all the same, the PCI did not lose all its earlier gains as shown both in 1979 and again in the regional and local elections of 1980. Furthermore, it must not be forgotten that Tuscan politics, whatever the merits of this case-study, cannot be divorced from the national political context, and that while the PCI enjoyed the role of senior party in the regional government the DC, albeit in opposition regionally, still remained the leading party of national government, which role of course was far more powerful and prestigious. This last factor was not without some influence on the Tuscan DC's insistence on or belief in maintaining its own independent identity in the face of PCI hegemony in the region.

By the end of the decade, therefore, PCI strategy seemed to have suffered a setback compared with the optimism in party circles around the the mid-1970s. In an important speech to the party Central Committee following the 1979 national election, Berlinguer drew some mixed conclusions from the experience of seeking convergence with the DC and other parties.[130] While he generally confirmed the strategy of the 'historic compromise', and claimed that in the latter half of the decade the PCI had been able to 'develop a more incisive action in the country' (i.e. in policy-making), he referred to disillusionment with the DC's lack of positive co-operation and admitted the PCI's mistaken 'tendency, on both the national and local level, to tone down the differences between ourselves and the DC', which had given the latter some advantages. This change of tone in PCI strategy was reflected in some revival of Communist polemics against the DC in Tuscany.[131]

The changes or fluctuations in inter-party relationships, on the other hand, also evidenced some new longer-term developments, as the case of Tuscany demonstrates. First, DC strategy during the 1970s implicitly if not explicitly acknowledged the PCI as a viable party of government at least at the sub-national level (while in national politics international constraints did play some part). Once having engaged in greater *de facto* co-operation with the PCI within the institutional framework, thereby according the PCI more legitimacy than ever before, it was difficult for the DC to deny this development. In fact, as noted on several occasions in this chapter, the political atmosphere of inter-party relationships had evolved from a state of ideologically-motivated polarisation to one of more 'normal' party competition. This was inevitable given the relatively greater electoral strength of the PCI and its much increased governing role sub-nationally.

Secondly, the PCI's strategy itself, while (not without reason) emphasising its continuity with the party's approach in the 1950s and 1960s, nevertheless involved in practice a qualitative change in its relationships with other parties, both with the DC and PSI especially. This again promoted a competitive rather than antagonistic relationship with these other parties, although the PCI's stress on the over-riding importance of broad alliances tended to underplay the competitive motive behind the 'historic compromise'.

Thirdly, the new sub-national institutional structures in the Italian state, notably the regions, were of course a permanent feature of the political scene. This meant that so long as the PCI did not suffer any major relapse in voting support, and possibly even increased it again in the future, it would be assured of an important governing role — all the more so if, as in 1977, the regions acquired further constitutional powers over different areas of policy-making. Consequently, the DC both at the level of regional politics and in exercising responsibility as the national party of government had to operate with this new fact of Italian political life and invariably co-operate with the PCI.

These three factors of longer-term change had as developed in the 1970s promoted a state of convergence between the different political parties, even if other factors mentioned before continued to condition inter-party relationships in a short-term sense. Thus, while new national party alliances might be formed — as the resumption of a DC/PSI coalition in Rome in 1980 replacing the former situation of the PCI's and other parties' co-operation with the DC in government — the existence of the regions did mean that respective party strategies were more difficult to co-ordinate right down the vertical state structure, and that conflicting alliances might have to be tolerated. Indeed, Berlinguer's strategy speech of July 1979 acknowledged this possibility, hence modifying the PCI's earlier emphasis on 'coherence', and this general likelihood was the subject of different party positions at the time of the 1980 regional and local elections. This did not necessarily suggest that national party strategies would cease to be the prior motive or consideration in sub-national politics; but departures from the model of national alliances might well be regarded less controversially in the future. Whether a DC/PCI coalition might after all be attempted in one of the Italian regions remained to be seen, although as a precursor to developments in Rome there had been no sign of this in the 1970s.

Table 5.2: Party Representation in the Tuscan Regional Assembly (Seats Won in Regional Elections)

	1970	1975	1980
PCI	23	25	25
PSI	3	4	5
DC	17	15	15
PRI	1	1	1
PSDI	3	2	1
PLI	1	-	1
PdUP	-	1	1
PSIUP	1	-	-
MSI	1	2	1

Total: 50 seats

Notes

a. See above, Chapter 1 (a), p. 2.
b. See above, Chapters 3 (d) and 4 (d).
c. See above, Chapter 1 (b), p. 12.
d. The idea of a consociative democracy involves the replacement of rotation in office by 'organic' co-operation between political elites and a de-emphasis on direct confrontation, as in defence of the political system against social fragmentation or for solving fundamental and pressing national matters. According to the PCI, such co-operation was necessary for dealing with 'the Italian crisis'. See A. Pappalardo, 'La Politica Consociativa nella democrazia italiana' in *Rivista Italiania di Scienza Politica*, No. 1, 1980.
e. On the PCI position towards this question, see below, Chapter 5 (c), pp. 229-31.
f. See above, Chapter 3 (d), p. 101.
g. A vague term translated as 'confrontation' or 'entente' which recognised the PCI as a partner in dialogue and granted the necessity for certain common points of co-operation, but rejected the idea of a political alliance with the PCI underlining the 'profound' ideological differences between the DC and that party.
h. See above, Chapter 4 (d), pp. 172-3.
i. See above, Chapter 4 (a), p. 12, and 4 (d), p. 177.
j. See above, Chapter 4 (c), pp. 151-3.
k. See above, Chapter 4 (d), p. 171.
l. See above, Chapter 3 (d), pp. 106-8.
m. See above, Chapter 4 (c), p. 165.
n. See above, Chapter 2 (a), pp. 29-30, and 2(b).
o. See above, Chapter 2 (c), p.141.
p. See above, Chapter 4 (a), pp. 122-3.
q. E.g. see above, Chapter 4 (b), pp. 132-3, on the effects of the Divorce Referendum in the province of Lucca.

r. See above, Chapter 1 (c).
s. Ibid., p. 24.
t. See above, Chapters 3 (c), pp. 182-8 and 4 (c), pp. 154-7 on party regionalisation in the PCI and DC respectively.
u. See above, Chapter 5 (c), pp. 229-30.
v. The PCI of course exploited this development, e.g. the message of its poster in Tuscany for the 1979 national election: 'Tuscany is an example of how in the regions, provinces and communes administered by the PCI and the Left political stability and capacity for government do not need to be protected by swindle laws (*leggi truffa*); it is the arrogance of the DC which blocks the efficiency of democracy: For a government capable of leading the country; Vote on the Left; Vote PCI!'
w. See above, Chapter 1 (c), pp. 20-2.
x. See above, Chapter 4 (c), pp 161-3.

References

1. See Sidney Tarrow, *Partisanship and Political Exchange in French and Italian Local Politics* (1974).
2. The October 1979 issue of *West European Politics* contains some useful articles on party strategies, especially on those of the PCI and PSI. So far as academic interest has dwelt on the question of party strategies, the PCI has of course received the most attention.
3. This point is discussed generally by Jean Blondel, *Political Parties: a genuine case for discontent?* (1978), Chapter 5.
4. For a full discussion of the PCI strategy in the 1970s, see Peter Lange, 'Crisis and Consent, Change and Compromise: dilemmas of Italian Communism in the 1970s' in *West European Politics*, October 1979, pp. 110-32. For an earlier assessment, see G. Sani, 'The PCI on the threshold' in *Problems of Communism*, November–December 1976, pp. 27-51.
5. Alessio Pasquini in PCI Comitato Regionale Toscano, *1° Congresso Regionale dei Comunisti Toscani* (1977), p. 25.
6. Speech of Vannino Chiti, secretary of PCI Pistoia federation, at its provincial congress, March 1977, p. 70. Cf. comment of secretary of PCI Pisa federation, in speech to 1975 provincial congress, that 'the historic compromise is not a formula, but a policy that starts with the need for progressing towards a new stage of democratic and anti-Fascist revolution in the direction of Socialism'.
7. Speech of secretary of PCI Arezzo federation to provincial congress, March 1977, p. 14d.
8. Alessio Pasquini, editorial in *Politica e Società*, July–August 1977, pp. 3-4.
9. ·*Toscana, Consiglio Regionale*, 31 July–15/30 August 1975, p. 481.
10. A. Messeri, 'Politica e amministrazione locale' in *Città e Regione*, March 1975, p. 120.
11. *Politica e Società*, January 1977, pp. 12-13.
12. Speech of Fanfani to DC National Council, January 1975, in *Compromesso con il PCI, rapporti con il PSI, scelte della DC* (1975), p. 14.
13. Interview No. 62.
14. *Appunti per il dibattito in Comitato Regionale D.C.*, 25 November 1977.
15. Interview No. 84.
16. Interview No. 13 (1977).
17. See A. Parisi (ed.), *Democristiani* (1979), pp. 177-8.

18. Ibid., pp. 184-5, that DC leaders felt constrained by their voters, who were more rigid about an alliance with the PCI.
19. A. Zuckerman, *Political Clienteles in Power: power factions and cabinet coalitions in Italy* (1975), p. 41.
20. *La Nazione*, 29 July 1975.
21. Speech by R. Cantini at Tuscan DC regional congress, *Il Popolo*, 13 April 1976.
22. E.g. the remark in the Tuscan regional council of one DC leader that his party would not be co-opted by the Left regional government 'because it believes in the essential role of democratic opposition in any representative democracy' (*Toscana, Consiglio Regionale*, 31 July–15 August 1975, p. 489) C.f. Ivo Butini, DC regional secretary, that 'I belong to the Western world: I believe in the clear-cut separation between government and opposition' (*La Nazione*, 31 May 1975).
23. Interview No. 24.
24. See David Hine, 'The Italian Socialist Party under Craxi: surviving but not reviving' in *West European Politics*, October 1979, pp. 133-48.
25. E.g. the final document of the 2nd Tuscan PSI regional congress, January 1976, that: 'the policy of the historic compromise risks making static present class relations in the country; if carried into effect, this policy would obstruct the energies of reforming forces by constraining them through a general and permanent agreement with the DC, which continues to affirm its own conservative role' (PSI, Comitato Regionale Toscano, *Alternativa Socialista*, 1976, p. 48).
26. *La Nazione*, 12 May 1978.
27. Ibid.
28. Hine, 'The Italian Socialist Party under Craxi', pp. 136-42.
29. On this see Alan Stern, 'Political Legitimacy in Local Politics: the Communist Party in Northeastern Italy' in D. Blackmer and S. Tarrow (eds.), *Communism in Italy and France* (1975), pp. 221-58.
30. G. Amendola, 'Una funzione d'avanguardia nello sviluppo democratico' in *Rinascita*, 8 May 1970.
31. E.g. Peter Lange, 'The PCI at the Local Level: a study of strategic performance' in Blackmer and Tarrow, *Communism in Italy and France*, pp. 259-304, which looks at the implementation of party strategy in the local context taking the case of the PCI Milan federation at the beginning of the 1970s. Cf. Mario Caciagli, *Democrazia Cristiana e potere nel Mezzogiorno* (1977), which looking at the DC in Catania, Sicily, comments that 'national events rarely provide the real reasons for changes of course at the local level; they rather offer the convenient motivation for settling internal party and *corrente* affairs and in the final instance power manoeuvres' (p. 453).
32. Interview No. 48.
33. Interview No. 40.
34. Interview No. 14 (1977).
35. G. Chiaromonte, *L'Accordo Programmatico e l'azione dei comunisti* (1977), pp. 13-14.
36. E.g. see speech of Giulio Quercini, PCI regional secretary in Tuscany, about the forthcoming local elections in 1980, in *Politica e Società*, November–December 1979, pp. 4-9.
37. Interview No. 42.
38. *L'Unità*, 4 January 1976, document of PCI Tuscan regional committee of 20 December 1975.
39. *Bollettino della sezione Regioni ed autonomie locali del CC del PCI*, No. 4, 1977, document of the PCI regional committee for the Marches, p. 54.

40. Interview No. 1.
41. Speech by Sergio Pezzati, DC provincial secretary for Florence, 18 April 1970.
42. The DC campaign in 1975 concentrated on preventing the PCI conquering Florence and thus 'closing the ring of its power in Tuscany' (*La Nazione*, 1 March 1975).
43. *La Stampa*, 25 May 1977.
44. *La Nazione*, 7 December 1977.
45. Ibid, 2 February 1978.
46. Press statement of DC Lucca provincial committee, early 1978, given to the author by DC Lucca.
47. Interview No. 93.
48. Interview No. 56.
49. Interview No. 13 (1978).
50. Vannino Chiti, 'Analisi di una provincia: Pistoia' in *Critica Marxista*, No. 5, 1975, p. 86.
51. *Politica e Società*, January–February 1978, report on 3rd regional congress of PSI, pp. 36-8.
52. Interview No. 79.
53. *Corriere della Sera*, 3 June 1970; *La Nazione*, 12 June 1970; and *La Nazione*, 21 June 1975, on PSI strategy over local alliances in Tuscany.
54. See Lange in Blackmer and Tarrow, *Communism in Italy and France*.
55. Interview No. 79.
56. See *I Comunisti umbri: scritti e documenti, 1944–1970* (1977), pp. 396-7, 416-19, 424-6, on the similarly painful experience of the Centre-Left in the 'Red' region of Umbria.
57. G. Amendola, article in *Rinascita*, 8 May 1970.
58. Interview with T. Codignola in *Politica e Società*, July–August 1977, p. 35.
59. Lange in Blackmer and Tarrow, *Communism in Italy and France*, esp. pp. 291-5.
60. R. Seidelman, 'PCI, decentramento e politica delle alleanze: il caso di Firenze' in *Il Mulino*, May–June 1978, esp. pp. 471-2.
61. Published by Vallecchi, Florence. This featured contributions from Left-wing Catholics and PCI leaders, though not all were Florentines. The PCI and Togliatti in person showed great interest in this publication, but it was ignored by the DC.
62. *Panorama*, 18 January 1977, report on the Florence area.
63. Interview No. 40.
64. *L'Unità*, 5 June 1977; PCI comitato comunale Lucca, *I comunisti e l'intesa programmatica al comune di Lucca*, June 1977.
65. Interview No. 53.
66. E.g. the PCI admitted this problem in the province of Pistoia, where the importance of an agreement with the DC and other parties was emphasised by the PCI with the following result: 'Our stressing it in this manner provoked reactions from the Christian Democrats and Republicans, who strongly differentiated themselves politically from us and accused the Communists of "wanting to instrumentalise the agreement" . . .' (*Politica e Società*, July–August 1977, p. 14).
67. This distinction is made by Robert Wade in his study of inter-party relationships in a small commune in the province of Grosseto; see two references under his name in the Bibliography.
68. The electoral programme of the PCI Versilia federation for the 1975 elections stressed the need for 'a sharp defeat of the policy of the DC leadership and of the Right as the essential precondition for opening up new prospects for

Italy' (PCI Versilia, *Una grande avanzata del PCI*, p. 2); interview with Michele Ventura, PCI secretary for Florence federation in *Il Nuovo*, 14 June 1975; 'The possibility for recoupment by the more progressive forces of the DC is only through a defeat of this party and therefore breaking the system of Christian Democratic power.'
69. *PCI, Almanacco '77* (1977), p. 30.
70. *Corriere della Sera*, 4 May 1975.
71. *La Nazione*, 22 November 1975.
72. Interview No. 13 (1977).
73. *Corriere della Sera*, 26 October 1975.
74. F. Ferraresi and P. Kemeny, *Classi Sociali e Politica Urbana* (1977), p. 19.
75. Giulio Quercini, PCI regional secretary, in *Politica e Società*, November–December 1979, p. 5.
76. G. Galli and A. Prandi, *Patterns of Political Participation in Italy* (1970), pp. 243-4; Robert Fried, 'Communism, urban budgets and the two Italies: a case study in comparative urban government' in *Journal of Politics*, November 1971, pp. 1016, 1045.
77. PCI Sesto Fiorentino, *Impegni, ruole e struttura del Partito a Sesto*, document for 6th communal conference of Sesto PCI, February 1978, p. 5.
78. Ferraresi and Kemeny, *Classi Sociali e Politica Urbana*, pp. 10, 28.
79. Ibid., p. 10.
80. On this change of approach, taking the example of the PCI in Emilia-Romagna, see Marco Cammelli, 'Politica istituzionale e modello emiliano: ipotesi per una ricerca' in *Il Mulino*, September–October 1978, pp. 743-67. CF. in the case of the Tuscan PCI, *Politica e Società*, November–December 1979, pp. 51-2, on the PCI local administrations: 'In recent years these administrations have had to measure up suddenly to a series of new problems, which are difficult to approach and to solve only with the instruments of good government and a correct budget policy ... the Left administrations have not been able always to provide quick and thorough answers to growing demands for intervention in very much broader areas than was the case at one time.'
81. Ferraresi and Kemeny, *Classi Sociali e Politica Urbana*, p. 29.
82. *Bollettino della sezione Regione*, No. 4, 1977, p. 55.
83. *L'Espresso*, 21 September 1975. One such party school was opened at Cascina, near Pisa, early in 1977, the aim of which was to train PCI administrators 'not only on the ideological and political level, but also regarding the major questions for which specific training is necessary', and that 'the school is therefore an irreplaceable instrument for instructing new cadres on a concrete and realistic plane, so they may rise to the new tasks which the Party is called on to perform' (speech of PCI secretary of Pisa federation to 13th congress of Pisa PCI, March 1977, p. 32).
84. *Politica e Società*, October 1977, p. 27: 'Relations with the DC, with the lay parties and with the PSI have been shown to be more positive in the supra-communal institutions, because they are less conditioned by the pure logic of alignments.' The DC president of the *comunità montana* for the Media Valle Serchio in the province of Lucca agreed with this judgement, and added that co-operation at this higher level also improved relations between the parties in the communes themselves, for the fact that the DC and PCI had administrators together in the *comunità montana* meant that while one or other was in opposition in the communes 'there is no longer that state of broken relations, of a closed attitude, of no dialogue ... DC mayors also look on those in opposition in municipal councils with a certain respect, because they are administrators in the *comunità* (Interview No. 26).'

85. Speech of PCI secretary for Versilia federation to 8th congress of Versilia PCI, March 1977, p. 16.
86. Messeri, 'Politica e amministrazione locale', p. 121.
87. Giulio Quercini, PCI regional secretary, in *Politica e Società*, November–December 1979, p. 6.
88. Interview No. 81.
89. Seidelman, 'PCI decentramento e politica delle alleanze', pp. 480-2. This composite picture of the Left administration at Florence is based on interviews with different party sources and newspaper reports during the later 1970s. For portraits of Gabbuggiani, see *La Nazione*, 28 August 1970; *Corriere della Sera*, 23 October 1975; and *Panorama*, 2 November 1976 and 8 August 1978.
90. Gianni Riccamboni, 'Regioni: una nuova classe politica?' in *Rivista di sociologia*, No. 31, 1976, p. 173.
91. Ibid., p. 173.
92. Ibid., pp. 139-43.
93. E.g. article by Piero Bassetti, former DC president of the Lombardy regional government in the *Guardian*, 26 March 1975: 'From the regions we can also expect the answer to the prospective rapport between the Catholics and the Communists, that "historic compromise" which would be impossible in the central government for a number of reasons of an international and strategic nature which no one underestimates. This offers the Italians the best opportunity to accept the Communist Party's challenge at the lowest risk and on a terrain which we all cherish, the terrain of freedom which we must encourage the Communists to explore.' Bassetti was on the DC Left and has been exceptional as a regionalist figure in his party.
94. Interview No. 71 (1978).
95. Interview No. 48.
96. Interview No. 50; interview also with Antonio Tortori, section for local government, PSI national office, Rome, 16 November 1977.
97. See articles on Lagorio in *La Nazione*, 25 August 1970, and *Panorama*, 3 October 1978; interviews with *La Nazione*, 28 December 1977 and 20 September 1978; and his book, *Presidente in Toscana* (1977).
98. *I comunisti umbri*, pp. 496-7.
99. Interview No. 54 (1978).
100. *La Nazione*, 4 October 1977 and 28 December 1977; Interview No. 15.
101. Interview No. 7.
102. L. Cavalli (ed.), *Classe Dirigente e Sviluppo Regionale* (1973), p. 118.
103. Vannino Chiti, 'Le Regioni "Rosse" ' in *Politica e Società*, December 1976, pp. 65-7.
104. Elio Gabbuggiani, 'Che cos'è una "regione aperta" ' in *Rinascita*, 8 May 1970.
105. Interview with Gabbuggiani, in *La Nazione*, 28 August 1970.
106. On PCI regional policy in Tuscany, see P. Giovannini in Cavalli, *Classe Dirigente*; and *Politica e Società*, January–February 1978, pp. 50-7, and November–December 1979, pp. 6-7, on PCI regional programmes.
107. *La Nazione*, 19 January 1972.
108. Interview No. 13 (1978).
109. 'Why Italy's regions are in conflict with Rome' in *The Times*, 8 January 1975.
110. *La Nazione*, 23 August 1970.
111. Interview No. 65; see also *La Nazione*, 21 June 1975.
112. *La Nazione*, 22 June 1978.

248 *Inter-party Relationships*

113. E.g. Lagorio's series of interviews on Radio Tuscany in the autumn of 1977, published as his book, *Presidente in Toscana* (1977).
114. *Toscana, Consiglio Regionale*, 31 July-15/30 August 1975, p. 496.
115. *La Nazione*, 30 December 1977.
116. Speech at provincial conference of Florentine DC, 18 April 1970.
117. Speech by Sergio Pezzati, at meeting of provincial DC leaders, 25 October 1970.
118. Ibid.
119. *La Nazione*, 16 September 1970.
120. Interview No. 12 (1977).
121. Interview No. 13 (1978).
122. *La Nazione*, 12 June 1970 and 17 June 1970.
123. Interview No. 13 (1978).
124. *Traccia di Proposta Politico-Programmatica*, adopted by DC Lucca provincial congress, December 1976, then presented to DC regional committee. Copy given author by Piero Angelini, DC provincial secretary for Lucca.
125. Interview No. 16.
126. Nello Balestracci, discussion in *Politica e Società*, January-February 1978, p. 52.
127. *La Stampa*, 25 May 1977.
128. Interview No. 13 (1978).
129. Ibid.
130. Speech of July 1979 in *L'Unità*, 4 July 1979.
131. *Politica e Società*, March-April 1980, p. 98 on PCI/DC relations at Viareggio.

CONCLUSION: CHANGE AND CONTINUITY IN THE ITALIAN PARTY SYSTEM

The theme 'change and continuity' may have a certain platitudinous ring, but it nevertheless is especially applicable to the Italian political situation in the 1970s. This is because, while patterns of political development in the postwar period from the Cold War up to this decade evidenced a remarkable degree of continuity, different changes have profoundly affected political behaviour since the late 1960s.

In particular, many assumptions made in the past about Italian politics have been called into question if not modified as a result of developments during the 1970s. These include notably the assumption about the continued dominance of the ruling Christian Democrats, the immutability of the polarised divide between the two main parties representing Right and Left with the Communists in firm opposition and also the strong stability of voting tendencies.

These changes are recognisable to the regular student of Italian affairs, but the object of an analytical study is to evaluate the intensity or depth of their impact, their exact significance and, if possible, their likely permanency. The main overall conclusion from looking at its development in the 1970s is that the Italian party system, unlike in earlier decades, can no longer be viewed as 'static', which had been a frequent observation or criticism of those writing on Italian politics before the 1970s. For example, Giorgio Galli's well-known book, *Il Bipartitismo Imperfetto* (1966), opened with the comment that Italy was essentially a *lentocrazia* (literally a 'slow-ocracy') because its postwar political system had during 1945-1966 remained behind the enormous developments in society and the economy: 'something acts as a brake on executive and legislative power, so that their specific interventions are inadequate and always too slow'. In view of Italy's *partitocrazia*, whereby her state structure functioned according to the will and effectiveness of the political parties, Galli indicated as the principal source of this problem the absence of alternation between the main political forces in power. He criticised here not only the means by which the DC retained its power position, but also (writing from a non-Marxist Left point of view) the PCI's 'immobilistic' approach which contributed to the static condition of Italian politics because it represented important sectors of society (Conclusion, pp. 407-8).

It is precisely in this respect that political change has been most evident during the 1970s. For, while the political spectrum of Italy has comprised the same individual parties, there has been significant movement in their respective political positions and strengths and concurrently their strategic courses and inter-relationships. The outcome of this development in the third decade of the postwar republic has been what is commonly referred to as 'convergence'. That is, the former polarised divide between the two main parties especially has been replaced by movement towards common political ground and their formal or *de facto* co-operation, but more generally by a competitive situation in which all parties concerned (except the neo-Fascist MSI) are regarded as viable and legitimate actors on the political stage and not disqualified from it (as the PCI was previously for ideological reasons). In particular, the greater electoral appeal of the PCI has combined with the decline in DC dominance to promote such a competitive situation. These changed circumstances, with a qualitative reduction in political 'distance' between them, may be regarded in longer-established liberal democracies as 'normal', whereas in Italy this has not been able to develop until the 1970s because of her relatively young parliamentary democracy, her historical background of Fascism and the postwar imprint of the East/West ideological conflict on her domestic politics. Paradoxically, although the Italian political system became stable during the first two decades after the War, it took the country's socio-economic crisis of the 1970s to make 'convergence' emerge. The new competitive situation resulting from this has not, however, undergone the ultimate test of a real alternation in power — which in Italy would mean a Left majority expelling the DC from national government — and indeed, the question of PCI participation in government in a formal coalition with the DC is still as of the early 1980s controversial.

In view of its significance, it is important to assess the specific effects of 'convergence' so far as it has developed during the 1970s. This study commenced with various fundamental questions concerning the role of the political parties in Italy, considering their central importance in the functioning of that country's political system. Have they in the difficult context of the 1970s had a unifying or integrative effect in the operation of the state structure? Have they in some way controlled or conditioned the changing socio-economic environment, or merely responded to it — or not at all? In short, has the 'Italian crisis' of this decade been caused in part at least by the behaviour of the political parties, individually and in relation to each other? What do the above-mentioned political changes represent in this broader light?

Conclusion

It is here that a case-study approach offers many advantages over a (perhaps too generalised) survey focusing on the national level of politics, as discussed in Chapter 2 (a). Most importantly, a complete answer to these various questions requires thorough attention being given to the role of the parties both vertically, acting as the channel of political communication between sub-national and national levels as well as horizontally at the different sub-national levels. Therefore, by way of summarising the main results of this regional example of party development in the 1970s use will be made again of the reference framework identifying three essential relationships in the role of parties, introduced and discussed in general terms in Chapter 1 (a): their relationship to the state, their relationship with society and the relationship between themselves.

First, the parties' relationship with the state has undergone change during the decade examined in the sense that their individual political positions within it have altered. The relative decline of DC dominance has been accompanied by a growing importance of the PCI as a party in power, thus underlining the extent to which the two principal parties have predominated within Italy's multi-party system. This change has been visible at the national level particularly with the PCI's support for the governments of 'national solidarity' during 1976-1979, but it has in fact been a more widespread trend at the sub-national level of politics. The 1970s witnessed a major advance by the PCI in control of local government, especially in the large cities, but even more significant was its emergence as a ruling party in the new regional structures.

This reduction in the previous imbalance, whereby the DC monopolised authority in the state structure, had significant effects on both main parties. The DC responded defensively to this decline in its dominance, but it nevertheless came to terms with it thereby implicitly if not explicitly accepting the PCI as a viable party of power — both vertically through its own relations as national ruling party with the regions of the Left, and horizontally in that the DC as opposition party in these regions necessarily had to deal with the PCI as the party of government. Internally, the DC suffered a major crisis of confidence following the rise of the PCI, for the latter's increased governing role together with its unprecedented electoral success of 1975-1976 resulted in a changed balance of forces within the DC. At the same time, this challenge from the PCI had a stimulating effect on the DC and was crucial in explaining its own eventual revival.

In the case of the PCI, its enhanced role of authority had two important consequences. Externally, it led to the party defining more clearly than ever before its own particular relationship to the Italian state which above all involved its abandonment of the concept of the 'Red' regions and municipalities as isolated entities within the DC-dominated state system. In fact, building on its newly won positions of power, the PCI became a strong advocate of 'reform of the state', whereby decision-making should be devolved more to the sub-national levels with new co-ordinative mechanisms to strengthen local political activity and complement the new regions. The experience of Tuscany, under PCI government from 1970, showed that the party was able to exercise its authority to promote this change. Internally, the PCI's increased political role had some impact on its own structural relationships. This was partly deliberate in that the leadership attempted to adapt the party organisation to the new regional state structures, but more importantly the PCI's greater responsibility in office created new strains on internal party solidarity. The concrete application of the 'historic compromise' meant that the PCI became co-responsible for the ineffectiveness of the Italian state in solving the country's fundamental problems. The very socio-economic crisis, which had been one factor in the DC's decline and the PCI's rise, rebounded on the latter after gaining office in the form of severe constraints on policy initiative and implementation. The consequence was disillusionment within the ranks of the PCI, although this was more pronounced in the south, where socio-economic conditions were most acute and party organisation weaker than in the 'Red' regions. Even so, the fact that the party encountered this problem also in Tuscany indicated the seriousness of this new problem for the PCI.

The introduction of the new regions should not, however, be overrated in political importance. While they offered the PCI, as the main party not in national government, a new outlet for policy-making similar to that enjoyed by the opposition party in the *Länder* of West Germany, this change was not equivalent to the initiation of a federal system, if only because the regions were very restricted in their constitutional powers and politically remained dependent on the central state for finance. In this sense, the change was evolutionary, although the granting of further powers to the regions in 1977 represented a small step in such a direction. Furthermore, the fact that the actual introduction and subsequent operation of the regional structures was so controlled by the political parties themselves underlined the strong element of continuity in that this whole process of change confirmed the predominant *partitocrazia* element in Italy's political system. It was also significant that, although regionalisation constitutionally involved a centrifugal procedure, politically it tended to act centripetally because it combined with the greater entrenchment of the PCI in the state structure. The PCI's own strategy for 'convergence' which claimed to reinforce the legitimacy of Italian democracy assured this.

Secondly, the relationship of the parties to society has been a salient feature of the 1970s because Italy's socio-economic environment became more unstable than in the preceding two decades. This change was reflected most obviously in new patterns of electoral mobility, which modified the country's previous renowned voting stability and resulted in a relative change in the balance of strength between the two main parties. It is, however, more interesting in this context to look at the parties' organisational links with the various sectors of society as a measure of their continuing mass character and integrative capacity in this difficult decade and hence of their general adaptability. In both major cases, the picture was more one of their responding or reacting to socio-economic change rather than foreseeing or directing it, although the basic contrasts between the PCI and DC as political parties determined that their responses differed.

The PCI was as a mass-structured class party very conscious of the social-integrative dimension of its political activity. In the region of Tuscany, one of its strongholds in the country, it had of course performed an important role as a force with strong roots in different sectors of society both urban and rural, although rapid postwar economic development in the region disrupted its organisational links for a time. In the 1970s, the PCI found itself dealing with a more urbanised society and one in which some social groups — notably, the younger generation — evidenced less predictable forms of political involvement, not to mention that the severe economic climate had inevitable repercussions on political behaviour. The party was inhibited in its response as a consequence of its customary bureaucratic methods of organisation, which were less appealing to the new younger and middle-class groups it was attracting. As a result, although the PCI extended its mass base quantitatively, its structural links here suffered qualitatively with the weaker social coherence of its membership. There were also some signs even in this traditionally 'Red' region that the PCI's sub-cultural roots were weakening as a result of the growth of urban society. This was all the same a relatively minor decline, since up to the 1970s at least the party's sub-cultural loyalties had by and large withstood social transformation with the movement in this region from the countryside to the towns. So far as this incipient change presaged any future development, it was likely that the strictly 'Marxist' nature of the PCI's sub-cultural roots would be permeated by more 'secular' values.

The DC being in comparative analytical terms a very different kind of political party from the PCI — it was voter rather than class-oriented, and organisationally loose-associational more than structured — it was no surprise that its response to social change differed from the PCI's. Furthermore, its belated and also particular form of response was influenced by its continuing occupation of national office (despite its decline in political dominance), and by the fact that when it responded this was transmitted not so much through the 'party' as an organisation as through the various Catholic associations which comprised the 'movement' supporting the DC. All these different factors were present in the Tuscan case, even though sociologically the DC in this region was not absolutely representative of the party nationally. The social challenge to the DC came in two ways. First, there was the long-term trend of secularisation that, at least in Tuscany, eroded the DC's sub-cultural roots more than in the case of the PCI, and was demonstrated politically in the Divorce Referendum of 1974. Secondly, the DC's general loss of credibility as a political force — which formed the main background to the electoral breakthrough by the PCI in 1975–1976 — was reflected socially in that the party lost favour among its less traditionalist supporters, in addition to its failure to attract newly emerging groups. During the period under discussion, however, this combined societal weakness of the DC was to a large degree counterbalanced by the politically mobilising effect on its supporters of the rise of the PCI. Whether this stimulation from party competition would continue to carry the DC remained an open question. Indeed, survey research from the late 1970s on underlying trends of DC support indicated serious future vulnerability for it as a socio-political force.

This discussion of the social dimension of the parties' role has identified various features of change, but it is also evident throughout that the factor of continuity has above all been present in the nature of the parties themselves. That is, the two principal parties have remained essentially within their same respective categories as types of political party, structurally and sociologically, even though within them they have revealed some modification. As a result of both parties being relatively weakened in their social aggregative or integrative ability, the question arises as to whether the future development of the Italian party system is not less certain than it has been in the past with its clear and combined predominance of the two main forces. Again, Tuscany is an instructive example in this respect to assess the potential

Conclusion

of the PCI and DC, because their combined electoral strength in this region has been that much higher than the national average (by 5.8 per cent to 7.2 per cent above it in the 1970s, compared with 5.4 per cent to 6.0 per cent above it in the 1960s — see Tables 1.1 and 2.2).

The third relationship of that betwen the parties themselves has also exhibited aspects of both change and continuity during the 1970s. Accommodation between different parties has in Italy's postwar political system been a crucial feature not merely for the purpose of majority-building or coalition formation, but also more broadly for creating consensus as a necessary prelude to political action in view of the country's fragile democratic tradition and ineffective bureaucratic structures. Hence, the key question behind these inter-relationships is whether they have contributed or not politically to the 'Italian crisis', or alternatively helped to alleviate what might have been even more critical.

The most obvious area of change in the 1970s has been, as already noted, a growing 'convergence' between the parties, especially the two main ones. The central party-political stimulus to this development has been the pursuit of the 'historic compromise' by the PCI. Tuscany is appropriate as a case-study here, because the PCI saw its predominance in this region as providing a key element in promoting the party's strategic objectives. There was a distinct trend in Italian politics whereby the PCI not only seized the initiative from the DC in strategic debate, but also emerged from relative isolation to strengthen or enlarge its alliances, notably with the PSI in Tuscan politics but also with cautious signs of a more 'open' attitude from the small centre parties. With the DC, the PCI's hopes for a formal alliance failed to transpire, although there was a growth in *de facto* co-operation between the two main parties. There was some evidence of this in local politics, while at the Tuscan regional level a difference was apparent between the first legislative period of 1970-1975, marked by polarised relations between the Left government and the DC opposition, and the second period of 1975-1980 when 'convergence' began to occur, though only gradually and somewhat behind the same development nationally.

The decade of the 1970s was distinguished by greater fluidity in inter-party relationships, which derived both from the DC's decline in dominance and the qualitative change in the PCI's approach to other parties. It was also a consequence of the fact that, with the reduction of political 'distance' between the DC and PCI, the inherent ambiguity in the PSI's strategy as a third force came more to the fore. This put into a wider context what might otherwise appear to be the vagaries of national coalitional behaviour, with some reversal in the PCI's political position at Rome at the end of the decade. Alongside short-term currents of political fortune, there were various features which suggested that party-political 'convergence' could well be a long-term or even permanent development. These included the very precedent of the national entente between the PCI and DC during 1976-1979, which would make it difficult for the latter to revert to its earlier intransigent anti-Communist consensus to justify its claim as ruling party; the profound and critical socio-economic state of the country, which hardly seemed likely to succumb to any short-term solution and did provide a compelling argument for 'convergence'; and the establishment of the regions, which ensured that in the future any party of national government would continue to have to operate with the PCI as a party of government sub-nationally, and that consequently the competitive basis for relations between the two main parties in particular remained less weighted against the PCI than had been the case in the 1950s and 1960s. It was also interesting in this respect that the introduction of a regional level of government created a new factor preventing the coherence of alliance formation at all levels of the Italian state structure. This new feature was inevitable considering the regional variation in party strength throughout the country.

While these foregoing factors were significant, involving a qualitative change in inter-party relationships, there were features of continuity which must be evaluated alongside them. These invariably confirmed previous patterns of party alliance behaviour, though some of them were partly modified by the aforementioned factors of change. First, party strategies at the sub-national levels of politics were predominantly determined by the national leaderships of the parties, despite the creation of an institutional framework for regional political activity. This confirmed the strong vertical mechanisms of control exerted by national leaders, although their success in implementing party strategy could be influenced in a secondary way by local factors, such as the balance of political forces in an area, or factors of diversity inherent to one party or another; e.g. geographical variation in *correnti* strength within the DC, an element of deliberate autonomy given the PSI locally to rationalise its general strategic ambiguity. Secondly, this case-study demonstrates that party elites were by no means entirely free in their pursuit of strategic aims or more specifically alliance formations. They were constrained here by real or assumed pressures from their party's membership or electorate. Once more, basic differences were apparent between the PCI and DC. The latter continued to reveal a low degree of internal party participation, but a distinct sense of party identity among its elites together with their belief that DC voters would not abide a formal alliance with the PCI strongly influenced their reserve towards that party. On the PCI side, problems arose for the party elites in that at the base ideological mistrust towards the DC surfaced with the concrete application of the 'historic compromise', while a growth of a less passive attitude among some groups of the membership, notably younger ones, emphasised that the leadership had to work hard to carry the party base in their choice of practical strategic options. This change in participation at the party base represented a possible new development in party life, modifying the traditional operation of 'democratic centralism'. In general, however, this regional case-study has revealed how much inter-party relationships were conditioned by internal party considerations, as well as vice versa. Thirdly, the growth of 'convergence' with *rapprochement* between the PCI and DC brought into relief the conceptual differences of interpretation over the very nature of inter-party relationships between the PCI on the one hand, with its idea of a consociative democracy building on its older line of broad social alliances; and on the other hand the other political parties, especially the DC, with their more Anglo-Saxon definition of inter-party relationships as being determined by the separation of government and opposition roles within the institutions.

Any definitive answer as to whether party-political 'convergence' has exacerbated or contained the 'Italian crisis' is impossible to give, for writing in 1980 this demands some foreknowledge of longer-term developments in the new decade. Based on the 1970s, an interim conclusion is possible but is somewhat hindered by contradictory evidence. On the one hand, the greater involvement of the PCI — as the main alternative party to the DC — in positions of responsibility at different levels of the state structure could not but reinforce the legitimacy of both the PCI and the political system. On the other hand, the translation of 'convergence' into actual broad co-operation over government between the different parties, at least as occurred at the national level during 1976-1979 and increasingly in the regions, opened up the possibility that political discontent might be attracted to extra-parliamentary or even disruptive movements because of the lack of a protest or oppositional force within the institutions. In a period of continued social disaffection and also political terrorism, this was no idle consideration. Indeed, the relatively weaker social-aggregative capacity of the two main parties was not unrelated to this problem.

If there were therefore any explanation for these contradictory signs about the effects of 'convergence', a valid distinction could be made between a growing commitment to the political system among party elites and to some extent their activists across the political spectrum, but broadening disillusionment among the electorate and public at their inability to provide convincing and effective answers to Italy's mounting problems. The one small consolation was that party elites were only too aware of this public disaffection, which ensured that the political parties would remain that much less immobilistic than they had done before the 1970s.

At the level of inter-party relationships, this likelihood was strengthened further by the more competitive party system, for the DC albeit remaining in national government was less able to take its power for granted. This was not merely because of the shock administered to it by its crisis of confidence from the mid-1970s, which had in any case relapsed somewhat by the turn of the decade, but because its decline in dominance in a deeper sense appeared to be a permanent development. Equally, the stronger role now exercised by the PCI in the state, both nationally and sub-nationally, meant that the DC was more subject than before to the pressures and strictures normally expected from an opposition in a parliamentary democracy. Otherwise, the main over-riding conclusion arising from this study is that predictions about the future of the party system in Italy are hedged with greater uncertainty than ever before. This in fact substantiates how much that party system has changed in the 1970s and become less immobilistic, despite its various elements of continuity.

NOTES ON SOURCES

Research on political parties demands utilising a variety of different sources to establish the accuracy of information, verify particular patterns of party development and test hypotheses.

The material for this book was drawn from four main sources: personal interviews, party documentation, newspaper reports and published work, whether academic, official or political. Details on these different sources and the use made of them are given in the introductions to the appendices which follow, except for party documentation which is acknowledged in the source lists of the five chapters. This documentation usually consisted of party speeches and proceedings of congresses and conferences, party newspapers and journals, statistical material, reports on party activity and internal memoranda. Finally, material on the political parties in Tuscany has been related to general studies of Italian parties and politics.

LIST OF TUSCAN COMMUNES VISITED FOR RESEARCH AND INTERVIEWS

The following is the list of the 30 communes visited in Tuscany in the process of in-depth research for this book. They were selected on the basis of three criteria: economic structure, size of population and political tendency (i.e. strength of the PCI vote as of 1976, and conversely that of the DC). Individual factors, such as the availability of contacts, were sometimes influential in choosing one case over another in the same category; also, other communes in addition to these 30 were investigated through research and discussions at the provincial level of the parties. Personnel interviewed were mayors and local secretaries of the two main parties in particular.

The three criteria were arranged in the following manner, including the number of communes under each sub-division:

Economic Structure

Agricultural 6
Industrial 7
Agricultural/industrial/tertiary 5
Industrial/tertiary 5
Tertiary 7

Size of Population (1971 census)

Up to 3,000   4
3,001-5,000   3
5,001-10,000   6
10,001-30,000   8
More than 30,000   9

Political Tendency (Vote of PCI)

10-20%   1
20-30%   4
30-40%   2
40-50%   11
50-60%   7
60-70%   5

The brief details on each commune include the categorisation under these criteria (population as in 1971 census); also, the party composition of the local government (elected in 1975), the name of the province where located and any individual features:

1. *Altopascio* (Lucca) Pop. 8,688 (1951: 7,254), industrial, especially textiles and clothes. In agriculture, predominance after the War of sharecropping, now of direct cultivators. 1976 Election: PCI 45.4%, DC 33.3% (1946: PCI 17.9%, DC 33.7%, PSI 28.3%). Local government: PCI-PSI with PSI mayor, as before 1975. One of the few 'Red' communes in the 'White' Lucchesia.

2. *Capannori* (Lucca) Pop. 41,403 (1951: 41,874). Industrial, especially footwear. In agriculture, predominance of direct cultivators, remained so. 1976 Election: DC 56.6%, PCI 27.0% (1946: DC 48.8%, PCI 9.9%, PSI 12.0%). Local government: DC as pre-1975.

3. *Castelnuovo Berardenga* (Siena) Pop. 5,110 (1951: 9,937). Agricultural: predominance of salaried workers. 1976 Election: PCI 52.6%, DC 32.9% (1946: PCI 41.9%, DC 22.3%). Local government: PCI-PSI with PCI mayor, before 1975: PCI-PSIUP-Ind. Left.

4. *Castelnuovo di Garfagnana* (Lucca) Pop. 6,316 (1951: 6,309). Industrial/tertiary. 1976 Election: DC 57.0%, PCI 22.6% (1946: DC 61.2%, PCI 10.0%, PSI 12.3%). Local government: DC, as before 1975. From 1945-1975 the mayor was the *fanfaniano* Loris Biagioni.

5. *Castelnuovo Val di Cecina* (Pisa) Pop. 3,336 (1951 : 5,022). Industrial especially presence of an ENEL establishment. In agriculture, postwar predominance of sharecropping system. 1976 Election: PCI 52.0%, DC 24.8%, PSI 15.1% (1946: PCI 46.2%, DC 14.8%, PSI 30.6%). Local government: PCI-PSI with PCI mayor, as before 1975.

6. *Colle Val d'Elsa* (Siena) Pop. 14,812 (1951: 12,063). Industrial: footwear, minerals and metal industry. In agriculture, postwar predominance of sharecropping system. 1976 Election: PCI 68.6%, DC 20.5%, PSI 4% (1946: PCI 59.8%, DC 20.6%, PSI 13.4%). Local government: PCI (became PCI-PSI in 1976), before 1975 PCI-Independent Left. One of the first Socialist communes in Italy — Socialist local administration formed 1897.

7. *Fiesole* (Florence) Pop. 14,111 (1951: 11,873). Industrial/tertiary. 1976 Election: PCI 54.0%, DC 25.6% (1946: PCI 33.4%, DC 23.4%, PSI 34.6%). Local government: PCI-PSI with PCI mayor, before 1975: PCI.

8. *Firenze* (Florence) Pop. 457,803 (1951: 374,625). Tertiary — tourist and artistic centre, capital of the region of Tuscany. 1976 Election: PCI 40.9%, DC 33.9% (1946: PCI 25.9%, DC 28.2%, PSI 24.4%). Local government: PCI-PSI since 1975: DC-led from 1951 until 1975, including one of first experiments in Italy of Centre-Left from 1960 (Giorgio La Pira mayor 1951-57

and 1961–64). PCI mayor since 1975: Elio Gabbuggiani.

9. *Gaiole in Chianti* (Siena) Pop. 2,894 (1951: 5,437). Agricultural: mainly salaried. 1976 Election: DC 49.8%, PCI 36.4% (1946: DC 41.0%, PCI 24.6%, PSI 20.8%). Local government: DC–PSI with DC mayor, before 1975: DC. Known for local prominence of the Ricasoli family, one of whom was a DC mayor.

10. *Greve in Chianti* (Florence) Pop. 10,061 (1951: 13,233). Agricultural/industrial/tertiary. 1976 Election: PCI 48.1%, DC 30.6%, PSI 15.7% (1946: PCI 33.2%, DC 23.0%, PSI 34.4%). Local government: PCI–PSI with PSI mayor, as before 1975.

11. *Livorno* (Leghorn) Pop. 174,791 (1951: 142,333). Tuscany's second largest city after Florence. Tertiary. Famous as a major Italian port, the fourth largest in the country. 1976 Election: PCI 53.0%, DC 24.0% (1946: PCI 44.9%, DC 19.1%, PSI 17.3%). Local government: PCI–PSI with PCI mayor, as before 1975. Socialist local administration before Fascism.

12. *Lucca* (Lucca) Pop. 90,995 (1951: 88,302). Industrial/tertiary. 1976 Election: DC 54.2%, PCI 22.8% (1946: DC 49.5%, PCI 12.2%). Local government: DC, as before (DC mayors since 1946). Noted for its religious tradition. Lucca was an independent republic until early nineteenth century, formally annexed to Grand Duchy of Tuscany in 1847.

13. *Marradi* (Florence) Pop. 4,539 (1951: 7,350). Agricultural/industrial/tertiary. 1976 Election: DC 41.4%, PCI 40.6%, PSI 11.5% (1946: DC 37.7%, PCI 22.0%, PSI 24.3%). Local government: DC–Ind. Left with DC mayor, before 1975: DC–PSI–Ind. Centre. Mountainous area in Apennines.

14. *Montalcino* (Siena) Pop. 6,297 (1951: 10,203; 1961: 8,825). Agricultural: predominance of salaried workers. 1976 Election: PCI 60.0%, DC 25.8% (1946: PCI 51.8%, DC 12.9%, PSI 20.4%). Local government: PCI, as before 1975. Was an independent republic until mid-sixteenth century.

15. *Monte Argentario* (Grosseto) Pop. 13,676 (1951: 10,692). Tertiary – tourism. 1976 Election: DC 32.9%, PCI 26.1%, PRI 17.5% (1946: PRI 44.3%, DC 25.9%, PCI 7.6%). PRI has maintained a higher vote in local than in national elections, e.g. the strongest party in communal elections 1975, second strongest in 1970. Local government: PRI (mayor: Susanna Agnelli), before 1975: PRI–DC. Wealthy residential area on the Mediterranean.

16. *Peccioli* (Pisa) Pop. 5,774 (1951: 8,371). Agricultural/industrial/tertiary – predominance of sharecropping system after War in agriculture, now salaried workers – development of light industry, notably furniture. 1976 Election: PCI 36.8%, DC 40.7%, PSI 14.0% (1946: DC 37.3%, PCI 20.7%, PSI 31.2%). Local government: PCI–PSI–PSDI with PSI mayor, before 1975: DC–PSI–PSDI with DC mayor.

Tuscan Communes Visited

17. *Pescaglia* (Lucca) Pop. 3,859 (1951: 5,897). Agricultural/industrial/tertiary — predominance after the War of direct cultivators in agriculture, development of some light industry since. Mountainous, the commune consists of small villages. 1976 Election: DC 68%, PCI 17.6%, PSI 5.4% (1946: DC 64.3%, PCI 1.4%, PSI 6.4%). Local government: DC, as before 1975.

18. *Pisa* (Pisa) Pop. 103,415 (1951: 77,722). Tertiary — tourist and communications centre, university city. 1976 Election: PCI 40.4%, DC 31.3%, PSI 10.2% (1946: PCI 34.7%, DC 27.9%, PSI 14.1%). Local government: PCI-PSI-Ind. Left with Ind. Left mayor before 1975: PCI-PSI-PSIUP-ex-DC (the mayor was ex-DC and became the Ind. Left mayor after 1975). There was a short period of Centre-Left in later 1960s.

19. *Poggibonsi* (Siena) Pop. 25,386 (1951: 14,387). Industrial — metal industry, furniture. Severe bombing in War, strong industrial development since. Predominance of sharecropping system in agriculture after War. 1976 Election: PCI 68%, DC 21.3%, PSI 5.9% (1946: PCI 58.8%, DC 16.9%, PSI 16.9%). Local government, PCI, as before 1975.

20. *Pontedera* (Pisa) Pop. 26,538 (1951: 19,124). Industrial/tertiary — noted for the Piaggio factory, which produces motor scooters. 1976 Election: PCI 43.4%, DC 32.1%, PSI 12.6% (1946: PCI 36%, DC 26.1%, PSI 24.8%). Local government: PCI-PSI with PSI mayor, as before 1975.

21. *Prato* (Florence) Pop. 143,232 (1951: 77,361). Industrial — traditional centre of textile industry (known as the 'Tuscan Manchester'), expansion since War — in ten years, the number of factories increased from 3,000 to over 5,000. Now the third most populous city in Tuscany. Predominance of sharecropping system in agriculture after War. 1976 Elections: PCI 51.7%, DC 31.8%, PSI 7.8% (1946: PCI 40.2%, DC 28.7%, PSI 22.3%). Local government: PCI-PSI with PCI mayor, as before 1975. PCI mayors since the War, Prato was a Socialist commune before Fascism.

22. *Radda in Chianti* (Siena) Pop. 1,588 (1951: 2,932). Agricultural — salaried workers. 1976 Election: PCI 44.4%, DC 41.1%, PSI 9% (1946: PCI 36.6%, DC 33.4%, PSI 20.8%). Local government: PCI-Ind. Left with Ind. Left mayor, from 1964-75 Centre-Left. Highest commune in the Chianti hills.

23. *Radicofani* (Siena) Pop. 1,605 (1951: 2,748). Agricultural — poor area. 1976 Election: DC 41.9%, PCI 40.9%, PSI 12.3% (1946: DC 33.9%, PCI 30%, PSI 25.7%). Local government: DC, before 1975: Centre-Left. Until 1964 PCI-PSI.

24. *San Gimignano* (Siena) Pop. 7,673 (1951: 11,297). Agricultural/industrial/tertiary — tourist town. 1976 Election: PCI 63.4%, DC 23.5%, PSI 6.7% (1946: PCI 57.3%, DC 15.7%, PSI 20.6%). Local government: PCI, as before 1975.

25. *Santa Croce sull'Arno* (Pisa) Pop. 11,107 (1951: 7,627). Industrial — metal

and leather industries, industrialisation since the War. 1976 Election: PCI 53.3%, DC 30.9%, PSI 8.1% (1946: PCI 49.3%, DC 23.7%, PSI 21.4%). Local government: PCI-PSI with PCI mayor, before 1975: PCI.

26. *Santa Luce* (Pisa) Pop. 1,647 (1951: 3,571). Agricultural – prevalence after War of sharecroppers, now of direct cultivators. 1976 Election: PCI 46.8%, DC 36.4%, PSI 12.5% (1946: PCI 35.9%, DC 27.1%, PSI 28.8%). Local government: PCI-PSI with PSI mayor, as before 1975.

27. *Sesto Fiorentino* (Florence) Pop. 41,973 (1951: 18,657). Industrial/tertiary – strong industrialisation since War, on outskirts of Florence. 1976 Election: PCI 60.1%, DC 22.9%, PSI 8.8% (1946: PCI 50.8%, DC 23.7%, PSI 20.6%). Local government: PCI-PSI-Ind. Left with PCI mayor, before 1975: PCI-PdUP with PCI mayor. Left-wing stronghold before Fascism – first became Socialist commune in 1899.

28. *Siena* (Siena) Pop. 65,634 (1951: 52,566). Tertiary – tourist city and centre of the Monte dei Paschi bank. 1976 Election: PCI 45%, DC 32.1%, PSI 9.6% (1946: PCI 30%, DC 29.8%, PSI 16.6%). Local government: PCI-PSI with PSI mayor, before 1975: PCI-PSI-Ind. Left with PSI mayor. Medieval independent republic, and strong rival then of Florence. Strong municipal traditions, noted for its annual Palio, the medieval-style horse-race between the 17 city districts (*contrade*).

29. *Viareggio* (Lucca) Pop. 55,737 (1951: 41,764). Tertiary – a growing tourist centre on the coast in the Versilia. 1976 Election: PCI 39.9%, DC 35.5%, PSI 12.4% (1946: PCI 30.6%, DC 35.4%, PSI 21%). Local government: PCI-PSI with PSI mayor, before 1975: DC-PSI-PSDI-PRI with DC mayor.

30. *Volterra* (Pisa) Pop. 15,888 (1951: 17,840). Tertiary. Some tourism, well-known for its alabaster industry. 1976 Election: PCI 54.3%, DC 26.3%, PSI 11.4%(1946: PCI 38.4%, DC 22.1%, PSI 26.9%). Local government: PCI-PSI with PCI mayor, before 1975: PCI, 1946-70: PCI-PSI, 1970-75 PCI with PSI external support. Medieval city, once an Etruscan city.

LIST OF INTERVIEWS

The following interviewees were selected partly from within the communes visited in Tuscany (see preceding appendix), and partly according to their positions in the provincial and regional structures of the parties here. Interviews were mainly conducted during two periods in Italy in 1977 and 1978, and lasted on average 1½-2½ hours each. They had two purposes: a) objective — seeking information and verifying information from other sources; b) subjective — probing attitudes and interpretations of party development. Interviews were conducted using open-endedly systematic questionnaires, with separate ones for regional, provincial and local party leaders. In general, these questionnaires were sub-divided as follows: personal political background, information on the area concerned, party organisational matters, ideological and policy matters, inter-party relationships and miscellaneous questions. In addition, the author also conducted written questionnaires in the autumn of 1977 with Tuscan regional councillors from all parties, and with members of the DC regional committee (for which he wishes to thank Giuseppe Matulli, DC regional vice-secretary, for his assistance). These written questionnaires concerned inter-party relationships in Tuscany as well as the regionalisation of party structures.

The following abbreviations for the nine Tuscan provinces have been used in this list (in brackets after names of towns):

Arezzo (Ar)   Massa Carrara (Ms)
Florence (Fi)   Pisa (Pi)
Grosseto (Gr)   Pistoia (Pt)
Livorno (Li)   Siena (Si)
Lucca (Lu)

Capogruppo = chairman of a party group in a communal council or in the regional assembly.

1. Sergio Marchetti, vice-secretary of PCI sezione San Gusme, at Castelnuovo Berardenga (Si), 5 September 1975.

2. Mario Ciappi, DC provincial vice-secretary Siena, at San Gusme (Si), 13 September 1975; DC capogruppo Radda in Chianti, at Siena, 1 December 1977.

266 *Interviews*

3. Andro Cesarini, DC local party leader Montalcino (Si), at Montalcino, 27 August 1977 and 9 September 1978.

4. Maurizio Buffi, PCI sezione secretary Montalcino (Si), at Montalcino, 30 August 1977.

5. Gino Vigni, PCI local functionary Montalcino (Si), at Montalcino, 30 August 1977.

6. Ilio Raffaelli, PCI mayor of Montalcino (Si), at Montalcino, 31 August 1977.

7. Alberigo Sonnini, DC mayor of Radicofani (Si), at Radicofani, 1 September 1977.

8. Corrado del Grosso, functionary of DC provincial committee Lucca responsible for organisation, and formerly the same for DC Siena, at Lucca, 9 September 1977 and 25 September 1978.

9. Franco Chilleri, press officer DC sezione Franco Martelli of Florence, at Florence, 11 September 1977 and 29 August 1978.

10. Paolo Cappeletto, PCI functionary federation of Florence, at Florence, 12 September 1977.

11. Claudio Pacini, official of DC regional committee for Tuscany, at Florence, 12 September 1977 and 19 September 1978.

12. Giuseppe Matulli, DC regional vice-secretary for Tuscany; and former vice-mayor of Murradi (Fi) and regional councillor, at Florence, 20 September 1977, 29 November 1977, 12 September 1978 and 30 July 1980.

13. Ivo Butini, DC vice-capogruppo Tuscan regional council and former DC regional secretary 1973–76, at Florence, 24 September 1977, 1 September 1978 and 5 September 1978.

14. Flavio Mocenni, Independent Left communal councillor and administrator (*assessore*) for education, Castelnuovo Berardenga (Si), at S. Piero in Barca, 25 September 1977 and 15 September 1978.

15. Mauro Mancini, journalist of *La Nazione*, at Florence, 26 September 1977.

16. Enzo Pezzati, DC provincial secretary for Florence and vice-president of Tuscan regional council, at Florence, 27 September 1977.

17. Giuseppe de Felice, PCI press officer of regional committee and former secretary of PCI Pisa federation 1969–76, at Florence, 27 September 1977 and 16 December 1977.

18. Marco Marcucci, PCI secretary of Lucca federation, at Lucca, 6 October

Interviews 267

     1977 and 25 September 1978.

19. Luigi Arzilli, PSI mayor of Peccioli (Pi), at Peccioli, 9 October 1977.

20. Dino Fornai, DC capogruppo Peccioli (Pi), at Peccioli, 9 October 1977.

21. Pierluigi Falagiani, DC capogruppo Santa Luce (Pi), at Santa Luce, 10 October 1977.

22. Piero Paoli, political correspondent of *La Nazione*, at Florence, 13 October 1977.

23. Palmiro Bini, DC mayor of Pescaglia (Lu), at San Martino in Freddana, 17 October 1977.

24. Rolando Armani, PCI secretary of Pisa federation, at Pisa, 18 October 1977.

25. Silvano Marchi, DC provincial secretary Pisa, at Pisa, 18 October 1977.

26. Giancarlo Bianchi, DC president of Comunità Montana Media Valle del Serchio (Lu) at Borgo a Mozzano, 19 October 1977.

27. Piero Angelini, DC provincial secretary Lucca and regional councillor at Lucca, 20 October 1977; at Florence, 19 September 1978; at Lucca, 27 September 1978.

28. Lenzi Moreno, functionary responsible for youth (FGCI) of PCI federation Lucca, at Lucca, 21 October 1977.

29. Milziade Caprili, PCI provincial secretary for the Versilia (Lu), at Viareggio, 21 October 1977.

30. Angiolo Dionelli, PCI secretary of Zona del Cuoio (Pi), at Santa Croce sull'Arno, 24 October 1977.

31. Massimo Baldacci, PCI secretary of sezione Santa Croce sull'Arno (Pi), at Santa Croce sull'Arno (Pi), 24 October 1977.

32. Giuseppe Vivaldi, DC secretary of sezione Pontedera (Pi), at Pontedera, 25 October 1977.

33. Piero Lazzeroni, PCI secretary of sezione Pontedera (Pi), at Pontedera, 25 October 1977.

34. Bruno Dolo, PCI secretary of sezione at Piaggio factory at Pontedera (Pi), at Pontedera, 25 October 1977.

35. Augusto Simoncini, PCI vice-secretary of Livorno federation, at Livorno, 25 October 1977.

268 *Interviews*

36. Roberto Brilli, functionary responsible for organisation PCI federation of Livorno, at Livorno, 25 October 1977.

37. Sergio Dardini, functionary of PCI federation Lucca and formerly secretary of the federation until 1970, at Lucca, 26 October 1977.

38. Francesco Borghini, PRI vice-mayor of Monte Argentario (Gr), at Porto S. Stefano, 1 November 1977.

39. Umberto Corsi, DC provincial secretary for Grosseto, at Grosseto, 2 November 1977.

40. Flavio Tattarini, PCI secretary of Grosseto federation, at Grosseto, 2 November 1977.

41. Celso Ghini, head of statistics department at PCI national headquarters, Rome, 7 November 1977.

42. Lino Milani, functionary of organisation department at PCI national headquarters, Rome, and national deputy, at Rome, 10 November 1977.

43. Armando Gigli, functionary of PCI Livorno federation and former co-founder of PCI at Livorno in early 1920s, at Livorno, 18 November 1977.

44. Bruno Bernini, PCI secretary of Livorno federation 1965-72 and national deputy, at Livorno, 18 November 1977.

45. Vittorio Lepri, official responsible for membership and elections of DC provincial committee Livorno, at Livorno, 18 November 1977.

46. Gildo Tognetti, PdUP communal councillor Capannori (Lu), 1970-75, at San Martino in Freddana, 2 October 1977 and 20 November 1977.

47. Giorgio Bianchi, Independent Left mayor of Radda in Chianti (Si) at Radda, 26 November 1977.

48. Nello Balestracci, DC capogruppo at Tuscan regional council and former DC provincial secretary for Massa Carrara 1964-70, at Florence, 29 November 1977.

49. Michele Ventura, PCI secretary of Florence federation, at Florence, 30 November 1977.

50. Silla Cellino, functionary of PSI regional committee responsible for local government, at Florence, 30 November 1977.

51. Dario Cecchini, PCI communal councillor Greve (Fi) at Panzano, 1 December 1977.

Interviews

52. Gianfranco Gigli, DC secretary of sezione San Gimignano (Si), at S. Gimignano, 9 December 1977.

53. Gabriello Mancini, DC capogruppo San Gimignano (Si), at S. Gimignano, 9 December 1977.

54. Enzo Sammicheli, PCI mayor of Colle di Val D'Elsa (Si), at Colle di Val D'Elsa, 9 December 1977 and 25 August 1978.

55. Luigi Testi, PCI functionary San Gimignano (Si), at S. Gimignano, 10 December 1977.

56. Tullio Innocenti, DC provincial secretary for Arezzo, at Arezzo, 12 December 1977.

57. Vasco Giannotti, PCI secretary of Arezzo federation, at Arezzo, 12 December 1977.

58. Ottaviano Colzi, PSI vice-mayor of Florence and former PSI provincial secretary for Florence, at Florence, 13 December 1977.

59. Franco Pardini, member of PRI provincial directorate for Florence and secretary of PRI sezione Figline Valdarno (Fi), at Florence, 13 December 1977.

60. Luigi Luciano, functionary of PSI provincial federation for Florence and communal secretary for Greve (Fi), at Greve, 14 December 1977.

61. Alessandro Vigni, functionary of PCI Siena federation, at Siena, 15 December 1977.

62. Enzo Martinelli, DC communal councillor Siena, at Siena, 15 December 1977.

63. Pietro Burresi, DC capogruppo at Poggibonsi (Si), at Poggibonsi, 15 December 1977.

64. Marino Marchetti, PCI secretary of sezione Poggibonsi (Si), at Poggibonsi, 15 December 1977.

65. Marco Majer, PCI vice-capogruppo at Tuscan regional council, at Florence, 16 December 1977.

66. Giorgio Gianni, member of PSDI provincial federation executive for Florence, at Florence, 16 December 1977.

67. Giulio Maestrini, DC secretary of communal committee Gaiole in Chianti (Si) at Gaiole, 17 December 1977.

68. Nella Montagnani, PCI secretary of sezione Gaiole in Chianti (Si), at Gaiole, 17 December 1977.

69. Orlando Fabbri, PCI secretary of Prato federation, at Prato (Fi), 19 December 1977.

70. Romano Boretti, PCI capogruppo communal council Prato (Fi) at Prato, 19 December 1977.

71. Vannino Chiti, PCI secretary of Pistoia federation, at Pistoia, 19 December 1977; and functionary responsible for organisation at PCI Tuscan regional committee, at Florence, 14 September 1978.

72. Michele Rossi, PCI mayor of Castelnuovo Val di Cecina (Pi), at Castelnuovo VC, 19 August 1978.

73. Francesco Gherardini, PCI administrator (*assessore*) for education Castelnuovo Val di Cecina (Pi), at Castelnuovo VC, 19 August 1978.

74. Mario Geppini, ex-PCI functionary and head of cooperative at Monterotondo (Gr), at Monterotondo, 20 August 1978.

75. Angiolino Poli, PSI vice-mayor of Castelnuovo Val di Cecina (Pi), at Sasso Pisano, 20 August 1978.

76. Benso Cheli, PSI trade unionist, at Sasso Pisano, (Pi), 20 August 1978.

77. Alvo Bastieri, DC capogruppo Castelnuovo Val di Cecina (Pi), at Castelnuovo VC, 20 August 1978.

78. Federigo Ciampoli, DC provincial secretary Grosseto 1947–52, at Montieri, 22 August 1978.

79. Carlo Benvenuti, PSI vice-mayor Volterra (Pi) at Volterra, 23 August, 1978.

80. Paolo Paggetti, DC secretary of sezione Volterra (Pi), at Volterra, 23 August 1978.

81. Pier Luigi Marrucci, PCI mayor of San Gimignano (Si) at S. Gimignano, 25 August 1978.

82. Rolando Giannelli, PCI communal councillor Volterra (Pi), 25 August 1978.

83. Emilio Gori, PCI administrator (*assessore*) Volterra (Pi), at Volterra, 25 August 1978.

84. Mario Signorini, DC provincial secretary for Florence 1975–77, at Florence, 7 September 1978, 11 September 1978 and 12 September 1978.

Interviews

85. Paolo Gorelli, CGIL functionary Montalcino (Si), at Montalcino, 10 September 1978.

86. Luciano Stanghellini, DC regional councillor, at Florence, 12 September 1978.

87. Massimo Pacetti, PCI communal secretary Sesto Fiorentino, (Fi), at Sesto Fiorentino, 13 September 1978.

88. Giorgio Conciani, former secretary of Radical Party at Florence, at Florence 13 September 1978.

89. Marcello Billi, DC official of Florence provincial committee responsible for local government, at Florence, 13 September 1978 and 20 September 1978.

90. Giovanni Pallanti, acting DC provincial secretary Florence, at Florence, 13 September 1978 and 20 September 1978.

91. Alberto Cecchi, PCI national deputy and former PCI Tuscan regional secretary 1970-72, at Florence, 14 September 1978.

92. Vincenzo Mattolini, DC capogruppo Sesto Fiorentino (Fi), at Florence, 15 September 1978.

93. Giancarlo Carrozza, DC capogruppo Fiesole (Fi), at Florence, 18 September 1978.

94. Pier Luigi Ballini, DC communal councillor Florence, at Florence, 19 September 1978.

95. Maria Martini, DC national deputy, at Lucca, 24 September 1978.

96. Leonardo Andreucci, DC mayor of Castelnuovo di Garfagnana (Lu), at Castelnuovo, 26 September 1978.

97. Piero Pratali, DC communal councillor Altopascio (Lu) and member of Lucca provincial committee, at Altopascio, 27 September 1978.

PUBLISHED SOURCES AND BIBLIOGRAPHY

The following list is not definitive, for it does not repeat the party and other documentation detailed in the individual source references at the end of each chapter. This list includes only published material, both general and relating to the region of Tuscany.

(1) Documentation: Tuscan Region, Political Parties and General

Agenzia di Ricerche e Legislazione (AREL), *Risultati di un sondaggio tra gli iscritti alla D.C.*, Rome, August 1977.

Bollettino della sezione regioni ed autonomie locali del Comitato Centrale del PCI

Comitato Regionale del PCI, *Toscana Comunità Montane*, Florence, January 1973

Comune di Livorno, *Elezioni Politiche 20 giugno 1976, Camera dei Deputati: Il Voto della Città*, Livorno, 1976

Comune di Livorno, *Elezioni Politiche 20 giugno 1976, Senato: Il Voto della Città*, Livorno, 1976

Decentramento Regionale e Riordinamento della Pubblica Amministrazione, leggi 22 luglio 1975, n.382 e 27 novembre 1976, n.894, Rome 1977

DC, Comitato Regionale Toscano, *1968–1970–1972: tappe di una battaglia, 1–Circoscrizione Firenze-Pistoia*, Florence, 1973

DC, Comitato Regionale Toscano, *1968–1970–1972: tappe di una battaglia, 2–Circoscrizione Siena-Arezzo-Grosseto*, Florence, 1973

Gruppo Consiliare DC, *Un primo giudizio sull'operato della maggioranza 'rossa' in Toscana*, Florence, 1975

ISTAT, *Compendio delle Statistiche Elettorale Italiane dal 1848 al 1934*, Rome, 1947

—, *Le Regioni in Cifre*, Rome, 1976

PCI Comitato Regionale Toscano, *1° Congresso Regionale dei Comunisti Toscani, Firenze, 31 marzo – 3 aprile 1977: sintesi degli atti e risoluzioni*, Florence, 1978

PCI federation Pisa, *La federazione comunista pisana dall' 11° at 12° congresso provinciale*, Pisa, 1975

PCI federation Pisa, *L'impegno dei comunisti per l'agricoltura: le lotte contadine e la programmazione regionale*, Pisa, 1975

PCI federation Pisa, *Materiale per uno studio statistico sul partito a Pisa*, Pisa, 1975

Regione Toscana, Giunta Regionale, *Linee del programma regionale di sviluppo economico*, Florence, 1973

Regione Toscana, Giunta Regionale, *Proposta di documento programmatico pluriennale*, Florence, 1977

Regione Toscana, Giunta Regionale, Dipartimento statistica, elaborazione dati, documentazione (SEDD), *Il comportamento elettorale in Toscana: una prima interpretazione*, Florence, 1975

—, *Le comunità montane della Toscana*, Florence, 1977

Regione Toscana, Giunta Regionale, Dipartimento statistica, elaborazione dati, documentazione (SEDD), *Dalla costituente alla regione: il comportamento elettorale in Toscana dal 1946 al 1970*, Florence, 1972
  1. Provincia di Arezzo
  2. Provincia di Firenze
  3. Provincia di Grosseto
  4. Provincia di Livorno
  5. Provincia di Lucca
  6. Provincia di Massa Carrara
  7. Provincia di Pisa
  8. Provincia di Pistoia
  9. Provincia di Siena
—, *Le elezioni amministrative del 26 novembre 1972*, Florence, 1972
—, *Le elezioni amministrative del 14-15 maggio 1978*, Florence, 1978
—, *Le elezioni del 15-16 giugno 1975 in Toscana*, Florence, 1975
—, *Elezioni Senato e Camera del 20-21 giugno 1976*, Florence, 1976
—, *Il Governo Locale in Toscana*, Florence, 1975
—, *Il Governo Locale in Toscana*, volume II, Florence, 1976
—, *Mappa politico-amministrativa della Toscana*, Florence, 1975
—, *Elezioni Senato e Camera del 3-4 giugno 1979*, Florence, 1979
—, *Elezioni Regionali dell' 8-9 giugno 1980*, Florence, 1980
—, *Elezioni Amministrative dell' 8-9 giugno 1980*, Florence, 1980
—, *I referendum dell' 11-12 giugno 1978 in Toscana*, Florence, 1978
—, *Il referendum del 12 maggio 1974 in Toscana*, Florence, 1974
Regione Toscana, *Statuto*, Florence, 1971
Studi-Ricerche-Documentazioni del Comitato Regionale Toscano DC, *Il Partito: Quaderni di Toscana Più 3*, Florence, 1964
Toscana Consiglio Regionale, proceedings of the Tuscan regional council, fortnightly, published since 1971, Florence
Ufficio Elettorale e di Statistica del PCI, *Elezioni Regionali e Amministrative Generali: 15 giugno 1975, Composizione delle giunte prima e dopo le elezioni regionali, provinciali, comunali*, Rome, 1976
—, *Raccolta di Dati sull'Organizzazione, 1971-1975*, volume II, Rome, 1976

(2) Reviews in Tuscany

Amministrazione Provinciale di Lucca, *La Provincia di Lucca*, quarterly, published since 1961
Chamber of Commerce, Pisa, *Pisa Economica*, quarterly, new series
Chamber of Commerce, Siena, *Siena Rassegna Economica*, monthly
Città e Regione, monthly review, published from 1975, Florence, pro-Socialist
  March 1975, *Verso la seconda legislatura regionale*
  April 1975, *La 'questione Firenze'*
  July 1975, *Le elezioni del 15 giugno in Italia, in Toscana e a Firenze*
  May 1976, *Il Partito Socialista Italiano: politica e programmi*
  June 1978, *La democrazia di partito*
Giunta Regionale, IRPET e Gruppo di Studio sul Comportamento Elettorale in Toscana, *Quaderni dell'Osservatorio Elettorale*, Florence, published since 1977, 1, 2, 3, 4, 5
Opposizione Democratica, fortnightly publication of DC group in Tuscan

regional council.

Politica e Società, monthly review of PCI Tuscan regional committee, published from 1976.

Testimonianze, Catholic monthly, Florence, published since 1958

(3) Books and Publications

AAVV, *Tutto il potere della DC*, Rome, 1975
Allum, P.A., *Politics and Society in Postwar Naples*, Cambridge, 1973
Badaloni, N., *Democratici e socialisti livornesi nell'ottocento*, Rome, 1966
Badaloni, N. and Bortolotti, F.P., *Movimento Operaio e Lotta Politica a Livorno, 1900-1926*, Rome, 1977
Barberis, G., *Le migrazioni rurali in Italia*, Milan, 1960
Barnes, Samuel, *Party Democracy: Politics in an Italian Socialist Federation*, New Haven, 1967
Becattini, Giacomo (ed.), *Lo Sviluppo Economico della Toscana*, Florence, 1975
Belloni, Frank, 'Factionalism, the Party System and Italian Politics' in F. Belloni and D. Beller, *Faction Politics: Political Parties and Factionalism in Comparative Perspective*, Santa Barbara, 1978
Bertolino, Alberto, *Problemi di politica economica territoriale*, Florence, 1975
Bettin, Gianfranco, *Partito e comunità locale*, Bologna, 1970
Blackmer, D. and Tarrow, S., *Communism in Italy and France*, Princeton, 1975
Braga, Giorgio, *Sociologia elettorale della Toscana*, Rome, 1963
Brunelli, Luigi *et al.*, *La presenza sociale del PCI e della DC*, Bologna, 1969
Burgalassi, Silvano, *Il comportamento religioso degli italiani*, Florence, 1968
Caciagli, Mario, *Democrazia Cristiana e Potere nel Mezzogiorno*, Florence, 1977
Camera di Commercio, Livorno, *Rapporto sulla economia della provincia*, Livorno, 1974
Cantelli, F. *et al.*, *L'organizzazione partitica del PCI e della DC*, Bologna, 1968
Castellacci, Claudio, *Mani pulite: i comunisti e le amministrazioni degli enti locali*, Milan, 1977
Catalano, I., 'The Rebirth of the party system, 1944-48', in S.J. Woolf (ed.), *The Rebirth of Italy, 1943-50*, London, 1972
Cavalli, Luciano (ed.), *Classe Dirigente e Sviluppo Regionale*, Bologna, 1973
Cervetti, Gianni, *Partito di Governo e Lotta*, Rome, 1977
Chiaromonte, Gerardo, *L'Accordo Programmatico e l'Azione dei Comunisti*, Rome, 1977
Compromesso con il PCI, Rapporti con il PSI, Scelte della DC; il dibattito al al Consiglio Nazionale DC, 31 gennaio – 3 febbraio 1975, Rome, 1975
Coppetti, M. and Vaselli, F., *Giorgio La Pira, agente d'Iddio*, Milan, 1978
Corsi, H., *Le origini del fascismo nel Grossetano, 1919-1922*, Rome 1973
Cossutta, A., Stefanini, M. and Zangheri, R., *Decentramento e Partecipazione*, Rome, 1977
Farneti, P., *Il sistema politico italiano*, Bologna, 1973
Ferraresci, F. and Kemeny, P., *Classi Sociali e Politica Urbana: destra e sinistra nelle amministrazioni locali*, Rome, 1977
Francovich, C., *La Resistenza a Firenze*, Florence, 1962
Fried, R.C., *The Italian Prefects*, New Haven, 1963
Galli, Giancarlo, *Il Piave Democristiano: i protagonisti della DC che cambia*, Milan, 1978

Galli, Giorgio, *Fanfani*, Milan, 1975
—, *I partiti politici in Italia, 1861-1973*, Turin, 1975
—, *Storia della DC*, Bari, 1978
Galli, Giorgio and Prandi, A., *Patterns of Political Participation in Italy*, New Haven, 1970
Ghini, Celso, *Il Terremoto del 15 giugno*, Milan, 1976
Gozzini, Mario (ed.), *Il Dialogo alla prova: cattolici e comunisti italiani*, Florence, 1964
Graziano, L. and Tarrow, S. (ed.), *La Crisi Italiana*, Turin, 1979
I Comunisti Umbri: scritti e documenti, 1944-1970, Perugia, 1977
IRPET, *Toscana decifrata*, Florence, 1975
Lagorio, Lelio, *Presidente in Toscana*, Florence, 1977
Martelli, Claudio, *Socialisti a confronto*, Milan, 1976
Martinelli, Renzo, *Il Partito Comunista d'Italia, 1921-26: politica e organizzazione*, Rome, 1977
Menapace, L., *La Democrazia Cristiana*, Milan, 1974
Orfei, R., *L'Occupazione del potere: i democristiani, 1945-75*, Milan, 1975
Ottone, Piero, *Fanfani*, Milan, 1966
Parisi, Arturo (ed.), *Democristiani*, Bologna, 1979
Parisi, Arturo and Pasquino, Gianfranco, *Continuità e mutamento elettorale in Italia*, Bologna, 1977
Ragionieri, Ernesto, *Storia di un comune socialista: Sesto Fiorentino*, Rome 1976
Regioni, enti locali per lo sviluppo nella libertà, Rome, 1975
Rodano, Franco, *Questione democristiana e compromesso storico*, Rome, 1977
Rossi, Raffaele, *Il PCI in una regione rossa: intervista sui comunisti umbri*, Perugia, 1977
Sani, Giacomo, 'L'immagine dei partiti nell'elettorato' in Caciagli, M. and Spreafico, A. (eds.), *Un sistema politico alla prova*, Bologna, 1975
Tamburrano, G., *L'Iceberg democristiano*, Milan, 1974
Tarrow, Sidney, *Partisanship and Political Exchange in French and Italian Local Politics*, London, 1974
—, *Peasant Communism in Southern Italy*, New Haven, 1967
Testimonianze, *Giorgio La Pira*, Florence, April-July, 1978
Tradition et Changement en Toscane, cahiers de la fondation nationale des sciences politiques, no. 176, Paris, 1970
Unione Regionale delle Camere di Commercio, Industria, Artigianato e Agricoltura della Toscana, *Quadri di Economia Toscana: gli ultimi venti anni*, Milan, 1974
Unione Regionale delle Province Toscane, *La Toscana nel regime fascista, 1922-1939*, Florence, 1971, 2 vols
Unione Sindicale Regionale Toscana, *Questa regione: Toscana in zone*, Florence, 1975
Valenzi, Maurizio, *Sindaco a Napoli*, Rome, 1978
Vanni, R., *Fascismo e antifascismo in provincia di Pisa*, Pisa, 1967
Wade, Robert, 'The Base of a "Centrifugal Democracy": party allegiance in rural central Italy' in J. Boissevain and J. Friedl (eds.), *Beyond the community: social process in Europe*, The Hague, 1975
—, 'Political Behaviour and World View in a Central Italian Village' in F.G. Bailey (ed.), *Gifts and Poison: the politics of reputation*, Oxford, 1971

Zuckerman, Alan, *Political Clienteles in Power: party factions and cabinet coalitions in Italy*, London, 1975

(4) Articles

Allum, P.A. and Amyot, G., 'Regionalism in Italy: old wine in new bottles?' in *Parliamentary Affairs*, winter 1970-71
Barbagli, Marzio and Corbetta, Piergiorgio, 'Partito e movimento: aspetti e rinnovamento del PCI' in *Inchiesta*, January-February 1978
—, 'Una tattica e due strategie: inchiesta sulla base del PCI' in *Il Mulino*, November-December 1978
Bibes, Geneviève, 'Le système des partis italien' in *Revue Francaise de Science Politique*, April 1979
Cammelli, Marco, 'Politica istituzionale e modello emiliano: ipotesi per una ricerca' in *Il Mulino*, September-October 1978
Cazzola, Franco, 'Partiti, correnti e voto di preferenza' in *Rivista Italiana di Scienza Politica*, 1971
Clark, M., Hine, D. and Irving, R.E.M., 'Divorce – Italian Style' in *Parliamentary Affairs*, autumn 1974
Cotta, Maurizio, 'Il rinnovamento del personale parlamentare democristiano' in *Il Mulino*, September-October, 1978
Dalton, Richard, 'Generational change within the Italian Christian Democratic party elite' in *European Journal of Political Research*, June, 1977
Fried, Robert, 'Communism, urban budgets and the two Italies: a case study in comparative urban government' in *Journal of Politics*, November 1971
Galli, G., 'L'influenza dell'organizzazione partitica sul voto' in *Rassegna Italiana di Sociologia*, January-March 1972
Gori, Neri, 'Attivismo tradizionale e crisi della partecipazione nel PCI: il caso di Firenze' in *Rassegna Italiana di Sociologia*, 1975
—, 'L'organizzazione del PCI a Firenze, 1945-1971' in *Rassenga Italiana di Sociologia*, 1974
Graziano, L., 'On Political Compromise: Italy after the 1979 elections' in *Government and Opposition*, Spring 1980
Hellman, Stephen, 'Generational differences in the bureaucratic elite of Italian Communist Party provincial federations' in *Canadian Journal of Political Science*, 1975
Hine, David, 'The Italian Socialist Party under Craxi: surviving but not reviving' in *West European Politics*, October 1979
—, 'Euro-communism and Social Democracy: the Italian case' in *West European Politics*, May 1978
—, 'Italian Socialism and the Centre-Left Coalition: strategy or tactics?' in *Journal of Common Market Studies*, June 1975
Lanchester, Fulco, 'La dirigenza di partito: il caso del PCI' in *Il Politico*, December 1976
—, 'I dirigenti del PCI: continuità e cambiamenti' in *Il Mulino*, May-June 1978
Lange, Peter, 'Crisis and Consent, Change and Compromise: dilemmas of Italian Communism in the 1970s' in *West European Politics*, October 1979
Leonardi, Robert, 'Opinioni politiche delle correnti democristiane in Emilia-Romagna' in *Rivista Italiana di Scienza Politica*, 1974
Lombardo, Antonio, 'Sistema di correnti e deperimento dei partiti in Italia' in

Rivista Italiana di Scienza Politica, April 1976
Marradi, Alberto, 'Analisi del referendum sul divorzio' in *Rivista Italiana di Scienza Politica*, December 1974
Parisi, A. and Pasquino, G., '20 giugno: struttura politica e comportamenti elettorali' in *Il Mulino*, May–June 1976
Pasquino, Gianfranco, 'Crisi della DC e evoluzione del sistema politico' in *Rivista Italiana di Scienza Politica*, December 1975
—, 'Italian Christian Democracy: a party for all seasons?' in *West European Politics*, October 1979
—, 'Before and after the Italian national elections of 1976' in *Government and Opposition*, Winter 1977
Pridham, Geoffrey, 'The Italian Christian Democrats after Moro: Crisis or Compromise?' in *West European Politics*, January 1979
Riccamboni, Gianni, 'Regioni: una nuova classe politica?' in *Rivista di Sociologia*, December 1976
Sani, Giacomo, 'Le elezioni degli anni settanta: terremoto o evoluzione?' in *Rivista Italiana di Scienza Politica*, August 1976
—, 'Ricambio elettorale e identificazioni partitiche: verso una egemonia delle sinistre?' in *Rivista Italiana di Scienza Politica*, December 1975
—, 'Profilo dei dirigenti di partito' in *Rassegna Italiana di Sociologia*, January–March 1972
—, 'The PCI on the threshold' in *Problems of Communism*, November–December 1976
Sartori, G., 'Proporzionalismo, frazionismo e crisi dei partiti' in *Rivista Italiana di Scienza Politica*, December 1971
Sechi, Salvatore, 'L'austero fascino del centralismo democratico' in *Il Mulino*, May–June 1978
Seidelman, Raymond, 'PCI, decentramento e politica delle alleanze: il caso di Firenze' in *Il Mulino*, May–June 1978
Sivini, Giordano, 'Gli iscritti alla Democrazia Cristiana e al Partito Comunista Italino' in *Rassegna Italiana di Sociologia*, 1967
Stern, Alan, 'The Italian CP at the grass-roots' in *Problems of Communism*, March–April 1974
Tarrow, Sidney, 'The Italian Party System between crisis and transition' in *American Journal of Political Science*, May 1977
Tassani, Giovanni, 'Laicità della DC e "ricomposizione" cattolica' in *Il Mulino*, September–October 1978

(5) **Periodicals and Newspapers**

Avanti, PSI daily
L'Avvenire, Catholic daily
Corriere della Sera
Critica Marxista, PCI review
La Discussione, DC weekly
L'Espresso, weekly
Le Libertà, monthly of DC Tuscan regional committee
La Nazione, Florence daily
Nuovo Corriere Senese, pro-PCI weekly, Siena
Paese Sera, Rome daily

Panorama, weekly
Il Popolo, DC daily

Rinascita, PCI weekly
La Stampa
Il Tirreno (formerly *Il Telegrafo*), Livorno daily
L'Unità, PCI daily

(6) Local Party Newspapers in Tuscany

Il Campanone, PCI San Gimignano
Circoscrizione 3, DC south Florence
La Città, PCI Poggibonsi
Il Corvo delle Torri, DC San Gimignano
Democrazia Cristiana Spes, DC Lucca
Democrazia Politica, DC Florence
Dibattito Democratico, DC Pistoia
L'Informatore Politico, PCI Montalcino
Montalcino Più, DC Montalcino
Note di Confronto, DC Pisa
Notizie, PCI Buonconvento
Orientamenti Sociali, MCL Florence, Catholic
Il Piaggista, PCI Pontedera
Siena Spes, DC Siena
Siena Sport, Libertas (DC) Siena
Il Taglio, DC Poggibonsi

INDEX

Agnelli, Susanna 262
Altopascio (Lucca) 261
Amendola, Giorgio 198-9, 207
Andreotti Government 68, 103, 104, 105, 108
Angelini, Piero 165
Anti-clericalism 32-3, 125, 127-8, 143
Anti-Communism 5, 16, 17, 21, 104, 118, 124-5, 154, 170, 171, 176, 177, 193, 194, 197, 207, 236
Anti-Fascism 10, 101, 189
Apennines 35
Arezzo, province of 35, 71, 87, 122, 123, 160, 163, 203, 236
Association of Catholic Parents (AGE) 136

Balducci, Ernesto 35, 129
Balestracci, Nello 237, 238
Bambi, Moreno 130, 180
Banca Toscana 136
Barga (Lucca) 211
Bartolomei, Giuseppe 151
Benelli, Cardinal 129, 131
Benelli, Paolo 195, 196
Berlinguer, Enrico 48, 84, 92, 102, 103, 108, 109, 189, 190, 240
Berlinguer, Giovanni 95, 97
berlingueriani 94, 104
Biagioni, Loris 175, 261
Bisagno, Tommaso 202
Bologna 30, 68
Butini, Ivo 155, 160-1, 192, 217, 235-6, 236, 237, 238-9

Calabria, region of 65
Campania, region of 65
Campo nell'Elba (Livorno) 132
Capannori (Lucca) 59, 130, 261
Capraia, island of (Livorno) 214
Careggine (Lucca) 56
Case del Popolo 33, 67, 72
Castelnuovo Berardenga (Siena) 261
Castelnuovo di Garfagnana (Lucca) 261
Castelnuovo Val di Cecina (Pisa) 261
Castiglione Garfagnana (Lucca) 56
'Catch-all' parties 8, 46-7, 121
Catholic Action 127, 129

Cecina (Livorno) 60
Centre-Left coalitions 9, 22, 23, 30, 104, 185, 186, 195, 196, 201, 202, 204, 204-5, 207, 210, 214, 215, 226, 233, 235
Cervetti, Gianni 78, 101
Chianti area 209
Chiaromonte, Gerardo 200
Christian Democratic Party, Italian (DC) – in general: and introduction of regional government 20-2; anti-Communism of 5, 16, 17, 21, 124-5, 154, 170, 171, 176, 177, 193, 194, 236; as governing party 5, 16; as party of dominance 11, 15-18; as type of political party 120-6; *correnti* in 17, 144; decline in dominance 250, 251; electoral orientation of 121, 123-4, 177-8, 193; relations with Catholic Church 16, 122, 123; role of ideology in 124-5, 180; social structure of membership in 141, 142; voting strength 5, 7, 8, 14, 15, 37; weak internal cohesion 4-5
Christian Democratic Party, Italian (DC) – in Tuscany: alliance strategy in Tuscany 201-4, local politics 199-225, regional politics 225-42; and Catholic associations 127, 128-9, 129-30; and Church influence 131, 133; and Divorce Referendum 132-5, 143-4, 161, 172, 180, 192; andreottiani *corrente* 163, 164; and share-cropping system 39; Base *corrente* 157, 160, 163, 170, 174; 'Battle of Tuscany' 235-6, 238; dorotei *corrente* 124, 160, 163, 164, 192, 236; economic power of 122-3, 136-8; effect of threat from PCI 135-6, 143-4, 153; effect on of loss of role in local government 150-1; electoral strength 37, 126, 152, 176-7; fanfaniani *corrente* 149, 157, 159, 160-3, 164, 170, 192, 209, 235, 236, 237; forlaniani *corrente* 163; Forze Nuove *corrente* 163, 170; 'Friendship festivals'

279

175-6; greater awareness of organisational weakness 148-9; *Libertas* association 132, 180; organisational structure of 144-67; regionalisation of party structure 153-7, 182; regional office 146; relations with PCI, internal party dimension of 167-78; representation in local government 148, 150-1, 214-18; role of *correnti* in 152, 157-66, 183, 203; social structure of membership 138-43; sociological structure 125-6; strategy of *confronto* 168-73, 191-4, 237, 238-9; strength of in province of Lucca 35-6, 125-6, 132, 138, 141, 148, 214; tradition of voluntary element in 145-8; weak membership participation in 151-2; 'Zaccagnini line' 149, 158, 160, 163, 164, 165, 171, 203

City district councils (*quartieri*) 24, 80, 150-1, 209, 223
Civic Committees 127
Coldiretti 130
Cold War 10, 94, 104, 186, 212, 218
Colle Valdelsa (Siena) 62-3, 74, 131, 261
Communist Party, Italian (PCI) — in general 4, 9, 11-12, 16, 17; and introduction of regional government 21, 22-3; concept of 'reform of the state' 229-32; electoral losses 18, 48; electoral strength 37; evolution as party and movement 45-50; greater role in state structure 16, 17-18, 18, 251-3; growth in electoral support 8, 18, 37; membership 51, 64, 65; party schools 221, 246; political alliances 16, 102; role in Resistance 5-6; strategy of the 'historic compromise' 1, 10, 17, 23, 30, 46, 101, 102, 103, 103-4, 104, 107, 108, 109, 187-91, 197-8, 212-13, 240, 243, 244, 247, 252, 257
Communist Party, Italian (PCI) — in Tuscany: alliance strategy in Tuscany 200-1, local politics 199-225, regional politics 225-42; and experience of Fascism 34-5; and 'Red' tradition 32-5; artisans in 51, 52, 59-60; change in attitude to local government role 218-20; degree of participation among membership 98-100; democratic centralism in 95-100, 104; development after World War II 49-50; doctrine of 'the open region' 231-2; electoral strength 37, 109-10; entrepreneurs in 61-3; growing prominence of young middle-class intellectuals as party functionaries 89, 90-5; 'historic compromise' strategy, internal party acceptance of 100-12; industrial workers in 51, 52, 56-9; local party newspapers 73-4; membership, strength and composition of 51-70; membership recruitment 56, 106, 118; nature of political discussion in 96-8; party bookshops 72-3; performance in local government 220-5; ratio members/voters 55-6; ratio PCI members/population 56, 57; regionalisation of party structure 82-8; regional policy of 232-3; rejuvenation of party functionaries 88-95; representation in local government in Tuscany 206, 207, 213-16; sharecroppers in 49, 51, 52, 53, 59, 63; 'Stalinists' in 107-8; structural adaptation 78-82; *Unità* festivals 75-6; urban middle classes in 59-64; women in 69-70; youth in 64-9; youth organisation (FGCI) 67-8, 92, 103, 116-17

Comunione e Liberazione (CL) 135
Concordat (1929) 4
Constitution, Italian (1948) 4, 17, 19, 23
Correntocrazia 10
Cossutta, Armando 83
Craxi, Bettino 104, 196, 204, 228, 239
Credito Lombardo 137

De Gasperi, Alcide 17, 120
De Martino, Francesco 204
De Pasquale, Pancrazio 22
Divorce Referendum (1974) 24, 69, 128, 132-5, 254
Donat-Cattin, Carlo 171

Elba, Isle of 40, 132, 163
Emilia-Romagna, region of 30, 32, 33, 51, 69, 71, 72, 102, 103, 109, 118, 155, 206, 226
Empoli (Florence) 41, 61, 72

Fanfani, Ameglio 166
Fanfani, Amintore 121, 123, 124, 126, 132, 133, 147, 155, 159, 160, 161, 162, 163, 166, 174, 179-80, 191, 192, 204
Fiesole (Florence) 203, 261
Florence, city of 30, 31, 34, 35, 41, 42, 53, 59, 66, 72, 80, 81, 93, 103, 114, 122, 125, 129, 132, 135, 150-1, 151, 153, 160, 202, 204, 207, 209, 214, 222-3, 224, 225, 230, 234, 236, 261-2
Florence, province of 32, 33, 35, 49, 51, 62, 69-70, 71, 72, 79, 123, 138, 163, 236
Forte dei Marmi (Lucca) 202, 202-3
Friuli-Venezia Giulia, region of 19

Gabbuggiani, Elio 223-4, 224, 231, 234, 262
Gaiole in Chianti (Siena) 262
Gallicano (Lucca) 58-9
Garfagnana 130, 130-1, 133
Giustarini, Mario 112-13
Gori, Giorgio 137
Gozzini, Mario 129, 209
Greve in Chianti (Florence) 262
Gronchi, Giovanni 126
Grosseto, city of 227
Grosseto, province 163
Groups of Political Involvement (*Gruppi di Impegno Politico* – GIP) 130, 145, 153, 179

Ideology, in Italian politics 12
'Imperfect two-party system', thesis of 13-14, 15, 18, 19
Ingrao, Pietro 22
Innocenti, Tullio 166
Inter-communal districts (*comprensori*) 80, 221
Inter-party relationships, change in during 1970s 1, 10, 18
Inter-party relationships, in Italy 9-10, 185-6, 187
Italian Association of Christian Workers (ACLI) 129
Italian Confederation of Workers' Trade Unions (CISL) 71, 130
Italian General Confederation of Workers (CGIL) 57, 71-2, 227
Italian Union of Labour (UIL) 71

Lagorio, Lelio 228-9, 234

La Nazione, newspaper 74, 223
La Pira, Giorgio 35, 124, 126, 129, 159, 160, 175, 207, 209, 223, 261-2
Lazio, region of 226
Leone, Mario 234
Liberal Party, Italian (PLI) 9, 23, 196-7
Liberal political class, pre-Mussolini 3, 5, 6
Licheri, Pier Giorgio 174
Liguria, region of 226
Livorno (Leghorn), city of 30, 41, 58, 60, 153, 209, 210, 227, 262
Livorno (Leghorn), province of 35, 91, 138, 160, 163
Local traditions in political life 19-20, 29-30, 73, 74, 79-80
Lombardy, region of 51, 155
Lucca, city of 125, 127, 128, 209, 210, 211, 262
Lucca, province of 30, 35-6, 55, 56, 71, 72, 125-6, 127, 132, 132-3, 138, 141, 148, 151, 163, 172, 214
Lucchesia 35, 43, 59, 71, 72, 121, 122, 128, 130, 133, 151

Macaluso, Emanuele 93-4
Marches, region of 32
Marradi (Florence) 262
Martini, Maria 133, 163
Massa (Massa-Carrara) 204
Massa-Carrara, province of 35, 40, 56, 71, 138, 160, 216, 217
Michels' theory of party bureaucracies 78, 81, 86
Milan 135, 208, 214, 221
Montalcino (Siena) 73-4, 75, 97-8, 115, 131-2, 262
Monte Argentario (Grosseto) 262
Montecatini Terme (Pistoia) 42
Monte dei Paschi Bank 123, 136, 137-8, 149, 166
Montieri (Grosseto) 146
Moro, Aldo 180, 237
'Mountain communities' (*comunità montane*) 24, 221, 246
Movement of Christian Workers (MCL) 130, 180
Mugello 122

Naples 32, 214
Neo-Fascist Party, Italian (MSI) –
 in general 13, 23, 197, 250

Index

Neo-Fascist Party, Italian (MSI) – in Tuscany 132
Nuova Pignone industry 41

Pacini, Senator 163, 235
Partitocrazia 4, 249
Party identification 7-8
Pasquini, Alessio 85, 87
Peccioli (Pisa) 43, 143, 153, 262
Pescaglia (Lucca) 263
Pezzati, Enzo 165, 237, 238
Pezzati, Sergio 160
Piaggio firm 41, 58, 74, 145, 153
Piedmont, region of 226
Piombino (Livorno) 41
Pisa, city of 31, 41, 58, 59, 66, 209, 263
Pisa, province of 32, 49, 60, 69, 72, 123, 160
Pistelli, Nicola 160, 164
Pistoia, city of 41, 72
Pistoia, province of 72
Poggibonsi (Siena) 41, 59, 74, 134, 263
'Polarised pluralism', thesis of 13, 18, 19
Politica e Società, Tuscan PCI review 58, 85, 224
Pontedera (Pisa) 41, 58, 67, 74, 153, 263
Popular Party, Italian (PPI) 3, 5, 6-7, 9, 20, 36, 147
Portoferraio (Livorno) 132
Prato (Florence) 41, 79, 227, 263
Provincialism in political life 4-5, 19-20

Quercini, Giulio 87

Radda in Chianti (Siena) 263
Radicofani (Siena) 263
Referendum on monarchy (1946) 34
Regional government 16, 17, chap. 1(c), chap. 5(c)
Regionalism in political life 4-5, 19-20, 29-30
Religion 32-3
Republican Party, Italian (PRI) – in general 9, 23, 196-7
Republican Party, Italian (PRI) – in Tuscany 205, 214, 215, 216, 228
Resistance movement 5-6, 10, 20, 33, 34, 34-5, 42-3, 43-4, 49-50, 59, 73, 125-6, 146, 147

Ricasoli family 262

San Gimignano (Siena) 74, 102, 103, 134, 211, 263
Santa Croce sull'Arno (Pisa) 41, 58, 79, 263-4
Santa Luce (Pisa) 264
Sardinia, region of 19
Scandicci (Florence) 55, 103
Semama, Paolo 21
Sesto Fiorentino (Florence) 54-5, 61, 72, 79, 99, 113, 143, 153, 162, 174, 264
Sharecropping system (*mezzadria*), sharecroppers (*mezzadri*) 32, 38, 39, 40, 43, 49, 51, 52, 53, 59, 63-4, 123
Sicily, region of 19, 32
Siena, city of 30, 31, 66, 74, 81, 103, 209, 264
Siena, province of 32, 35, 49, 52, 55, 56, 62, 66, 71, 72, 79, 122, 131, 138, 149-50, 161-2, 163, 210
Signorile, Claudio 194, 204
Smallholders, peasant (*coltivatori diretti*) 36, 40, 52, 130, 141, 177
Social Democratic Party, Italian (PSDI) – in general 9, 196-7
Social Democratic Party, Italian (PSDI) – in Tuscany 205, 214, 215, 216, 228
Socialist Party, Italian (PSI) – in general: and introduction of regional government 21, 22; and political alliances 16, 23, 30; electoral strength 37; pre-Fascist 6-7; strategy of 194-6
Socialist Party, Italian (PSI) – in Tuscany: and PCI dominance 32; electoral strength 37, 224; regionalisation of party structure 228; representation in local government 207, 214-16; strategy in Tuscany 204-5, 206, local politics 199-225 *passim*, regional politics 225-42 *passim*.
Soldati, Ferdinando 168
Sorano (Grosseto) 214
Speranza, Edoardo 124
Stefanini, Marcello 22
Sub-cultures, political 3, 6, 14
Suffrage, extension of 6-7

Terrorism 25, 257

Testimonianze, Catholic review 35, 129
Togliatti, Palmiro 61, 64, 92, 101, 102, 190
Togni, Senator 175
Trasformismo, as political practice 3, 8-9, 9
Trentino-Alto Adige, region of 19
Turin 214, 220, 221
Tuscany, region of 30-1; Catholic tradition in 35-6; political traditions in 31-6; 'Red' tradition in 32-5; socio-economic structure 38-42, 43

Umbria, region of 30, 226, 229, 233, 234
Val d'Aosta, region of 19
Val d'Elsa 41, 62
Veneto, region of 35, 122, 211, 218
Venice 214
Versilia 35, 41, 42, 78, 209
Viareggio 81, 93, 133, 204, 264
Volterra (Pisa) 42, 59, 112-13, 206, 264
Voting Behaviour, background of stability 7
Voting Behaviour, mobility in 1, 7

Zaccagnini, Benigno 162, 165, 166, 166-7, 173-6, 202, 237
Zangheri, Renato 22